COMMUNITY FORMATION

in the Early Church
and in the Church Today

COMMUNITY FORMATION

in the Early Church
and in the Church Today

RICHARD N. LONGENECKER, *Editor*

HENDRICKSON
PUBLISHERS

Hendrickson Publishers, Inc.
P. O. Box 3473
Peabody, Massachusetts 01961-3473

Printed in the United States of America

First Printing—November 2002

Library of Congress Cataloging-in-Publication Data

Community formation in the early church and the church today /
    edited by Richard N. Longenecker.
        p. cm.
    Includes bibliographical references and indexes.
    ISBN 1-56563-718-6
    1. Church polity.   2. Church polity—History—Early church,
    ca. 30–600.   I. Longenecker, Richard N.
        BV647.3 .C66 2002
        262'.009—dc21

                                    2002151528

Contents

List of Contributors   vii

Abbreviations   ix

Introduction   xi

I. The Social Context

1. Greco-Roman Philosophic, Religious, and Voluntary Associations   3
   Richard S. Ascough

2. The Jewish Experience: Temple, Synagogue, Home, and Fraternal Groups   20
   Alan F. Segal

3. Building "an Association *(Synodos)* . . . and a Place of Their Own"   36
   Peter Richardson

II. The New Testament

4. The Ministry of Jesus in the Gospels   59
   Craig A. Evans

5. Paul's Vision of the Church and Community Formation in His Major Missionary Letters   73
   Richard N. Longenecker

6. Divine Power, Community Formation, and Leadership in the Acts of the Apostles   89
   S. Scott Bartchy

7. Congregation and Ministry in the Pastoral Epistles   105
   I. Howard Marshall

III. The Early Centuries

8. Christian Ministry in Three Cities of the Western Empire (160–258 C.E.)   129
   Alan L. Hayes

 9. Ministerial Forms and Functions in the Church Communities
    of the Greek Fathers   157
    Frances Young

IV. The Church Today

10. The "Self-Organizing" Power of the Gospel: Episcopacy and
    Community Formation   179
    John Webster

11. The Sanctified Life in the Body of Christ: A Presbyterian Form of
    Christian Community   194
    David C. Hester

12. Community Formation as an Image of the Triune God: A
    Congregational Model of Church Order and Life   213
    Miroslav Volf

Index of Subjects   239

Index of Modern Authors   243

Index of Ancient Sources   245

Contributors

Richard S. Ascough, Ph.D. (St. Michael's). Assistant Professor of New Testament, Queen's Theological College, Queen's University, Kingston, Ontario, Canada.

S. Scott Bartchy, Ph.D. (Harvard). Professor of Christian Origins and the History of Religion, Department of History, and Director of the Center for the Study of Religion, University of California Los Angeles, Los Angeles, California, U.S.A.

Craig A. Evans, Ph.D. (Claremont). Payzant Distinguished Professor of New Testament at Acadia Divinity College, Wolfville, Nova Scotia, Canada.

Alan L. Hayes, Ph.D. (McGill). Bishops Frederick and Heber Wilkinson Professor of Church History, Wycliffe College, University of Toronto, Toronto, Ontario, Canada.

David C. Hester, Ph.D. (Duke). Professor of Christian Education, Louisville Presbyterian Theological Seminary, Louisville, Kentucky, U.S.A.

Richard N. Longenecker, Ph.D. (Edinburgh), D.D. (Wycliffe). Professor Emeritus of New Testament, Wycliffe College, University of Toronto, Toronto, Ontario, Canada.

I. Howard Marshall, Ph.D. (Aberdeen), D.D. (Asbury). Honorary Research Professor of New Testament, University of Aberdeen, Aberdeen, Scotland, U.K.

Peter Richardson, Ph.D. (Cambridge). Professor Emeritus, Centre for the Study of Religion, University of Toronto, Toronto, Ontario, Canada.

Alan F. Segal, Ph.D. (Yale). Professor of Religion and Ingeborg Rennert Professor of Jewish Studies, Barnard College, Columbia University, New York, New York, U.S.A.

Miroslav Volf, Dr.Th., Dr. Th.habil. (Tübingen). Henry B. Wright Professor of Systematic Theology, Divinity School, Yale University, New Haven, Connecticut, U.S.A.

John Webster, Ph.D. (Cambridge). The Lady Margaret Professor of Divinity, University of Oxford, and Canon of Christ Church, Oxford, England, U.K.

Frances Young, Ph.D. (Cambridge), D.D. (Aberdeen). Edward Cadbury Professor of Theology, University of Birmingham, Birmingham, England, U.K.

Abbreviations

BDAG	F. W. Danker, ed. *A Greek-English Lexicon of the New Testament and Other Early Christian Literature*. 3d ed. Chicago: University of Chicago Press, 2002.
BGU	*Aegyptische Urkunden aus den Königlichen Staatlichen Museen zu Berlin: Griechische Urkunden*. 1895–.
CIJ	J.-B. Frey, ed. *Corpus Inscriptionum Judaicarum*. New York: Ktav, 1975.
CIL	*Corpus Inscriptionum Latinarum*. 1863–.
I. Alex.	François Kayser. *Recueil des inscriptions grecques et latines (non funéraires) d'Alexandrie impériale*. Cairo: Institut français d'archéologie orientale, 1994.
IG	*Inscriptiones Graecae*. 1873–.
LSJ	H. G. Liddell, R. Scott, H. S. Jones. *A Greek-English Lexicon*. 9th ed., with a revised supplement. Oxford: Oxford University Press, 1996.
MM	J. H. Moulton and G. Milligan. *The Vocabulary of the Greek Testament*. London: Hodder & Stoughton, 1930. Repr. Peabody, Mass.: Hendrickson, 1997.
OTP	J. H. Charlesworth, ed. *Old Testament Pseudepigrapha*. 2 vols. Garden City, N.Y.: Doubleday, 1983.
P. Kar.	E. J. Goodspeed. *Karanis Papyri*. Chicago: University of Chicago, 1932.
P. Lond.	*Greek Papyri in the British Museum*. 1893–1874.
P. Oxy.	*Oxyrhynchus Papyri*. 1898–.
SEG	*Supplementum Epigraphicum Graecum*.
SIG	W. Dittenberger, ed. *Sylloge Inscriptionum Graecarum*. 4 vols. 3d ed. Leipzig: Hirzel, 1898–.
TDNT	G. Kittel and G. Friedrich, eds. *Theological Dictionary of the New Testament*. Translated by G. W. Bromiley. 10 vols. Grand Rapids: Eerdmans, 1964–1976.

Introduction

Richard N. Longenecker

Community formation, or what has commonly been called "church order" in ecclesiastical circles, has to do with the way the Christian church is structured and its life expressed. It is an issue of real importance, not only for church leaders and scholars but also for all believers. Is the organization of the church a divine ordinance or a social necessity? Does the New Testament present a normative pattern of church order, or does it reflect a diversity of forms, structures, and expressions? Is the formation of the church's life to be primarily determined theologically, or should it be understood as largely conditioned sociologically? Are ecclesiastical structures intrinsic to the gospel, and therefore fixed, or to be seen as the result of contextualizing the gospel in particular places, at certain times, and in various circumstances, and so somewhat fluid? Is the relation between the spiritual life of the church and its external structures to be viewed as analogous to the union of a person's soul and body, and so indissolubly joined, or a person and his or her clothes, with fabrics and colors conditioned by particular locations and occasions? These are questions asked by every follower of Jesus.

AN ERA OF INTENSIVE DEBATE: 1868–1950

Roman Catholicism and Anglo-Catholicism, as well as Eastern Orthodoxy, build on the conviction that church order has been divinely ordained, and therefore cannot be changed or adjusted without diluting or destroying the gospel—as witness, for example, Charles Gore, *The Church and the Ministry* [1888], and Kenneth E. Kirk, ed., *The Apostolic Ministry* [1946], who bracket the period in question from an Anglo-Catholic perspective. A similar stance has been taken by various "restorationist" groups and denominations within Protestantism as well.

During the latter part of the nineteenth century, however, what Olof Linton has called a "consensus of scholarship" (cf. *Das Problem der Urkirche*) began to be formed among Protestants, which viewed the church of the first century—as well as the church throughout the succeeding ages—as, in the words of W. D. Davies, made up of individual Christians who formed a religious society, which in itself, as a society, was by no means necessary for salvation, and whose organised life could be adequately understood in the light of that of similar contemporary religious groups, of which there were many in the Hellenistic as in the Jewish world. (*Normative Pattern of Church Life*, 2)

Linton has documented this shift, focusing particularly on Edwin Hatch in Britain and Adolf Harnack and Rudolf Sohm in Germany—though with references also to Georg Heinrici in Germany and J. B. Lightfoot, William Sanday, and B. H. Streeter in Britain (cf. *Das Problem der Urkirche*). A brief history of the rise of such a "consensus" in the English-speaking world, however, is pertinent here, with an emphasis on those scholars who were particularly important and highlighting the issues in the debate that ensued.

The period really began with the work of J. B. Lightfoot, who took the occasion in his 1868 commentary on Philippians to develop an eighty-nine-page "dissertation" on "The Christian Ministry"—drawing his rationale for such a discussion from the fact that "the mention of 'bishops and deacons' in the opening of this letter furnished a good text" (*Philippians*, 2). In many ways, Lightfoot's treatment of the early church and its orders of ministry was revolutionary. Lightfoot argued that the organization of the church is to be seen not as a divine ordinance but as arising out of social necessity: "It must be evident that no society of men could hold together without officers, without rules, without institutions of any kind; and the Church of Christ is not exempt from this universal law" (ibid., 181). Furthermore, Lightfoot proposed that it was circumstances that called for the creation of the three "permanent" orders of ministry within the church: first the diaconate, which was "an entirely new creation, called forth by a special emergency and developed by the progress of events" (ibid., 191); then the presbyterate, which had parallels in the religious, philosophic, and social clubs of the Greco-Roman world (ibid., 191–95); and finally the episcopate, which developed during the last three decades of the first century, becoming widely and firmly established in the early second century, and which "was formed not out of the apostolic order by localisation but out of the presbyteral by elevation" (ibid., 196).

Lightfoot continued to speak of the diaconate, presbyterate, and episcopate as "divine appointments." But he did so more in the sense of principles of church order that are inherent in the gospel and what would be called today the "indigenization" or "contextualization" of those principals in particular localities, times, and circumstances, rather than in terms of established offices or divine ordinances—that is, of "divine providence" rather than "divine command."

Twelve years later in his 1880 Bampton Lectures at Oxford, which were published in 1881 as *The Organization of the Early Christian Churches*, Edwin Hatch asserted (1) that the organization of the church was a gradual evolution, and (2) that the clue to the various organizational features observable in the early churches was to be found in the Greco-Roman religious, philosophical, and social societies of that day. In particular, he argued that the terms "elders" (*presbyteroi*) and "bishops" *(episkopoi)* referred to the same persons but to different roles—that is, as members of a church's council they were called *presbyteroi,* but as administrators they were called *episkopoi* (as well as *epimeletai,* which was the more common term for administrators or financial officers). Furthermore, he insisted that the office of bishop achieved prominence in postapostolic churches simply because of the need for a financial administrator to handle matters pertaining to almsgiving in the societies of Christians, much as in other religious and philosophical societies of the Greco-Roman world.

Hatch was more radical than Lightfoot, principally in crediting church order only to a human desire to externalize religion and in arguing that the development of offices in the church was patterned largely on Greco-Roman religious, philosophical, and social structures of the day. Hatch wrote at a time when many viewed the teaching of Jesus and the proclamation of the apostles as having been overlaid with hellenized viewpoints and Catholic structures, so that the purity of the original Christian message and simplicity of the earliest believers' lifestyle had become distorted by later ecclesiastical dogma and organization. His Hibbert Lectures, which were published in 1888 as *The Influence of Greek Ideas on Christianity,* articulated this view with great clarity. And his earlier study of church order took such a stance as well.

F. J. A. Hort, who was Lightfoot's colleague and who (compared to Lightfoot) "had the strongest feeling for the institutional side of the Christian religion" (cf. Neill, *The Interpretation of the New Testament,* 34; 2d ed., 36) lectured at Cambridge during the Michaelmas terms of 1888 and 1889 on "The Early History and the Early Conceptions of the Christian Ecclesia." These lectures built on the work of Lightfoot and were published posthumously in 1897 as *The Christian Ecclesia.*

In his "recapitulation" at the close of his lectures, Hort affirmed the following regarding the organization of the church in the apostolic age:

> The offices instituted in the Ecclesia were the creation of successive experiences and changes of circumstances, involving at the same time a partial adoption first of Jewish precedents by the Ecclesia of Judea, and then apparently of Judean Christian precedents by the Ecclesiae of the Dispersion and the Gentiles. There is no trace in the New Testament that any ordinances on this subject were prescribed by the Lord, or that any such ordinances were set up as permanently binding by the Twelve or by St Paul or by the Ecclesia at large. Their faith in the Holy Spirit and His perpetual guidance was too much of a reality to make that possible. (*The Christian Ecclesia,* 230)

And though Anglo-Catholic in many of his commitments, Hort concluded those lectures with the following warning and observations:

> In this as in so many other things is seen the futility of endeavouring to make the Apostolic history into a set of authoritative precedents, to be rigorously copied without regard to time and place, thus turning the Gospel into a second Levitical Code. The Apostolic age is full of embodiments of purposes and principles of the most instructive kind: but the responsibility of choosing the means was left for ever to the Ecclesia itself, and to each Ecclesia, guided by ancient precedent on the one

hand and adaptation to present and future needs on the other. The lesson-book of the Ecclesia, and of every Ecclesia, is not a law but a history. (Ibid., 232–33)

A further step in the construction of a Protestant "scholarly consensus" on church order was taken by B. H. Streeter, who in 1929 published *The Primitive Church, Studied with Special Reference to the Origins of the Christian Ministry*, which incorporated material from his lectures on "Primitive Church Order" at the University of London in 1925, his Oxford post-graduate Seminars of 1927 and 1928, and his Hewett Lectures of 1928. In *The Primitive Church* Streeter argued for "a far greater diversity and variegation in Primitive Christianity than is commonly recognised" (p. vii), summarizing his position in the following two points:

(1) In the New Testament itself there can be traced an evolution in Church Order, comparable to the development in theological reflection detected by scholarship of the last century.

(2) The most natural interpretation of the other evidence is that, at the end of the first century A.D., there existed, in different provinces of the Roman Empire, different systems of Church government. Among these, the Episcopalian, the Presbyterian, and the Independent [i.e., Congregational] can each discover the prototype of the system to which he himself adheres. (*The Primitive Church*, ix)

What Streeter argued was that all three positions on church order can be found in the New Testament and continued to be expressed in various localities and to various degrees within the postapostolic churches. And while not rigid in his identifications, he tended to equate (1) the Jerusalem church with an episcopal model of ministry, which espouses the transmission of authority from Christ through the apostles and a monarchical system of ecclesiastical order; (2) the Antioch church with a presbyterian model, which holds to a ministry that all of its recipients have the power to confer on others and an oligarchical or representative system of church legislation and order; and (3) the Gentile churches established by Paul with a congregational model, which bases ministerial vocation on recognition by a local congregation and advocates a more collegial form of ecclesiastical structure and practice.

Not everyone, of course, was happy with the developing "consensus" represented by Lightfoot, Hatch, Hort, and Streeter. Michael Ramsey, then Archbishop of York (later Archbishop of Canterbury), for example, published in 1936 *The Gospel and the Catholic Church*, which in Part I appeals to the theology of Christ's death and resurrection in arguing for episcopacy as the only form of ecclesiastical order that truly expresses the gospel and in Part II claims Christian history in support of the papacy. Kenneth E. Kirk, Anglican Bishop of Oxford, edited in 1946 *The Apostolic Ministry*, a volume authored by ten Anglo-Catholic and Roman Catholic scholar-theologians (himself included), which argues for what he called "the true view" of church order:

The episcopate is the divinely ordained ministerial instrument for securing to the Church of God its continuous and organic unity, not as a club of like-minded worshippers or aspirants to holiness, but as a God-given city of salvation. (*The Apostolic Ministry*, 8)

On the other hand, most Protestant scholars of the day, such as C. H. Dodd ("The Church in the New Testament"), R. Newton Flew *(Jesus and His Church)*, George Johnston *(The Doctrine of the Church in the New Testament)*, and T. W. Manson *(The Church's Ministry)*, applauded and built on the work of Lightfoot and Hort—with most also commending that of Streeter and some that of Hatch.

Postulating a radical difference between the centrality and freedom of the Spirit in the apostolic church and the church's later focus on hierarchical structures and juridicial orders, Rudolf Sohm in Germany *(Kirchenrecht)* and Vernon Bartlet in Britain *(Church-Life and Church-Order during the First Four Centuries,* the Birkbeck Lectures of 1924, published posthumously in 1943) went quite a bit further than most Protestants in arguing that not only are the structures and orders of the postapostolic church of no dogmatic significance, but they actually represent a departure from the original purity of the apostolic message and spiritual fellowship of the earliest believers, who had no need of any outward structures. For Sohm and Bartlet, the former was "the Church of the Spirit and of love" whereas the latter was a "legalistic Church"—so the "apostolic" and "pneumatic" ordering of the early church was quite different from later "juridical" and "hierarchical" orders. But the great majority of Protestants, whether Lutheran, Reformed, "Low Church" Anglican, or "Nonconformist," agreed with Hort, Streeter, Flew, Johnston, and others—as well as with Adolf Harnack on this point (see Appendix I, Harnack, "Sohm's Theory," in *Constitution and Law of the Church,* 176–258), whose writings were translated and read widely in the English-speaking world—that (1) whereas the New Testament does not teach a specific form of church order, it nonetheless enunciates principles for the structuring of the church and evidences that the earliest Christian communities were organized from their beginnings; and (2) freedom of the Spirit and ecclesiastical structures cannot be so summarily contrasted as being contradictory or mutually exclusive.

THE SITUATION DURING THE LAST HALF CENTURY: 1950–2000

Much of the discussion in the Western world during the latter part of the nineteenth century through to the middle of the twentieth century was not only dogmatic in nature, pitting Protestant views against Catholic views, but also methodological, setting what would be called today a "Biblical Theology" method of historical inquiry against a theological method of argumentation. Differences between the two stances and methods seemed insurmountable, and it became something of an embarrassment in an age of rising ecumenical interest to continue such discussions.

For Catholics the issue was clear: (1) "apostolic succession" had been established by Christ himself and is a primary datum of church history; (2) by means of apostolic succession the governing of Christ's church has been passed on to the church's bishops; and, therefore, (3) a monarchical form of church order, supervised by local bishops under the direction of one supreme bishop, is the only true form of government for the Christian church. It is not, of course, an apostolic succession *to* the apostolate as such, for no one can "succeed" to having seen the risen Christ, but a succession *from* the apostles, which guarantees the continuance of the apostolic office among duly ordained bishops of the church.

For Protestants, however, while united in opposition to viewing church order as a localization of the apostolic office—that is, opposed to an "apostolic succession of office," though espousing an "apostolic succession of doctrine and faith"—the issue was more complex. Three somewhat different positions regarding church order, in fact, came to be fairly common among Protestants—whether Lutheran, Reformed, "Low Church" Anglican, or "Nonconformist"—during the second half of the twentieth century, with various attempts made to combine either the first two or the last two: (1) that church order is a matter of divine providence, not divine command, and that it springs from the interaction of the principles of the gospel and the circumstances of both time and place (J. B. Lightfoot, F. J. A. Hort, B. H. Streeter); (2) that church order arises from a human desire to externalize religion and that organizational developments in Paul's Gentile churches were patterned after the Greco-Roman religious, philosophical and social societies of the day (E. Hatch, G. Heinrici, A. Harnack); and (3) that church order represents a departure from the pristine purity of the original gospel and the spiritual fellowship of the earliest believers in Jesus (R. Sohm, J. V. Bartlet).

In large measure, discussions among scholars and church leaders during the second half of the twentieth century turned away from matters having to do with church order to issues concerning the nature of the church, the mission of the church, the renewal of the church, and the church's interaction with society. A great deal of very significant work, in fact, was done during this period on these matters—particularly on the church as rooted in the theology of the Old Testament and early Judaism, the church as the eschatological "People of God," the unity of the church as being "in Christ," the dynamic of the church being "by the Holy Spirit," and the mission of the church as being the extension of the gospel. Little attention, however, was paid to matters pertaining to church order or the external organization of the church. Probably the best of the studies on church order coming out of the latter part of the earlier era of intense debate were the works of Eduard Schweizer, *Church Order in the New Testament,* expressing a Lutheran perspective, and Rudolf Schnackenburg, *The Church in the New Testament,* expressing a Roman Catholic perspective—both of which are historical-exegetical works of great importance. But positions seemed entrenched and further discussion seemed fruitless.

W. D. Davies has characterized studies on the church at the midpoint of the twentieth century as a "curious dichotomy":

> On the one hand, there has emerged a marked unity as to the essential nature of the Church as the eschatological people of God in Christ. On the other hand, there has emerged an equally marked disagreement as to the way or ways in which that people was organised, if, indeed, in its earliest stages we could speak of its being strictly "organised" at all. The nature of the Body of Christ has become clear; but there is division as to the form or forms that the Body has assumed. (*Normative Pattern of Church Life,* 7)

There have been a number of efforts during the final two decades of the twentieth century to resurrect discussions of early church community formation—principally sociologically oriented studies, which have to do with such matters as the urban setting of early Christianity, the existence and function of house churches, the impact of the Jewish synagogue on the worship and structures of the early church, and the influence of Greco-Roman religious, philosophic, and social structures on church order (as will be noted in the chapters to follow in this volume). But agreements reached during the past century and a quarter between Catholics and Protestants on church order have been mainly "agreements to disagree." So rather than continue such discussions, issues having to do with the nature, mission, and message of the church—which, of course, are themselves vitally important topics—have taken first place on the agenda of both church leaders and scholars during the second half of the twentieth century.

THE PERSPECTIVE, FOCUS, METHOD, AND PURPOSE OF THE PRESENT VOLUME

Yet questions about community formation continue to be asked by many church leaders and Christians today. This is particularly true because of (1) the collapse of an atomistic individualism, which characterized so much of nineteenth- and early twentieth-century western thought; (2) the position the church finds itself in vis-à-vis the state in many European, Asian, African, Central American, and South American countries; (3) the continuing desire among Christians for improved ecumenical relations between churches; (4) the recent rise of sociological studies pertaining to the situation of early Christianity and the course of church history; and (5) a growing realization of the need to understand better and bring about more adequately the "indigenization" or "contextualization" of the gospel not only in distant lands but also at home. Thus, though the topic has been often shunned during the past half century or so, it seems necessary to return once again to questions of Christian community formation—dealing with them in a manner that takes into account recent studies about the church in its past and present social contexts, makes the conclusions of such research more widely available for ministers, theological students, and inquiring lay people, and introduces the data at hand and issues at stake in a more readable and comprehensive fashion.

Most of the chapters in this volume were originally presented at the Bingham Colloquium, held June 26–27, 2000, at McMaster Divinity College, Hamilton, Ontario, Canada. They are avowedly written from a Protestant perspective and largely espouse a historical or "biblical theology" method. Their focus is fairly restricted, with matters having to do with organizational structures, functions, offices, and the like to the fore. There is no desire in any of the presentations, however, to assert a "primitivist" or "restorationist" thesis. Rather, the controlling themes of the entire enterprise are (1) that community formation within the Christian church must be understood primarily as an expression of the Christian gospel; (2) that ecclesial formation, structures, and order are matters having to do with the contextualization of the Christian gospel in forms that are both conducive to the church's mission and appropriate to the situations where that mission is expressed; and (3) that the church can profit in its attempts to contextualize its ministry by comparative studies of how such contextualizations have taken place in the past and are taking place today.

Admittedly, the subject of community formation within the Christian church is large. To do it justice would require much more by way of coverage, research, and explication than is possible here. Our desire for this volume is only that it will provide some direction for both the earnest reader and the Christian church at large by setting out selected topics of great pertinence, each of which is written by an informed expert, in the four general areas of "Social Context," "The New Testament," "The Early Centuries," and "The Church Today"—with further guidance provided by the bibliographies appended to each chapter. Such a relatively small volume as this cannot be expected to deal with everything that could or should be said on the subject. All that is hoped for is that it will raise significant issues, deal with important data, give perspective and guidance for thought, and provide resources for further study.

BIBLIOGRAPHY

Bartlet, J. Vernon. *Church-Life and Church-Order during the First Four Centuries.* Edited by C. J. Cadoux. Oxford: Blackwell, 1943.

Burtchaell, James T. *From Synagogue to Church: Public Services and Offices in the Earliest Christian Communities.* Cambridge: Cambridge University Press, 1992.

Davies, W. D. *A Normative Pattern of Church Life in the New Testament: Fact or Fancy?* London: James Clarke, 1950.

Dodd, C. H. "The Church in the New Testament." Pages 1–16 in *Essays Congregational and Catholic.* Edited by Albert Peel. London: Congregational Union of England and Wales, 1931.

Flew, R. Newton. *Jesus and His Church: A Study of the Idea of the Ecclesia in the New Testament.* London: Epworth, 1938.

Gore, Charles. *The Church and the Ministry.* London: Longmans, Green, 1888.

Harnack, Adolf. *The Constitution and Law of the Church in the First Two Centuries.* Translated by F. L. Pogson. London: Williams & Norgate, 1910. ET of *Entstehung und Entwickelung der Kirchenverfassung und des Kirchenrechts in den zwei ersten Jahrhunderten.* Leipzig: Hinrichs, 1910.

Hort, F. J. A. *The Christian Ecclesia. A Course of Lectures on the Early History and Early Conceptions of the Ecclesia.* London: Macmillan, 1897.

Hatch, Edwin. *The Influence of Greek Ideas on Christianity.* London: Williams & Norgate, 1888.

———. *The Organization of the Early Christian Churches.* London: Rivingtons, 1881.

Johnston, George. *The Doctrine of the Church in the New Testament.* Cambridge: Cambridge University Press, 1943.

Kirk, Kenneth E., ed. *The Apostolic Ministry: Essays on the History and the Doctrine of Episcopacy.* London: Hodder & Stoughton, 1946.

Lightfoot, J. B. "The Christian Ministry." Pages 181–269 in *Saint Paul's Epistle to the Philippians.* London: Macmillan, 1868.

Linton, Olof. *Das Problem der Urkirche in der neueren Forschung: Eine kritische Darstellung.* Uppsala: Almquist & Wiksells, 1932.

Manson, T. W. *The Church's Ministry.* London: Hodder & Stoughton, 1948.

Neill, S. *The Interpretation of the New Testament, 1861–1961.* London: Oxford University Press, 1964. 2d ed., S. Neill and T. Wright, 1988.

Ramsey, A. Michael. *The Gospel and the Catholic Church.* London: Longmans, Green, 1936.

Robinson, J. A. "The Christian Ministry in the Apostolic and Sub-Apostolic Periods." Pages 57–92 in *Essays on the Early History of the Church and the Ministry.* Edited by H. B. Swete. London: Macmillan, 1918.

Schnackenburg, Rudolf. *The Church in the New Testament.* Translated by W. J. O'Hara. New York: Herder and Herder, 1965. ET of *Die Kirche im Neuen Testament.* Freiburg: Herder, 1961.

Schweizer, Eduard. *Church Order in the New Testament.* Translated by F. Clarke. London: SCM, 1961. ET of *Gemeinde und Gemeindeordnung im Neuen Testament.* Zurich: Zwingli, 1959.

Sohm, Rudolf. *Kirchenrecht.* Bd. I, *Die geschichtlichen Grundlagen.* Bd. II, *Katholisches Kirchenrecht.* Leipzig and Munich: Von Duncker & Humblot, 1892–1923.

Streeter, B. H. *The Primitive Church, Studied with Special Reference to the Origins of the Christian Ministry.* London: Macmillan, 1929.

Part I

The Social Context

Chapter 1

Greco-Roman Philosophic, Religious, and Voluntary Associations

Richard S. Ascough

A "group" is generally defined as a collection of persons with a feeling of common identity, goals, and norms. For example, slaves working the Roman mines in Spain had—whether they liked it or not—a common social identity (slave), a common goal (mining), and shared norms of behavior (work or be punished). "Associations," however, are more formal than groups. Associations are composed of persons who not only share common interests and activities but also have deliberately organized for some specific purpose or purposes. As such, associations have established rules of organization and procedure and established patterns of leadership.

Associations can be divided into two basic categories: involuntary and voluntary. Involuntary associations have a membership based on birth or compulsion. This was generally the case with the *demes* and *phratries* of ancient Athens. It is also true of a conscripted army. Voluntary associations, however, are formed by persons who freely and deliberately choose to join and who can likewise choose to resign. Examples would be a guild of actors or a gathering of Isis-worshipers.

Voluntary associations in the Greco-Roman world have a long history, going back at least to the laws of Solon in sixth-century B.C.E. Athens. Such associations continued to grow through the classical period and were flourishing in the Hellenistic period. During the first century C.E. their presence was felt throughout the entire Roman Empire in cities and villages alike—although, of course, there is considerably more attestation for associations in urban centers than in rural areas. A variety of extant sources attest to various voluntary associations in antiquity. These include literary texts, papyri, inscriptions, and archaeological remains. All of these sources are important in an investigation of community-formation in Greco-Roman associations.

This chapter will focus on three types of associations in the Greco-Roman world: (1) philosophical associations, which are sometimes called philosophical

schools; (2) public religious associations, which are often called "mystery religions"; and (3) private religious and professional associations, which are usually
referred to more generically as "voluntary" associations.

1. PHILOSOPHICAL ASSOCIATIONS

The word "school" can mean different things in different contexts. When
applied to philosophical thought in antiquity it generally refers to persons who
follow the same founder and propagate similar ideas and doctrines. Schools in
this sense generally had as their goal the creation of a pathway to human flourishing. In so doing they focused on intellectual discourse and followed a particular
way of life. Philosophical schools, however, were not always "groups" in terms of a
sociological definition. That is, members of a school may be considered to be
those who held related ideas, but these same persons may not—and generally did
not—meet together as a group of one sort or another.

Our focus here, however, is not on the varying ideas of the many philosophical schools of antiquity, such as the Platonists, the Aristotelians, the Stoics, the
Epicureans, the Pythagoreans, the Cynics, or the Skeptics. Rather, we want to
focus attention on how philosophical associations were organized. In so doing,
however, we run into a problem concerning our sources: most of the extant
sources for the philosophical schools are interested in their ideas and founders,
not in the form and organization of the schools themselves.

Alan Culpepper has set out some of the characteristics that were shared by
a number of the philosophical schools of antiquity:

> (1) they were groups of disciples which usually emphasized *philia* and *koinōnia*; (2)
> they gathered around, and traced their origins to, a founder whom they regarded as
> an exemplary, wise, or good man; (3) they valued the teachings of their founder
> and the traditions about him; (4) members of the schools were disciples or stu-
> dents of the founder; (5) teaching, learning, studying, and writing were common
> activities; (6) most schools observed communal meals, often in memory of their
> founders; (7) they had rules or practices regarding admission, retention of mem-
> bership, and advancement within the membership; (8) they often maintained some
> degree of distance or withdrawal from the rest of society; and (9) they developed
> organizational means of insuring their perpetuity. (*Johannine School*, 258–59)

Furthermore, Culpepper notes that the organizational complexity of a school was
usually tied to its understanding of the role of fellowship *(koinōnia)*: "The more a
school emphasized 'fellowship' the more likely it was to have a developed, structured organization and rules governing its communal life" (ibid., 254).

If we focus our attention on philosophical schools for which evidence from
around the first century C.E. indicates that members formed themselves into associations, we are really limited to two particular groups—the Pythagoreans and
the Epicureans, with less evidence for the former than the latter. The Epicureans,
in fact, are the only group for which we have direct first-century evidence. The

Pythagorean school, however, probably influenced the organization of the other philosophical schools in antiquity and so also deserves attention.

The Pythagorean School

During the sixth century B.C.E., Pythagoras (d. ca. 497 B.C.E.) founded a closely knit school at Croton in southern Italy in which he emphasized asceticism and ritual purity, with a focus on the deliverance of the soul. It is difficult to determine the exact organizational structure of the Pythagorean school, for membership in it required secrecy and many of its traditions were passed on by memory alone. Those writers who do discuss the school's structure, such as Diogenes Laertius, Porphyry, and Iamblichus, are late in date (all third to fourth century C.E.) and somewhat unreliable. It is even unclear whether Pythagoras himself actually intended to found a school at all, since "Pythagoreanism was more of a way of life than a philosophy" (Culpepper, *Johannine School*, 247, 249).

Nonetheless, the Pythagorean school welcomed candidates for membership. Pythagoras's preaching attracted some adherents by calling people away from a life of luxury to a life of simplicity. According to one report, which may very well have been inflated, two thousand men, plus their wives and children, did not return home after hearing Pythagoras, but pooled their property and built an auditorium *(homakoion)* as large as a city (Iamblichus, *Life of Pythagoras* 6, citing Nicomachus). Other sources, however, suggest that the school was composed mostly of young, aristocratic men, some of whom were hand-picked by Pythagoras himself. These aristocratic connections provide the most likely reason for the school's political connections as well as for the fact that conflicts seem to have sometimes been a part of the school's life.

A description of the initiation procedure into the Pythagorean school can be found in a number of sources, particularly in Iamblichus, *Life of Pythagoras* 17—although, again, these descriptions may be only later, apocryphal reconstructions. According to our sources, initiation into the school began with a scrutiny of the devotees' family background, their way of life (e.g., leisure time, joys, disappointments), their physique, and their gait. They were then ignored for three years as a means of testing the strength of their desire to learn. Should they pass this testing period, they entered a five-year novitiate during which time they could not speak. At the end of this period, those who were approved underwent rites of purification and were initiated into the association. For those who were rejected, however, a tomb was raised as if they were dead. And if in the future a Pythagorean encountered those rejected, they were treated as if they were strangers.

Once membership was attained, the candidates became disciples *(mathē-tai)* and were considered to be members of the fellowship *(koinōnia)* or school *(scholē)*. According to Diogenes Laertius, Pythagoras "was the first to say 'Friends have all things in common' and 'Friendship is equality'; indeed, his disciples put all their possessions into one common stock" (8.10, citing Timaeus). This communal practice may have been short-lived or only applicable to an inner group.

But when the policy was operative, property was submitted at the beginning of the five-year silent probationary period. If after five years as a novitiate a candidate was rejected, double the amount contributed was returned; if the candidate was accepted, the property was held in common by the community.

Pythagorean communal life was structured around an ordered daily schedule and included common meals. Restrictions were placed on the members' diet (no beans or meat, only uncooked food), their drink (pure water alone), their clothing (no wool), and certain materials (e.g., cypress could not be used in coffins). It is difficult to know all that occurred in the community, simply because the traditions of the school were to be kept secret and those who violated this code were punished or expelled. Control rested with Pythagoras when he was living or his successor after his death. Leadership was passed on through election or by appointment made by the previous leader, with leadership positions being held for life.

The Pythagoreans memorized the teachings of their founder and were in some ways more interested in commitment to the person and principles of Pythagoras than in acquiring knowledge. Nonetheless, they also studied Homer and perhaps some science and mathematics, and they probably used music for edification. Members were divided into two ranks: the students (*mathēmatikoi*), who received the full teachings and participated in debate, and the hearers (*akousmatikoi*), who were given only a summary (Iamblichus, *Life of Pythagoras* 18). Although Iamblichus notes that both of these two groups were recognized as Pythagoreans, those designated students looked down on the so-called hearers as not having received their instruction directly from Pythagoras.

Daily life in the Pythagorean school was fairly routine. Iamblichus describes a typical day of the members, although his description seems to apply most directly to those not living in the community and so probably reflects a later form of the school. Upon waking they took a lonely morning walk and then met together for discussion. Following some exercise they had breakfast of bread and honey. The afternoon was spent fulfilling civic obligations, although in the late afternoon they took another walk—this time in pairs or threesomes in order to review their disciplines. After a bath they met for a meal that began with libations and the burning of incense. Eating ceased before sunset and the meal was closed with libations and a public reading. Moral admonishments concluded the evening before members went to bed (cf. *Life of Pythagoras* 21). Whatever the date of this description, it gives us a sense of the lifestyle of the Pythagoreans generally. And it is not difficult to see how such a regime might have occurred in a communal setting, with instruction replacing political activities in the afternoon.

At the end of the fourth century B.C.E. the Pythagorean school had all but disappeared. There is little evidence for it until the first century B.C.E. at Rome, where Neo-Pythagoreanism continued the traditions of Pythagoras and venerated his name. Eventually, however, both classical Pythagoreanism and Neo-Pythagoreanism were subsumed by Neo-Platonism in the second century C.E.

The Epicurean Garden

Epicurus (ca. 341–271 B.C.E.) formed his Garden in Athens during the later part of the fourth century to the early third century B.C.E. Sources for understanding this community are better than for many of the other philosophical schools, since Epicurus himself wrote much and some of what he wrote survives. Other extant reports about Epicurus, though less reliable, can help round out our picture of the organization of the Epicurean school—particularly those by Diogenes Laertius, Cicero, and Plutarch.

Epicurus is usually considered to be the first to have intentionally set out to form a philosophical association. Born on the island of Samos, a citizen of Athens by birth, and having studied at Athens as a youth, he returned to Athens in 306 B.C.E. As an Athenian citizen he was able to purchase both a house and adjacent land for a garden outside the city wall, and it is at his house and garden, rather than the gymnasium, that he established his school. Members lived together in the house and pursued their daily regime in the garden. And although the Epicurean community withdrew from the world to seek a better way of life, it is probable that the house and garden was located within a densely populated, busy quarter of Athens. As such, the school was not particularly well secluded, and the withdrawal of its members from public life led, at times, to disfavor among the general population.

Epicurus's Garden "placed more emphasis on community and friendship than any other philosophical school" (Culpepper, *Johannine School,* 101). Epicurean associations were formed as fictional kinship groups and based on a household model. The goal was friendship, and the Epicureans sought to produce love and intimacy among all members. Cicero (106–43 B.C.E.), the Roman orator, philosopher, and statesman, writing in the first century B.C.E., records that "in just one household—and a small one at that—Epicurus assembled such large congregations of friends which were bound together by a shared feeling of the deepest love. And even now the Epicureans do the same thing" (*On Goals* 1.65).

Eusebius, the fourth-century Christian apologist, church historian, and bishop of Caesarea in Palestine from 313 until his death in 339, cites Numenius as saying: "The school of Epicurus resembles a true commonwealth *(politeia),* altogether free of factionalism, sharing one mind and one disposition, of which they were and are and, it appears, will be followers" *(Praep. ev.* 14.5). Such a close relationship among its members contributed to the overall success of Epicureanism. Nevertheless, goods were not held in common, for Epicurus considered such a practice to imply mistrust. Rather, the simple lifestyle of the Epicureans was supported by wealthier members and adherents through patronage. At the same time, Epicurean associations outside of Athens paid some form of dues to the Athenian Garden.

The Epicurean schools were dominated by their founder, who provided them with an organizational model and practical wisdom. In some respects, Epicureanism was closer to a "sect" or "cult" than a philosophical association, for not only were Epicurus's teachings held in high esteem but he himself was venerated as "father" and "the wise one" by his followers. Seneca (ca. 4 B.C.E.–65 C.E.), the Roman philosopher, tells us that an oath of allegiance to Epicurus was taken by his disciples and suggests that his teachings were followed with vigor: "We will be obedient to Epicurus, according to whom we have made it our choice to live" (*Epistles* 25.5). The Epicureans met for a banquet once a month in honor of their founder and his early disciple, Metrodorus. After Epicurus's death, regular funeral offerings were undertaken for him and his family, and a celebration was made on his birthday. By the first century C.E., it appears, Epicurus was worshiped as "a god who had revealed wisdom" (Culpepper, *Johannine School,* 109; cf. DeWitt, *Epicurus and His Philosophy,* 97–101).

There is some debate over the nature of leadership among the Epicureans. While there was no official leadership structure, there seems to have been a hierarchy of leadership based largely on the level of attainment in the philosophy of Epicurus. Epicurus, or his successor, held the highest place of honor as "the wise one." Below were "associate leaders" *(kathēgēmones),* who were called "philosophers." These were followed by "assistant leaders" *(kathēgetai)* or "instructors," who each had a group of students over whom they were responsible. A distinction was made between advanced students *(synētheis)* and novices *(kataskeuazomenoi).* Once admitted to the association, a novice was taught full submission to the instructor. Each member was trained to respect and obey the person who was more advanced. "On this principle," as Norman DeWitt observes, "one member could be said to be better than another only so far as he had made more progress" (*Epicurus and His Philosophy,* 100). But all members, especially younger members, were subject to admonition and reproof from one another, and all were expected to accept it willingly and learn from the correction. Furthermore, once admitted into the association a person was warned against all other forms of knowledge—such as music, rhetoric, or geometry—which were thought to interfere with the pursuit of happiness.

A clear distinction was made between "friends" *(philoi)* or associate members of the group and those who were "devotees" *(gnōrimoi)* or part of the inner circle close to Epicurus or his successors. Membership included both males and females, whether slaves or free. The presence of women is suggestive of the pleasure-seeking goal that formed part of Epicurus's philosophy. There is, however, some evidence that these women were full participants in the lifestyle and teachings of the school. And slaves probably worked as secretaries and copyists for the large-scale publishing endeavors of Epicurus and his followers.

Epicureanism is considered a missionary movement, for Epicurean centers were established throughout the Mediterranean world and attracted many adherents. Epicurus himself maintained contact with these various centers through his letters to them, although none of these letters are extant. Along with his maxims, he also wrote principles of conduct for his followers in various locations as well as summaries of his teaching. Yet, despite the presence of such groups throughout the Mediterranean world, little is known about Epicureanism beyond the Garden in Athens. The house and garden were still operative in the first century B.C.E., but much in need of repair. The movement finally died out in the second century C.E.

2. PUBLIC RELIGIOUS ASSOCIATIONS

When discussing "religious associations" the primary focus is usually on the ancient mysteries, which are often misnamed "mystery religions." Walter Burkert distinguishes three types of organization around the ancient mysteries: (1) the itinerant practitioner; (2) the sanctuary; and (3) the association of worshipers (*Ancient Mystery Cults,* 31). In the case of the itinerant, "there was no backing by a corporation or community" (ibid., 31). The remaining two categories can be characterized as "public" and "private" religious associations, respectively. And although they had some similar organizational characteristics, they were dissimilar enough to warrant separate investigation.

Public religious associations were most often found connected to a public sanctuary and fell under the administration of the city *(polis).* Within this realm lies the mystery cults, which themselves were often tied to the *polis*—as was the case of the mysteries of Demeter at Eleusis, near Athens. Other well-known and popular mysteries include those of Dionysus, Demeter, Isis, and Mithras. For the most part these mysteries began as local cult groups but, at least by the first or second century C.E., grew to have a broader appeal throughout the Greco-Roman world.

Initiation into one or another of the mysteries was usually a matter of choice. One participated in a ritual of status transformation that was usually a collective experience. For the most part the ceremonies were tied to the cycle of nature. Otherwise, very little is known about the actual rites themselves, since, as the name implies, their rituals were closely guarded secrets. Apuleius, the second-century C.E. Roman rhetorician and Platonic sophist, says concerning the mysteries of Isis: "If I were allowed to tell you, and you were allowed to be told, you would soon hear everything; but, as it is, my tongue would suffer for its indiscretion and your ears for their inquisitiveness" (*Metam.* 18). Once initiated, persons could return for special ceremonies or festivals. Noninitiates, however, were barred from participation.

The Mysteries at Eleusis

The Eleusinian mysteries provide an interesting, and somewhat representative, case study of the larger mystery cults, since, as Everett Ferguson points out, they "exercised a formative influence on the mysteries of the eastern cults" and, by at least the first century C.E., were open to anyone who wished to join (*Backgrounds,* 200). The association began as a domestic cult at Eleusis, although it soon broadened out to include not only citizens of Eleusis, but also of Athens and eventually all Attica. Following Alexander the Great's conquest of Greece, the appeal of the Eleusinian mysteries was broadened still further. Despite the initial expense of initiation into the cult, its benefits—particularly its promise of a happy afterlife—were considered worthy of the cost and it became popular with many. Initiation into the Eleusinian mysteries was open to all men and women, and sometimes even to children.

Initiates underwent three stages. In or around February or March they were purified through the "lesser mysteries" by fasting, the sacrifice of a pig, a water ritual (either sprinkling or bathing), the singing of hymns, and the bearing of a sacred vessel of some sort—though much of this, admittedly, remains a "mystery" to us. The "greater mysteries" took place during a ten-day period in September and involved a great procession from Athens to Eleusis, along with various rituals involving purification, sacrifices, and rites for the dead. A third level of initiation, "overseer" *(epoptēs),* could be attained one year after initiation into the greater mysteries. At the conclusion of the nocturnal rites in a large hall on the eighth day of the festival, those who were so designated remained behind to be shown some sacred objects called *hiera*—the nature of which is unknown, but perhaps consisted of cut wheat, sacred chests or baskets, and poppy flowers. The central rites of initiation seem to have included "things enacted" (*drōmena,* perhaps a sacred pageant recounting the foundational myth), "things said" *(legomena),* and "things shown" *(deiknymena).* Those initiated then considered one another to be "brothers" *(adelphoi).*

Other mysteries, such as those of Dionysus, Isis, and Mithras, had initiation rituals and levels of adherence similar to that at Eleusis. The Isis mysteries had three classes of adherents: (1) those who attended the daily ceremonies and joined processions; (2) initiates who had the right to enter the temple and participate in the ceremonies; and (3) various levels of priests. The male-only mystery of Mithraism had seven grades of initiation, corresponding to the order of the seven planets in astrology.

There is most often found at the sanctuaries of these mysteries a group of priests or priestesses (or both) who oversaw the administration of the cult. Priesthood could be obtained through inheritance, through election, or through purchase. For the most part, such officials were paid professionals whose numbers would never increase beyond the ability to be funded by the revenues from the cult. Walter Burkert somewhat overstates the case when he says, in comparing public mysteries with private religious associations, that "a corporation of this kind cannot develop into a self-sufficient, alternative religious community in the full sense" (*Ancient Mystery Cults,* 44). Indeed, private religious associations comprised of officials from the public mysteries existed in antiquity (as we will discuss below). Nonetheless, Burkert is correct insofar as the public mysteries, like the civic cults, remained less intimately organized than the private religious associations.

The Mysteries of Andania

Before discussing private religious associations in detail, it is worthwhile first to look at a private religious association that gained enough civic importance to become, in effect, a public mystery cult in the city of Andania, which was located in the southwestern part of the Greek Peloponnesus. In fact, the Andanian mystery cult was regarded by Pausanius, a second-century C.E. geographer and traveler, as second in importance only to the cult of Eleusis (see his *Description of Greece* 4.33.3–6). The lengthy regulations of the Andanian cult are recorded in an inscription that dates from 92/91 B.C.E. (see *IG* 5/1.1390; trans. Meyer, *The Ancient*

Mysteries, 51–59). Little is revealed in the inscription concerning the initiation rituals and sacrifices. Rather, much of the inscription is taken up with regulations to be followed by those participating in the mysteries. In so doing, however, the inscription also reveals the organizational structure of this private religious association that became in southern Greece something of a public mystery cult.

The Andanian mysteries were laden with layers of officials. At the top stood Mnasistratos, with his wife and children, who was the founder (or refounder) of the cult as a result of his having donated a chest and books and who was duly honored with a crown, the lead position in sacred processions, and portions of the sacrifices. Under Mnasistratos was a supervisory council of ten male citizens, who were to be at least forty years old and appointed by general election. This group was to oversee the administration of the sacred officials. Under the supervisory council were the sacred officials, both male and female, who were appointed on the basis of their capabilities. From among the sacred officials were chosen mystagogues and twenty rod-bearers. The category of rod-bearers designates those who were to enforce the regulations of the association through physical punishment. The entire body of sacred officials was required to swear an oath of purity and of maintenance of the secrets of the mysteries. Once sworn, they received from the previous year's officials the cultic objects. The supervisor of the female sacred officials also was to appoint by lot one woman to oversee a group of sacred virgins to participate in the mysteries.

Other officials are mentioned in the regulations regarding the procession, including the priests and priestesses of the gods of the mysteries (particularly "the Great Mother" Demeter, the divine benefactress of humanity), the director of the games, the mistress of the banquet and her assistants, and various entertainers (i.e., "flute players"). There is a clear distinction between the initiated and the uninitiated, with the latter being banned from certain areas in the sacred grove. Some of the civic officials would continue in a related supervisory role during the time of the festival. Thus the supervisor of the market was in charge of the selling of goods in the area of the sacred grove, and the scribe of the magistrates administered the oath for the sacred officials appointed for the festival. The city treasurer was to oversee and audit five (wealthy) persons elected to manage the funds from the mysteries. These five were responsible for all the revenues and disbursements, and they were to provide a balanced financial account at the end of the festival, for the festival was to be financially self-sustaining, with any extra revenue reverting back to the city.

The sacrificial animals were to be chosen carefully according to specific criteria. Once sacrificed, portions were allotted to various officials and the remainder was consumed as part of a sacred meal. There is a clear concern in the Andanian cult inscription for orderly behavior during the festival—especially during the performance of the sacred rites. Disorderly behavior is regulated through the threat of fines, floggings, and expulsions, as designated by the officials and administered by the rod-bearers. In addition, the names of convicted offenders and their offenses were to be permanently inscribed on a building in the sacred area.

Little differentiation is made in the inscription between male and female or slave and free in terms of their participation in the sacred rituals. The sacred area itself is to be treated as a place of refuge for slaves. Differentiation, however, is made in terms of purity regulations (e.g., a female official is to take an additional oath of fidelity to her husband) and punishments (e.g., free persons are fined, whereas slaves are fined double and scourged). The Andanian cult inscription ends with the words: "The rule is to be authoritative for all time."

3. "VOLUNTARY" ASSOCIATIONS

Whereas the philosophical associations ("philosophical schools") and public religious associations ("mystery religions") were legal within the Roman Empire, private religious associations and professional associations (usually referred to more generically as "voluntary" associations) were technically barred under various Roman laws enacted as early as 184 B.C.E. Exceptions were granted to associations considered to have been established for some time—as, for example, the Jewish synagogues, which used this exemption to claim protection from local civic authorities. Yet despite occasional suppression by the authorities, voluntary associations never completely disappeared, and they were always able to reassert themselves as a viable presence in Greco-Roman society.

Private Religious Associations

Private religious associations met for the primary purpose of religious worship, but did so outside of the larger, civically sanctioned mysteries and cults of the day. Their domain was generally domestic—although a number of associations met in public spaces, and some even met as private religious associations within a larger public cult. Membership in a private religious association was based primarily on the attraction of the particular deity or deities worshiped. As such, they tended to draw persons from all strata of Greco-Roman society—although the elites of society were probably not as numerous in such associations as were the urban poor, slaves, and freed persons. Religious associations were generally gender-inclusive, at least in admitting to membership both males and females. As one inscription puts it, they are open to "men and women, freeborn and slaves" (*SIG*, 3d ed., 985). One even finds instances of the membership of children in Dionysiac religious associations. Nevertheless, there were also religious associations that were gender-exclusive—either all male or all female. And in mixed gender associations positions of leadership tended to be predominantly male, although there were a number of exceptions.

Professional Associations

Professional voluntary associations, or guilds, were made up of artisans or manual laborers. Guilds from a wide range of professions existed throughout the Greco-Roman world. Among laborers there were guilds for almost every profession, including leather-workers, purple-dyers, carpenters, bakers, tanners, silver-smiths, and the like. Domestic workers tended to stick together and so formed associations comprised exclusively of such. Entertainers had their own guilds; evidence exists for such associations as actors ("Dionysiac artists"), gladiators, and athletes. Professional musicians even formed themselves into professional associations, with their members being employed each year for the various cultic celebrations—such as those of the Andanian mysteries. There are, in fact, very few professions not represented in the extant records of the professional voluntary associations of antiquity.

Although the central commonality among members of professional associations was their occupation, the religious aspect of such associations should not be discounted. In every instance professional associations claimed the patronage of a deity or deities, and they took seriously their worship of such deities; whenever they met, the gods were invoked, and special festivals and rituals were central to their communal life. Often the deity or deities chosen had some connection to the particular profession. Thus we find such connections as a Delian association of shippers who worshipped Poseidon, the god of the sea, or an association of gardeners dedicated to the earth goddess Demeter. A number of different professions were associated with Dionysus, such as winegrowers, cowherds, actors, and pantomimes.

Professional associations, as well as private religious associations, were generally small in terms of membership, averaging perhaps fifteen to one hundred—although at times they could reach as high as four hundred or even twelve hundred members. The social status of the members was generally tied to the status of their particular profession within Greco-Roman society. As a highly structured culture, each profession would have had its place within the social stratification of the day. It is therefore safe to assume that, being laborers, the majority of the members of professional associations were of the artisan class, and so generally poor. Within this underclass, however, professional associations could include slaves, freed persons, and free persons. In a number of instances, in fact, recorded members of professional associations have three names, which indicates that they were Roman citizens. Likewise, the professional associations of antiquity had some wealthy members and drew on patrons to sponsor their activities.

Unlike many of the private religious associations, professional associations tended to be gender-exclusive. This was due in large part to gender separation in the work force. Thus professions dominated by males had professional associations comprised only of males and professions dominated by females tended to have all-female associations. What little crossover there was reflects elites of one gender patronizing an association of the opposite gender. For example, in one Roman association we have the case of a woman patron of an all-male association who is publicly thanked in an inscription for her patronage, but who does not herself participate in the banquet that her generosity has funded (cf. *CIL* 10243; dated 153 C.E.).

Organizational Structure

Professional associations often organized themselves by modeling the civic structures. This can be seen in the variety of civic titles used to designate associations, such as *phylē, hetairia, kollēgion, synedrion, synodos, ekklēsia,* and *politeuma.* The term for "citizenship" (*politeuma* and its cognates), for example, is found in use in two Egyptian associations, one religious and one professional (comprised of soldiers), in a Carian association dedicated to Zeus, and in a number of associations formed on the basis of a common homeland by those living outside their home city (e.g., the Tyrian Merchants at Ostia). There are also at least five instances of the use of *ekklēsia* as a community designator, from Samos, Asia Minor, and Delos, all from the second century B.C.E. to the second century C.E. In light of this evidence, it is especially interesting to note that Luke, who uses the designation *ekklēsia* for Christian groups, also calls the assembly of professional silversmiths at Ephesus an *ekklēsia* (Acts 19:32).

Community founders played a key role in the maintenance of the association, often presiding over the association or acting as its patron. We find instances of founders dedicating rooms or buildings for the use of the association. But founders could also maintain a high degree of control over the group. Such was the case with Xanthos, who would not allow the sacrifices to be undertaken if he were not present and reserved the right of succession for his designate (cf. *IG* 2, 2d ed., 1366).

Much has been made of the inclusive, egalitarian nature of voluntary associations, and, for the most part, this seems to have been the case at a very general level. Belonging to an association often brought about opportunities to participate in the organizational structure of the association. We also, however, find a degree of hierarchy in associations in so far as there are levels of leadership and honors to which members may aspire. Voluntary associations did not have a uniform organizational structure. This is not to say that they did not have any organizational structure. Indeed, they tend to reflect complex organizational behavior, albeit with local differences in structures and titles.

Voluntary associations were adaptive, well able to transform their structures in order to respond to new situations arising either internally or outside the group. Associations that shared a common designator and common leadership terminology did not always assign similar functions to those titles. This is well illustrated in the cases of eight associations of Sarapiastai found throughout the Greco-Roman world, which show no similarity of organization.

The range of titles found for functionaries within both religious and professional voluntary associations is vast. Some of the more common titles include "priest" and "priestess" (those who were responsible for the cult of the association), "treasurer" (*tamias,* who oversaw the collection and disbursement of funds), "secretary" (*grammateus,* who recorded the minutes of the meeting and insured that inscriptions were commissioned), "manager" (*epimeletēs*), and "examiner" (*exetastēs*). Many other titles are given on the basis of function, such as "water bearer" or "casket bearer" or "bouncer." The leader of the association could go by a number of titles, including *patēr, matēr, archōn,* and *prostatēs*—the latter found only occasionally in the sense of "patron." It is interesting to note that in at least six non-Jewish associations, five of which are in Macedonia, the title *archisynagōgos* is used of a leader. Such leaders would convene and chair meetings, oversee the rites, arrange for banquets and funerals, and enforce the regulations and decrees of the associations. They often also served as patrons or benefactors and were so designated through honorific statements.

Among leadership titles in associations we even find the occasional use of *episkopos* and *diakonos*. Only in some cases can it be determined what such titles indicate. Furthermore, the titles seem to have connoted different job descriptions from association to association. *Episkopos* was used to indicate a financial officer, a cult functionary, and a person who oversaw the honorific matters of the association. *Diakonos* was used of sacral officials, including a priest, and of liturgical functionaries. It is clear that the latter title was not restricted to the role of a table functionary, as is so often assumed.

Positions of leadership could be gained through appointment (particularly by the founder of the association), election, or, in some cases, through purchase, with the position going to the highest bidder. Funds, of course, would go to the administration of the association. Serving as a leader in an association brought with it great status within the association and, if the association was large enough, brought status within the larger social context. At the same time, positions of leadership could be financially burdensome, for cash-flow problems and revenue shortfalls were expected to be alleviated by those in leadership. This is particularly true in the case of the treasurer. An inscription from Kallatis records the situation of a treasurer who had to repay, with interest, association money he had lost in a maritime investment gone sour (cf. *SIG*, 3d ed., 1108; dating from the third century B.C.E.).

Patronage was also an important feature of association life, as it was generally in the Greco-Roman world. Wealthy patrons would bestow on a particular association financial donations to be used for operating costs, religious festivals, commemorative events, or social occasions. Such benefaction was recognized through public proclamations and honorary inscriptions. In fact, such benefaction was often encouraged among the membership by setting up some sort of agonistic situation—as witness, for example, an inscription from the Piraeus which, in the midst of honoring one benefactor, states that the statute was set up "so that also the others shall be zealous for honor among the members, knowing that they will receive thanks from the members deserving of benefaction" (*IG* 2, 2d ed., 1263; from the third century B.C.E.).

Such benefaction could be costly, and those who fell on hard times would have to withdraw their patronage. Among the Egyptian papyri we find the following letter:

> To Thrax, the president, and to the fellow members of the association, from Epiodoros. Since I am impoverished and unable to act as benefactor to the guild, I ask that you accept my resignation. Farewell. (*P. Kar.* 575; dated 184 C.E.)

One can certainly feel the pathos of the sender of this letter.

The other primary means for obtaining money for the association was through the collection of membership dues, either on entrance into the association or during attendance at each meeting. Membership into an association located in the Roman city of Lanuvium during the second century C.E., for example, was gained through the payment of an initiation fee of one hundred sesterces and an amphora of good wine (*CIL* 14.2112). Dues would go toward the association's expenses—although, in most cases, without patronage membership dues were not enough to cover all the group's expenses. Expenses would include the association's banquets, festivals, burial of members, and general expenses. In some cases money might be collected toward the upkeep of buildings or the erection of statues and inscriptions. Occasionally associations used their common funds to help out needy members.

Associations evidenced strong bonds among members. It is common to find kinship language used within the group, with members referred to as "brothers" and leaders and patrons designated as "fathers" or "mothers." These strong bonds were also expressed by the use of such a designation as "friends" for the associates of the group (cf. *IG* 2, 2d ed., 1369). The communal bond itself is often designated by the term *koinon* and its cognates.

It would be misleading, however, to suggest that internal community relations were completely amicable. We have, in fact, abundant evidence to the contrary. Inscriptions were often set up outlining the internal community regulations of associations. Members were warned against such abuses as "disorderliness" *(akosmeō),* taking another member's seat, insulting another member (or a member's mother), or physically abusing another. In general, failure to meet the moral or communal standards set by the association would result in one or more of any number of the following punishments: fines, flogging, restrictions from the association's rituals, temporary expulsion, or loss of membership. In some cases, a special group of "bouncers" was in place to remove violators of the association's regulations (see *IG* 2, 2d ed., 1368).

Although sometimes accused of all sorts of vices—not only in antiquity, but also today in scholarly literature—many religious associations included moral codes of conduct for both personal ethics and social morality. In a well-known inscription from Philadelphia in Lydia, for example, men and free women are prohibited from having sexual intercourse with anyone other than their spouse on pain of restricted access to the association's meeting place for the men and "evil curses" for the women (*SIG,* 3d ed., 985).

In addition to intragroup tensions, voluntary associations seem to have been also at times in conflict with one another. This is implied in the cry of the Athenian Iobacchoi: "Now we are the first of all the Iobacchoi!" (*IG* 2, 2d ed., 1368). It is also suggested in the stipulation of a priestess of Dionysus at Thessalonica that when she dies, if the designated association does not carry out her wishes, her bequest is to be transferred to a different association (*IG* 10/2.260). To be sure, the latter association will be watching the first group.

Membership in a number of voluntary associations included initiation rites. An Attic inscription dating from the second century C.E., for example, describes a process whereby a candidate must be examined by a number of officials to see whether he is "holy, pious, and good" before gaining entry into the association (*IG* II² 1369). Likewise, the fragmented ending of *IG* 10/2.255 from Thessalonica seems to indicate that one of the priestesses violated the association's code by involving noninitiates in the sacred rites of the association, which suggests that an initiation was required for full participation.

One particularly illustrative text from Philadelphia, in Egypt, records on papyri the "authoritative" laws of the association *(synodos)* of Zeus Hypsistos *(P. Lond.* 7.2193; dated about 69–58 B.C.E.). The association met in a public temple and elected a president and his assistant for a one-year term. No other officers seem to exist. The association itself was formed not by a single individual but by the members themselves. A monthly banquet is stipulated at which there are to be libations, prayers, and "other customary rites on behalf of the god." The text then goes on to set forth the association's communal regulations:

> All are to obey the president and his assistant in the matters pertaining to the association *(koinon),* and they shall be present at all command occasions to be prescribed for them and at meetings and assemblies *(synagōgai)* and outings. It shall not be permissible for any one of them to [. . . . .] or to make factions or to leave the brotherhood of the president to join another brotherhood or for men to enter into one another's pedigrees at the banquet, or to abuse one another at the banquet, or to chatter or to indict or charge another or to resign for the course of the year or again to bring the drinking to nought. (For text, translation, and commentary, see Roberts, Skeat, and Nock, "The Guild of Zeus Hypsistos.")

Unfortunately, the text becomes fragmented at this point. The exclusivity clause forbidding the joining of another association is particularly interesting since such a clause is not found in the extant regulations of other associations.

4. CONCLUSION

Further nuancing of the data regarding the various types of associations in Greco-Roman antiquity is certainly possible and necessary. For example, in addition to the two types of private associations described above—religious and professional—there are other types, some of which overlap with these two broad categories, such as associations based on common ethnic or geographic origin or residence in the same neighborhood.

Furthermore, it is difficult to demarcate the different types of associations as clearly as one might wish. The Pythagorean school, for example, was one of the earliest philosophical schools, yet its organization may have been influenced by Greek political associations *(hetaireiai)* or by Orphic associations *(thiasoi).* Indeed, the philosophical schools of the Pythagoreans and the Epicureans have often been understood as religious associations (cf. Strabo 17.1.8; Tertullian, *Apol.* 38.1.5; but see Culpepper, *Johannine School,* 248, 252). An example of a less well-known group comes from Egypt, where we have the following inscription:

"The philosophers [honored] Aelius Demetrius, rhetor, after Flavius Hierax their fellow diner dedicated [this statue of] . . . and father" (*I. Alex.* 98; dating from the second half of the second century C.E.). The public mysteries often contained within their structures smaller, private religious associations; these were sometimes composed entirely of members of the same occupation without formally being professional associations (see *SEG* 45 [1995], no. 2074).

One result of treating these usually separated associations together in this chapter is to underline the necessity of seeing all of them—and I would include here as well Jewish and Christian associations—as somewhat differing manifestations of the same phenomenon: as differing manifestations of voluntary associations. As further explorations of these varieties of voluntary associations are undertaken, we will undoubtedly begin to understand more fully the array of associative models that were operative in antiquity and under whose influence those who worshiped Jesus began to form themselves into associations. In doing so, we will see how much, as Ilias Arnaoutoglou has reminded us, "cultural context influences and shapes the forms of organisational structure" ("Between *koinon* and *idion*," 75).

BIBLIOGRAPHY

Arnaoutoglou, Ilias. "Between *koinon* and *idion:* Legal and Social Dimensions of Religious Associations in Ancient Athens." Pages 68–83 in *Kosmos: Essays in Order, Conflict and Community in Classical Athens.* Edited by P. Cartledge, P. Millett, and S. von Reden. Cambridge: Cambridge University Press, 1998.

Ascough, Richard S. "Translocal Relationships among Voluntary Associations and Early Christianity." *Journal of Early Christian Studies* 5 (1997): 223–41.

———. "The Thessalonian Christian Community as a Professional Voluntary Association." *Journal of Biblical Literature* 119 (2000): 311–28.

———. "Voluntary Associations and Community Formation: Paul's Macedonian Christian Communities in Context." Ph.D. diss., University of St. Michael's College, Toronto School of Theology, 1997.

———. *What Are They Saying about the Formation of Pauline Churches?* New York: Paulist, 1998.

Burkert, Walter. *Ancient Mystery Cults.* Cambridge, Mass.: Harvard University Press, 1987.

Cotter, Wendy. "The Collegia and Roman Law: State Restrictions on Voluntary Associations 64 B.C.E.–200 C.E." Pages 74–89 in *Voluntary Associations in the Graeco-Roman World.* Edited by J. S. Kloppenborg and S. G. Wilson. London: Routledge, 1996.

Culpepper, R. Alan. *The Johannine School: An Evaluation of the Johannine-School Hypothesis Based on an Investigation of the Nature of Ancient Schools.* Society of Biblical Literature Dissertation Series 26. Missoula, Mont.: Scholars Press, 1975.

DeWitt, Norman W. "Organization and Procedure in Epicurean Groups." *Classical Philology* 31 (1936): 205–11.

———. *Epicurus and His Philosophy.* Minneapolis: University of Minnesota Press, 1954.

Ferguson, Everett. *Backgrounds of Early Christianity.* Grand Rapids, Mich.: Eerdmans, 1987.

Harland, Philip A. "Claiming a Place in *Polis* and Empire: The Significance of Imperial Cults and Connections Among Associations, Synagogues and Christian Groups in Roman Asia (c. 27 B.C.E.–138 C.E.)." Ph.D. diss., Centre for the Study of Religion, University of Toronto, 1999.

Inwood, Brad, and L. P. Gerson. *The Epicurus Reader: Selected Writings and Testimonia.* Indianapolis: Hackett, 1994.

Kloppenborg, John S. "Collegia and *Thiasoi:* Issues in Function, Taxonomy and Membership." Pages 16–30 in *Voluntary Associations in the Graeco-Roman World.* Edited by J. S. Kloppenborg and S. G. Wilson. London: Routledge, 1996.

Meeks, Wayne A. *The First Urban Christians: The Social World of the Apostle Paul.* New Haven, Conn.: Yale University Press, 1983.

Meyer, Marvin W., ed. *The Ancient Mysteries: A Sourcebook.* New York: Harper & Row, 1987.

Roberts, Colin, T. C. Skeat, and Arthur Darby Nock. "The Guild of Zeus Hypsistos." *Harvard Theological Review* 29 (1936): 39–88.

Van Nijf, Onno M. *The Civic World of Professional Associations in the Roman East.* Dutch Monographs on Ancient History and Archaeology 17. Amsterdam: Gieben, 1997.

Chapter 2

The Jewish Experience: Temple, Synagogue, Home, and Fraternal Groups

Alan F. Segal

There is something quite anachronistic about studying the Jewish background of Christianity in order to illuminate Christian institutional structures. It is true that today Christianity is a major world religion with literally billions of adherents, while Judaism can muster but several million if every Jew is counted, regardless of religious sentiments. So it is easy to think that Jewish life is only one aspect of the enormous Christian movement—though, certainly, Christianity was influenced by a variety of forces beyond its original Jewish environment.

In the first century it was the other way around. Since Christianity was an eccentric form of Judaism, it is an enormous understatement to ask in what way Judaism influenced it. It is like asking how water influences fish. Furthermore, Judaism was an extremely widespread movement throughout the Persian and Roman Empires. The Jewish religion existed in a large variety of different forms, both in the land of Israel and elsewhere. The sects that Josephus mentions—Sadducees, Pharisees, Essenes, and Zealots—must surely be only a small part.

On the other hand, the Jewish community of the first century was but a small minority in a very culturally plural, individualistic, cosmopolitan world. And by comparison to Jewish life in the first century, the entire Christian movement—including everyone whose existence is attested in the New Testament, as well as in the noncanonical early documents—was but a tiny fraction. Whatever small percentage of the Roman Empire Judaism may have been, it was in the first century so vast by comparison to nascent Christianity that the mind boggles at any attempt to capture it in a few pages.

With this disclaimer about the impossibility of accomplishing the task given me, and with the recognition that it can be but hundreds of times harder to attempt the same thing for the pagan culture of late antiquity, I take up the topic "The Jewish Experience: Temple, Synagogue, Home, and Fraternal Groups," with some attention to the relationship of these matters to Christianity.

1. THE TEMPLE

The Jerusalem temple had been part of Israel's government since the days of Solomon. The desert tabernacle was the temple's forerunner and, according to priestly traditions, its explicit model. Although during David's time the building of a temple for YHWH was a controversial idea, the temple eventually became an integral part of the government and religious life of Judeans and later the Jews. Thus, the temple and the priesthood were the easiest institutions to justify in terms of the biblical record.

The Place of God's Presence

According to Scripture, the Temple was the place where God was manifested and where his presence was to be found. The Bible uses the root *s-k-n* to describe God's presence in the tabernacle. Later when bereft of a temple, Judaism used the same root to describe God's presence, his Shekinah. But while the temple stood, the Holy of Holies in the center of the temple complex was well understood as the place where God's presence was to be found.

For Christians, the presence of God, which was eventually symbolized by the Jerusalem temple for most of Judaism, was replaced by the spiritual presence of the risen Christ. For rabbinic Judaism, the only other major surviving development of the Judaism of those times, the presence of the Lord is to be found in prayer, study, acts of loving-kindness, and the community. The Gospels make several statements about the destruction of the temple—a topic that figures prominently in the charges against Jesus (cf. Mark 14:58, Matt 27). Jesus' action of overturning the tables of the money changers (Matt 21:12–13 par.) depicts the opposition as beginning in the ministry of Jesus—which, of course, may be debatable, but is also quite credible. But whether these traditions actually go back to the time of Jesus, they certainly reflect Christian opposition to the temple cult.

This impatience with the temple was not unique to the Christian movement. There were times, especially during the time of Jesus, when temple administration did not appear to live up to its august history. And everybody recognized that the second temple was not identical with the first, whose idealized presence is to be found in hundreds of places in the Bible.

The Political Importance of the Second Temple

During the Persian period the Second Temple was far more important politically than the First Temple had been. The high priest in First Temple times was an important figure but was not the source of direct governmental power while a Davidic king sat on the throne. The Persians, however, elevated the high priest to the status of the highest political leader within the country, thereby politicizing the Jerusalem temple far more than it had been during First Temple times.

Furthermore, the Second Temple, as the administrative center of the native Judean government, had functions that went far beyond those of the First

Temple. The Persians continued to confirm the high priests at the temple throughout their period of rule. And during the subsequent Hellenistic period, the Ptolemies were able to develop the same kind of confidence in the high-priestly family. But when the Seleucids conquered the area from the Ptolemies, the Greek ruler Antiochus IV intervened in the succession to fill his empty coffers. His tampering started a civil war, which resulted in the establishment of the Maccabean monarchy.

The Maccabees were neither in the Davidic line nor part of the high-priestly family. So although they had delivered the people from Seleucid rule, their taking of the high-priestly diadem and the kingly scepter was held to be a usurpation by large sections of the Judean community. Thus the high priesthood became entangled in the country's complicated political life.

The temple, therefore, became one of the major organs of the state. Indeed, the temple at Jerusalem took on much of the national administration. Since the administration was handled from the temple courtyards, which had evolved by the first century B.C.E. into an institution in their own right, some of the governmental functions became imbued with holiness. Some of the temple's courtyards, however, were secular enough to be visited by Gentiles or unclean Israelites. To be sure, neither the Persian governors nor the procurators of Rome could legally enter very far into the temple precincts, for, being Gentiles, they were too impure. So the purity of the temple also acted as a barrier, ensuring a measure of independent deliberation on the part of the priesthood. At the same time, however, during Herodian and Roman times ultimate power was clearly vested in the ruler or the Roman procurator, no longer in the priesthood.

Criticism and Veneration of the Temple

Whereas the institution of the temple could be justified on the basis of the Torah and the historical prophets, critical voices were often raised against the contemporary temple administration. Many Israelites felt that the new temple, which had been modeled partly on Hellenistic conventions, did not live up to the ideals of the ancient institution. Furthermore, as had become clear during the Maccabean revolt, the high priest was not an independent ruler but subject to confirmation or manipulation by the ruling authority—be it Persian, Ptolemaic, Seleucid, Roman, or native Hasmonean. The Hasmonean successors of the original Maccabees, in fact, were severely criticized by many sects—including the Essenes, the Pharisees (and later the rabbis), and the Christians—for having subverted the institution. The claim of the Maccabees to the offices of both king and high priest, which was viewed by many as a constitutional violation, may have been responsible for some of their unpopularity.

Although Herod, who followed the Hasmoneans, was roundly hated by almost everyone, his extensive renovations and beautification of the Jerusalem temple enhanced Jewish pride and the reputation of Jerusalem all over the Roman empire. The high priest and the priesthood, therefore, were accused and criticized far more often than the building itself. Because the temple symbolized

God's presence as well as the government, people who were unhappy with the state could frame that disquiet as opposition to the administration of the temple cult, and vice versa.

The most obvious critics of the Jerusalem temple were the Qumran sectarians. Josephus tells us that they did not participate in the temple cult. The documents of the sect tell us far more. The *Temple Scroll (11QT)* and the more recently published document called *Miqṣat Maʿaśê ha-Torah (4QMMT)*, as well as the many writings already known, portray the Dead Sea Scroll community as priestly in character and holding entirely different views as to how the temple ought to be run.

The implications of these critiques of the temple were far-reaching, for the temple was not solely a religious building. From the sixth century B.C.E. to the end of the first century C.E., it was also one of the central organs of government, since the priesthood became the highest and most stable internal political power. This was in keeping with Persian notions of imperial rule. The result was that charges against the temple were seen not just as opposition to the management of the temple but also as impiety and even disloyalty to the state.

Jews living in exile, who evidently had no detailed knowledge of the temple's administration, saw the Jerusalem temple more unambiguously as a symbol of national pride. They waited to hear messengers from the temple proclaim the holidays, feasts, and festivals. All who lived close enough and could afford the journey made the trip to the temple on the three great pilgrimage holidays—on Passover, Pentecost, and Sukkoth.

Holiness and Purity Associated with the Temple

Holiness surrounded the Jerusalem temple in concentric circles of increasing purity. At the very center of holiness was the dark chamber of the Holy of Holies, which was to be entered only by the high priest and only once a year, on Yom Kippur. When Pompey brought Judea under Roman control in 63 B.C.E., he broke this rule by entering the Holy of Holies. And when Titus destroyed the temple in 70 C.E., he suffered, according to rabbinic legend, apt retribution—for God caused an insect to crawl into his ear and kill him, thereby violating his own inner sanctum, as it were, and showing Titus's true stature in the eyes of God.

Priests and Levites Serving in the Temple

The basic duties of the temple were performed by the Levites, who were professional assistants trained in specific services. Serving the Jerusalem priesthood was a much larger cadre of amateur priestly volunteers. Most of these priests served on a regular schedule, taking leave from their ordinary occupations to come to Jerusalem for their prestigious service.

The Grandeur of the Temple and Its Service

As enlarged and rebuilt by Herod on the earlier Persian structure, the temple at Jerusalem was widely admired by Jews and Gentiles alike as a grand edifice in a mixed semitic and hellenistic style. Gentiles could and did donate sacrifices as an act of piety toward the Jewish state and people. At holiday times Jews and Gentiles from all over the world converged on Jerusalem for pilgrimage. After special occasions, such as childbirth, Jews also made the journey. Whether or not they traveled to Jerusalem, all Jews were expected to contribute to the upkeep of the institution. Most honored that obligation, wherever they lived. As a result the temple was an extremely well supported and maintained institution in spite of its growing obsolescence.

No more dramatic description of the temple and its service exists than that provided in the *Letter of Aristeas*, which was written by an Alexandrian Jew sometime between the second century B.C.E. and the first century C.E.:

> The ministering of the priests was absolutely unsurpassable in its vigor and arrangement of its well-ordered silence: All work hard of their own accord, with much exertion, and each one looks after his appointed task. Their service is unremitting, sharing the sacrifices, some undertaking the carrying of wood, others oil, others wheaten flour, others the sweet spices, others offering burnt offerings of the parts of the flesh—all of them exerting their strength in different ways. They divide the legs of the bullocks with both hands, though they are more than two talents in weight in almost every case, and then with an upward movement rip off with each hand in an amazing way a sufficiently large portion with unerring accuracy. The sheep and the goats are similarly treated in a remarkable way, weight and fat notwithstanding. Those whose concern it is choose in every case spotless specimens outstanding for fatness: Thus the aforesaid procedure is carried out. They have a rest room set aside, where those who are resting sit down. When this happens, some of those who are rested stand up with alacrity, but no one orders the arrangements of their ministry. A general silence reigns, so that one might think that there was not a single man in the place although the number of ministers in attendance is more than seven hundred, in addition to a large number of the assistants bringing forward the animals for sacrifice: Everything is carried out with reverence and in a manner befitting supreme divinity. It was an occasion of great amazement to us when we saw Eleazar engaged on his ministry, and all the glorious vestments, including the wearing of the "garment" with precious stones upon it in which he is vested; golden bells surround the hem [at his feet] and make a very special sound. Alongside each of them are "tassels" adorned with "flowers," and of most beautiful colors. He was clad in an outstandingly magnificent "girdle," woven in the most beautiful colors. On his breast he wears what is called the "oracle," to which are attached "twelve stones" of different kinds, set in gold, giving the names of the patriarchs in what was the original order, each stone flashing its own natural distinctive color—quite indescribable. Upon his head he has what is called the "tiara," and upon this the inimitable "mitre," the hallowed diadem having in relief on the front in the middle in holy letters on a golden leaf the name of God, ineffable in glory. The wearer is considered worthy of such vestments at the services. Their appearance makes one awe-struck and dumbfounded: A man would think he had come out of this world into another one. I emphatically assert that every man who comes near the spectacle of what I have described will experience astonishment and amazement beyond words, his very being transformed by the hallowed arrangement on every single detail. (*Letter of Aristeas* 92–99; trans. R. J. H. Shutt, *OTP* 2:19).

2. THE SYNAGOGUE

The other major Jewish institutions of Hellenistic times—the synagogue and the Sanhedrin—were defined by tradition rather than biblical statute, although a pretext had to be found in the Torah to justify the institutions after the fact. Many institutions were firmly rooted in tradition but not mentioned explicitly in Torah, just as political parties and the president's cabinet are not mentioned in the U.S. constitution but are fixed features of the political system. The synagogue, in particular, was not mentioned by the Torah.

Origin and Purpose of the Synagogue

No one knows how the synagogue came into being or what its original function was. Synagogues are known to have existed in the Holy Land in the first century only because they were described in the New Testament and in the writings of Josephus. There is still little unambiguous archaeological evidence for synagogues in Judea until after the destruction of the temple.

The purpose of the synagogue was threefold: to be (1) a place of assembly, both for public discussion and for the celebration of various meals; (2) a place of study; and (3) a place of prayer. Public assembly might also include the secondary functions of lodging travelers and catering dinners. The Talmud describes synagogues in terms of these three functions, and they are well supported by archaeological discoveries. All three functions are ancient, and much scholarly energy has been expended on efforts to ascertain which was the original function.

Whatever and whenever its origin, however, the synagogue was legitimated by its functions. It was a place where the Torah was read, studied, and interpreted and from which the author of the Torah was addressed in prayer. This is clarified by the New Testament, as well as by Philo and Josephus, in describing synagogues in various places outside Judea. Almost everything that is currently known about ancient synagogues may be found in S. Safrai's article "The Synagogue" and Lee Levine's book *The Ancient Synagogue.*

Synagogues in the Diaspora and Galilee

According to Philo, synagogues were plentiful in the Diaspora even before the destruction of the Jerusalem temple. Many synagogues were to be found in the Jewish parts of the city of Alexandria, the greatest city of the ancient world and home to enormous numbers of Jews. Some were neighborhood-based; others were founded by various trade guilds. Philo remarked that each trade—whether glassblowing, goldsmithing, silversmithing, or whatever—had its own synagogue in Alexandria. In the center of the city was the Great Synagogue, which, according to Philo, reached enormous proportions. When it was full for a Jewish feast, semaphore signals were needed to guide the congregation to the correct prayers.

Galilean synagogues are now famous to us, not only on account of references to them in the New Testament but also because of the well-preserved mosaic floors that have been uncovered in the excavations of synagogues in Galilee that existed in the third century and later. Judea, evidently, had a lesser need for synagogues while the Jerusalem temple stood, and so they seem to have arrived there later.

We do not, in fact, have archaeological evidence for synagogues in Judea until the second century. But there is an inscription that attests to a synagogue in Galilee, which probably comes from the first century:

> Theodotus, son of Vettenus, priest and *archisynagogos*, son of an *archisynagogos*, grandson of an *archisynagogos*, built the synagogue for the reading of the Law and the teaching of the commandments, and the guest house and the rooms and the water supplies as an inn for those who come from abroad; which his fathers had founded and the elders and Simonides. (*CIJ* 2.1404)

The term "synagogue" refers first of all to the congregation gathered, and not primarily to a building. It was used of edifices earlier in the Diaspora than in the Holy Land. Rabbinic tradition maintains that there was a synagogue within the precincts of the Jerusalem temple, but this may be an anachronism.

The Governance of the Synagogues

Evidence about the governance of the synagogues has come down from ancient writings and archaeological remains. The synagogue leaders were called *archontes*, which was a standard term for "rulers" or "those in authority" in many Greek organizations. A prominent congregant might refer to himself or herself as a mother (*mētēr*) or father (*patēr*) of the synagogue on a burial inscription. The president of the synagogue was called the *archisynagōgos*. Laypersons led prayers and Torah readings. The epigraphy seems to demonstrate far more participation by women than later practices would imply (cf. Brooten, *Women Leaders in the Ancient Synagogue*).

There was nothing, however, that corresponded to the modern practice of hiring a rabbi to supervise the religious life of the congregation—both because the rabbinic movement was in its infancy and because the whole idea of a specific ministry to a community had not yet evolved. The synagogue was the focus of Jewish activity in the Diaspora, but the life that centered there was quite different from the one that the rabbis were later to ordain.

The "God-Fearers"

Besides Jews, a group of Gentiles called "God-fearers" (*sebomenoi* or *phoboumenoi*) is mentioned in the New Testament and in synagogue inscriptions. They were evidently an unorganized and undefined group of fellow travelers who might contribute to the upkeep of a synagogue and even attend services and observe some of the Jewish laws, as they saw fit. Some of them wanted to convert to Judaism. Others, favorably impressed with the Jewish religion, wanted only to bestow some civic honor on the local synagogue. In an inscription from Aprodisias, a list of synagogue patrons is followed by a list of the God-fearers, who have Greek names and occupations. The contention that early Christian support in synagogues came from these God-fearers, based on reports in Acts, can no longer be dismissed as the imagination of Luke.

3. FRATERNAL ASSOCIATIONS

Jewish society, like the ancient Near Eastern and Hellenistic societies before it, depended on private organizations for a number of different social functions. Especially in the Diaspora, Jewish communities were organized into what may have looked like fraternal associations.

Political Organization of Diaspora Jews

Many ethnic groups in the Greco-Roman world were organized into communities and licensed. The constitutional license in Greek law was known as a *politeuma* (plural *politeumata*). In Alexandria, the Jewish *politeuma* was maintained by a board of directors, of whom one was "the first among equals" (Latin *primus inter pares*). This board of directors maintained a court system and kept the community's civil records of marriages, births, divorces, deaths, and community events. The Jewish community in Alexandria was a kind of city within a city, operating autonomously—except for taxes and other duties due to the municipality. Jews, therefore, had a kind of anomalous existence, for they were citizens in a way and not citizens in another way.

This ambiguity was the cause of much suffering in first-century Alexandria. It was contested both by the Greeks of the city, who were headed by the *gymnasiarch* and the Roman governor, and by the Jewish community, which wanted citizenship, access to these institutions, and exemption from various taxes on noncitizens. Riots ensued. When the rioting was over and both groups sent embassies (actually the Jewish group sent two embassies with differing aims) to Emperor Caligula at Rome, it was up to the Roman central authority to decide what status the Jews would enjoy.

Fortunately for the Jews, Caligula was assassinated while the embassies were awaiting a decision. Unlike Caligula, who would surely have sided against the Jews, the new emperor, Claudius, wrote a more evenhanded rescript that guaranteed the Jews a continuation of their ancient rites and rights but did not automatically advance them to full citizenship. Rather, they were to remain with lawful rights *(isopoliteia)* that were equal to citizenship. And thus the Jews remained until Christian emperors repealed their toleration in the fifth century.

Jewish Guilds and Societies

Professional guilds also existed among the Jews. Although there is not much evidence of such Jewish guilds before rabbinic times, we know that there were Jewish guilds of wool dealers and dyers, bakers, mule drivers, butchers, and weavers. For instance, a Jewish inscription from Joppa, which is datable to the second century C.E., mentions a guild of fishermen (*CIJ* 945:142–32).

The reason for guilds is obvious. They represented the positions of particular economic groups. If they were strong, they could affect the pricing of their commodity. And they may well have somehow participated in the training of apprentices.

There were also various societies that met for other functions. The rabbis mention the *ḥăbûrôt*, which were groups of more pious followers of the rabbinic lifestyle who kept purity on a higher level than most other Jews. These would naturally have overlapped with the Hellenistic notion of philosophical schools, which were primarily organized to teach and inculcate the philosophies of their founders. The famous Aphrodisias Inscription tells us that in Late Antiquity there was a synagogue charitable society that had been organized for the purpose of feeding the hungry, and that God-fearing Gentiles as well as Jews contributed to its upkeep.

A considerable amount of research in recent years has focused on ancient voluntary associations and their relationship to Judaism and Christianity. There is no doubt that to outside pagan observers, both Judaism and Christianity sometimes appeared to be a kind of voluntary association or philosophical school.

Burial Societies

The most obvious private organization of the synagogue, which began in medieval times and continued later, was the *hevra kadisha* or the burial society. Unfortunately, we have no clear references to these groups in antiquity, though we have a considerable number of cemeteries.

Starting in the third century, the Jewish and Christian communities of Rome used catacombs to bury their dead, as did many pagan families and the Etruscans. That the catacombs were also used to shelter their respective communities in times of trouble is secondary to their primary function. We have clear distinctions between Jewish and Christian communities, as witnessed by the different catacombs. That does not mean, however, that pagans would have understood—or even cared to understand—the difference between them, for the most part. And it seems easy to see why pagans sometimes understood Christianity, at least, as a kind of burial society, given the facilities for prayers and services that existed in the catacombs.

4. THE HOME

The Israelite family was not the nuclear family that people in the Western world know today. It was composed of a much larger group of relatives, who might live together or near each other in groups that usually comprised several generations. Generations and branches of a family might settle close to each other, sharing a courtyard between them. In good weather the courtyard served as the scene for most of the family's activity. (Cf. S. Safrai, "Home and Family," for a detailed description of the talmudic home.)

Rituals and Observances of the Home

After the destruction of the Jerusalem temple, the synagogue and the Jewish home took over a great many of its functions. Many Jewish holidays that were proclaimed by the temple and celebrated there now became the purview of either the synagogue or the home. Synagogue ritual is adapted from temple ritual. But virtually every Jewish holiday and ritual has a focus in the home, and only secondarily, in addition, at a synagogue location.

Since Jews are enjoined by rabbinic law to pray three times a day, the home is the natural locus for at least morning and evening prayers. At the same time, the synagogue may also have public prayer three times a day, based on the temple service. All the laws of personal status and purity are centered around the home, though they may also be performed at synagogues.

The Hebrew purity laws outlined in Scripture, for example, postulate that several substances are able to transmit states of impurity. These rules need to be practiced everywhere, but the main focus for them is the home and table. The Bible suggests that impurity could be removed by various rituals involving the passage of time, full bodily immersion (for all purification was accomplished by the immersion of the entire body), and temple sacrifice. After the destruction of the temple only two remained. The community might erect baptismal fonts, called mikvehs, for use in purifying. But it is also clear from archaeology that well-to-do homes contained their own mikvehs—sometimes several of them. Synagogues were often constructed near the ocean, which could serve as a mikveh. Or they might even construct a mikveh for the use of the community.

Purity rules, however, were mostly enforced within the home. Contact with a corpse might transmit impurity, but so did childbirth or menstrual blood. Though impurity did not necessarily imply sin, there were cases in which contact with various materials—such as pigs or pork products—was always forbidden and did imply sin. On the other hand, a woman was unclean, not immoral, because of her menstrual period. A man who touched her would also be contaminated. These might not imply anything more than impurity, which had to be ritually removed. But it might also imply immorality if it was consciously contracted. For example, corpses and sexual relations both cause impurity; yet the dead must be buried, and marital relations are stipulated as positive actions. If, however, a couple knowingly had relations when the wife was in her menses, that would imply sinfulness.

Purity Rules

It is easy to get confused about these complicated rules and content oneself with the simplistic and wrong implication that Christianity had nothing to do with them. It is growing increasingly clear today, however, that the different sects of the first century, including Christians, each had their own interpretation of how the Jewish purity rules should be observed (cf. Klawans, *Impurity and Sin in Ancient Judaism,* showing how the different sects of Jews interpreted the ambiguous biblical rules).

The Qumran sectarians, who are comparable to Josephus's description of the Essenes, were committed to staying as close as possible to absolute ritual purity. They thought they would be called on to fight alongside the angels to remove the enemies of God in the soon-to-arrive apocalyptic end. There is also evidence that they viewed themselves as worshiping together with the angels. So they reasoned that since purity was necessary to worship in the Jerusalem temple, it was also necessary in order to come into the presence of the divine through ascents to the heavenly temple. And since they were celibate, at least for the most part, they tended to equate sinfulness and impurity, since any sexual activity was usually viewed as a violation of the community's vows.

The rabbis, by contrast, tended to separate sin and impurity as completely as possible. They were neither apocalyptic in orientation nor interested in celibacy. Thus, for them, impurity and immorality were entirely different realms of life. The rules for impurity might operate, as much as possible, without interfering one with another. They used the notion of intention to distinguish between simple impurity and sin, where it was unclear. The rabbinic insistence on purity was a practical device that functioned to enforce Jewish identity. In point of fact, such great differences in interpretation are possible because the Bible is ambiguous on many of the fine points of how purifications should to be carried out.

Jesus' few pronouncements on purification seem to put him much closer to the Qumran group than to the rabbis. This is in line with the portrait of earliest Christianity as an eschatological community—in fact, one that valued celibacy quite highly, even if it was not universally practiced.

Tithe Offerings and Food Prohibitions

The Hebrew tithe offerings were special duties or taxes on produce that were owed to priests. The Pharisees, and especially the *hăbûrôt,* refused to eat food from which the tithes had not been properly taken. Though the rabbis ruled that these laws were only relevant within the land of Israel, tithe offerings obviously had the effect of distinguishing the more pious from the less pious.

Hebrew Scripture also contains a series of food prohibitions, including (among other things) not eating blood, a kid seethed in its mother's milk, any shellfish, or any of the birds and animals which themselves scavenged or violated these rules by predation. The rabbinic party greatly expanded these ordinances into what is today known as "the kosher rules." It is a bit difficult to isolate how much of what observant Jews do today was present in the first few centuries. But the rabbinic movement stipulated that all animal slaughter be done in a humane way, so as not to give excessive pain to the animal, and that meat and milk be kept strictly separate—stipulations that were effected as a safeguard against violating the biblical rules.

The Bible says not to eat a young goat boiled in its mother's milk. It says nothing, however, about keeping separate utensils for meat and milk—or about eating a fowl, which provides no milk for its young, at the same meal as cheese. Yet as the biblical rules were interpreted, poultry was treated like meat and cheese was treated like milk, so that combining them became illegal as well.

Purity Rules, Food Prohibitions, and Group Coherence

It is extremely difficult for modern society, which has few such rituals, to understand the complex messages implied by rabbinic notions of purity and kashrut. Christian writings, in fact, have traditionally portrayed the Pharisees as hypocritical, and this has been reflected in Christian views of Jewish practice generally. But purity rules and food prohibitions are typical not only of Jews but also of many of the world's religions.

In the context of the first century C.E., Jewish purity rules functioned to separate Jews from their Hellenistic social context and imposed on them a degree of group coherence, which had been destroyed when the nation-state was dismantled by the Romans. In such a group consciousness, the traditional role of the priests was acknowledged by having duties payable to them properly set aside as a provision for both them and the poor. And in such a group consciousness, the ritual status of those Pharisees who practiced purity was raised.

Just as upward mobility can be achieved in a modern society by means of higher income or the more tasteful spending of one's newly gotten financial resources, so too upward mobility could be achieved in ancient Israel by seeking greater ritual purity, which granted higher prestige and status. The Pharisees represented many in the trades classes, as did a few Christians. Thus just as people with ambiguous status could, in later times, remove that ambiguity by joining the Christian community, so Pharisaic Jews of the first century could raise their status and eliminate ambiguity by taking on a higher ritual obligation.

The continuance of the purity and kashrut customs has been enormously important for Judaism. With the destruction of the temple, the purity and food laws have been not only greatly adumbrated, but the locus of the laws is now the home and the other social institutions of the community. The kitchen receives the supervision of the whole family and the table has the sanctity of the Jerusalem temple. Every meal in the Jewish home, therefore, becomes a reenactment of the cosmic role of the temple in bringing God's presence to earth.

5. CHANGE IN PERSONAL STATUS

All of the preceding discussion has assumed a relatively stable social system. To be sure, we have seen both the temple and the synagogue develop and change—and, eventually, the temple destroyed. But there is no doubt that the temple, the synagogue, and the home were all meant to further the stability of the Jewish people and to reestablish that stability after the fateful revolts against

Rome. As such, they are institutions designed for stability. Nonetheless, in outlining them we would be remiss if we did not also consider the forces for change that were equally strong.

Conversion, Cosmopolitanism, and Individualism

It was during the Second Temple period that the notion of conversion developed. Conversion was virtually impossible during the period of the first temple. All over the ancient Near East people remained what they were when they were born. It is during the period of the Second Temple, however, that people began to get the notion that they could change from one religious group to another. In order for that to happen, two conceptions had to exist: cosmopolitanism and individualism. These quite modern values were stimulated by Hellenization.

The Greek word *hellēnizō*, which is cognate with the English word "hellenization," means literally "to speak Greek" or "to learn to speak Greek." This is an apt term, for the Hellenistic age was characterized by the learning of Greek by non-Greek peoples all over the Mediterranean. Greek remained the dominant language of trade in the area throughout the Roman period.

With the Greek language came the ability to find out about other people living quite differently in other cultures and worshiping other gods. This developed a sense of cosmopolitanism—literally, the conception that one was a citizen of the universe and not just a citizen of one's own city. At the same time, comparison between the lives of others and one's own life brought with it the realization that one was an individual, not just a member of a group. It was these features, especially visible in Hellenistic Jewish writings, that made religious change both possible and, indeed, desirable.

It was desirable because a people who had access to so many different ways of understanding themselves needed a variety of sects, denominations, or parties, to handle and accommodate the change. This is quite obvious in our own society, which has even more cosmopolitanism and individualism to offer. Many people see the denominationalism of Protestantism or of Judaism, for example, as a great detriment. Taken to an extreme, it may be. But it is the basic way that every religion has accommodated itself to our very cosmopolitan and individualistic world.

Hellenization among the Jews

Although Hellenization affected all parts of Jewish society—not only in the Diaspora, but also within the land of Israel itself—it did not infuse all parts of Jewish society equally. The community living in the land of Israel may have kept more of its native ways, but Hellenization was pronounced even there. The geographical size of the nation changed several times, and most of the time the district of Judea was not even as big as the modern state of Israel. It was closer, in fact, to the geographical limits of metropolitan Jerusalem today. And, surrounded by cities that had been founded or resettled on Greek models, it could hardly ignore Hellenistic culture.

The Hellenization of Jewish society was also true because there was a good deal of Hellenistic influence within the confines of Jerusalem itself, a city where Hellenization took on unique forms but nevertheless flourished—as evidenced, in part, by the amphitheater and gymnasium constructed there in the second century B.C.E. The process of Hellenization was similar to two contemporary types of cultural contact—that is, to modernization, which is a phenomenon in the Third World, and to secularization, which is a phenomenon of religious transformation in Western societies.

These transformations are stimulated by a society's need to acculturate a new world system. They also involve a breakdown of the power, wholeness, and appeal of the traditional religion. In modernization, the stimulus comes from Western industrial or colonial rule. In secularization, the stimulus comes from the intellectual structures of a philosophy that challenges traditional religion. In both cases the traditional unity of the culture is broken down. Often this outcome is accompanied by parties that seek pluralism and free competition between varieties of religious expression. But it can just as easily spark fundamentalism, which seeks to privilege a form of religion that presents itself as being traditional, as a way of warding off the dangers of acculturation.

Both notions are obviously at home in our own society today. With care, they can be seen to have functioned in ancient Jewish society as well. The common feature in the two developments is that the particular religious establishment in question can no longer take for granted the allegiance of its population. As a result, the religious tradition—which was an almost unconscious, self-evident assumption about the world—becomes a set of beliefs that has to be marketed. And this is true for whatever sect or denomination we might study or discuss.

New Perceptions and Outlooks

The situation in Second-Commonwealth Israel was similar, in that Greek culture and the spread of trade eroded the automatic assent of Judeans to the religion of their forefathers and made an entirely new world perception necessary. The religion had to evolve new ways of understanding itself in a Greek environment and explain itself in new contexts. Furthermore, the process of Hellenization progressed at different rates in different social classes, making more distinct separations between the social classes in Judea and exacerbating class conflicts.

Those people who were interested in a life of leadership within the community and could afford an education sought out Greek educational institutions. They consisted mostly of the traditional aristocrats and priests, who were entrusted with running the country. A developing trades class also learned rudimentary Greek for use in international exchange. These Jews felt that Greek philosophy and culture did not necessarily interfere with their Jewishness.

The Pharisees appear to have been a client group whose rulings were fairer for the developing trades class and, as they grew in power, the landowners. Immediately one has to ask whether the Christians competed directly with the Pharisees. Although we see Jesus disputing with the Pharisees, he is clearly not a member of that class. An interest in how Torah is to be understood does not make one a Pharisee, it merely makes one a Jew.

6. THE STANCES OF THE CHRISTIAN NEW TESTAMENT

Jesus preached a radical overturning of the community and an apocalyptic end. These features mark him as a member of the more rural, more traditional voice of Judea and Galilee. His critique of Pharisaism was not that it was not radical enough but rather that it was too radical. It broaches immorality by making changes. Jesus' teaching "Be perfect as your heavenly Father is perfect" (Matt 5:48) was meant to bring people back to older notions of truth and justice, not to institute new ones.

But that, of course, was not the only way that Christianity competed with Judaism. The community represented in the Gospel of Matthew appears to have been in competition with the Pharisees for the hearts and minds of the synagogue. In Matthew, Jesus' love commandment is a legal position, in competition with the Pharisees' legal enactments, while in Luke and Mark it is meant to explode the Jewish legal system. The latter is clearly the position of a predominantly Gentile branch of Christianity. But Matthew is different. His perspective makes legal sense within the Jewish community.

Paul clearly represents the model of a Jewish convert. He moves from the conservative side of Pharisaism, likely a Shammaite or yet more conservative. By his own admission he was zealous to bring others around to his understanding of piety. His conversion was effected because of visions and revelations, which Luke attributes to his audition on the road to Damascus. This fits the events that Paul tells us. And it is clear from his own brief accounts of his life that his conversion experience was but the first of a number of religious visions and revelations of the risen Christ.

It does not seem to me that the kinds of categories available to understand the positions of Mark, Matthew, and Luke make much sense of Paul. He believes himself to be still a Jew, albeit a messianic one. And he believes that God will soon make his plan manifest to all the world, insuring the conversion of the rest of the Jewish community. Paul, therefore, seems to represent a convert from one variety of Judaism to another—at a time before it became clear that Christianity would not exist within the sectarian structure of Judaism (cf. my *Paul the Convert* for a more extensive treatment of Paul along these lines).

BIBLIOGRAPHY

Akenson, Donald Harman. *Saint Saul: A Skeleton Key to the Historical Jesus.* New York: Oxford University Press, 2000.

Brooten, Bernadette J. *Women Leaders in the Ancient Synagogue: Inscriptional Evidence and Background Issues.* Chicago: Scholars Press, 1982.

Cohen, Shaye J. D. *The Beginnings of Jewishness: Boundaries, Varieties, Uncertainties.* Berkeley: University of California Press, 1999.

————. *From the Maccabees to the Mishnah.* Philadelphia: Westminster, 1987.

Hayward, C. T. R. *The Jewish Temple: A Non-Biblical Sourcebook.* London: Routledge, 1996.

Klawans, Jonathan. *Impurity and Sin in Ancient Judaism.* Oxford: Oxford University Press, 2000.

Kloppenborg, John S., and Stephen G. Wilson, eds. *Voluntary Associations in the Graeco-Roman World.* London: Routledge, 1996.

Levine, Lee I. *The Ancient Synagogue: The First Thousand Years.* New Haven: Yale University Press, 2000.

Moxnes, Halvor, ed. *Constructing Early Christian Families: Families as Social Reality and Metaphor.* London: Routledge, 1997.

Rutgers, Leonard V. *Subterranean Rome: In Search of the Roots of Christianity in the Catacombs of the Eternal City.* Leuven: Peeters, 2000.

Safrai, Shmuel. "Home and Family." Pages 728–92 in vol. 2 of *The Jewish People in the First Century: Historical Geography, Political History, Social, Cultural and Religious Life and Institutions.* Edited by S. Safrai and M. Stern in cooperation with D. Flusser and W. C. van Unnik. Philadelphia: Fortress, 1996.

————. "The Synagogue." Pages 908–44 in vol. 2 of *The Jewish People in the First Century.*

————. "The Temple," Pages 865–907 in vol. 2 of *The Jewish People in the First Century.*

Satlow, Michael. *Tasting the Dish: Rabbinic Rhetorics of Sexuality.* Atlanta: Scholars Press, 1995.

Segal, Alan F. *Paul the Convert: The Apostolate and Apostasy of Saul the Pharisee.* New Haven, Conn.: Yale University Press, 1988.

————. *Rebecca's Children: Judaism and Christianity in the Roman World.* Cambridge, Mass.: Harvard University Press, 1986.

Stanton, Graham N., and Guy G. Stroumsa, eds. *Tolerance and Intolerance in Early Judaism and Christianity.* Cambridge: Cambridge University Press, 1998.

White, Michael. *The Social Origins of Christian Architecture.* Vol. 1, *Building God's House in the Roman World: Architectural Adaptation among Pagans, Jews, and Christians.* Vol. 2, *Texts and Monuments for the Christian Domus Ecclesiae in Its Environment.* Harvard Theological Studies 42. Valley Forge, Pa.: Trinity Press International, 1996, 1997.

Chapter 3

Building "an Association *(Synodos)* . . . and a Place of Their Own"

Peter Richardson

In the opinion of most scholars, early Christian church buildings derived from house churches, on the one hand, and Roman basilicas, on the other. These are two useful and relevant models. I propose, however, an architectural background for early church buildings that includes both of these models but is much broader—that is, that of the voluntary associations of the ancient world. My title for this chapter attempts to capture this focus in the words of a Roman official, as quoted by Josephus, who spoke of Jews at Sardis in 50–49 B.C.E. as having "an association *(synodos)* . . . and a place of their own" (*A.J.* 14.235).

Since both synagogues and churches were viewed in antiquity as "associations," the suggestion that Jews and Christians adopted various organizational structures and architectural forms from Greco-Roman structures and forms of the day should come as no surprise. And if early church buildings drew much of their inspiration from the various philosophical, religious, and professional associations, we need to take account of this fact in assessing the community formation of the early church.

I suggest the following general picture: In the earliest period (say, to 150 C.E.), people of the Roman empire viewed Christian communities on the analogy of Jewish synagogues, which were themselves viewed as associations. In the creative middle period (approximately 150 to 325 C.E.), when Christianity and Judaism veered apart, churches continued to be thought of as associations. In the post-Constantinian period (325 C.E. onward), however, when the association analogy was less relevant, Christian use of the basilica—an architectural form that consciously expressed power, with civic and imperial implications—contributed to the church being viewed as part of the power elite, though other Christian groups fell outside that power structure and continued to be more like voluntary associations.

1. RECENT STUDIES AND ISSUES

A recent symposium volume—*Voluntary Associations in the Graeco-Roman World,* edited by John S. Kloppenborg and Stephen G. Wilson—provides the grounding and sets out the issues for our subject. After an overview (Stephen Wilson) and taxonomy (John Kloppenborg), contributors examine *collegia* and *thiasoi* (John Kloppenborg), *philosophiai* (Steve Mason), and *ekklēsiai* (Wayne McCready). Others investigate synagogues as *collegia* (Peter Richardson), Egyptian Jewish associations (Valerie Heuchan and Peter Richardson), associations in Philo's Alexandria (Torrey Seland), Mithraism (Roger Beck), Pergamon's Asklepieion (Harold Remus), Delos associations (Hudson McLean), the Dead Sea Scrolls (Eileen Schuller; Sandra Walker-Ramisch), women in synagogues (Sharon Lee Mattila), and the Roman legal situation (Wendy Cotter).

These studies establish the following points: that voluntary associations included religiously discrete groups such as Mithraea, synagogues, and churches, in addition to other associations such as trade, merchant, and philosophical groups; that most voluntary associations valued patrons and benefactions highly; that most associations carried on a similar range of functions, such as communal meals, cultic actions, and burials, despite substantial variations in emphasis; that the Roman state dealt with these varied groups on much the same basis, even if it sometimes needed to differentiate among them; and that the architecture of these associations was varied but shared certain common features. These studies provide much of the basis for this chapter.

Does an analysis of the architecture and artifacts of ancient associations have any direct relevance for an understanding of those groups? The architecture and art of Mithraea, for example, proclaimed the aims, values, and ideals of the group. Yet though Mithraea were self-revealing, Mithraic art was mainly for insiders and not meant for public display. How, then, are we to interpret their cave-like spaces with a pair of parallel inward-facing benches on which a small group of participants evidently reclined or knelt at their communal meetings? Written descriptions of the Mithra cult might suggest a strongly hierarchical organization. But the architectural bench arrangement seems to presuppose a more democratic group. Should we, therefore, read the social experience of the Mithra cult from the written descriptions or from the archaeological evidence?

The social character of a group was expressed in the form of its building—whether called a *synodos,* a *collegium,* a *thiasos,* a *philosophia,* or an *ekklēsia.* This was for two complementary reasons: (1) groups consciously constructed buildings that expressed their character, as in the case of Mithraea; and (2) groups adapted to the character imposed on them by the structure of their meeting space, as happened with the churches' early use of houses. Deliberate architectural expression—that is, the first reason given above—must lie behind the choice of building type for structures of associations, as I will highlight later. Also important, however, though more controversial, is the second reason cited, which is perhaps best termed architectural determinism. Examples from both the past and today suggest that the form of one's surroundings influences socioreligious developments—whether a church, a synagogue, or a mystery cult. Groups take on the character of the spaces they occupy.

Social character was also expressed in the various architectual details included in the physical structure that housed a Greco-Roman association. Statues, busts, and portraits, along with inscriptions on the walls, colonnades, columns, and mosaic floors, as well as frescoes—all of which were in honor of the patrons of the association—provided an implicit *cursus honorum* among the members. Members and visitors alike were reminded of the rewards of generosity, especially the "honor" *(timē)* that accrued to the patrons. Dedications attested to the privileges of wealth and social status, to patron-client obligations, and to hierarchical relationships.

Inscriptions attest, as well, to the use of this practice among both Jews and Christians. To judge from synagogue structures from the second century B.C.E. to the fifth century C.E. and from church epigraphs in the fourth and fifth centuries C.E., there was no difference in this regard between associations, synagogues, and churches. Both synagogues and churches sought benefactions and engaged enthusiastically in patronage and honor systems similar to those of other private associations of antiquity.

Association buildings, however, have attracted relatively little attention. This is, perhaps, partly because the category is flexible and partly because most were unassuming. *Collegia* or *thiasoi* turn up in urban centers, but they have not frequently been identified as buildings of intrinsic archaeological or architectural interest. Many associations have simply disappeared from view because of the vagaries—or the strategies—of excavators (as at Ephesus and at Miletus), not because they were unimportant. Sometimes buildings of associations were readapted later for other uses, occasionally by Christian churches (as at Mactaris), so that some associations have disappeared beneath later uses. Only very extensive excavations (as at Ostia) have revealed enough associations to permit generalizations.

Because many association buildings were adapted from the houses of patrons and benefactors, even in antiquity an association might have been publicly invisible and become visible only when extensively renovated. Groups were small. A house renovation might have accommodated from fifteen to one hundred members. A group of three houses in Priene, each of which housed a voluntary association, illustrates such residential locations away from the city center. And being away from the city's center, they illustrate also the scholarly lack of attention to such structures.

2. RELATIONS BETWEEN SYNAGOGUE AND CHURCH ARCHITECTURE

Investigations of Egyptian Judaism have led to the conclusion that Egyptian synagogues, as well as synagogues elsewhere, were seen by their members and by society as associations. The inscriptional evidence for Egyptian synagogues is especially strong and includes the following features: (1) the buildings were dedicated to the Ptolemaic king and queen; (2) donors were named alongside the honorees; (3) the buildings were called *proseuchai* ("prayer houses"); and (4) architectural features such as a gateway, *peribolos, exedra,* holy garden, and appurtenances were mentioned.

These features describe the typical Egyptian-Jewish "house of prayer" *(proseuchē)* as a complex structure, not unlike an association. But since the inscriptions derive from different buildings, the details cannot be combined to provide a description of any one Jewish synagogue. Nonetheless, these early Jewish community buildings represented an important stage on the way to self-definition among Jewish communities. For alongside the community itself—that is, a "synagogue" *(synagōgē)* in the root sense, a group of people—went the creation of a building—that is, a "house of prayer" *(proseuchē)* for communal use. Gradually the terminology altered so that *synagōgē,* which originally expressed the communal character of the group, later came to be used also of the building.

Equally important is the fact that monastic Jewish groups preceded monastic early Christian groups. An ascetic monastic establishment near Alexandria—the Therapeutae referred to in Philo's *De vita contemplativa*—was an early eremitic or hermitlike experiment that emphasized withdrawal, worship, and contemplation. Some of its inspiration came from Egyptian religious practices—especially, it seems, its surprising paralleling of men's *(therapeutai)* and women's *(therapeutrides)* roles. The Therapeutae formed a first-century B.C.E. or C.E. monastery. Similarly, the Qumran community on the northwest shore of the Dead Sea is a coenobitic or communal establishment that dates from the same period. Both communities—the Therapeutae and the Dead Sea covenanters—had ceased functioning by the early second century C.E.

The actual sources of early Christian monasticism are unclear. It is remarkable, however, that when significant documentary evidence for Christian monasticism begins to appear in the late third century, both eremitic (i.e., individual, hermitlike) and coenobitic (i.e., communal) monastic structures were being developed in both Egypt and Palestine. The only relevant models for these two forms of monastic life appear to be those of Jewish monasticism in Egypt and Palestine about two centuries earlier. This typological analogy remains somewhat perplexing. Yet the parallelism emphasizes the natural Christian takeover of Jewish models. And this inclusion of monastic development expands the range of early Christian building types that need to be studied.

Two points emerge from this brief review: (1) that there are close architectural relationships between synagogues and churches, and (2) that both synagogues and churches are to be seen as part of the larger category of voluntary associations. The association model is particularly important during the formative period of Christian development in understanding the variety of influences on early Christian architecture. For while it is true that the architecture of churches developed along several main tracks—the three main forms being house churches, meeting houses, and basilicas—the overall set of developments should be interpreted within the context of ancient Greco-Roman associations. Architectual differences between the various types of association structures should not be exaggerated, since all forms were utilized by the associations.

Christian use of the three main architectural forms can be traced within the third century, paralleling synagogue developments exactly. House churches were the earliest, but there were also meeting houses and purposely built basilicas already before Constantine. Following Constantine's conversion, however, there were speedy and sweeping changes. House churches and meeting houses tended to die out, and monumental basilica structures—together with octagonal or round memorial buildings—took over. But even when the basilica became the norm, the form was altered by the influence of features derived from the functional solutions for association buildings.

3. ARCHITECTUAL FEATURES OF ASSOCIATION BUILDINGS

A large number of association buildings have been identified in the excavations of various cities of the ancient world. Here I will set out the basic architectural features found in some of these excavations, beginning with structures and artifacts found in western Asia Minor, moving on to those found on a small but significant island of the south Aegean Sea, then to those found in Italy, then those in North Africa, and concluding with the situation in Syria-Palestine. The following section will briefly assess what those architectural features tell us about what took place in the various voluntary associations.

Priene

Priene was located in southwest Asia Minor, in the region of Caria, north of Miletus. It was one of the twelve Ionia cities of Asia. According to tradition it was colonized by Ionians and Thebans. In the fourth century B.C.E. it was rebuilt on a rectangular "gridiron" plan. The site contains many ruins and is a fine example of ancient town planning.

Three small religious structures, which had been adapted from normal houses, were located at the west end of Agora Street beside the city wall. They provided facilities for Jews, adherents of Cybele, and the Alexander cult, respectively. The earliest of the three structures, which was built relatively soon after Alexander's death, housed a *heroōn* for Alexander the Great. Another housed the orgiastic cult of Cybele, the "Great Mother *(Mater Magna)* of Phrygia," with its strong sense of initiation and the mysteries, whose priests castrated themselves. The third, and latest, was a house of prayer *(proseuchē)* or synagogue *(synagōgē)*, where Jews and affiliated non-Jews studied, worshiped, and established a communal identity.

The juxtaposition of the three cults in neighboring houses implies that all three originated in similar communal conditions. Each had matured sufficiently that a benefactor emerged to provide a permanent home, thereby encouraging communal formation and accelerating further development. The three buildings collectively reflect the conditions of many voluntary associations—that is, located on the town's edge, relatively invisible, and relying on patrons. When the associations were endowed with a building, each adapted the house in successive alterations to serve their needs for meeting, dining, worship, administration, and storage, so that they grew increasingly useful for meeting ritual and communal needs.

The Alexander and Cybele buildings are so ruined that little can be said about them. A sacrificial pit and a statue of Cybele identified one cult building as that of Cybele. In the house next door Alexander reputedly lived while he was at Priene in 334 B.C.E. An inscription from elsewhere in the city mentioned an *Alexandrium,* and another inscription on the door post of this second house warned that only the pure clothed in white garments could enter the sanctuary. Figurines, including a bust and partial torso of an Alexander-like figure, were also found in the excavations of this house. And the living area and a room on the north of the courtyard had been modified for cultic purposes.

More can be said about the synagogue, which dated from the second or third century C.E. and was located at the end of a short lane off Agora Street. A stele with a menorah, which indicates a Jewish community, was discovered in the excavations, as well as a smaller relief with a menorah. Remains of a Doric order, which was part of a colonnade that carried the roof over the new assembly hall, were also found. Benches provided seating. Later, it appears, the Jewish community had negotiated with its neighbor to the east for an additional one square meter for a Torah niche, which suggests a developing ritual need. Other rooms surrounded the main assembly hall and a new entrance was arranged on the west.

A well-known inscription from Stobi amplifies the Priene synagogue's functional character. Polycharmus, a patron of the second or third century C.E., had donated a house as a synagogue but reserved a portion for his family's use. After two phases of synagogue structures, the building was rebuilt as a Christian church. The original donor, Polycharmus, was named in the floor inscriptions of stratum I of the building, while the following inscription on a column was still in use during the church phase:

> [Claudius] Tiberius Polycharmus, also called Achyrius, father of the synagogue in Stobi, who has conducted himself with all the prescriptions of Judaism, in accordance with a vow, [gave] a house as the holy place, and the *triclinium* with the colonnades [*tetrastoa*], from his own funds, without touching in any way the funds of the sanctuary. But the right to and ownership of the upper story, I, Claudius Tiberius Polycharmus, reserve for myself and my heirs for life. If anyone wishes to make alterations contrary to my decisions, he shall pay the patriarch [of the synagogue] 250,000 denarii. This agreement was made by me. Repairs of the tiles of the upper level are to be made by me and my heirs. (Adapted from *CIJ*, 694)

A similar but earlier inscription from Acmonia in Phrygia (ca. 60 C.E.), which mentions several patrons, is also relevant to Priene:

> This building constructed by Julia Severa was restored by Publius Tyronius Clades, head of the synagogue for life [*dia biou archisynagōgos*], and Lucius, son of Lucius,

head of the synagogue, and Popilius Zotikos, *archōn,* from their own funds and from money contributed: the walls and the ceiling; and they made safe the gates; and all the remaining decorations. The community [*synagōgē*] honored these men with a golden shield on account of their virtuous life and their good will and zeal for the community [*synagōgē*]. (Adapted from *CIJ,* 766)

These inscriptions attest to the selective alteration of various parts of the building, embellishments to the structure, the combination of communal and individual gifts, acknowledgment of patrons, and even the reservation of some parts of the building for patronal use. They flesh out the social-historical background of gifts of houses to associations, such as the three houses found at Priene. And they make it clear that the use of houses should be seen as part of the larger pattern of association buildings.

Miletus

Miletus was located in southwest Asia Minor, in the region of Caria, and situated on the coast opposite the mouth of the Maeander River. The city was thought to have been founded about the twelfth century B.C.E. by Ionian Greeks, and it became the principal settlement of the twelve Ionian cities in Asia. It was a flourishing trading city and a center of literature and philosophy—the birthplace of the philosophers Thales and Anaximander, the traveler Hecataeus, and the courtesan Aspasia.

Though no buildings of associations have been found in Miletus, some evidence is still relevant. Surviving inscriptions on the seats of the very large Roman theater, which dates from the second century C.E., indicate that various associations held reserved seats. These inscriptions have not been published, so the full range of groups reserving seats is uncertain. Two groups, however, illustrate associative life in a city of the Greek East. Side by side in the theater were seats reserved for the "Jews and God-fearers" of Miletus, hinting at a synagogue group, and for the "emperor-loving [*philaugoustoi*] goldsmiths." That Jews and Imperial cult members might sit side by side underscores the range, importance, and visibility of associations that had seats in the theater in a city such as Miletus.

Ephesus

Ephesus was located on the west coast of Asia Minor, in the region of Lydia, and situated on the Caÿster River near its mouth, south of Smyrna. Because of its importance as a port of trade the city flourished. Subsequently it fell to the Persians but continued to thrive. Alexander the Great established a democratic constitution there. The city was taken by the Romans in 133 B.C.E. But it still remained great and powerful. Through ancient times Ephesus, the city of the goddess Artemis, was celebrated for its temple of Artemis and as a great commercial city whose wealth was proverbial.

It is surprising, given the extensive excavations at Ephesus, that no buildings for associations have been identified. About one hundred of the 4000–5000 inscriptions from Ephesus, however, refer to private voluntary associations, with a total of sixty groups referred to in these inscriptions—forty-one trade associations (in fifty-two inscriptions) and nineteen cultic associations focused on gods and emperors (in twenty inscriptions). Of the inscriptions referring to cultic associations, seven refer to the Jewish god, one to Isis/Sarapis, one to Nero along with his mother and his wife, one to Trajan, three to Hadrian, and five generally to the *sebastoi*. Only eight inscriptions, however, mention buildings or building renovations. But since inscriptions require structures on which they can be mounted, there must have been substantially more than eight buildings.

The epigraphic information provided by these inscriptions covers a wide range of associations, from low-status trade associations (e.g., fishermen, fishmongers, cowherds, wool-workers, linen-workers, and bread mixers) to high-status professional associations (e.g., bankers and physicians), through various midrange groups (e.g., master builders, mystics, silversmiths, and coppersmiths). Religious-cultic associations included Demeter, Dionysus, Hermes, Poseidon, Zeus, Asklepios, as well as the God of the Jews, and Isis/Sarapis. Among imperial figures, Nero was the earliest named by a private association. No Flavians are named on the inscriptions found at Ephesus, though one inscription is dated to Domitian's reign, that is 88/89 C.E.

Of particular interest is an inscription at Ephesus that describes an association of fishery tollhouse workers, who dedicated a building to Nero, Agrippina, and Octavia (ca. 54–59 C.E.), together with the *dēmos* of the Romans and of the Ephesians. Eighty-eight members, both males and females, contributed, with their gifts ranging from four columns at the top end to five denarii at the bottom. The structure, which was evidently located near the southeast corner of the harbor, has not been found. It was, however, publicly prominent, to judge from the stele's inscription that lists the following architectural elements: eighteen columns (including one painted column), Phokaian stone paving in an "open area" and in the "colonnade beside the stoa," a tile roof of three hundred tiles, and a brick structure of four thousand bricks—with the stoa's floor being covered with rush mats. The inscription also tells us that L. Fabricius Vitalis, the construction superintendent, donated two of the eighteen columns—the ones beside the temple of the Samothracian gods—plus the adjacent altars.

The main structure of the association was probably a utilitarian, freestanding, brick building with tile roof. Its most impressive feature was likely the courtyard with its stoa—perhaps four columns wide by seven columns long, making up a total of eighteen columns. Both the courtyard and the stoa were paved attractively in Phokaian marble, which suggests that the courtyard where the group assembled was the focus of this association building. This inscription is the closest we get to precision concerning the architectural character of an association building in Ephesus.

Sardis

Sardis was the capital of the region of Lydia in western Asia Minor, being located at the foot of Mount Timolus. From the sixth century B.C.E. on it was an important inland city. It was burned about 498 B.C.E. in the revolt of the Ionian cities against the Persians. But it was rebuilt by the Persians and became the residence of the Persian satraps of western Asia. Alexander the Great took it without a struggle in 334 B.C.E., after which it flourished under both the Greeks and the Romans.

The imperial court-bath-gymnasium-synagogue complex at Sardis is well known. A monumental Roman bath and a Greek *palaestra,* whose gymnasium rooms have survived in the mostly unexcavated north wing, sandwiched the imperial cult facilities. The synagogue, which dates from the third century C.E., occupies the matching south wing of the gymnasium, which dates from the second to the third centuries C.E. Since the gymnasium had educational and philosophical functions, it may have seemed appropriate that the "association" *(synodos)* of Jews at Sardis continued those study activities when they took over this already remodeled portion of the gymnasium. The intermediate use of the space between gym and synagogue has not been identified.

Even though the synagogue structure was probably not the direct successor of the earlier building that Josephus describes, the decree he records is still relevant:

> Lucius Antonius, son of Marcus, proquaestor and propraetor, to the magistrates, council and people of Sardis, greeting. Jewish citizens of yours [v. l.: "ours"] have come to me and pointed out that from the earliest times they have had an association [*synodos*] of their own in accordance with their native laws and a place of their own [*topon idion*], in which they decide their affairs and controversies with one another. . . . (*Antiquities* 14.235, citing a decree of 50–49 B.C.E.)

Despite the lack of a demonstrable connection between this decree and the earlier synagogue structure, it may be surmised that the Jewish community at Sardis was considered an association *(synodos)* since at least the mid-first century B.C.E. and that it had "a place of its own" where it decided its own affairs. Later the synagogue was moved into grander quarters in the gymnasium's south wing, which was a major public structure and where it was juxtaposed with the imperial cult (as also at Miletus). The synagogue building was larger than those of most other associations (though see below on Pergamon, Ostia, Pompeii, and Sufetula). Its rich decoration, extensive inscriptions, large forecourt, and adjacent shops can be paralleled among other associations.

Pergamon

The name Pergamon (also Pergamum; modern Bergama) means "citadel" or "stronghold." The city was located in the region of Mysia in northwest Asia Minor, about fifty miles (or eighty kilometers) north of Smyrna. It became famous because of the victory of Attalus I over the Gauls in the latter half of the third century B.C.E. Eumenes II, the son of Attalus I, extended the city and greatly adorned it architecturally. He also founded a famous library in the city and built governmental buildings on a succession of terraces at the summit of the acropolis, which rises nine hundred feet above the plain. During his reign occurred the remarkable development of Pergamene sculpture, which was more modern in spirit than the older Greek art. The city remained prosperous under the Romans, and during the time of the empire many fine buildings were erected on the acropolis and beside the river below.

Three important association structures in Pergamon are particularly relevant: a philosophical hall, a "hall of benches," and a Sarapeion. These three structures illustrate clearly the broad range of association buildings. For though these three buildings were purposely built on the main street to house their respective associations, and though their respective associations shared strong cultic concerns, their formal differences prohibit facile generalizations about buildings for associations.

The philosophers' association building, which can be dated to the early first century B.C.E., comprised an entry hall, which faced the processional way, together with a bath, a meeting hall, and a cult area, with these latter three opening off the entry hall. The meeting hall was a raked theatral or theaterlike seating area—with thirteen curved rows averaging six meters, which would have held about 150 persons, and a wide opening to the entry. East of this was a handsomely finished room with busts, and a niche opposite the door, probably used as a *herōon;* one bust was of Diodorus Pasparos, to whom the association was dedicated, whose benefactions probably included the decorative marble work that identified this as a high-status association. West of the theatral room was a multiroom bath. Unlike the hall of benches, with its communal arrangements, this *philosophia* had formal theaterlike arrangements—like an *odeion* or *ekklēsiastērion*—that distinguished audience from teacher.

Adjacent to this, the hall of benches was part of a complex of shops and houses on a lane off the processional way, overlying earlier houses but not constructed from them. Atypically, its main space was like two large dining rooms *(triclinia),* whose open ends faced each other. Members reclined on high, wide dining benches around the room's perimeter. It was also atypical in that the fronts of the benches, which had niches in them, were so high that stairs were needed. The diners focused on two cult altars associated with Dionysus. There may have been ancillary service rooms on the south, but these cannot be clearly identified. The hall of benches represents a form continuous with the triclinium-centered adaptations of houses familiar from other associations.

The Sarapeion or "Red Hall," which was located in the lower town and dated from the early second century C.E., was entered through a large *peribolos* of one hundred by two hundred meters, with landscaped gardens. The courtyard probably held an earlier temple to Isis, in addition to the large basilica of twenty-six by sixty meters, with reversed apse and stairs to the roof. Below the basilica floor, a tunnel gave access to a huge seated statue of Sarapis on a large platform, so that priests could speak from Sarapis's mouth. The high brick walls of the basilica, which have survived to a height of nineteen meters, were originally faced with marble and alabaster and still give the impression of wealth, power, and influence.

Delos

Delos was the smallest island of a group of islands called the Cyclades in the south Aegean Sea. The city of Delos was the seat of a great sanctuary in honor of Apollo, which was one of the most famous religious foundations of antiquity. From the time of Solon (ca. 638–559 B.C.E.), the Athenian law-giver, Athens sent an annual embassy to the Delian festival, in which the "tunic-trailing Ionians" honored Apollo with boxing, dance, and song. After the Persian War the city became the center of the Delian League, which was formed to resist Persian aggression. With its conquest by Alexander the Great, it first became an Athenian dependency and then was semi-independent. It was made a free port by the Romans and developed into a great commercial center. After 88 B.C.E., however, when it was raided by the forces of Mithridates VI, it soon fell to the status of an almost uninhabited place.

Twenty-four voluntary associations are attested on Delos, including groups based on ethnic, geographical, or professional factors—as, for example, the Italian *Hermaïstai,* the *Hēraclēsiastai* of Tyre, the *Poseidōniastai* of Berytus, two Sarapeia, and a synagogue. Most noteworthy is the similarity of several of the buildings—especially the Hellenistic houses, which had been adapted for use by various associations—with cultic adaptations that, though different from each other, had common elements.

The synagogue, which dated from the early second century B.C.E., may have been an adaptation of a Hellenistic house that was built around a large peristyle courtyard (though that is disputed). On one side were two large adjacent rooms, one with benches and a marble *thronos,* together with a suite of smaller rooms. The main entrance was the peristyle courtyard.

Before 153 B.C.E. the Poseidōniasts of Berytus—that is, the merchants, shippers, and warehousemen—had constructed a building, which also had a peristyle courtyard and off which were two other courts, one the cult center with three altars. Off the cult center were four small parallel rooms, three of which were small shrines. And along another side of the main courtyard was a suite of rooms—partly for commercial purposes, partly for living areas—with a long inscription describing the building and its patrons.

Sarapeion A, dated about 220 B.C.E., was an early adaptation of a house for cultic purposes, which a lengthy epigraph refers to as being those of the "Therapeutae." A small temple was raised slightly above a sunken courtyard, off which were other rooms at different levels. Sarapeion B had a courtyard with a stoa on one side, a small temple fronting the court on another side, and a large meeting room with altars and small rooms that served as shrines.

Pompeii

Pompeii, a flourishing provincial town of southern Italy, was situated on the Bay of Naples some thirteen miles southeast of Naples, at the foot of Mount Vesuvius. It contained many villas, but was severely damaged in 63 C.E. by an earthquake and totally destroyed in 79 C.E. by an eruption of Vesuvius. Owing to the preservation of the town by layers of ash and pumice that buried it, the remains of Pompeii afford in many ways the most complete information we possess about Roman material civilization.

The extensive excavations of Pompeii have not disclosed as many associations as might be expected—perhaps because associations were suppressed after the riots of 59 C.E. (cf. Tacitus, *Ann.* 14.7.4). The Villa Imperiale, with its long promenade, three or four meeting rooms, a barrel-vaulted banquet hall, a ladies' dining room, and other facilities, was likely "hired for an evening by a collegium or sodalicum that had no clubhouse of its own" (L. Richardson, *Pompeii*, 220). The Temple of Isis, which had been rebuilt *a fundamento* by a patron, N. Popidius Celsinus, just north of the large theater, was a small temple within a four-sided peristyle, from which five wide doorways opened onto a large rectangular hall for ritual meals, with Egyptianizing frescoes. The building's form repeats remarkably closely a nearby fresco of the worship of Isis—with priests, altar, and two facing choirs or groups of worshipers.

Outside the walls of Pompeii, the Villa dei Misteri was a large country villa with atrium, peristyle, *tablinum,* several *triclinia,* a large winepress and an even larger kitchen. While it may never have been used as an association building, the frescoes in one large room illustrate clearly the ritual of a Dionysiac cult in the period and so are useful evidence for the character of cult-associations. The Insula Iuliae Felicis was a military association with bath, swimming pool, dining areas, shops with mezzanines, upper story apartments, colonnades, and gardens.

Ostia

Ostia was located in Latium, Italy, and situated on the left bank of the Tiber near the ancient mouth of the river, about fifteen miles southwest of Rome. According to Roman tradition, it was the oldest colony of Rome and dated from the seventh century B.C.E. Excavations, however, have revealed nothing earlier than the fourth century B.C.E., and most historians think the city was first established as a Roman military camp about 340 B.C.E.. Rome's need for grain, other foodstuffs, and building materials, which were imported from Spain, North Africa, Sicily, and Egypt, caused Ostia to grow rapidly as the commercial port of the empire's capital city. Marcus Agrippa built a theater there, and behind it was a vast colonnade where the corporations that organized the import-export trade and barge services on the Tiber had their offices. For centuries the ancient city was quarried by Roman princes for building materials and art objects, but it remains one of the most impressive archaeological sites of ancient Italy.

Since Ostia's guilds were not suppressed, numerous important—sometimes imposing—*collegia* can be identified. Perhaps there were as many as fifty-nine. Two buildings across the street from one another, located near the western end of town, reflect Ostia's wealthy ambiance. On the south side of the Decumanus was a handsomely articulated Schola of Trajan, while on the north side was an equally substantial Association of Shipbuilders. Perhaps the same association built both as a coordinated effort to impress Ostia with the ship-builders' influence.

The Schola of Trajan had a columned entrance that was calculated to impress. Within, a formal courtyard was dominated on one side of the axial approach by a statue of Trajan; beyond, a long raised pool down the center dominated another courtyard, at the end of which was a fine *triclinium*. Across the street, the shipbuilders had an association building with entry, courtyard, raised axial temple, stoas, and another courtyard beyond. It was one of five similarly designed complexes in Ostia.

The guild of the *Vigiles*, Ostia's firefighters, was altogether different. The barracks centered on a large courtyard, which was surrounded by a portico and rooms on several floors and shops along one side. The courtyard focused on an imperial cult chapel. Inside the chapel was a low platform, with altars to Antoninus Pius, Lucius Verus, L. Septimius Severus, and two to Marcus Aurelius. Outside around the portico were statues of other imperial figures.

Similarly, the association of builders met in a building with an open courtyard, a portico, five *triclinia*, a chapel, a kitchen, and other rooms. An inscription records details of another association building and lists various contributions, among which were a statue and two busts of Marcus Aurelius, five busts of Antoninus, and busts of Lucius Verus, Commodus, and Concordia. Also recorded were six benches, four tables and two stools, hot baths with heating apparatus, candelabra, six mattresses and four cushions, along with distributions of gifts to all the members. It is notable in this group of associations how closely tied they were to the members of the imperial family.

An imposing triangular courtyard just inside the Porta Laurentina held temples for Cybele, Attis, and Bellona. It also included separate guild buildings for "the reed-bearers" *(cannophori)*, "the tree-bearers" *(dendrophori)*, and "the spear-carriers" *(hastiferi)*, where the *taurobolium* was practiced. Near the Via della Foce was a building for Sarapis, dated about 127 C.E., with living quarters. There was also a cult to Isis, though the building has not yet been found. And there were at least fifteen Mithraea throughout the city, though with none suggesting wealth.

Outside the Porta Marina was the well-known first-century C.E. (and later) synagogue, with successive adaptations of an earlier house. A large hall with an *aedicula* or Torah shrine dominated the eventual scheme. There was also a second main room with benches for community meetings and meals, an adjacent kitchen, and ancillary spaces. The Ostia synagogue, in fact, is a good example of a house adaptation that must, at first, have been fairly invisible, but with successive renovations came to be quite a visible feature in the neighborhood.

North Africa

Among a number of relevant association structures in North Africa, only two will be here noted. The first is at Mactaris (modern Makhtar), where was found an imposing association building for the *Iuventutes*—an imperially sponsored, quasi-military youth association aimed partly at keeping the peace—that was designed around an attractive peristyle courtyard and included a variety of other facilities. A church, which was a later conversion of the Iuventutes's building and entailed a substantially new structure built from the earlier materials, overlies part of the original association building. The second is at Sufetula (modern Sbeitla), where was found a very large and rather finely designed association building that provided for the needs of a guild of craftsmen—with hall, apsidal triclinium, and workshops, all of which were laid out around a handsome peristyle courtyard.

These two structures represent two of the larger associations that existed in North Africa. And in the case of the association at Mactaris, the appropriateness of the transition from voluntary association with imperial overtones to church demonstrates an important aspect of the close relationship of associations and churches.

Syria-Palestine

Evidence from the ancient east for associations is not especially strong, despite the existence of important eastern cults and extensive trade activities. The eastern evidence, however, is important for understanding the relevance of association structures for early Christian communities.

The destruction about 257 C.E. of Dura Europos, which was a military town on the Empire's fringe, preserved important second- and third-century C.E. evidence of several significant adapted buildings—in particular, those of Mithra, Gaddes, Zeus, and the Palmyrene gods, as well as a synagogue and a church— where the underlying houses can still be traced with varying degrees of success. Their urban locations parallel those of the Priene associations, which were in mainly residential areas beside the city wall. And all of these buildings seem to have been richly decorated in a common Syrian/Parthian style.

This group of association buildings at Dura provides a striking snapshot of developments as one moves from the second through fourth centuries. Houses were still being adapted for the use of associations, but such adaptations were beginning to show differentiated features—in some cases, in fact, monumental features—that were specific to the developing needs of the group.

Here we will leave to one side the growing body of pre-70 C.E. synagogues in the Diaspora and Palestine, which I have discussed elsewhere (cf. my "Early Synagogues as Collegia"; also "An Architectural Case")—as well as other relevant structures of the late first century C.E. (e.g., the Mithraeum at Caesarea Maritima)—to allude almost parenthetically to early church architecture in Jordan and Syria.

The Dura Europos church, which was adapted for Christian use about 230 C.E., is usually considered the earliest significant church structure. Recently Thomas Parker and Mary Louise Mussell have claimed that Aqaba in Jordan, only half a century later, boasted a structure that was purposely built as a church sometime about 290 C.E. (cf. Rose, "Early Church"). If they are correct, this is the oldest known structure that was originally built as a church. The excavators claim it was built in a somewhat crude basilical style, though that is not apparent from the photographs. Such pre-Constantinian evidence of Christian structures—which, on the one hand, were wholly similar to other cult-association buildings, and yet, on the other, rather novel in an informal adaptation of a basilical style for a purposely built structure—is extremely important for understanding the development of early Christian communal buildings.

The situation in Jordan and southern Syria during the Byzantine period, however, seems rather startling, for the archaeological evidence suggests that Madaba in Jordan had at least fourteen churches, that nearby Umm er-Rasas had fifteen, that Gerasa (Jerash) and Umm al-Jimal each had fifteen, and that Khirbet es-Samra had eight. By contrast, Pella in southern Syria had six churches, Bostra three, and Qanawat two. These are, of course, minimum numbers, since debris or the still-inhabited areas of some cities may hide other churches.

No similarly small area had such a remarkable concentration of churches. This suggests that Jordan may have been a significant early center of Christianity—much more important and influential than standard histories allow. And with the lone exception of Jerusalem, which had comparable but smaller numbers of churches (eleven in Jerusalem proper and eight on the Mount of Olives, by my count, though an ancient pilgrim reports twenty-four churches on the Mount of Olives alone!), nowhere else in Judea had similar concentrations of early church structures.

Even if one interprets the evidence from Madaba, Umm er-Rasas, Gerasa, Umm al-Jimal, and Khirbet es-Samra as churches for neighborhoods, there were still more churches in Jordan than one would expect. Larger urban centers such as Ephesus, Hierapolis, Laodicea, Corinth, Philippi, and Thessalonica—to name only some with early Christian and strong Pauline connections—had nothing like these numbers. The combination of these large numbers (i.e., sixty-seven churches in five provincial towns) and the (admittedly selective) evidence for early church buildings at Dura Europos (about 230 C.E.) and at Aqaba (about 290 C.E.) underscores the importance of Jordan and southern Syria for the developing history of early Christian communities. It may be that thinking about churches as association buildings will help us understand these numbers.

4. ARCHITECTURAL TYPOLOGY OF ASSOCIATION BUILDINGS

Analysis of the architectural typology of associations described above can shed light on their contributions to an understanding of community formation and life in the early Christian churches.

Domestic

Domestic-style associations—as at Priene (Alexander, Cybele, synagogue), Dura (church, synagogue, Gaddes, Mithra), Delos (synagogue, Sarapeia), and

Pompeii (mysteries)—were often cultic in function, with a patron's religious convictions prompting the gift of a house for the cult's needs. In their initial phases they borrowed the general domestic character of the patron's house. Gradually, however, they diverged from that model as their buildings were renovated and adapted to meet developing needs of the community. So their structures came to be quite differentiated.

Domestic-style associations were organized architectonically around the house's peristyle courtyard. But the room most often used as the association's center was the *triclinium,* which often continued to dominate the facilities. Patrons continued to play significant roles in the life of domestic associations (e.g., Stobi, Acmonia), and might even continue to use parts of the house.

Christian associations with domestic origins were formally indistinguishable from other religious or secular associations. Christian cultic activities were often integrated with community-building activities. And the use of domestic facilities, especially the important *triclinium,* is often noted in Christian writings—as, for example, in Luke–Acts, Paul's letters, 1 Peter, 2–3 John, Didache, and Ignatius.

Odeion-like

The theater-style seating found at Pergamon, where the group was a *philosophia,* must have been uncommon, as the implications of "academy," "garden," and "stoa" would also suggest. This association's building distinguished between philosopher and audience, and so emphasized the role and authority of the speaker in a kind of one-directional conversation. The group might still have functioned as a genuine community—as the bath and the cultic area with niche, altar, and statues alongside the lecture hall suggest—but its structures underplayed that communal character. A theater model for church structures seems not to have been pursued. There are no known churches from antiquity with raked seating, though churches developed a similar directional, focused, authority-based model of communal organization.

Study

Collective study was emphasized in several diverse association settings—as at Aphrodisias (philosophical building); Priene, Sardis, Delos, Dura (synagogues); and Sardis and elsewhere (gymnasia for philosophical study). The use of benches around several sides of a hall in synagogues conveyed architecturally the formal importance of study to the community—with some early synagogues having a separate Beth ha-Midrash or "House of Study," especially in the Holy Land as at Gamla and Chorazin. While a special seat sometimes identified a "president" in the "seat of Moses," this was mainly a functional differentiation that probably signaled some social or status differentiation—for in selecting a "president" or *archisynagogos,* wealth or benefactions probably played a role. Surprisingly, with but few exceptions (e.g., two churches at Herodium that had benches), this was not a model adopted by the church, which suggests that communal study was rarely articulated as a communal priority.

Prayer

It was common to conduct prayers in association buildings—as, for example, in the Mithraea, synagogues, and cultic spaces. So far as I know, however, only the Jewish community explicitly created "prayer houses" *(proseuchai).* And though early Christians shared this religious activity with Jews, Mithraists, and most other cult groups, churches were not specifically prayer houses.

Important as prayer was, architectural expressions of prayer were not widely implemented in the ordinary communal settings of early Christianity. Monastic complexes, of course, were exceptions. Eremitic or hermit-type monasteries, whether Jewish or Christian, had cells for individual monks that were specifically designed at a very early stage for prayer and meditation—often focusing on a niche to which devotion was directed.

Dining

Dining in a *triclinium* is a core communal model for associations—as at Pergamon (Hall of Benches), Ostia (trade associations, Schola of Trajan), Pompeii (Isis, Villa of the Mysteries), and Sufetula (trade association). Much of the life of the *collegia, thiasoi, synodoi, philosophiai,* or *ekklēsiai* focused on this most fundamental community-formation activity. The fact that the *triclinium* was the main space used in adaptations of private houses for associations of various kinds—whether synagogue, church, or Mithraeum—emphasizes the importance of communal meals as a formative model.

Among churches, this activity seems to have been crucial for two or three centuries, while house churches were the norm. After Constantine, however, this activity disappeared, except in monastic—especially coenobitic or communal—structures, where the refectory appears to have replaced the *triclinium.* In churches, the community-forming common meals were replaced by liturgical and cultic celebrations within the main basilica meeting space.

At Ostia, with its military and trade associations, and no doubt in other large cities, *insulae* were used to accommodate voluntary associations. Churches could also have been accommodated in rooms of an *insula,* as slender but significant archaeological evidence attests at least for Rome. This development is probably best thought of as a subcategory of the dining function of associations, since some of the associations that can be assessed accommodated their needs within street-front taverns, which were usually ground floor *tabernae* or *cauponae* in *insulae.*

Legal-cultic

Small local "basilical" churches—as at Pergamon (Sarapeion) and Aqaba (church), particularly in the early period (Aqaba)—were modeled, unlike later imperial-style basilicas, either on adaptations of basilicas for associations or on basilica synagogues. When associations adopted a basilical model, with an apse as the place of cultic veneration housing a god's, emperor's, or patron's statue, they might utilize various configurations—with ancillary rooms, the basilica structure on one side of a courtyard, narthex, and so on. Some such structures were later adapted for use as churches, as at Mactaris in Tunisia and the Sarapeion at Pergamon—suggesting, thereby, that this form of building was considered appropriate for a Christian community.

The basilica became the architectural model of choice for churches after Constantine adopted Christianity—primarily, but not exclusively, in cases of imperial patronage, as, for example, Bethlehem's Church of the Nativity, Jerusalem's Church of the Holy Sepulcher, the Eleona Church, and Rome's St. Peter's. Some of the features of these monumental basilicas that are uncharacteristic of earlier Roman basilicas appear to have derived from association complexes—as, for example, the entry, the courtyard, the narthex, and ancillary rooms—so that the basilica form, when taken over into Christianity, was not a pure "basilica" but a hybrid, one part of which was akin to buildings for associations.

Initiation-Sacrificial

Associations whose main purpose was cultic—as at Ostia (Cybele, Attis, Bellona, shipbuilders, and others), Pompeii (Isis), and Delos (Sarapeion A, Sarapeion B)—tended to have structures whose forms reflected the sacrificial needs of the cult. Typically this meant the provision of a *naos*-like structure for the cult statue, with additional facilities surrounding this—including provision for the group to meet, usually in a courtyard, and provision for communal dining. Often the courtyard-temple was raised on a podium above the courtyard, an arrangement not ordinarily found in churches, though occasionally other elements of the layout and massing of a cultic association can be found in Christian buildings.

In some strongly communal associations with sacrificial practices (e.g., Dionysus at Pergamon, Isis at Pompeii, and elsewhere), exclusion and controlled access were important. Christianity as a mystery may have drawn from these models, especially in the privacy of the Christian mysteries and the emphasis on entry into the community and ritual. There was soon extensive refinement and elaboration of provision for baptisms in churches and monasteries, usually in a symbolically significant location—and even with symbolically significant tanks shaped, for example, as a vulva, symbolizing the new birth (as at Sufetula). The inspiration for these developments may have come more from mystery associations than from inherently necessary theological or communal concerns within early Christianity.

5. CONCLUSIONS

This rather broad, preliminary analysis of buildings that were used, renovated, or originally built for various types of voluntary associations in the ancient world was prepared as "grist for the mill" in understanding early Christian practices. Such a study, of course, should be carried out more fully and for its own sake—particularly with narrower chronological and geographical limits.

For our present purpose, however, a few conclusions seem valid and may be made here:

1. Voluntary associations were a widespread fact of life, but buildings for such associations fitted no one common pattern. As a functional grouping of related activities, they formed a complex matrix of architectural types.

2. Synagogues looked and behaved like voluntary associations. As they developed first in the Diaspora, they mimicked architecturally the characteristics of associations (with communal emphasis, benches, meals, worship, courtyards, ancillary spaces, etc). Within the life of the *polis*, they adopted patterns of behavior similar to associations, such as reserving seats in the theater (as at Miletus) or finding a donor to provide a house for their needs (as at Priene, Dura, etc.).

3. Churches, too, behaved like associations, sometimes even taking over voluntary associations and reusing them (as at Mactaris and Pergamon). Only rarely did a church take over and reuse the *cella* of a pagan temple (as it did at Olba in Turkey); more often the temple was torn down and the site reused (as at Gerasa, Jerusalem, and Damascus). With the Constantinian triumph, the dominant architectural solution was the use of the basilica as the prototype for churches. But for a period and in some places, voluntary associations (along with house churches) were influential models for communal development, and some elements in a typical church building of antiquity seem, almost necessarily, to derive from association buildings.

4. Practices shared with associations include patronage and benefaction, along with the typical memorials to them in inscriptions and images (and the veneration of images of influential figures) found in numerous churches in all areas. Also borrowed were such architectural features as atria, enclosed courtyards, narthexes, and complex ancillary spaces. Additional association features can be found in monastic complexes, especially in coenobitic monasteries.

Recognition of the links between association building practices and early-Christian building practices could fundamentally alter our understanding of the social-historical factors operative on the church. These links reinforce an understanding of Christianity's rootedness in associational customs (e.g., patronage, benefaction), practices (e.g., initiation, membership, devotion to the gods, dining), and building typologies (e.g., adaptation of domestic spaces, utilization of sacrificial and basilica models). The tendency has been to view the relevance of associations rather narrowly. One of the purposes of this chapter is to encourage a more extensive appropriation of this model in understanding early Christian patterns of community.

It hardly needs to be added that the shift to a formal, official, and powerful model of church building—that is, the basilica—and away from communally oriented buildings commonly used by associations represented a development that continues to influence parts of the church and its ministry today.

BIBLIOGRAPHY

Beck, Roger. "The Mysteries of Mithras." Pages 176–85 in *Voluntary Associations in the Graeco-Roman World.* Edited by J. S. Kloppenborg and S. G. Wilson. London: Routledge, 1996.

Harland, Philip. "Association and Empire: A Social-Historical Study of Associations in Ephesus (I–II C.E.)." Unpublished paper, University of Toronto, 1995.

———. "Claiming a Place in *Polis* and Empire: The Significance of Imperial Cults and Connections among Associations, Synagogues and Christian Groups in Roman Asia." Ph.D. diss., University of Toronto, 1999.

———. "Honouring the Emperor or Assailing the Beast: Participation in Civic Life among Associations (Jewish, Christian and Other) in Asia Minor and the Apocalypse of John." *Journal for the Study of the New Testament* 77 (2000): 99–121.

———. "Honours and Worship: Emperors, Imperial Cults and Associations at Ephesus (First to Third Centuries C.E.)." *Studies in Religion/Sciences religieuses* 25 (1996): 319–34.

Hermansen, Gustav. *Ostia, Aspects of Roman City Life.* Edmonton: University of Alberta Press, 1982.

Horsley, G. H. R. "A Fishing Cartel in First-Century Ephesus." Pages 95–114 in vol. 5 of *New Documents Illustrating Early Christianity.* North Ryde, N.S.W.: Ancient History Documentary Research Centre, Macquarie University, 1989.

Jewett, Robert. "Tenement Churches and Communal Meals in the Early Church: The Implications of 2 Thess. 3:10." *Biblical Research* 38 (1993): 23–43.

Kloppenborg, John S. "Collegia and *Thiasoi:* Issues in Function, Taxonomy and Membership." Pages 16–30 in *Voluntary Associations in the Graeco-Roman World.* Edited by J. S. Kloppenborg and S. G. Wilson. London: Routledge, 1996.

Koester, Helmut, ed. *Pergamon, Citadel of the Gods: Archeological Record, Literary Description, and Religious Development.* Harvard Theological Studies 46. Harrisburg, Pa.: Trinity Press International, 1998.

McLean, B. Hudson. "The Place of Cults in Voluntary Associations and Christian Churches on Delos." Pages 186–225 in *Voluntary Associations in the Graeco-Roman World.* Edited by J. S. Kloppenborg and S. G. Wilson. London: Routledge, 1996.

Meiggs, Russell. *Roman Ostia.* Oxford: Clarendon, 1960.

Richardson, L., Jr. *Pompeii: An Architectural History.* Baltimore: Johns Hopkins University Press, 1988.

Richardson, Peter. "An Architectural Case for Synagogues as Associations." In *The Ancient Synagogue from Its Origins until 200 C.E.: Papers Presented at an International Conference at Lund University, October 14–17, 2001.* Edited by Birger Olsson and Dieter Mitternacht. Stockholm: Almqvist & Wiksell, 2002.

————. "Architectural Transitions from Synagogues and House Churches to Pur-pose-Built Churches." Pages 373–89 in *Common Life in the Early Church: Essays Honoring Graydon F. Snyder.* Edited J. V. Hills et al. Harrisburg, Pa.: Trinity Press International, 1998.

————. "Augustan-Era Synagogues in Rome." Pages 17–29 in *Judaism and Chris-tianity in First-Century Rome.* Edited by K. Donfried and P. Richardson. Grand Rapids, Mich.: Eerdmans, 1998.

————. "Early Synagogues as Collegia in the Diaspora and Palestine." Pages 90–109 in *Voluntary Associations in the Graeco-Roman World.* Edited by J. S. Kloppenborg and S. G. Wilson. London: Routledge, 1996.

————. "Philo and Eusebius on Monasteries and Monasticism: The Therapeutae and Kellia." Pages 334–59 in *Origins and Method: Towards a New Under-standing of Judaism and Christianity: Essays in Honour of John C. Hurd.* Ed-ited by B. H. McLean. Sheffield: JSOT, 1993.

Richardson, Peter, with Valerie Heuchan. "Jewish Voluntary Associations in Egypt and the Roles of Women." Pages 226–51 in *Voluntary Associations in the Graeco-Roman World.* Edited by J. S. Kloppenborg and S. G. Wilson. London: Routledge, 1996.

Rose, Mark. "Early Church at Aqaba." *Archaeology* 51/6 (1998): 18. Online: http://www.archaeology.org/9811/newsbriefs/aqaba.html.

White, L. Michael. *The Social Origins of Christian Architecture.* Vol. 1, *Building God's House in the Roman World: Architectural Adaptation among Pagans, Jews and Christians.* Vol. 2, *Texts and Monuments for the Christian Domus Ecclesiae in Its Environment.* Harvard Theological Studies 42. Valley Forge, Pa.: Trinity Press International, 1996, 1997.

————. "Synagogues and Society in Imperial Ostia: Archaeological and Epi-graphic Evidence." Pages 30–68 in *Judaism and Christianity in First-Century Rome.* Edited by K. Donfried and P. Richardson. Grand Rapids, Mich.: Eerdmans, 1998.

Part II

The New Testament

Chapter 4

The Ministry of Jesus in the Gospels

Craig A. Evans

The paradigm of ministry for Christians was established by Jesus himself, whose example was followed—even though not always successfully or willingly—by his disciples and those who came to believe in him. Every model of ministry, therefore, if it is to be truly Christian, must be guided by the teaching and example of Jesus.

The purpose of this chapter is to assess the essential elements of the ministry of Jesus as presented in the New Testament Gospels. It begins with a survey of the language and imagery of ministry in the Bible. Its focus, however, is on five major features of Jesus' ministry: (1) the proclamation of good news; (2) healing and exorcism; (3) forgiveness and fellowship; (4) instruction in worship; and (5) service and sacrifice.

1. THE LANGUAGE AND IMAGERY OF MINISTRY

The English word "ministry" occurs only sixteen times in the entire Bible, at least as translated by the NRSV—twice in the Old Testament, the remainder in the New Testament. The one occurrence of "ministry" in the Gospels is in Luke 3:23 ("Jesus, when he began his ministry, was about thirty years of age"), but there is no corresponding term in the Greek text (which has only *archomenos*, "when he began"). Most of the remaining examples are found in Acts and Paul's letters, translating the noun *diakonia*, "service." Verbal forms of "to minister" are more numerous. In the Old Testament the Hebrew word is usually *šrt*, which can mean to "minister," "serve," or "attend." Often it is used with reference to Israel's priests serving the Lord in the tabernacle or the temple (cf. Exod 28:35, 43; 29:30; 30:20; Num 3:6; Deut 10:8; etc.). The Septuagint or LXX, which is the Greek translation of the Hebrew Old Testament, often translates *šrt* by the verb *leitourgein*, "to serve" (the verb *douleuein*, "to serve," being used usually to render various forms of *ʿbd*).

The verb *diakonein*, "to serve," which plays such a prominent and important role in the New Testament—including utterances ascribed to Jesus—does not appear at all in the LXX. The noun *diakonia*, "service," occurs only once in the LXX, in 1 Macc 11:58, but not in a sense of any significance for our present concerns. We must conclude, therefore, that for the most part concepts and imagery, and not specific vocabulary, provide the relevant backdrop for an understanding of Jesus' own model of ministry.

The verb *therapeuein*, however, needs more careful consideration. For while *therapeuein* in the LXX sometimes means "to heal" or "cure"—as in 2 Kgs 9:16 ("Joram king of Israel was getting well [*etherapeueto*] from the arrows" with which he had been wounded); Tob 12:3 ("For he has led me back to you safely, he cured [*etherapeusen*] my wife, he obtained the money for me, and he also healed [*etherapeusen*] you"); and such other passages as Wis 16:12 and Sir 18:19; 38:7— the more common use of *therapeuein* in the LXX is to "minister to" or "serve" God, his people, or a human king.

Examples of this more usual use of *therapeuein* in the LXX are seen when King Josiah tells the priests: "You need no longer carry it [the ark of the covenant] upon your shoulders. Now worship the Lord your God and serve *(therapeuete)* his people Israel" (1 Esd 1:4). In the LXX additions to Esther, Mordecai is described as "a Jew, dwelling in the city of Susa, a great man, serving *(therapeuōn)* in the court of the king" (11:3; 1.1b), and we are told that "the king ordered Mordecai to serve *(therapeuein)* in the court and rewarded him for these things" (12:5; 1.1q). The LXX's translation of Hebrew Esther says that "Mordecai served *etherapeuen* in the court" (2:19; cf. 6:10). And this same use of *therapeuein* is found in Judith ("For your servant is religious and serves *[therapeuousa]* the God of heaven day and night" [11:17]) and in Tobit ("Of all my produce I would give a tenth to the sons of Levi who ministered *[tois therapeuousin]* at Jerusalem" [1:7]).

Examples of this usage also appear in the Wisdom literature of the LXX. In Proverbs, for example, it is said: "Evil men shall fall before the good; and the ungodly shall serve *(therapeuousin)* at the gates of the righteous" (14:19); "Many serve *(therapeuousin)* faces of kings" or "rulers" (19:6; 29:26)—with the expression "serve the faces of" being used in the sense of sycophancy or obsequious flattery to mean "court the favor of." Personified Wisdom, we are told in Wisdom of Solomon, rescued from troubles "those who served *(tous therapeuontas)* her" (10:9). The sage Jesus ben Sira avers: "He whose service *(therapeuōn)* is pleasing to the Lord will be accepted, and his prayer will reach to the clouds" (Sir 35:16). A sage in the Isaianic tradition adds: "In this is the inheritance for those who serve *(tois therapeuousin)* the Lord, and you will be righteous to me" (Isa 54:17). The word *therapeuein* can also be used of "those who serve *(hoi therapeuontes)* idols" (Bar 6:25, 38). And in his vision of the divine court, Daniel says that "thousand thousands ministered *(etherapeuon)* to him [God], and ten thousands attended upon him" (Dan 7:10).

This use of *therapeuein* approximates what we find in secular Greek texts, where it means "to serve" and is roughly synonymous with such verbs as *douleuein*, *latreuein*, *leitourgein*, and *hypēretein* (cf. Beyer, *therapeuō*, TDNT

3:128–31; MM 288–89; BDAG; LSJ). *Therapeuein,* Plato explains, "has in view something good and the advancement of the subject to which it applies" (*Euthyphr.* 13a). Indeed, "servants *(douloi)* serve *(therapeuousin)* their masters" (13d). More particularly, however, *therapeuein* often has in mind medical service. It may mean "to heal" or "cure" (e.g., Josephus, *A.J.* 17.150; cf. *BGU* 956), but it frequently means simply "to treat medically." For example, in *P. Oxy.* 1088, which was written in the early first century C.E., a nurse is told to apply an ointment and "then lay the man on his back and treat [*therapeue*] him" (line 30). That *therapeuein* in a medical context may mean simply "to treat medically," and not necessarily "to heal," is also evident in *P. Oxy.* 40, a second-century text, where a physician suggests to his colleague: "Perhaps you treated [*etherapeusas*] them wrongly" (lines 7–8). Obviously, his statement cannot be translated "Perhaps you healed them wrongly"! Furthermore, *therapeuein* was used in secular Greek texts when speaking of "treating"—certainly not "healing"—dead bodies (cf. *P. Turin* 1, col. ii, line 22, which dates from about 117 B.C.E.).

In the Gospels, while *therapeuein* usually means "to heal" or "cure"—that is, to signify actual healings performed by Jesus, and not merely medical treatment generally or some type of service or ministry—nuances of "service" or "ministry" are also present in its usage. Thus it needs to be recognized that such healings would have been interpreted by Jesus' contemporaries as significant acts of ministry—that is, as service rendered by Jesus to those who suffered various physical afflictions.

2. THE PROCLAMATION OF GOOD NEWS

The ministry of Jesus is first and foremost grounded in his proclamation of "the good news" of "the reign of God"—or, in more literalistic parlance, the good news of "the kingdom of God." For reasons of clarity, however, we will refer in what follows to Jesus' proclamation of the good news of "the kingship of God."

The evangelist Mark summarizes and contextualizes Jesus' proclamation as follows:

> Now after John was arrested, Jesus came into Galilee, preaching the gospel of God, and saying, "The time is fulfilled, and the kingship of God is at hand; repent, and believe in the good news." (Mark 1:14–15)

In the Gospels of Matthew and Luke, Jesus is presented as saying:

> The blind receive their sight and the lame walk, lepers are cleansed and the deaf hear, and the dead are raised up, and the poor have good news preached to them. (Matt 11:5; cf. Luke 7:22)

And in the Lukan form of the Nazareth sermon (Luke 4:16–30; cf. Mark 6:1–6), Jesus declares that the words of Isa 61:1–2 have been "fulfilled" in the ears of his compatriots in his hometown synagogue:

The Spirit of the Lord is upon me, because he has anointed me to preach good news to the poor. He has sent me to proclaim release to the captives and recovering of sight to the blind, to set at liberty those who are oppressed, to proclaim the acceptable year of the Lord. (Luke 4:18–19)

It is evident from the above verses that Jesus' proclamation of the kingship of God was fundamentally indebted to the language and vision of the prophet Isaiah, especially as found in Isa 40:9 and 61:1–2. And so it is most probable that Jesus' "gospel" or "good news" (*bĕśōrāh* in Hebrew and Aramaic; *euangelion* in Greek) derived directly from these passages.

In Isa 40:9 God's message and directive, which was given through the prophet, is as follows:

> Get you up to a high mountain,
>   O Zion, herald of good tidings;
> lift up your voice with strength,
>   O Jerusalem, herald of good news,
>   lift it up, fear not;
> say to the cities of Judah,
>   "Behold your God!"

In the Aramaic tradition, however, which has ancient roots—some of which may well have reached back to the time of Jesus—the prophet is to declare: "The kingship of your God is revealed!"

The verbal coherence is not to be missed. For the good news of which Isaiah speaks is the announcement of the revelation of God's kingship. It seems most probable, therefore, that the meaning of the "kingship" or "reign" of God has to do with the powerful presence of God. And this seems to be the underlying assumption in Jesus' rebuttal to the charge that his exorcisms were empowered by Satan rather than God: "But if it is by the finger of God that I cast out demons, then the kingship of God has come upon you" (Luke 11:20; cf. Matt 12:28).

The "good news" of Jesus is the inbreaking reign of God. God's powerful presence is at hand in Jesus' ministry to redeem, save, and restore. This proclamation, of itself, would have been understood by Jesus' contemporaries as the single most important part of his ministry. The joy of receiving such good news is captured, once again, in the vision of Isaiah:

> How beautiful upon the mountains
>   are the feet of him who brings good tidings,
> who publishes peace, who brings good tidings of good,
>   who publishes salvation,
> who says to Zion, "Your God reigns." (Isa 52:7)

And once again that significant paraphrase "the kingship of your God is revealed!" appears in the Aramaic version of this passage.

Isaiah not only defines the essence of the "good news," that is, the revelation of God's reign, but the prophet also delineates several blessings of this reign—blessings that are witnessed in Jesus' ministry.

3. HEALING AND EXORCISM

In the Greek Old Testament, as we have seen, "to minister" is often rendered by the verb *therapeuein*, which also means "to heal." A similar semantic overlap occurs with reference to Jesus' acts of healing, with *therapeuein* signifying both "to heal" and "to minister." Jesus' healings and exorcisms, therefore, would have been viewed by his contemporaries as important features of his "ministry," and so it is quite appropriate to speak of Jesus' "ministry of healing."

This semantic overlap of "to heal" and "to minister" is further attested by that ancient, rather mysterious Egyptian group called the Therapeutae, who are thought to be related in some way to the Essenes. In fact, it is the derivation of the name "Essene" that immediately suggests this relationship. Pliny the Elder calls the Essenes *Esseni* (*Natural History* 5.17.4). Josephus usually calls them *Essēnoi* (e.g., *Antiquities* 13.171–172; 13.298). But he sometimes calls them *Essaioi* (*Antiquities* 15.371), which is the form of the name used by Philo (*Quod omnis probus* 13.91; *De vita Mosis* 1.1) and Eusebius (*Preparation for the Gospel* 8.11.1). It has been suggested that underlying these various Latin and Greek transliterations is the Aramaic *ʾāsyāʾ* ("healer"). If so, then it is probable that the Therapeutae (Greek: *therapeutai*), or "healers," were an Egyptian branch of the Essenes (which may also account for the presence of the *Damascus Document* in Egypt).

According to Josephus, the Essenes were interested in health: "They display an extraordinary interest in the writings of the ancients, singling out in particular those which make for the welfare of soul and body; with the help of these, and with a view to the treatment of diseases, they make investigations into medicinal roots and the properties of stones" (*War* 2.136). According to Philo, Essenes are *therapeutai theou*, "servants of God" (*Quod omnis probus* 12.75), in whose company "the sick are not neglected" (*Quod omnis probus* 12.87). But more importantly, Philo speaks of the meaning of *therapeuein*, from which the name Therapeutae derives, saying that it means either "cure, because they profess an art of healing better than that current in the cities which cures only the bodies" or "worship, because nature and the sacred laws have schooled them to worship" God (*De vita Mosis* 1.2). In contrast to the Therapeutae, Egyptian pagans, who worship various deities and animals, are said to be "incurable" (*atherapeutoi*) (*De vita Mosis* 2.10).

This dual meaning of healing and worship is reflected in various ways in Jesus' ministry, where we find acts of healing and service combined with instructions on the proper worship of God. Furthermore, the linkage of a ministry of healing and exorcism to the proclamation of the kingship of God is explicitly attested, as we have seen, by Luke 11:20, where the casting out of Satan is evidence of being overtaken by God's reign. So it is appropriate to say that Jesus' high-profile public healings would have been perceived in his day as an essential part of his ministry.

The celebrated Dead Sea text 4Q521 demonstrates a similar linkage of healing and the proclamation of "good news" among the Qumran covenanters:

[1][. . . For the hea]vens and the earth shall listen to his Messiah [2][and all w]hich is in them shall not turn away from the commandments of the holy ones. [3]Strengthen yourselves, O you who seek the Lord, in his service. *(vacant)* [4]Will you not find the Lord in this, all those who hope in their heart? [5]For the Lord seeks the pious and calls the righteous by name. [6]Over the humble his spirit hovers, and he renews the faithful in his strength. [7]For he will honor the pious upon the th[ro]ne of the eternal kingship, [8]setting prisoners free, opening the eyes of the blind, raising up those who are bo[wed down.] [9]And for[ev]er (?) I (?) shall hold fast [to] the [ho]peful and pious [. . .] [10]. . [. . .] . . shall not be delayed [. . .] [11]and the Lord shall do glorious things which have not been done, just as he said. [12]For he will heal the critically wounded, he will revive the dead, he will proclaim good news to the afflicted. . . .

This Qumran text echoes Isa 35:5 ("the eyes of the blind shall be opened"), Isa 61:1 ("anointed . . . to proclaim good news to the afflicted . . . liberty to prisoners . . . opening of the eyes"), Isa 26:19 ("your dead shall live, their bodies shall rise"), and possibly Isa 53:5 ("he was wounded for our transgressions, he was bruised for our iniquities . . . and with his stripes we are healed"). Also to be noted is the fact that there are several important points of contact between 4Q521 and Jesus' reply to John the Baptist as recorded in Matt 11:5 and Luke 7:22—which parallels further suggest that Jesus' ministry of healing was not only part of his anointed, or messianic, task, but also part of the "good news" he was to proclaim to the poor.

The linking of healing with "good news" is also attested in the pagan world, perhaps most interestingly in the case of the imperial cult. For when the Roman emperor Vespasian ascended to the throne, the event was hailed as "good news"—and, as confirmation of heaven's favor, the new emperor was urged to heal (cf. Josephus, *War* 4.618; 4.656–657). Vespasian was initially reluctant to attempt such a feat. But he finally yielded to the pressure of his counselors, and, to his own astonishment, successfully healed a blind man and a lame man (cf. Suetonius, *Divus Vespasianus* 7.2–3).

4. FORGIVENESS AND FELLOWSHIP

Jesus' healings were seen not only as evidence of the powerful presence of God, but also as proof of the forgiveness of sins. The link between healing and forgiveness is clearly seen in the account of the paralyzed man who was let down through the roof by his friends (Mark 2:1–12). Impressed by their act of faith, Jesus says to the paralyzed man: "My son, your sins are forgiven" (Mark 2:5; cf. Matt 9:2; Luke 5:20). In response to the scribes who are offended by this assertion, Jesus heals the man "so that you may know that the Son of man has authority on earth to forgive sins" (Mark 2:10; cf. Matt 9:6; Luke 5:24). Jesus' self-understanding as "the Son of man" who has "authority on earth" derives from the vision of Daniel 7, where "one like a son of man" approaches the divine throne and receives "kingship and authority" (Dan 7:13–14). This heaven-given authority is what authorized Jesus to proclaim the kingship of God and to demonstrate its presence through healing.

Forgiveness is also linked to fellowship and acceptance of the impure. This feature of Jesus' ministry is beautifully illustrated in the moving story of the woman who anointed Jesus' feet in Luke 7:36–50. Simon the Pharisee assumed that Jesus would not allow such a woman to touch him if he really knew who and what sort of a woman she was—that she was a sinner (7:37, 39). He reasoned that because Jesus evidently did not know, he must not be a true prophet. But Jesus turns the tables on Simon, challenging his assumptions. For, indeed, he does know the history of this woman, that she was a sinner (7:47). However, her thanksgiving and love for the proclaimer of the good news was evidence of her experience of grace. So in the presence of everyone there gathered, Jesus assures the weeping woman: "Your sins are forgiven" (7:48); "Your faith has saved you; go in peace" (7:50).

Jesus defends his understanding of God's will with the parable of the Two Debtors in Luke 7:41–42. Commentators have pointed out that the Aramaic ḥôbāʾ means both "sin" and "debt," thereby tying the parable closely to issues of sin, forgiveness, and thanksgiving. Recognition of this nuance brings us back again to Jesus' proclamation of good news, which recalls Isa 58:6 and 61:1–2 in the "letting go" (or "forgiveness") of prisoners and the oppressed. For Jesus assures the woman that she is released from the debt of her sins, which had burdened her and led to her estrangement from the God of Israel. And the woman, recognizing this release, expresses her love and gratitude to Jesus—a response that beggars that of the ungracious Simon.

Torah-observant Jews, who are frequently depicted in the Gospels as Pharisees and scribes, objected to Jesus' intimate association with "sinners"—that is, with those who did not observe the laws of purity, as Jesus' critics understood them. This criticism leveled against Jesus is ancient, being attested both by the tradition incorporated by Mark and by the sayings material used by Matthew and Luke. In Mark 2:15–17 we read:

> And as he sat at table in his house, many tax collectors and sinners were sitting with Jesus and his disciples; for there were many who followed him. And the scribes of the Pharisees, when they saw that he was eating with sinners and tax collectors, said to his disciples, "Why does he eat with tax collectors and sinners?" And when Jesus heard it, he said to them, "Those who are well have no need of a physician, but those who are sick; I came not to call the righteous, but sinners."

And in Matthew and Luke, Jesus is represented as repeating what his critics say of him: "Behold, a glutton and a drunkard, a friend of tax collectors and sinners!" (Matt 11:19; cf. Luke 7:34).

The authenticity of this tradition can scarcely be doubted, for the early Christians can hardly have wished to characterize their Lord as a "friend of [hated] tax collectors and [despised] sinners"—which would have reflected not only dubiously on Jesus himself but also very poorly on themselves. Such criticism, as attested in our earliest Gospel sources, harks back to an important and controversial aspect of Jesus' ministry.

It is clear that Jesus regarded the people to whom he ministered as "sinners" in need of redemption. He acknowledged, for example, that the sins of the woman who washed his feet were many and that she was a "debtor." Furthermore, by characterizing himself as a physician ministering to the sick and as one who came to call not the righteous, but sinners (Matt 11:19), Jesus unequivocally identified those to whom he ministered and with whom he fellowshipped as sinners. On this question he was in agreement with the scribes and Pharisees.

The issue, however, was what to do about the sinners. Were they to be shunned and condemned, as many of the religious leaders of the day apparently thought, or were they to be ministered to, as was Jesus' desire? Herein, it seems, lies a major difference between many of the Jewish teachers and Jesus.

5. INSTRUCTION IN WORSHIP

Issues of purity—that is, of determining what is clean and what is not clean—were inextricably tied to worship. Indeed, only pure, unblemished gifts could be presented at the temple. In Mark 7:14–23, however, Jesus declares that the evil that proceeds from one's heart is what defiles a person, not unwashed hands or (by implication) other external forms of contagion one might encounter. The parable of the Pharisee and the Publican in Luke 18:9–14 illustrates the point in a pithy and significant manner:

> He also told this parable to some who trusted in themselves that they were righteous and despised others: "Two men went up into the temple to pray, one a Pharisee and the other a tax collector. The Pharisee stood and prayed thus with himself, 'God, I thank you that I am not like other people, extortioners, unjust, adulterers, or even like this tax collector. I fast twice a week, I give tithes of all that I get.' But the tax collector, standing far off, would not even lift up his eyes to heaven, but beat his breast, saying, 'God, be merciful to me a sinner!' I tell you, this man went down to his house justified rather than the other. For all those who exalt themselves will be humbled, but those who humble themselves will be exalted."

The Old Testament background presupposed in this parable is Deut 26, which commands Israelites to bring their first fruits and tithes to the temple (it is implied) and to declare that they are children of Abraham and that they have obeyed God's law (see esp. Deut 26:3–10, 13–15). This is precisely what the Pharisee in the parable is doing. He thanks God for his privilege of election—though, of course, at the expense of sinners and the nonelect, such as the tax collector standing nearby—and he declares that he has tithed faithfully.

The Pharisee's behavior corresponds to a description of the conclusion of Jewish worship at the Jerusalem temple found in Josephus: "And when any man, after having done all this and having offered tithes of all, along with those for the Levites and for all the banquets, is about to depart to his own home, let him stand opposite the sacred precincts and render thanks to God. . . . Let him ask God ever to be favorable and merciful" (*Antiquities* 4.242–243). One may also hear an echo of the Pharisee's self-righteous prayer in rabbinic literature:

> I thank you, O Lord, my God, that you have assigned my portion with those who sit in the house of learning, and not with those who sit at street corners; for I am early to work on the words of Torah, and they are early to work on things of no importance. . . . I run towards the life of the Age to Come, and they run towards the pit of destruction. (*b. Berakoth* 28b)

In sharp contrast, the tax collector offers no gift and makes no self-assured statements about his covenant status. On the contrary, he confesses that he is a sinner and begs God to be merciful. Jesus' pronouncements regarding forgiveness and acceptance by God in Mark 7 and Luke 18—contrary to some rabbinic understandings of Deut 26, though undoubtedly in line with the theology of many others who were his Jewish contemporaries—teach that purity of heart and humility before God meet the test for purity and constitute true worship.

In material found only in Matthew's Gospel, we are presented with a picture where Jesus makes it possible for the marginalized to renew their worship. People who are grouped together as "maimed, halt (or lame), and blind" are in the Old Testament sometimes regarded as unqualified for certain religious ceremonies. Indeed, to have any of these defects was to be disqualified from the priesthood (cf. Lev 21:16–24, esp. v. 18). Sacrificial animals with similar defects were also to be excluded (cf. Lev 22:17–25, esp. v. 22; Deut 15:21). Such restrictions played an important role in the symbolism of purity. And some writings at Qumran appeal to these defects as grounds for excluding even their own members of the renewed covenant from participating in the final holy war (cf. 1QM VII, 4) and from attending the messianic banquet (cf. 1QSa II, 3–7).

According, however, to the evangelist Matthew: "The blind and the lame came to him in the temple, and he healed them. But when the chief priests and the scribes saw the wonderful things that he did, and the children crying out in the temple, 'Hosanna to the Son of David!' they were indignant" (21:14–15). Commentators have rightly heard in this passage an echo of 2 Sam 5:8:

> And David said on that day, "Whoever would smite the Jebusites, let him get up the water shaft to attack the lame and the blind, who are hated by David's soul." Therefore it is said, "The blind and the lame shall not come into the house."

David was angry for having been taunted by the Jebusites that he was so feeble that even the blind and lame of the city could defend against him. But David proved stronger than the Jebusites and was able to capture Jerusalem. The house that the "blind and lame" were not to enter was understood to be the temple of the Lord at Jerusalem—though this part of the verse is probably a later gloss.

The Aramaic paraphrase of 2 Sam 5:8 equates these handicapped persons with the sinful. According to this version David said: "The sinners and the guilty shall not go up to the house." In all probability, this Aramaic paraphrase reflects an understanding among priestly and Pharisaic interpreters. Because of their defects, the blind and lame were not permitted to enter the precincts of the

Jerusalem temple. But Jesus' ministry of healing made it possible for them to do so—that is, to worship God, like all other Israelites, in God's house.

Jesus also teaches his disciples to pray. The shorter and probably more original form of the Lord's Prayer in Luke 11:2–4 reads:

> Father, hallowed be your name.
>   Your kingship come.
> Give us each day our daily bread;
> and forgive us our sins,
>   for we forgive every one who is indebted to us;
> and lead us not into temptation.

Jesus' prayer is clearly an adaptation of the Jewish prayer known as the Qaddish—that is, "holy," "sanctified," or "hallowed":

> May His great name be glorified and hallowed in the world that He created according to His will.

> May He establish His kingship in your lifetime and during your days.

The original form of this prayer probably more closely paralleled the form of the first two petitions of the Lord's Prayer. Over time the Qaddish was embellished and expanded, as was the Lord's Prayer (cf. Matt 6:9–13).

Jesus adds three petitions to the two foundational petitions for the sanctity of God's name and the coming of God's rule or kingship: a petition for daily needs; a petition for the forgiveness of sins; and a petition for preservation from temptation. The petition for forgiveness calls for comment. The reciprocity of the plea for forgiveness should not be missed. For forgiving one's neighbor correlates to God's forgiveness of us. One immediately thinks of Jesus' parable in Matt 18:23–35 of the Unforgiving Servant, who had been forgiven a great debt but refused to forgive a fellow servant a much smaller debt. The unforgiving servant was severely punished. And in application of the parable, Jesus tells his disciples: "So also my heavenly Father will do to every one of you, if you do not forgive your brother and sister from your heart" (v. 35).

This is the negative side of Jesus' double commandment: "You shall love the Lord your God with all your heart, and with all your soul, and with all your mind, and with all your strength. . . . You shall love your neighbor as yourself" (Mark 12:30–31). It is also the negative side of the so-called Golden Rule: "So whatever you wish that people would do to you, do so to them; for this is the law and the prophets" (Matt 7:12). One can hardly love one's neighbor if one refuses to forgive him or her, and one would surely hope to be forgiven if one had caused offense.

The need to forgive one's neighbor and to be at peace also has a direct bearing on worship. In the first antithesis of the Sermon on the Mount in Matt 5:23–24, Jesus instructs his disciples: "If you are offering your gift at the altar, and there remember that your brother has something against you, leave your gift there before the altar and go; first be reconciled to your brother, and then come and offer your gift."

Although the linking of "love of God" and "love of neighbor" was probably not unique to Jesus, the link between obligations to one's fellow and the worship of God appears to be distinctive and should be viewed as one of the major features in Jesus' ministry.

6. SERVICE AND SACRIFICE

Jesus' ministry is marked by some rather startling teachings regarding service and sacrifice. Although not entirely unique, Jesus' exhortation that his disciples humble themselves and seek to serve is distinctive. Several sayings come to mind:

> He who is greatest among you shall be your servant; whoever exalts himself will be humbled, and whoever humbles himself will be exalted. (Matt 23:11–12; cf. Luke 14:11; 18:14)

> If any one would be first, he must be last of all and servant of all. (Mark 9:35)

> Let the greatest among you become as the youngest, and the leader as one who serves. (Luke 22:26)

In contrast to the Gentiles, who rule over people, and the mighty, who lord it over the weak and powerless, Jesus commands his disciples to pursue a different course of action:

> But it shall not be so among you; but whoever would be great among you must be your servant, and whoever would be first among you must be slave of all. (Mark 10:43–44)

We need to be reminded of how stark the contrast between servant and master was in the Roman world of late antiquity. Slavery was common; citizenship was treasured. Greatness in God's kingship, Jesus taught his disciples, is measured by service to others, not by the acquisition of wealth and power. According to Jesus:

> Blessed are those servants whom the master finds awake when he comes; truly, I say to you, he will gird himself and have them sit at table, and he will come and serve them. (Luke 12:37)

> For which is the greater, one who sits at table, or one who serves? Is it not the one who sits at table? But I am among you as one who serves. (Luke 22:27)

The authenticity of this tradition of service is supported by Acts 6:2: "And the twelve summoned the body of the disciples and said, 'It is not right that we should give up preaching the word of God to serve tables.'" Jesus' teachings regarding service, it seems, stand somewhat in tension even with apostolic leadership.

But Jesus demanded more of his followers than service only. He asked them to be prepared to suffer, even die, for his cause. In Mark 8:34 he is reported as saying: "Those who would come after me must deny themselves and take up their cross and follow me." Although some have argued that this saying arose in the post-Easter Church, there are good reasons for thinking that it, like similar sayings attributed to various itinerant philosophers of the day, was uttered by Jesus during his public ministry. Jesus was fond of hyperbole, and suggesting that becoming his disciple was tantamount to taking up a cross and carrying it to a place of execution was about as hyperbolic as one could be.

An expectation of martyrdom was consistent with Jesus' understanding of his mission—a mission greatly clarified by the struggle envisioned in Dan 7. Indeed, thrones had been set up (cf. Dan 7:9) on which Jesus and his disciples would someday sit as they administered the tribes of Israel (cf. Matt 19:28 // Luke 22:28–30), but before this could take place, a great ordeal would have to be endured. Satan and his allies will not go quietly.

Contrary to popular expectation—and even contrary to his disciples' wishes—Jesus the anointed anticipated his own death. This anticipation led him to subvert part of Dan 7. According to verse 14, all the nations were to serve "the son of man." But according to Jesus, "the Son of man also came not to be served but to serve, and to give his life as a ransom for many" (Mark 10:45 // Matt 20:28). This saying suggests not only that Jesus anticipated that suffering must precede vindication and glorification, but also that he understood his death as being vicarious for others.

Many critics have disputed the authenticity of this saying. But Jesus was not blind to events unfolding before him. He had heard of what had happened to his colleague and mentor, John the Baptist. He was aware of the struggle depicted in Dan 7. He had encountered stiff and unyielding opposition from the ruling priests in Jerusalem. In fact, had he not reckoned seriously with the probability of his own death, he would have been naive indeed. And had he not sought a meaning for it, he would have been uncharacteristically remiss in his theological reflections.

Jesus would have been well acquainted with the stories of the martyred faithful—especially the gruesome story of the tortured and murdered seven brothers in 2 Macc 7. These brave lads believed that their fidelity to God's law and their willingness to die for it would bring reconciliation between God and the nation of Israel (see esp. 2 Macc 7:33, 37–38). It is against such a backdrop that we should understand the words of institution: "This is my blood of the covenant, which is poured out for many" (Mark 14:24). Jesus' words allude to Exod 24:8 ("Behold the blood of the covenant which the Lord has made with you"), Jer 31:31 ("Behold, the days are coming . . . when I will make a new covenant with the house of Israel"), and Zech 9:11 ("because of the blood of your covenant, I will set your captives free").

Jesus anticipated his death, found meaning in it, and urged his disciples to be prepared to follow his example. This was no easy teaching. It was, in fact, a feature of Jesus' ministry that did not go over particularly well for either his disciples or himself. He had asked James and John, the sons of Zebedee, if they were prepared to drink the cup of suffering, and they responded "We can!"(Mark 10:38–39). But when he was arrested, his disciples fled. One of them betrayed him and another denied ever knowing him. And when the time came for Jesus himself to drink it, he preferred not to (Mark 14:36).

But the lessons Jesus taught his disciples apparently did take root, for in the aftermath of Easter, they testified boldly to Jesus' resurrection and messiahship and founded a church that within three centuries captured the Roman Empire. The young church, struggling to organize itself, attempted to emulate Jesus' example and to implement, augment, and interpret his teaching. Jesus' inclusiveness, his openness to the marginalized and ostracized, paved the way for a mission to Gentiles and set the pattern that the church has, with more or less success, followed down through the centuries.

7. CONCLUSION

Jesus' ministry was inaugurated and defined by the proclamation of the good news of the kingship of God. Apart from this message, there could not have been any meaningful ministry. The good news entailed the restoration and redemption of Israel, the renewal of the covenant, and the reclamation of the lost. The essence of this message concerning the kingship of God guided all other aspects of Jesus' ministry.

The reality and power of the good news that Jesus proclaimed was demonstrated in his healings and exorcisms—that is, in Jesus' freeing of hostages from the bondage of Satan and his allies. This freeing also entailed a forgiveness of sin that made renewed fellowship with God possible. Conversely, such a freely bestowed divine forgiveness made possible—indeed, required—a corresponding freely bestowed forgiveness of one human being for another. And on the basis of such forgiveness, it was then possible to worship God freely, to treat others humanely, and to view personal sacrifice, suffering, and death as imaginable—even, in fact, acceptable.

Jesus' ministry not only established the paradigm on which the Christian church's ministry would be founded, it also put in place the principal components out of which Christian theology developed. Thus Jesus' ministry must be regarded as an essential element of New Testament teaching. It should certainly not be pushed to the side to make room for the more systematic presentations found in the New Testament letters and epistles, as is sometimes done. For Christians, Jesus' ministry is not only inspirational but also doctrinally normative and ecclesiologically formative.

BIBLIOGRAPHY

Bayer, Hans F. *Jesus' Predictions of Vindication and Resurrection: The Provenance, Meaning and Correlation of the Synoptic Predictions.* Tübingen: Mohr (Siebeck), 1986.

Best, Ernest. *Disciples and Discipleship: Studies in the Gospel according to Mark.* Edinburgh: T&T Clark, 1986.

———. *Following Jesus: Discipleship in the Gospel of Mark.* Sheffield: JSOT Press, 1981.

Borg, Marcus J. *Conflict, Holiness, and Politics in the Teachings of Jesus.* Harrisburg, Pa.: Trinity Press International, 1998.

Evans, Craig A. "Jesus' Ethic of Humility." *Trinity Journal* 13 (1992): 127–38.

France, Richard T. *Jesus and the Old Testament: His Application of Old Testament Passages to Himself and His Mission.* London: Tyndale, 1971.

Hengel, Martin. *The Charismatic Leader and His Followers.* New York: Crossroad, 1981.

Jonge, Marinus de. *God's Final Envoy: Early Christology and Jesus' Own View of His Mission.* Grand Rapids, Mich.: Eerdmans, 1998.

———. *Jesus, The Servant-Messiah.* New Haven, Conn.: Yale University Press, 1991.

Kim, Seyoon. "Salvation and Suffering according to Jesus." *Evangelical Quarterly* 68 (1996):195–207.

Meye, Robert P. *Jesus and the Twelve: Discipleship and Revelation in Mark's Gospel.* Grand Rapids, Mich.: Eerdmans, 1968.

Sanders, E. P. *Jesus and Judaism.* London: SCM; Philadelphia: Fortress, 1985.

Schweizer, Eduard. "Ministry in the Early Church." Pages 835–42 in vol. 4 of *Anchor Bible Dictionary.* Edited by D. N. Freedman et al. New York: Doubleday, 1992.

Stein, Robert. H. *The Method and Message of Jesus' Teachings.* Rev. ed. Louisville, Ky.: Westminster John Knox, 1994.

Taylor, Vincent. *Jesus and His Sacrifice.* London: Macmillan, 1937.

Wright, N. Thomas. *Jesus and the Victory of God.* London: SPCK; Minneapolis: Fortress, 1996.

Chapter 5

Paul's Vision of the Church and Community Formation in His Major Missionary Letters

Richard N. Longenecker

All thirteen Pauline letters in the New Testament are missionary and pastoral, and all of them represent themselves as speaking with apostolic authority to particular issues or concerns. Nine are addressed to congregations (Romans, 1 and 2 Corinthians, Galatians, Ephesians, Philippians, Colossians, and 1 and 2 Thessalonians, to list them in canonical order), whereas four are addressed to individuals (1 and 2 Timothy, Titus, and Philemon, again in canonical order). None of them, however, is specifically evangelistic, setting out for us the nature of the earliest apostolic preaching—though there are reflections and recollections of what was earlier proclaimed. None of them is of the nature of an ecclesiastical encyclical, setting out for us final truth in unalterable form. For all of them, while working from firm convictions, are "works in progress" that speak to a variety of interests and topics and seek to contextualize the Christian gospel for particular readers in their specific circumstances.

Yet every Pauline letter—whether directly or derivatively—presents us with something of the apostle's own vision of the church and its formation. That is true not only for the seven generally accepted letters of Paul (Romans, 1 and 2 Corinthians, Galatians, Philippians, 1 Thessalonians, and Philemon), but also for those letters often credited to an immediate follower (Ephesians, Colossians, and 2 Thessalonians) or seen as arising out of a later Pauline school (1 and 2 Timothy and Titus). The latter three letters, the so-called Pastoral Epistles, deal specifically with issues regarding church order. The special character of these latter letters seems to have been recognized early within the Christian church, for the Muratorian Canon (ca. 180–200 C.E.) speaks of them not only as having been written to individuals (together with Philemon) but also as having to do with "ecclesiastical discipline." In the ten other letters, however, which I will here refer to as Paul's "major missionary letters," matters pertaining to community formation are included, but not as directly as in the Pastoral Epistles. Attention will later be directed to the Pastoral Epistles (see chapter 7). Here our concern is with Paul's vision of the church and community formation in his major missionary letters.

1. PRELIMINARY OBSERVATIONS ON PAUL'S USE OF EKKLĒSIA

The Greek word for "church" *(ekklēsia)* appears more frequently in the Pauline letters than in any of the other writings in the New Testament: sixty-three times in his major missionary letters—nine times in Romans, twenty-two times in 1 Corinthians, nine times in 2 Corinthians, three times in Galatians, nine times in Ephesians, twice in Philippians, four times in Colossians, twice in 1 Thessalonians, twice in 2 Thessalonians, and once in Philemon—though, interestingly, only three times in the Pastoral Epistles; whereas it appears three times in the Gospels (all in Matthew), twenty-one times in Acts, twice in Hebrews, once in James, three times in 3 John, and seventeen times in the Apocalypse. Word counts alone are inadequate for determining meaning; significance can be judged only by usage. Yet such a frequency shows that Paul had a great concern for both the church universal and the local churches to which he wrote, and also suggests that it would be profitable to investigate his vision of the church and community formation.

A number of preliminary observations regarding Paul's ecclesiastical vision can be based simply on how he used the word *ekklēsia*. First, he appears to have made little distinction between what we would call the church local and the church universal. Paul seems to have viewed every congregation at whatever time and in whatever locality as an embodiment of the church universal—that is, to have viewed each particular congregation as *the* church of God. Second, there seems to be a development in Paul's ecclesiastical consciousness, which appears to grow from a more localized understanding to a usage that includes a more universal understanding. This can be seen, for example, by comparing the salutations of his earlier letters with those of his later letters. For in his earlier letters he addresses "the churches in Galatia" (Gal 1:2), "the church of the Thessalonians" (1 Thess 1:1; 2 Thess 1:1), and "the church of God at Corinth" (1 Cor 1:2; 2 Cor 1:1), with *ekklēsia* being used largely in a localized fashion, whereas in his later letters the addressees are spoken of as "loved by God," "holy ones," and "faithful brothers and sisters," with *ekklēsia* not being used in these salutations (cf. Rom 1:7; Eph 1:1; Phil 1:1; Col 1:2) but left for more developed treatments of the church universal later in the letters.

A third observation regarding Paul's use of *ekklēsia* is the functional way he speaks about the church in his letters. This is true not only when he addresses various doctrinal and ethical issues of the particular churches but also when he writes about the nature, unity, mission, and activities of the universal church. And fourth, in the Pauline letters the church is "at the same time" both "central and peripheral" (cf. Barrett, *Church, Ministry, and Sacraments,* 9 *et passim,* who makes this "paradox" the central theme of his book). Paul's essential message had to do with "Christ crucified" (e.g., 1 Cor 1:23, 2:2; Gal 3:1) and being "in Christ" (e.g., Gal 3:26–28), not church order, church politics, or even church sacraments (1 Cor 1:13–17a). Yet being "in Christ" also meant for him being an integral part of "the body of Christ" (Rom 12:4–5; 1 Cor 12:12–27; Eph 1:22–23; 4:4, 12, 16; 5:23–33; Col 1:18, 24; 2:19). So individual and corporate relationships always cohered in his understanding and proclamation (cf. Best, *One Body in Christ*).

But these are only preliminary observations. Further explication requires going beyond merely linguistic considerations to investigate Paul's images of the church, his criteria for community formation, and reflections of church order in his letters.

2. IMAGES OF THE CHURCH AND SOME IMPLICATIONS

When we ask about church order, we find Paul talking about the nature of the church. And when we ask about the nature of the church, we find him setting out various images of the church—which imagery he evidently meant to signal certain vital features about the church's nature and to suggest certain important implications for its structures and order. Six major images of the church, with their attendant auxiliary images and corollaries, are particularly significant and suggestive in the Pauline letters.

The People of God

The identification of Christians as "the people of God" appears a number of times in the New Testament (e.g., Luke 1:17; Acts 15:14; Titus 2:14; Heb 4:9; 8:10; 1 Pet 2:9–10; Rev 18:4; 21:3). But it is used by Paul with special significance in Rom 9:25–26; 11:1–2; 15:10, and 2 Cor 6:16 to set the Christian church in the context of the long story of God's dealings with his chosen people Israel. "People of God," a covenant expression, speaks of God's choosing and calling a particular people into covenantal relationship (Exod 19:5; Deut 7:6; 14:2; Ps 135:4; Heb 8:10; 1 Pet 2:9–10; Rev 21:3). They are God's people not because of their own proclivities or efforts but because of God's gracious initiative and magnanimous action in creating, calling, saving, judging, and sustaining them. And as God's people, they experience God's presence working among them.

A whole galaxy of auxiliary images oscillate around the analogy of "the people of God" for Christians and the Christian church. These include in the Pauline letters the following: "God's elect" (Rom 8:33; Eph 1:4; Col 3:12), "Abraham's descendants" (Rom 4:16; Gal 3:29; 4:26–28), "the true circumcision" (Phil 3:3; Col 2:11), and even "the Israel of God" (Gal 6:16). All of these images assert, in some manner, an enduring solidarity of the people of the church with the people of Israel, whose history provides the church with an authoritative account of the principles and actions of God's past redemptive working. It is the task of exegesis and theology to spell out the nature of this relationship.

Certain implications, however, can be drawn from such a solidarity for our purposes here. We must see not only that Christian theology is rooted in the theology of the Old Testament and early Judaism, but also that church order has Jewish roots and that the earliest believers in Jesus organized their worship and communal lives in ways congenial to their Jewish experiences. Such implications have important ramifications for any discussion of community formation in the early church and the church today.

The Body of Christ

The non-Pauline writings of the New Testament allude a few times to believers' either partaking of or being in Christ's "body" (e.g., Mark 14:22 par.; Heb 13:3), but only the Pauline letters use "body of Christ" with direct reference to the church, first by way of illustration and then as an image depicting its nature. In fact, it is in Paul's "body of Christ" imagery that "his originality is incontestable and his deeper penetration into the idea of the Church is evident" (Schnackenburg, *The Church in the New Testament*, 77). Attention, therefore, has often been directed to the expression "the body of Christ" when dealing with Paul's vision of the church, with many considering that image to reflect the apostle's "decisive advance" and "creative achievement" in the area of ecclesiology (ibid., 84).

Paul's use of "body" (*sōma*), however, is "extremely flexible and elastic" (Minear, *Images of the Church*, 173), appearing in a number of ways and therefore not to be treated as simply a "verbalistic monism" (ibid., 197). In Romans, for example, the word is used as a synecdoche for the death of Christ (7:4, "You died to the law through the body of Christ"), as a collective expression to signify the sum total (7:24, "Who will deliver me from the body of this death?"), as a synonym for one's self (12:1, "Present your bodies as a living sacrifice"), and as an illustration of our interdependent relationship in the community of believers with other believers (12:4–5, "As in one body we have many members, and all the members do not have the same function, so we, though many, are one body in Christ, and individually members one of another"). In 1 Corinthians the apostle exhorts his converts not to use their bodies for immorality, and so sin against their own bodies, but to view their bodies as entering into relationship with Christ, with the Holy Spirit, and with God (6:12–20); to understand that as believers "in Christ" they are "one body" who participate in "the body of Christ" (10:16–17); to realize that the Lord's Supper signifies Christ's "body, which is for you" (11:24), and so to celebrate it in a manner that neither profanes "the body and blood of the Lord" (11:27) nor lacks discernment regarding "the body" (11:29); to recognize the interrelational features of being in "the body of Christ" (12:12–27); and to appreciate that the resurrection "body" will be as God ordains it—not just a resuscitated or revivified physical body, but a changed, spiritual body of material substance, which will be in continuity with our earthly bodies (15:35–50). And in Philippians he speaks of awaiting from heaven "a Savior, the Lord Jesus Christ, who will change our lowly body to be like his glorious body, by the power which enables him even to subject all things to himself" (3:21).

Nonetheless, in Rom 12:4–5 and 1 Cor 12:12–27 (cf. 6:15–17, 10:17) Paul uses "the body" as an illustration of the interrelation of believers with Christ and with one another. This imagery is developed further in Ephesians and Colossians, where the body of Christ is specifically identified with the church, Christ is spoken of as the head of the church, and the corporate relationship of believers with one another is emphasized (cf. Eph 1:22–23; 4:4, 12, 16; 5:23–33; Col 1:18, 24; 2:19)—though, again, other uses of the word "body" appear in these letters as well (cf. Col 1:22; 2:11, 17).

The imagery of the body when applied to the church carries with it a number of implications—not only with respect to believers' relationships with Christ ("the head") and with one another ("the many members"), but also having to do with the order and functioning of the church. Paul himself begins to spell out some of these implications in 1 Cor 12:12–31 when he uses the human body to illustrate both the unity of believers in "the body of Christ" (12:12–13, 27) and the diversity of functions within the church (12:14–31). Numerous suggestions can be drawn from Colossians and Ephesians regarding the order and functioning of the church. For the imagery of "the body of Christ, which is the church," suggests not only the personal theme of being "in Christ" (cf. Best, *One Body in Christ*) but also both the unity of believers and the functional diversity of orders and activities within the church.

The Household of Faith/God

At two places in the Pauline writings (one earlier letter and one later) the members of the community of believers in Jesus are called "household members" *(oikeioi):* "the household of faith" in Gal 6:10, and "the household of God" in Eph 2:19. Such a designation undoubtedly stems from the common parlance of the Old Testament and early Judaism in calling the place where God meets his people a "house" (uniquely the Jerusalem temple) and God's people a "household" (Hebrew: *bayit*). But it also seems to have arisen from the familial language used by both Jews and Christians, which spoke of God as "Father" (Rom 8:15; Gal 4:6; passim; cf. Isa 63:16; *Sir* 51:10; Matt 6:9//Luke 11:2; *Shemoneh Esreh*, Benediction 6) and of one another as "sons [and daughters] of God" (Rom 8:14; 2 Cor 6:18; Gal 4:5–7; cf. Hos 11:1).

Households in antiquity consisted of a number of persons: the immediate family members, comprising at least three and sometimes four generations; slaves and servants; various business associates or clients; and others who had for one reason or another been drawn into the family circle. Families in antiquity were patriarchal and hierarchical, with the father ruling the household (though, if the father were deceased, at times the mother would become the head of the household). Slaves and servants often had managerial roles as well as menial tasks. Everyone performed his or her assigned duties for the welfare of the household. Thus when the Christian church was referred to as a "household" (whether "of faith" or "of God"), ideas of order, structure, and functional responsibility would inevitably have arisen in the minds of both those who used and those who heard such terminology.

The Temple of God

Paul uses the imagery of "the temple of God" *(naos theou)* to characterize both believers in Jesus Christ and the church in 1 Cor 3:16–17, 6:19–20; 2 Cor 6:16–7:1, and Eph 2:20–22—with the oscillation of thought between the individual and the corporate being evidently only a particularization with respect to the former and a generalization with respect to the latter. He probably took over the imagery of a "new house" or "temple not made with hands" from Jewish apocalypticism and early Christianity (cf. *1 En.* 90:28–29; 91:13; *Jub.* 1:17; 1QS VIII, 5–6; Mark 14:58 par.). Through such temple imagery, Paul "depicts the church under its divine aspect as the society of the redeemed, which through sanctification by the Holy Spirit constitutes the inviolable dwelling-place of God" (McKelvey, *The New Temple,* 92).

The fullest reference to the Christian church as "the temple of the living God" in Paul's letters is to be found in 2 Cor 6:16: "What agreement is there between the temple of God and idols? For we are the temple of the living God. As God has said: 'I will live in them and walk among them, and I will be their God, and they will be my people'" (quoting from Lev 26:12; Jer 32:38; Ezek 37:27). This reference may be Paul's earliest surviving exposition of the subject, for it appears in a portion that many think was probably part of his "previous letter" to his converts at Corinth (i.e., 2 Cor 6:14–7:1; cf. 1 Cor 5:9).

But Paul also uses temple imagery in characterizing Christians generally. In 1 Cor 3:16–17, when dealing with the problem of divisions within the Corinthian church, he writes: "Don't you know that you are God's temple and that God's Spirit lives in you? If anyone destroys God's temple, God will destroy that person; for God's temple is sacred, and you are that temple." And in 1 Cor 6:19–20, when dealing with issues of sexual immorality in the church, he writes: "Don't you know that your body is a temple of the Holy Spirit, who is in you, whom you have received from God? You are not your own; you were bought at a price. Therefore honor God with your body." Ephesians 2:20–22 brings all of this temple imagery together: the church is "built on the foundation of the apostles and prophets," with "Christ Jesus himself as the chief cornerstone"; it is "in Christ," being joined together and rising "to become a holy temple in the Lord" (vv. 20–21)—with individual believers then spoken of as "in him" being also "built together to become a dwelling in which God lives by his Spirit" (v. 22).

Paul's use of temple imagery, however, does not extend to referring to the church as a place for sacrifice, as in 1 Pet 2:4–10, for in Pauline theology (1) Christ is the one "who loved us and gave himself up for us as a fragrant offering and sacrifice to God" (Eph 5:2; Col 1:22), (2) Paul and his associates are those who have offered to God and his people their ministries as a sacrifice (2 Cor 2:15–16; Phil 2:17), and (3) believers in Christ are urged to offer themselves and their service to God and others as sacrifices (Rom 12:1–2; 2 Cor 9:11–15; Phil 4:18)—which, of course, furnishes the basis for the Protestant doctrine of "the priesthood of all believers." Rather, the emphases in Paul's use of temple imagery for the church are (1) the place in the New Covenant where God dwells; (2) the place where God's

Spirit is now active; and (3) the holiness and purity that must necessarily charac-terize God's people, both individually and corporately. For both believers and the church, whether local or universal, have become habitations of God's Spirit.

The Community of the Spirit

A further image of the church—no less important than any of the others, yet one lacking a specific title in the apostle's letters—may be expressed as "the community of the Spirit." This image underlies much of what Paul writes, partic-ularly in his earlier letters, though often it is more implied than expressed.

In writing to his confused converts in the Roman province of Galatia, Paul lays particular emphasis on the fact that they are a community of the Spirit and so should not be giving heed to the nomistic enticements of the Judaizers. In his *probatio* of 3:1–4:31, where he develops his central arguments, he begins with questions that assume his converts' experience as a community of the Spirit: "Did you receive the Spirit by observing the law, or by believing what you heard?" (3:2); "Does God give you his Spirit and work miracles among you because you observe the law, or because you believe what you heard?" (3:5). In his *exhortatio* of 5:1–6:10, where he exhorts on the basis of what has been argued in the *probatio*, he urges them to "live by the Spirit," reflect "the fruit of the Spirit" in their lives, and "keep in step with the Spirit" (5:16–26).

Likewise in writing to converts at Thessalonica, Paul alludes to their corpo-rate life as being a community of the Spirit. Almost casually he speaks of the word of God "at work in you who believe" (1 Thess 2:13), affirming that this is so be-cause God "gives you his Holy Spirit" (1 Thess 4:8). It is, in fact, "the sanctifying work of the Spirit," coupled with their "belief in the truth," that makes effective God's salvation in their lives and gives them hope for the future (2 Thess 2:13–14). So they are admonished: "Do not quench ['stifle' or 'suppress'] the Spirit!" (1 Thess 5:19).

Being "the community of the Spirit" means many things for believers in Christ—both doctrinally and ethically, and both individually and corporately. It does not, however, mean that one must affirm only the spiritual and renounce everything natural; or that one be guided only by the Spirit and oppose everything traditional or ecclesiastical; or, as in our discussion here, that one should honor a ministry of the Spirit that exists without structures, forms, or order. Rather, the church as the community of the Spirit, whose activity necessarily finds expression in local congregations and particular situations, is urged to "keep in step with the Spirit" in whatever circumstances it finds itself, as Paul exhorted his converts at Galatia to do (Gal 5:25). And that holds true, it seems, not only in matters of faith and doctrine, but also with respect to ecclesiastical structures, forms, and order.

God's Eschatological Community

"People of God" and "community of the Spirit" came to have eschatological significance in early Judaism. When Paul applies them to the Christian church, they are associated with other expressions that identify the church as a society centered in heaven and striving toward eschatological fulfillment. In Gal 4:25–26 Paul speaks of the "mother" of believers in Christ as being "the Jerusalem above" *(hē anō Ierousalēm)*, not "the present Jerusalem" *(hē nun Ierousalēm)*; in 2 Cor 11:2 he calls the church at Corinth a "pure" or "chaste virgin" whom he wants to present to Christ at his parousia for the messianic marriage; and in Phil 3:20 he says that Christians have their citizenship "in heaven," which is their true home and final destiny.

In none of these three verses does the word "church" *(ekklēsia)* appear. Yet all of them speak of corporate existence in the New Covenant, and all of them use Old Testament and early Jewish imagery that suggests eschatological fulfillment. So all three of them, particularly in concert with the expressions "people of God" and "community of the Spirit," may be seen as alluding to the church as God's eschatological community. All of this imagery suggests that the real nature of the church—though presently, and of necessity, embodied in various shapes and forms—cannot be truly grasped simply by a study of any of the church's earthly shapes or historical forms, whether ancient or modern.

3. CRITERIA FOR CHURCH ORDER

Protestant studies of church order have all too often pitted the apostolic church, where freedom of the Spirit reigned, against the later church, where hierarchical structures and juridical order are seen to have dominated—frequently setting them out as contradictory and mutually exclusive. But such a scenario is superficial and specious, for while the New Testament gives no definitive constitution for church government, the Pauline missionary letters set out certain criteria for community formation and reflect various features of church order within Paul's Gentile churches.

The Divine Origin and Control of the Church

Basic to Paul's thought about the church—as well as that of all the other writers of the New Testament—is that the church is fundamentally different from every other humanly constituted community or society. Paul does not credit the founding, growth, or building up of the church to his own or any other missionary's abilities or efforts but only to God, Christ, and the Holy Spirit (cf. 1 Cor 3:5–9; Eph 2:20–22; 4:11–16). Therefore, as Rudolf Schnackenburg has rightly observed, the first matter of importance in any study of church government must be that "all the men [and women] who are entrusted with tasks and services in the Church are simply God's instruments, servants of Christ, organs of the Holy Spirit (1 Cor 4:1; 12:4–6), and so possess an essentially different character from all bearers of office appointed by merely human statute and constitution" (*The Church in the New Testament*, 25).

The most distinctive image of the church in the Pauline letters is, as noted above, that of the body of Christ—which suggests that, in Paul's mind at least, the essential nature of the church is not to be viewed simply in terms of some social compact theory. Indeed, the early Christians used the organizational forms of the day to structure their corporate lives. In Paul's vision of the church and community formation, however, the church is fundamentally different from any purely human community or society, for God is its founder, Jesus Christ is its chief cornerstone, and the Holy Spirit directs its affairs.

The Importance of Form and Order in Paul's Churches

The earliest believers in Jesus, as F. J. A. Hort long ago pointed out, were neither enthusiastic cranks nor "a mere horde of men ruled absolutely by the Apostles," and so without form or organizational structure (*The Christian Ecclesia,* 52). Although they viewed themselves as living in "the last days" of redemptive history and attempted to give free reign to the Spirit, they did not form purely spiritual societies that had no need of structure or order. As the new "people of God" and the new "temple of God," the earliest believers in Jesus were not neophytes in religion but drew on the long tradition of worship, discipline, and organization they had known in their Jewish synagogues and in the Jerusalem temple.

The earliest forms of worship in the Christian church, in fact, reflect in many ways patterns drawn from the Jewish experience of the earliest believers in Jesus. These patterns, undoubtedly through Paul's influence, also continued in large measure in Gentile churches. These inherited elements included praising God in "psalms, hymns, and spiritual songs," as well as through various other means of thankfulness (cf. 1 Cor 14:26; Eph 5:19; Col 3:16); the reading of Scripture (cf. Col 4:16; 1 Thess 5:27; 1 Tim 4:13); prayers (cf. 1 Tim 2:1–2); a sermon, exposition of Scripture, or exhortation (cf. 1 Cor 14:26); the amen (cf. 1 Cor 14:16); and various confessions of faith (cf. my *New Wine into Fresh Wineskins,* 1–66).

Order was important for Paul. He held, as with Judaism generally, that disorder was a characteristic of Hades (cf. Job 10:22), not of God or his people (cf. 1 Cor 14:33). He recognized a functional order in the hierarchy of God, Christ, man, and woman (1 Cor 11:3)—even while going on to highlight a redemptive order "in the Lord" where equality dominates (cf. 1 Cor 11:11–12). He spoke of an order in the resurrection: "Each in his own order: Christ the firstfruits; then at his coming those who belong to Christ" (1 Cor 15:23)—even to the extent of setting out an order of resurrection for first "the dead in Christ" and then "we who are still alive" at the time of the parousia (1 Thess 4:15–17). He exhorted his converts at Corinth, whose charismatic and spiritual enthusiasm seemed unbounded, to carry on their worship in "a fitting and orderly way" (1 Cor 14:40; cf. 14:26–40). And he wrote to believers at Colossae about his delight not only in their "firm faith in Christ" but also their "good order" (Col 2:5).

Likewise, form was important for Paul, though not a controlling criterion. In his thinking about a future resurrection, for example, he visualized the necessity of embodiment but was also cognizant of a variety of "bodies" created by God. He was sure that the precise form of a believer's body at the resurrection would be "as he [God] has determined" (1 Cor 15:35–50). Furthermore, he viewed disembodiment as something repugnant and was not at all interested in any "naked" or "unclothed" soulish resurrection, but looked for a time when both he and all believers in Christ would be "further clothed" (2 Cor 5:1–4).

The Creativity and Spontaneity of God's Spirit

No one can read Paul's letters without becoming acutely aware of the creativity and spontaneity of God's Spirit, at work in the early churches. "In Christ" and by the work of God's Spirit, nationality, class, and sex—the three divisive factors of history—are transcended (Gal 3:28); women are allowed to pray and prophesy openly in the local church (1 Cor 11:4–5); "the dividing wall of hostility" between Jews and Gentiles is broken down (Eph 2:11–22); and an unworthy slave is received back as a fellow human being ("in the flesh") and a fellow believer ("in the Lord")—in fact, as a "dear brother" (Phlm 8–21). Even traditional forms of worship, as drawn from early Judaism and reconstituted by early Jewish Christianity, were subject to the creativity and spontaneity of the Spirit's guidance—as witness, for example, Paul's handling of the abuses of the Lord's Supper at Corinth and his directive that its practice be changed, thereby putting an end to those abuses and being better able to signal the true intent of the celebration.

Believers in the churches involved may not have fully understood all these instances of the Spirit's creative and spontaneous working, and Christians during past centuries and today have not always seen them as significant. But the factor of God's Spirit at work in the church in ways that are both creative and spontaneous must always be held in high regard by Christians in their thinking about their lives, whether individually or corporately. Likewise, it must always be seen as an important principle for church order. For the task of the Holy Spirit is not only to bring to fruition the unity and universality of the church but also to guide the church and the churches in expressions of such unity and universality in ways that are appropriate for specific times and places—often in ways that are serendipitous, reflecting the Spirit's own creativity and spontaneity.

The Unity and Diversity of the Church

That Paul was actively interested in promoting the unity of the church can hardly be contested—though, of course, the unity he advocated was always in terms of the gospel he believed had been entrusted to him, not that of the Judaizers at Galatia, the party politicians, spiritualists or enthusiasts at Corinth, or the ascetic-mystical gnostics at Colossae. His emphasis on unity is well summarized in the exhortation of Eph 4:3–6:

> Make every effort to keep the unity of the Spirit through the bond of peace. There is one body and one Spirit—just as you were called to one hope when you were called—one Lord, one faith, one baptism; one God and Father of all, who is over all and through all and in all.

His practice on behalf of church unity is clearly exemplified by his strenuous efforts with regard to the Jerusalem collection, which he organized and eventually joined in taking to "the poor" of the Jerusalem church (cf. Rom 15:25–32; 1 Cor 16:1–3; 2 Cor 8:1–9:15). For though he differed in some respects from believers at Jerusalem, the unity of the church—even amidst its diversity and despite real dangers—was of great importance to him.

Nonetheless, the acceptance of diversity within his own Gentile churches seems also to have been a prominent factor in his thinking, as witness his somewhat differing lists of spiritual gifts in Rom 12:6–8 and 1 Cor 12:4–11 and of ecclesiastical functions in 1 Cor 12:28 and Eph 4:11. It may be difficult to catalogue or classify Paul's thought regarding such ecclesiastical ministries. J. B. Lightfoot distinguished between "temporary" and "permanent" ministries (cf. "The Christian Ministry," 185–86); Edwin Hatch between "episcopal-diaconal" and "presbyterial" ministries (*The Organization of the Early Christian Churches*, lectures II and III); and Adolf Harnack between "religious" or "charismatic" and "administrative" ministries (*The Constitution and Law of the Church*, 45–60). But however one arranges and identifies the items within Paul's lists of ministries in the church, they reflect his awareness of diversity in church order. In fact, they seem to suggest that for Paul the church is to be understood as a unity in diversity and a diversity in unity—that is, a unity that is diversely contextualized and a diversity that expresses various features of an essential unity.

4. REFLECTIONS OF CHURCH ORDER

But how did Paul's theology of the church and criteria for community formation work out in his own churches? His major "missionary letters" provide very little explicit information on the structures and order of his Gentile churches but do provide a few bits of data. To these we must now turn, asking such questions as: What do Paul's missionary letters suggest regarding church order in the Gentile churches of his day? How are the structures and order of Paul's churches to be related to what can be discerned in the other apostolic churches? How normative are the structures and order of Paul's churches for the church today?

The Data of the Letters

The ten Pauline letters with which we are here dealing indicate quite clearly that, at least at first, Paul considered himself to be the one to exercise supervision over the affairs of his Gentile churches. He had been called by God to be an apostle to the Gentiles (cf. Gal 1:15–16; 2 Cor 5:18–20); the "pillar" apostles at Jerusalem had recognized the validity of his commission "to preach the gospel to the Gentiles" (cf. Gal 2:6–9); he had strenuously exerted himself—risking even death—in his mission to bring "the good news" of Christ to the Gentile world (cf. Gal 4:13–16; 2 Cor 1:8–11; 4:8–12; 11:23–33; 2 Thess 3:7–10); he had been to his converts like both a mother and a father in their Christian birthing (cf. 1 Cor 4:15; Gal 4:19; 1 Thess 2:7–12); and he was responsible before God for all his converts to present them as pure or chaste virgins to Christ at the parousia for the messianic marriage (cf. 2 Cor 11:2). And not only did he feel himself responsible for the welfare of believers in the churches he founded, but he also felt responsible for believers in the Gentile churches founded by others (cf. Rom 1:5–6, 13; 15:15–16; Col 1:3–9). For he was preeminently the apostle to the Gentiles, who had been given grace by God "to be a minister of Christ Jesus to the Gentiles with the priestly duty of proclaiming the gospel of God, so that the Gentiles might become an offering acceptable to God, sanctified by the Holy Spirit" (Rom 15:15–16).

Paul did not, however, exercise his apostolic mandate to supervise his Gentile churches alone. He also delegated authority to his coworkers to represent him in the administration of his churches, providing them at times with letters of introduction. In particular, we read in his missionary letters of Timothy, who was sent as his delegate to Thessalonica (1 Thess 3:2–6), Philippi (Phil 2:19–23), and Corinth (1 Cor 4:17; 16:10–11; cf. 2 Cor 1:1, 19), and of Titus, who was twice sent to represent him at Corinth (2 Cor 2:13; 7:6–7, 13–16; 8:6, 16–24; 12:18). As E. Earle Ellis has pointed out, "In the Book of Acts and the canonical literature ascribed to Paul some 100 names, often coupled with a score of assorted titles, are associated with the Apostle" ("Paul and His Co-Workers," 437; see also 438–52, building on Ramsay, *St. Paul the Traveller and the Roman Citizen*, 397, and Redlich, *St. Paul and His Companions*, 200–86)—the most important of these associates mentioned in his missionary letters being not only Timothy and Titus, but also Barnabas (1 Cor 9:6; Gal 2:1, 9, 13), Silas (2 Cor 1:19; 1 Thess 1:1; 2 Thess 1:1), Apollos (1 Cor 3:4–9; 4:1–13; 16:12), Phoebe (Rom 16:1–2), Epaphras (Col 1:7–8; 4:12; Phlm 23), Tychicus (Eph 6:21; Col 4:7), Aristarchus (Col 4:10; Phlm 23), Mark (Col 4:10; Phlm 24), Demas (Col 4:14; Phlm 23), and Luke (Col 4:14; Phlm 24).

Furthermore, Paul recognized the presence of many local leaders in his churches. In 1 Thess 5:12–13, for example, he refers to various church leaders at Thessalonica, speaking of them as "those who work hard among you, who are over you in the Lord, and who admonish you," and asks his converts to "respect" them and "hold them in the highest regard in love because of their work." Such leaders were evidently drawn from the Thessalonian congregation itself—probably to fulfill some particular type of service and perhaps on a part-time or rotation basis, which would have allowed them to carry on their normal occupations as well. The fact that Paul does not name these leaders probably means not that he did not know them or their names but that he wanted his exhortations to be received as applicable to whoever held such positions of leadership in the congregation. Local leadership at Corinth seems implied in his words to his converts in 1 Cor 5:4–5: "When you are assembled in the name of our Lord Jesus and I am with you in spirit, and the power of our Lord Jesus is present, hand this man over to Satan, so that his sinful nature may be destroyed and his spirit saved on the day of the Lord."

Likewise, the greetings extended to "the overseers" (*episkopoi*) and "those who serve" (*diakonoi*) in Phil 1:1 reflect the presence of local leaders in Paul's church at Philippi. Some of these he names: Euodia and Syntyche, two women who had earlier served with him "in the cause of the gospel" at Philippi, but who were now at odds with one another (4:2); and Clement, who had also served with the apostle in that city and seems not to have gotten involved in the argument between the two women (4:3). As D. E. H. Whiteley has appropriately pointed out with respect to the greetings of Phil 1:1: "'Serving' and 'overseeing' were certainly functions; it is not clear whether in St. Paul's day they had hardened into 'offices'" (*Theology of St. Paul,* 203). And although Acts and the Pastoral Epistles frequently use the term "elder" *(presbyteros)* for church leaders (cf. Acts 11:30; 14:23; 15:2, 4, 6, 22, 23; 16:4; 20:17; 21:18; 1 Tim 5:1, 17, 19; Titus 1:5–6), it does not appear in Paul's major missionary letters—unless, of course, the reference to "pastors and teachers" in Eph 4:11 is a functional way of characterizing the work of "presbyters" or "elders," as J. B. Lightfoot held ("The Christian Ministry," 194).

Admittedly, there is much that is ambiguous in Paul's missionary letters about church order and leadership in his Gentile churches. We could wish, for example, that we knew more about the "house churches" referred to in Rom 16:3–5 (perhaps also vv. 10 and 11); 1 Cor 16:19; Col 4:15; and Phlm 2 (see esp. Malherbe, "House Churches and Their Problems," and Branick, *The House Church in the Writings of Paul*). Likewise, we might wish we knew more about how the Gentile churches chose their delegates to take the money they had collected to Jerusalem for the impoverished Jewish Christians there (cf. 1 Cor 16:1–4; 2 Cor 8:18–19; also Rom 15:25–26). Gunther Bornkamm's summation regarding church order generally, however, is apt: "there was no absence of organisation and offices in the Pauline congregations." His statement about leaders in the churches is also pertinent: "their authority derives from the ministry accepted and discharged by them, not from their status" (*"presbys, ktl,"* *TDNT* 6:664).

Even more suggestive regarding church order in Paul's thought is the way that he handles certain issues regarding the sacraments or ordinances of the church—that is, regarding baptism and the Lord's Supper. For while he highly values Christian baptism, as his words in Rom 6:3–7 clearly indicate, he also says in 1 Cor 1:14–17 with respect to the divisions in the church at Corinth:

> I am thankful that I did not baptize any of you except Crispus and Gaius, so no one can say that you were baptized into my name. (Yes, I also baptized the household of Stephanas; but beyond that, I don't remember if I baptized anyone else.) For Christ did not send me to baptize, but to preach the gospel—not with words of human wisdom, lest the cross of Christ be emptied of its power.

Such a disclaimer, coupled with an assertion about his true responsibility, indicates that Paul saw baptism, while vitally important, to be the responsibility of the church and not directly his as an evangelist—except, of course, in the founding of a local church, when he alone would be available to baptize.

His treatment of the Corinthians' abuses of the Lord's Supper in 1 Cor 11:17–34 is revealing as well. In the earliest days of the Jerusalem church, believers in Jesus probably celebrated two kinds of communal meals: (1) a paschal or sacred meal in their corporate gatherings, which commemorated the death of Jesus and followed the pattern of the Jewish Passover and Jesus' Last Supper with his disciples (cf. Acts 2:42), and (2) a joyful fellowship meal in their homes, which commemorated Jesus' resurrection and continued presence with his followers and was patterned along the lines of a Jewish *haburah* (fellowship) meal and

Jesus' eating with his disciples during his earthly ministry (cf. Acts 2:46b–47a). These two meals, however, seem to have been combined into one communal feast when the gospel penetrated Gentile regions outside Jerusalem and when Jewish influence ceased to play a dominant role in the development of Christian worship. But even though a one-meal tradition appears to have become fixed among Gentile Christians, Paul in dealing with abuses at Corinth felt free to change matters again by disengaging the Lord's Supper from the more expressly fellowship features of a communal meal (cf. 1 Cor 11:17–34). He was evidently willing to alter a seemingly established practice within his churches rather than to have that practice, when misused, pervert the essential principles of the gospel.

Such a vignette of church life in one of Paul's churches—even though it may reflect the circumstances of only one of his Gentile congregations—speaks volumes as to what Paul saw to be central in the Christian gospel and the extent to which he was prepared to be flexible in his contextualization of that gospel. More important for our purposes here, however, it encapsulates many of the criteria for community formation that are discernible in the Pauline letters, particularly those having to do with the unity and diversity of the church and the creativity and spontaneity of God's Spirit.

Paul's Churches vis-à-vis Other Apostolic Churches

But how do the structures and order of Paul's churches, as reflected in his missionary letters, correspond to the structures and order discernible in the other apostolic churches of his day? And how are the differences between them to be understood?

Admittedly, our knowledge of early Christian missionary activity and the founding of Christian churches is limited, being confined largely to the portrayals of the ministries of Peter and Paul in the Acts of the Apostles. Furthermore, Luke has put his own spin on what he relates in Acts, and the vignettes in his second volume can be variously interpreted. Nonetheless, it does appear that the church at Jerusalem was predominantly monarchical in its organization, with James "the Lord's brother," together with the apostles Peter and John, its overseers (cf. Gal 1:18–20; 2:1–10, 12; also Acts 15:13–21), and that the church of Syrian Antioch was principally oligarchic, with various "prophets and teachers" drawn from the congregation's own ranks taking leadership (cf. Acts 11:22–30; 13:1–3). Yet Paul's churches, however understood, seem not quite the same in their structures and order as the churches of Jerusalem and Antioch.

Some have viewed Paul's whole missionary activity and his founding of churches as "dangerous exceptions" to the established, monarchical structure of the early church, for Antioch was the base and axis of his ministry, not Jerusalem, and the authorization for his ministry came through certain "prophets and teachers" at Antioch, not the apostles at Jerusalem. Others have looked upon the churches he founded as being "provisional in nature," asserting that they represented only an initial stage in the growth of the church and that they would later develop properly into more orderly institutions.

But to characterize what is reflected in Paul's letters about church order as being either "exceptional" or "provisional" is to miss an extremely important point in the interpretation of both the New Testament and church history, for in the pages of the New Testament and the annals of church history we have presentations of the essential features of the Christian gospel, depictions of the central convictions of those who believed the gospel, and portrayals of how that gospel has been contextualized at various times and in differing situations—whether in the apostolic age or later, and whether at Jerusalem, at Antioch, in Paul's Gentile churches, in our own country, or in lands "overseas."

To understand the New Testament and church history properly, we must appreciate both the central features in the apostolic proclamation and comprehension of the gospel and also the various contextualizations of that gospel from the earliest days of the Christian church to the present day. Paul's missionary letters reflect contextualizations appropriate for a particular time, culture, and circumstance, which should be appreciated on their own merits—but should also guide us as we contextualize the Christian gospel for our own particular time, culture, and circumstances.

A Normative Pattern for Today?

How normative, then, is the pattern of church life and order reflected in Paul's major missionary letters—if, indeed, such a pattern can be detected with any degree of certainty—for the ordering of the Christian church today? Many have wanted to reproduce the structures and order not only of the New Testament churches generally but also of the Pauline churches in particular. Such a desire has frequently led either to ossification or to heresy, and sometimes to both. Little can be added to what F. J. A. Hort said in concluding his 1888–1889 Cambridge lectures on "The Early History and the Early Conceptions of the Christian Ecclesia" (lectures that built on J. B. Lightfoot's 1868 dissertation on "The Christian Ministry" and were published in 1897, five years after Hort's death):

> In this [i.e., the study of early church order] as in so many other things is seen the futility of endeavouring to make the Apostolic history into a set of authoritative precedents, to be rigorously copied without regard to time and place, thus turning the Gospel into a second Levitical Code. The Apostolic age is full of embodiments of purposes and principles of the most instructive kind; but the responsibility of choosing the means was left for ever to the Ecclesia itself, and to each Ecclesia, guided by ancient precedent on the one hand and adaptation to present and future needs on the other. The lesson-book of the Ecclesia, and of every Ecclesia, is not a law but a history. (*Christian Ecclesia*, 232–33)

BIBLIOGRAPHY

Ascough, Richard S. *What Are They Saying about the Formation of Pauline Churches?* New York: Paulist, 1998.

Barrett, C. K. *Church, Ministry and Sacraments in the New Testament.* Exeter: Paternoster, 1985.

Best, Ernest. *One Body in Christ: A Study in the Relationship of the Church to Christ in the Epistles of the Apostle Paul.* London: SPCK, 1955.

Branick, Vincent. *The House Church in the Writings of Paul.* Wilmington, Del.: Michael Glazier, 1989.

Burtchaell, James T. *From Synagogue to Church: Public Services and Offices in the Earliest Christian Communities.* Cambridge: Cambridge University Press, 1992.

Davies, W. D. *A Normative Pattern of Church Life in the New Testament: Fact or Fancy?* London: James Clarke, 1950.

Ellis, E. Earle. "Paul and His Co-Workers." *New Testament Studies* 17 (1971): 437–52.

Harnack, Adolf. *The Constitution and Law of the Church in the First Two Centuries.* Translated by F. L. Pogson. London: Williams & Norgate, 1910.

Hatch, Edwin. *The Organization of the Early Christian Churches.* London: Rivingtons, 1881.

Holmberg, Bengt. *Paul and Power: The Structure of Authority in the Primitive Church as Reflected in the Pauline Epistles.* Lund: Gleerup, 1978.

Hort, F. J. A. *The Christian Ecclesia: A Course of Lectures on the Early History and Early Conceptions of the Ecclesia.* London: Macmillan, 1897.

Lightfoot, J. B. "The Christian Ministry." Pages 181–269 in *Saint Paul's Epistle to the Philippians.* London: Macmillan, 1868.

Longenecker, Richard N. *New Wine into Fresh Wineskins: Contextualizing the Early Christian Confessions.* Peabody, Mass.: Hendrickson, 1999. See esp. "The Pauline Corpus," 48–63, and "Toward an Incarnational and Contextualized Theology," 154–73.

Malherbe, Abraham J. *Social Aspects of Early Christianity.* Philadelphia: Fortress, 1983. See esp. "House Churches and Their Problems," 60–91.

McKelvey, R. J. *The New Temple: The Church in the New Testament.* London: Oxford University Press, 1969.

Meeks, Wayne A. *The First Urban Christians: The Social World of the Apostle Paul.* New Haven: Yale University Press, 1983. See esp. "The Formation of the Ekklēsia," 74–110.

Minear, Paul S. *Images of the Church in the New Testament.* Philadelphia: Westminster, 1960.

Ramsay, William M. *St. Paul the Traveller and the Roman Citizen.* London: Hodder & Stoughton, 1908.

Redlich, E. Basil. *St. Paul and His Companions.* London: Hodder & Stoughton, 1913.

Schnackenburg, Rudolf. *The Church in the New Testament.* Translated by W. J. O'Hara. New York: Herder & Herder, 1965.

Schweizer, Eduard. *Church Order in the New Testament.* Translated by F. Clarke. London: SCM, 1961.

Streeter, B. H. *The Primitive Church, Studied with Special Reference to the Origins of the Christian Ministry.* London: Macmillan, 1929.

Whiteley, D. E. H. *The Theology of Paul.* Oxford: Blackwell, 1964.

Chapter 6

Divine Power, Community Formation, and Leadership in the Acts of the Apostles

S. Scott Bartchy

Why did Luke write his two-volume work? What changes in belief and be-havior among his Gentile readers did he seek to inspire? What did he seek to com-municate about the nature, character, and activity of Divine Power in his narrative called "the Acts of the Apostles"? What consequences did his under-standing of the "good news" of God's inbreaking "kingdom" have for traditional views about leadership? What does he portray regarding the character and struc-ture of the early Christian communities?

Answers to these questions hold the key to a deeper grasp of Luke's theol-ogy of ministry and leadership. The best answers, I believe, can be found by fo-cusing on two fundamental concerns: Luke's understanding of the character and purpose of God, and the cultural values and social codes of the ancient Mediter-ranean world. Ignoring these primary contextual considerations inevitably ren-ders inadequate, if not actually misleading, any analysis of the early Christian church. But highlighting these two matters provides the proper setting for a better understanding of Christian community formation and leadership in the Acts of the Apostles, which is what I will endeavor to provide in what follows.

1. THE CHARACTER AND PURPOSE OF GOD

What was it about Luke's understanding of Ultimate Reality—that is, of God—that the intended readers of the Acts of the Apostles did not yet under-stand and believe? Many would answer that Gentiles did not understand or be-lieve in monotheism, and so Luke had to contrast the many gods of the Gentile nations, who are designated "idols" in Acts 15:20, 29, and 17:16, with the one true God who has revealed his will definitively in the words and actions of a human being, Jesus of Nazareth. Placing the accent somewhat differently, I propose that for Luke what was "unknown" about God among the Gentiles (see 17:23) was not so much that there was only one true God among all the gods, but that this God, the God of Israel, had a strikingly different character from all the other divine powers known to them, and that this God sought to achieve a significantly different goal among human beings from those deities worshiped in Greco-Roman culture.

God as Creator of Human Community

The longest leap in a Gentile's conversion from polytheism to the God of Israel was not renouncing the Many for the One but embracing a transformed understanding of Ultimate Reality. For Gentiles who converted to either Judaism or Christianity, Divine Power became intimately linked to the values and practice of justice and mercy in interpersonal relationships and social institutions.

Children raised in a Greco-Roman culture soon learned that the traditional Greco-Roman divinities were not, in principle, concerned about how their worshipers treated each other or with the building up of human community. Indeed, from the stories they were told they knew that these divine powers were often in conflict with one another. "Polytheism," as Walter Burkert has observed, "encounters fundamental difficulties in giving legitimization to a moral world order. Its multiplicity always implies opposition: Hera against Zeus, Aphrodite against Artemis, Dionysos against Apollo" (*Greek Religion,* 248).

This absence of a clear connection between religious worship and the interpersonal behavior of the worshipers had far-reaching consequences. While religious concerns were enmeshed in every crevice of Greco-Roman life, the concept of "god" (Greek, *theos;* Latin, *deus*) did not bring to Gentile minds the practice of "fellowship," "community," or "close personal relationship" (Greek, *koinōnia;* Latin, *communitas* or *societas*). Despite earlier, classical Greek associations of some aspects of justice with Zeus—which seemingly had been forgotten by the first century—the deep interest of Israel's God in justice and mercy was generally unknown to the "nations" (cf. Lloyd-Jones, *Justice of Zeus,* 1–18). As Wayne Meeks points out: "Being or becoming religious in the Greco-Roman world did not entail either moral transformation or sectarian resocialization" (*Origins of Christian Morality,* 28).

In striking contrast, Judeans had in common the tradition that their god, as the creator of the world and the principal actor in history, had long sought to create a community characterized by interpersonal righteousness and social justice. According to the Mosaic covenant, this god's worshipers agreed to deal fairly and generously with one another without regard to social or economic status.

And this was true, as well, for the earliest Christians. Because of the teaching and actions of Jesus of Nazareth, the community they formed was redefined as a radically inclusive group in which all human beings were now called to honor this God primarily by obeying God's will regarding how they treated each other. And in the Acts of the Apostles the nature and purpose of God's *ekklēsia* ("assembly" or "church") is displayed both by such a radical inclusivity and by the giving of honor and aid to all followers of Jesus.

In continuity with the major traditions about God in Israel's Scriptures, Luke, therefore, must be seen in his Gospel and Acts to have sought to persuade non-Jewish converts to the Christian movement to conform their behavior to an understanding of God that had been largely unknown among them—that is, to an understanding of God as a community-forming and community-sustaining power. As such, this God desired above all to be worshiped by their practices of justice and mercy, especially on behalf of those who were poor, whether economically or socially, or both.

The Nature and Purpose of the Community

Luke's summary statement about the congregation at Jerusalem in Acts 4:32–35 presents the practice of such solidarity and compassion as the basis for the hearing given to the apostle's preaching about God raising Jesus from the dead. That is, the "one-heart-and-soul" manner of these believers in sharing with each other (v. 32) made plausible in Jerusalem their claim to be God's Spirit-filled people.

Especially important to note in 4:32–35 is the A-B-A′ construction of the passage and the force of the two uses of the causal connector "for" (*gar*) in verse 34:

> A All the believers were one in heart and mind. No one claimed that any of their possessions was for their own use, but they shared everything they had. (v. 32)
>
> B With great power the apostles continued to testify to the resurrection of the Lord Jesus, and they all were given great favor [by God]. (v. 33)
>
> A′ For (*gar*) there were no needy persons (*endeēs*) among them. For (*gar*) from time to time those who owned lands or houses sold them, brought the money from the sales and placed it at the apostles' feet. And it was distributed to anyone who had need. (vv. 34–35)

Verses 32 and 34–35 are like bread slices in a sandwich construction, with verse 33 being the meat. Since there are many English translations in which the first "for" (*gar*) of verse 34 is ignored, thereby giving the reader the impression that the sentences present a simple list of activities rather than highlight causal connections among them, I must stress here the importance of the Greek causal conjunction *gar* for the intended logic of the passage (see Bartchy, "Credibility Factor," 155–60).

Luke evidently used this *inclusio* structure to highlight the integral connection between the behavior of the early Christians, whose lives had been transformed to share possessions with each other, and the persuasiveness of the Christian message, which created the basis for such a striking behavioral change. I am pleased to note that Gerhard Krodel also calls attention to this causal connection between the powerful communication of the gospel of the resurrection and the readiness of the earliest believers in Jesus to share the goods of life (*Commentary on Acts*, 116–17).

Luke's conviction seems to be rooted, both in concept and in vocabulary, in the Greek translation (LXX) of Deut 15:4–5: "When the Lord God blesses you in your land, there will be no needy person *(endeēs)* among you . . . if you listen to God's voice and obey all these commands." The commands in question, which are stated in Deut 15:7–8, all have to do with the sharing of possessions. And this section of Deut 15 ends in verse 11 with these words: "Since there will never cease to be some in need *(endeēs)* on the earth, I therefore command you, 'Open your hand to the poor and needy neighbor in your land.'"

With the intention of using the Jerusalem Christians as an example for his readers, Luke claims that "there was not a needy person *(endeēs)* among them" (4:34). The Greek term *endeēs* ("needy person"), which Luke highlights in verse 34, appears in the New Testament only here. And with the first *gar* of that verse he links the generosity shown such persons among the believers in Jerusalem to the persuasiveness of the apostles' preaching and the great favor of God noted at the end of verse 33.

This description should not be seen as simply Luke's idealized projection into his narrative about the followers of Jesus at Jerusalem, but rather understood as his use of traditionally loaded terms to present what he regarded as the social reality practiced by these early believers and a practice that he desired to stimulate among all his readers (cf. Bartchy, "Community of Goods"). This intensity of caring for one another must have been all the more impressive as the believers extended it to the various Judeans whom "the Lord was adding daily" (2:47)—that is, to new believers who came from diverse social, economic, and cultural backgrounds and who certainly included some of those who had earlier called for Jesus' execution.

Writing in the generation after Paul for Christians in "house congregations" where those who had grown up knowing Israel's God were rapidly becoming a minority, Luke evidently intended to continue the process of resocializing the "nations" that was attempted by Paul: to bring the behavior of those "who had not known God" into harmony with the will of the "living and true God" (1 Thess 1:9). Their behavior should confirm their new belief by demonstrating the character of their new God. Thus the defining point in the conversion of these early believers was not their commitment to monotheism in some abstract sense, but their commitment to cooperation with this true God's character and purpose.

2. CULTURAL VALUES AND SOCIAL CODES OF THE ANCIENT MEDITERRANEAN WORLD

The nature and purpose of this new community, however, will be understood in depth only by the reader who has become well acquainted with the cultural values and social codes of the Mediterranean world in the first century of our era. In Acts 1:15, for example, at the first Pentecost Feast following Jesus' crucifixion, we read: "Peter stood up among the brothers and sisters (together they numbered about a hundred and twenty)." But what did it mean to these one hundred and twenty persons to regard each other as "brothers and sisters"? To facilitate an understanding of Luke's description of the Jesus communities, especially in his frequent use of the Greek term *adelphoi* (literally: "brothers" but more adequately translated "brothers and sisters"), I begin this section with a brief description of the obligations of kinship.

Obligations of Kinship

In first-century Mediterranean families, the closest family ties were conventionally experienced among brothers and sisters. This sense of solidarity among siblings stood in sharp contrast to the sense of competition that prevailed once a person stepped over the family threshold. In the patriarchal system of the world of Jesus, Paul, and Luke, both boys and girls were socialized to expect not only that men would routinely dominate women, but also that every male should seek to dominate as many other men as possible. Within all social classes, traditional male socialization produced human beings trained to pursue a never-ending quest for greater honor and influence in a culture where both honor and influence were in limited supply. Among strangers and those from other families, honor could be acquired only at the expense of someone else's honor. Thus retaliation was the only honorable response to a challenge to one's honor in any encounter beyond the family. And in such a situation, as Bruce Malina has succinctly phrased it: "Since honor is the pivotal value (much like wealth in our society), nearly every interaction with non-family members has undertones of a challenge to honor" (*New Testament World*, 34).

Inside the family, however, these values were inverted. Brothers were raised to give honor freely to all their siblings—thereby practicing what anthropologists today would call "general reciprocity"—and to refrain from responding in kind to any honor challenge from a member of one's own family. The tightest unity of loyalty and affection in the ancient Mediterranean world was experienced in the sibling group of brothers and sisters. This is in striking contrast to the family values of modern Western culture, where such loyalty and affection are experienced in the emotional bonds of marriage.

In our modern Euro-American kinship systems, persons conventionally find their strongest emotional bonds in marriage. So it follows that interpersonal treachery and breakdown in family values are epitomized in stories of spousal betrayal, adultery, and divorce—with such stories seeming to have unending power to captivate the public, as editors of supermarket tabloids know well. In the world of Jesus and his early followers, the breakdown of family values and treachery in its most extreme, despised, and engrossing form was epitomized in stories of strife and betrayal among blood brothers.

The story of Cain's murder of his brother Abel, for example, was told frequently by Second Temple Israelites and early Christians to illustrate the extreme possibilities of human wickedness (cf. *4 Maccabees* 18:11; *Testament of Benjamin* 7:5; 1 John 3:12; Jude 11; *1 Clement* 4:17; Josephus, *Antiquities* 1.52–66). In his *Metamorphoses,* the Roman poet Ovid supported his judgment about the extreme breakdown of social relations during the late Roman Republic by pointing out that "friend was not safe from friend . . . and even between brothers affection was rare" (1.127–51). Thus readers of Mark's Gospel would grasp immediately the seriousness of the warning that as God's judgment approached, social relations would become so badly broken that "brother will hand brother over to death" (Mark 13:12; cf. Matt 10:21; Luke 21:16).

Surrogate Kinship Groups

It was possible, to be sure, for a person to decide to become a member of a surrogate kinship group—such as the one established by the Essenes at Qumran, which remained hierarchical in structure, or the one described by Luke in Acts 2 and 4 at Jerusalem, which did not (as will be discussed later in this chapter). In both cases, it would have been expected that general reciprocity would have been practiced, that is, a sharing of the resources of the group according to need and without keeping score.

Other characteristics of practice within a surrogate kinship group included the following:

1. *Loyalty and trust.* In the first century there was no such thing as a sense of the "kinship of all human beings." Loyalty was to be given to blood kin. Beyond such kin, people were generally regarded as dishonorable until proven otherwise. Men of the same village or town who were not blood relatives conventionally related to each other with deep mistrust.

2. *Truth telling.* Since loyalty was owed only to kin, it followed that there was no obligation to tell the truth to outsiders. On the other hand, there was a high obligation to tell the truth within the blood family. The story of Peter, Ananias, and Sapphira in Acts 5:1–11 should be read with this factor in mind.

3. *Open homes to all in the extended kin group.* The report in Acts 2:46 that the new converts were "breaking bread from house to house" strongly suggests that the gift of the Spirit opened them up to regarding each other as kin. The later report in 12:12 of John Mark's mother opening her home for meetings of the believers further displays her leadership in practicing this kinship value, which had apparently become characteristic of the Jesus community at Jerusalem.

4. *Obligation to be sure the needs of everyone in the group are met.* Each member of a kin group was expected to provide assistance to anyone within the group who needed it, without specifying some return obligation. Members with substantial resources were expected to function as patrons for the kin group. An honored patron functioned as a river of blessing for his people. In turn, the honor of such a person of means depended on his or her sharing wealth rather than hoarding it— that is, in being a giver and not just a receiver of life's limited goods. Luke assumed his readers would understand the stories about Joseph Barnabas (Acts 4:36–37) and Ananias and Sapphira (5:1–11) with this cultural value in mind.

5. *A sense of shared destiny.* Scholars of the period agree that a sense of shared destiny prevailed in most ancient extended families. Throughout the Acts

narrative, the Jesus community remains highly energized by a sense of common purpose and shared destiny.

Embodying these cultural values within the surrogate kinship group at Jerusalem, Joseph, a Levite of Cyprus, was honored by the apostles with the name Barnabas, which means "Son of Encouragement" (4:36–37). By selling a field and humbly delivering the proceeds to the community via the apostles, he demonstrated that he had indeed cast his lot with the Jesus community. The attentive reader of Luke's two volumes might have noted the sharp contrast that the evangelist drew between the behavior of Barnabas in Acts 4:26–37 and that of the rich and pious ruler in Luke 18:18–25, who rejected Jesus' invitation to cast his lot with him and his followers. In any case, Barnabas revealed his sense of solidarity, trustworthiness, openness, and generosity to all in the community. He had, indeed, become a "river of life" to his people. He also revealed his humility by publicly honoring the apostles—who in the Judean society of that day were probably his social as well as his economic inferiors (cf. Bartchy, "Community of Goods," 309–18).

3. COMMUNITY FORMATION AND LEADERSHIP

What, then, can be said about the consequences of the "good news" of God's inbreaking "kingdom" for traditional views about leadership? And what does Luke portray with regard to the character, purpose, and structure of the early Christian communities?

God as Patron of the Community

According to Acts 2:33–47, the Spirit of God was perceived as having a "Jesus-shape," for in his Pentecost speech Peter claimed that the exalted Jesus poured out the Holy Spirit on that day, and the gift of this Spirit resulted in the extension of the historical Jesus' work—that is, in teaching, prayers, doing "signs and wonders," and "having all things in common" (v. 42). A careful reader of Luke's Gospel, therefore, will quickly recognize here in the evangelist's second volume, the so-called Acts of the Apostles, the direct influence of the Spirit of Jesus that is portrayed in his first volume.

In his second volume Luke presents the Holy Spirit in the role of the patron of the Jesus-community, for it is the Spirit who created the community and who continued to sustain it. "The gift of the Spirit," as Luke Timothy Johnson notes, "brought about a community which realized the highest aspirations of human longing: unity, peace, joy, and the praise of God" (*Acts of the Apostles*, 62). Indeed, it is not too strong to say that the "gift of the Holy Spirit" promised to those who repented and were baptized *is* the shared life in the new community itself.

In the context of such positive relationships, the story of Ananias and Sapphira in Acts 5:1–11—and, in particular, Peter's claim that Ananias lied to the Holy Spirit and not to Peter himself (v. 3)—takes for granted the reader's acquaintance with both kinship obligations and patron-client relations. By their deceit, first Ananias and then his wife Sapphira revealed themselves not only to have betrayed their brothers and sisters in the new community, but also to have rejected the Spirit as the patron and protector of the community and its integrity.

Peter asked, "How is it that you have agreed together to put the Spirit of the Lord to the test?" (v. 9). Lying was not and could not be tolerated in such positive relationships. As unreasonable as the story may seem to modern readers, ancient readers would have understood intuitively why the sudden death of each of these two betrayers was appropriate, even necessary. Of note also is the fact that Luke treated Sapphira as a moral agent in her own right and not, according to the prevailing cultural values, as simply embedded in her husband's honor.

On the other hand, Luke introduced Barnabas in Acts 4:36–37 as a creative agent of God's Spirit and a faithful patron for his new community. By his generosity and humility this man made credible his new community's claim that God had raised Jesus from the dead and that they were living in the age of the Messiah. And it will come as no surprise to the careful reader that later Luke presents Barnabas as a trustworthy broker between Saul of Tarsus, who had formerly been a persecutor of the followers of Jesus, and the apostles at Jerusalem (cf. 9:27) and also as a major leader in the early church (cf. 11:22–30; 12:25; 13:1–3, 7, 42–52; 14:12–20; 15:2–35, 36–39). As Luke's portrayal of the first apostles and Barnabas demonstrates, valid leadership was a direct expression of the Spirit's influence in the world.

Authority Based on Character and Commitment

Joseph Barnabas is just one example of a variety of persons in the narrative of Acts who became highly respected leaders among the early Christians without ordination or any other kind of appointment by the first apostles. Apparently the strength of his character and his loyalty to the community established his authority. He became a central figure among the Christians at Antioch (11:25–26), and soon he was counted among the prophets and teachers in the house congregations there (13:1). From there he became the leader of a mission to his native Cyprus (13:4–12)—although, of course, Saul/Paul quickly became more prominent. What needs to be particularly noted in this regard, however, is that in the commissioning of the apostolic witness of Barnabas and Saul, not one of "the Twelve" apostles was involved. Rather, a small group of four other prophets and teachers at Antioch laid hands on them—and perhaps all the Christians there did so as well (13:2–3).

Among the many other leaders in Luke's narrative who served without validation by the Jerusalem apostles were the prophet Agabus (Acts 11:28; probably also 21:10) and Philip's four daughters (21:9). Also without ordination or appointment by the Jerusalem apostles were such early Christian leaders as Ananias of Damascus, who baptized Paul (9:10–19; 22:12–16), Simeon called Niger, Lucius of Cyrene, and Manaen, who was a friend from his youth of Herod Antipas (13:1), Timothy (16:1; 17:14–15; 18:5; 19:22; 20:4), Lydia (16:14, 40),

Priscilla and Aquila (18:2, 18, 26), Apollos (18:24; 19:1), Crispus (18:8), Erastus (19:22), Tychicus (20:4), Trophimus (20:4; 21:29), and the "elders *(presbyteroi)* and overseers *(episkopoi)*" at Ephesus (20:17, 28). Furthermore, the appointment of "the Seven" by "the Twelve" in 6:1–6 apparently set no precedent for legitimating leadership in Luke's perspective. This observation is underlined by the facts that in the last thirteen chapters of his story the term "apostle" does not appear and "the Twelve" as such are noticeably absent from the narrative after chapter six.

House Churches as Surrogate Siblings

Earlier I emphasized that the early Christians shared a sense of solidarity and the obligations of general reciprocity that were typical of sibling relations. This fact had direct implications for the recognition of leaders and their exercise of authority in a nondominating manner. Here I extend this observation by adducing the sharp critique of patriarchal authority that begins in Luke's Gospel with Jesus' call to abandon patriarchal obligations in favor of participation in his community: "If anyone comes to me and does not hate his own father and mother . . . he cannot be my disciple" (Luke 14:26; cf. 9:59–60). Although Luke seems not to know Matthew's related tradition, "call no man father" (Matt 23:9), he refers to none of the early church's leaders as "father" (or "mother"). Rather, he challenges his readers to practice the general reciprocity and mutual support that characterized relations among siblings at their best.

In light of ongoing discussions among scholars and social analysts about patriarchy and egalitarian practice as opposing ends of the same power spectrum, it is important to argue here that it was not Luke's intent to present these Jesus communities as living in an egalitarian social structure. Rather, I am persuaded that Luke thought in antipatriarchal terms while not being egalitarian. How could this be? Three points, in particular, need to be noted: (1) that in the Greco-Roman world, two institutions provided the primary metaphors for all human relationships: kinship and politics; (2) that the term "patriarchy" belongs to the semantic field of kinship, whereas the term "egalitarian" belongs to the semantic field of politics and so refers to such things as equal access to the vote, positions of public leadership, and the ownership of property; (3) that, therefore, the opposite of patriarchy is not egalitarianism but something else—something else for which we may not have a better term than simply "nonpatriarchy"—while the opposite of egalitarianism is not patriarchy but monarchy, oligarchy, or despotism. Our confusion, I think, has been abetted by the fact that the Roman emperors sought to disguise their monarchy by selling it as a higher form of patriarchy—a monarchical patriarchy wherein the emperor was not a king, but simply the *pater patriae!*

To be sure, among blood-related siblings there were usually obvious differences in their respective capacities, strengths, and relative influence within the family. In basic agreement with Paul of Tarsus, Luke recognized differences in capacities and strengths among the early Christians. His apparent goal in writing as he did was not the creation of an egalitarian community in the political sense, but a well-functioning family in the kinship sense—a family in which each member used his or her strengths, whatever they were, first of all to enrich the quality of life in the family rather than for themselves as individuals. And it was undoubtedly this antipatriarchal perspective that had important consequences for Luke's view of leadership.

4. WHERE ARE THE MISSING APOSTLES?

The second volume in Luke's two-part writing, "The Acts of the Apostles," may well be the most misleadingly titled book in the canon of the New Covenant. For two persons, not twelve, are the primary actors presented to the reader in this engrossing narrative. Moreover, according to Luke's criteria in Acts 1:21–22 for being counted among the apostles, only one of these two qualified. The reader has already met Peter the apostle in Luke's Gospel, and his activities are the principal subjects of chapters 2–5 and 9–12 of Luke's Acts. But Paul of Tarsus is a latecomer, having played no role in the stories about the historical Jesus. This is why he cannot be an "apostle" according to Luke's criteria in Acts 1:21–22 (but see 14:4 and 14, where both Barnabas and Paul are called "apostles"). Saul/Paul does not enter Luke's narrative until Acts 7:28–8:3, which introduces him as an enemy of the followers of Jesus in Jerusalem. After this, Saul/Paul becomes the primary focus of the narrative in chapter 9 and throughout chapters 13–28.

The Original Apostles and Matthias

So what happened to the other ten "original" apostles and to the mysterious Matthias who was chosen to replace Judas, "the guide for those who arrested Jesus" (Acts 1:16)? To deal with the latter first, it needs to be noted that Matthias was, indeed, one of a number of men who did satisfy Luke's criteria for apostleship: he had been in the group around Jesus since John baptized Jesus, and he was among the apostles who received Jesus' revelations during the forty-day postresurrection period (1:21–26). But for the reader, Matthias comes out of nowhere and goes back there again! No further mention is made of him in Acts. If Luke was the novelist that some scholars claim him to have been, he certainly missed a grand opportunity to present Matthias in a cameo appearance in the Gospel, not to mention the later scenes in Acts into which he could have been inserted.

For Luke, Matthias's chief significance seems to have been his reconstitution of the symbolic number twelve, each of whom represented one of the ancient tribes of the House of Israel (cf. Luke 22:28–30). But once he and the other ten apostles stood up with Peter on the Day of Pentecost, the reader hears nothing more about this apostle. Why?

Furthermore, Acts 1:13 presents a list of the other eleven apostles—Peter, John, James, Andrew, Philip, Thomas, Bartholomew, Matthew, James son of Alphaeus, Simon the Zealot, and Judas son of James (repeating Luke 6:13–16)— thereby alerting the reader to anticipate stories of their various inspiring deeds. But no such stories are told. Only Peter, John, and James are mentioned again. John is Peter's companion in a number of circumstances: as a healer and preacher in the temple area (ch. 3), as a prisoner in Sadducean custody and a bold witness before the Sanhedrin to the healing power of the risen Jesus (ch. 4), and as a physical and spiritual connection between the followers of Jesus in Jerusalem and the new converts in Samaria (ch. 8). John the apostle, however, is not mentioned again in the entire narrative, except to identify his brother James.

James the apostle plays no named role in Acts after chapter one—until, of course, Luke reports that King Herod Agrippa I "had James, the brother of John, killed with the sword" (12:1–2). According to Luke's narrative, James is the first one of "the Twelve" to be eliminated from the Christian community. But in striking contrast to the case of Judas, no new apostle is appointed to replace him. Apparently the time when "the Twelve" were needed in their symbolic role as the twelve had long passed.

For most of the first half of Acts, Luke's narrative focuses on Peter, emphasizing his critical role as the first proclaimer of the gospel both to Jews and Jewish proselytes gathered in Jerusalem (chs. 2–5) and to Gentiles in the household of Cornelius at Caesarea (ch. 10). As the key player in the Holy Spirit's astonishing breakthrough of the ethnic barrier, thereby extending the radical inclusiveness advocated by Jesus, Peter then ordered the baptism of these Gentile believers (10:47–48), and he defended his reception of Gentiles before the congregation in Jerusalem (11:1–18).

A few paragraphs later, following the report of Herod Agrippa's arrest and imprisonment of Peter and his amazing, angel-led release, the reader is told that "Peter then went down from Judea to Caesarea and stayed there" (12:19). Not until three chapters later does Peter appear out of nowhere for his critical scene in Acts 15, "the Jerusalem Council," which is the reader's last sight of him in Acts. And although other "apostles" are reported to have been in Jerusalem for this meeting, neither their names nor their number are noted. In fact, "the Twelve" have not been mentioned as such since 6:2–6 and their commissioning of "the Seven."

In Acts 15 the elders are always mentioned alongside the apostles, suggesting that in Jerusalem they had gained equivalent dignity and respect. In the letter that both groups agree to send to Gentile believers, the apostles and elders together are referred to as "the brothers" (15:23)—a fact which may have new meaning for the reader in light of our discussion above of family kinship and a sense of solidarity among siblings.

The principal speech is once again on Peter's lips. His words help legitimate the reports of Paul and Barnabas, the only leaders mentioned by name alongside Peter and a certain James. This James was not one of the Twelve, but is identified by Paul in Gal 1:19 as both "the Lord's brother" and an "apostle."

Paul and Other Apostles

Paul in his letters not only repeatedly refers to himself as an "apostle" but also attests to a number of persons other than himself and the Twelve whom he regarded as apostles—that is, the aforementioned James in Gal 1:19, Adronicus and Junia in Rom 16:7, Barnabas in 1 Cor 9:5–6, and certain unnamed "apostles" in 2 Cor 8:23b–24. And this broadening of the category of "apostle" is reflected also in Acts, where Luke, after having clearly defined the criteria for replacing Judas in 1:21–22, seems to permit his source to shine through his editing when he refers to both Barnabas and Paul as "apostles" in 14:4 and 14.

Moreover, in Luke's view, Peter's role as one of the Twelve did not give him the preeminent authority in every situation. For in Acts 15 Luke clearly presents James, whom Paul identified as "the Lord's brother" and an "apostle," and not Peter as the chief executive among those Christians gathered in Jerusalem, who concluded his brief speech with the statement: "Therefore I have reached the decision [note the first person singular] that we should not trouble those Gentiles who are turning to God, but we should write to them" (15:19).

In contrast, "the apostles and the elders with the consent of the whole assembly" (15:22) made the decision to send Silas and Judas, who was called Barsabbas, to Antioch along with Paul, Barnabas, and the letter. Peter is not mentioned again. Indeed, these are the final acts of both James and Peter in the narrative of Acts, and Luke has just reached the halfway point in his story. The reader has thirteen chapters to go before reaching the climactic ending in Rome—and not one of the Twelve will be again mentioned in those final thirteen chapters of the narrative.

Summation

For Luke, none of the Twelve were necessary as ongoing guarantors of the traditions about "all that Jesus began to do and teach." They neither represented the beginning of church offices nor were they prototypes of later church leaders (cf. Bartlett, *Ministry in the New Testament,* 117). Luke seems to have viewed the ongoing leadership among the early Christians as Spirit-inspired fulfilling for necessary tasks and not as an office or a controlling position that was confirmed by Peter's appointment or that of any of the others among the Twelve.

5. AN EXCURSUS ON "THE TWELVE"

What was the intended significance of the tradition, which is currently frequently referred to and emphasized by some ecclesiastical authorities, that the Twelve whom Jesus appointed were all males? Would not the appointment of at least one female to this distinguished group have been worth a thousand words of theoretical argument?

Perhaps it should first be noted that, in contrast to the skepticism expressed by a previous generation of scholars about the actual existence of "the Twelve" (as distinct from their literary function), there is a growing consensus among contemporary historians that the historical Jesus did indeed choose twelve males whom he intended to represent the renewal of the twelve ancient tribes of Israel (see, for example, Lohfink, *Jesus and Community*, 9–11). But it is remarkable to observe in the ancient documents how small a role they are said to have played in the early Christian movement. Furthermore, the importance of the absence of women from this symbolic group has been exaggerated far beyond the group's own ongoing significance.

The Twelve are presented primarily as founders and preachers, and not as a ruling council at Jerusalem or elsewhere. When the early Christian movement addressed its greatest crisis to date—that is, the question regarding the basic unity of the Jewish-Christian group with the Gentile-Christian group, as represented in Acts 15—Luke did not even mention the Twelve. Apparently they rather quickly completed their symbolic function for the broader Judean population as a bridge from the activity of the historical Jesus to the early postresurrection community. Then they moved on as individuals to become involved in their respective missionary endeavors—as seems evident by the fact that no reference to "the Twelve" appears in Acts after 6:2.

It seems clear, therefore, that Luke did not intend for his readers to regard the Twelve as the primary decision makers or as an ongoing council of leaders in the early Christian movement. Jesus' claim to have the authority to select symbolic representatives of Israel's traditional twelve tribes was, no doubt, already highly controversial without increasing the tension by putting forward a woman as one of those representatives. In any case, women were soon functioning as prophets in the early Christian movement (cf. Acts 2:17–18; 21:8–9; 1 Cor 11:5). And in at least the Pauline mission area, at least one woman, named Junia, was known as an "apostle"—indeed, as one who was, in Paul's words, "outstanding among the apostles" (Rom 16:7).

A survey of the remaining books that the early Christians regarded as authoritative leads to the conclusion that they never understood these twelve men—the exact names of whom are somewhat uncertain from the traditions—to have constituted either an ongoing council of decision makers or a sanctified paradigm of exclusively male leadership for the rest of church history. In fact, it must be said that the Twelve as a group came to play a much larger role in the stained glass windows and statuary of medieval cathedrals than they ever did in their own time.

6. THERE IS NO CLERGY STATUS IN ACTS

The narrative of Acts does not present specific criteria or related titles for those in the Christian house congregations who planned or administered, who taught, preached, or prophesied, or who baptized or led the eucharistic meals.

Furthermore, Luke used no word for "priest"—except in Acts 6:7 to describe those Second Temple priests who left their ritual responsibilities and that title to become part of the Christian community in Jerusalem: "a great many of the priests became obedient to the faith." How can we account for this striking absence of the vocabulary of traditional religious leadership?

Alastair Campbell has argued persuasively that Acts presents information about the development of the church's structures and ministry "untendentiously" (*Elders*, 174). He concludes that "Luke does not have a special interest in 'church order,' and certainly does not write in order to show that a particular pattern was adopted 'everywhere and by all'" (ibid., 173; see also 150). In this judgment Campbell stands on the shoulders of both C. K. Barrett and Ernst Haenchen. For, as Barrett has aptly concluded, "if among the purposes he had in mind for his second volume Luke intended to include an account of the origin, authorization and functions of the Christian ministry, he was singularly unsuccessful in carrying out his intention" (*Church, Ministry and Sacraments*, 49–50).

Campbell correctly observes that "it is of the highest importance that the earliest Christian congregations of which we have firsthand knowledge came to birth within households or extended families" (*Elders*, 241). From this he concludes that "it is extremely likely that the principle of seniority that was taken for granted in the household was taken for granted in the congregation" that met in such a household (ibid.). At home it would not have been natural to refer to such a leader as an "elder," for there he or she was the father or mother, the uncle or aunt, or perhaps the older brother or sister. And to this judgment I add the antipatriarchal emphasis described above, which ideally resulted in a father or mother relating to all as a brother or sister.

Luke, as Campbell points out, used the general term "elder" as a collective term for "a group of leaders acting representatively," which became feasible only after the household congregations began to multiply and consolidate their position in a town (*Elders*, 256). And the fact that Luke refers in Acts 20:17 to a plurality of elders at Ephesus fits the scenario that Campbell has described. The Christian mission had been established at Ephesus for a number of years, and Paul himself spent about three years there (20:31). In his exceptionally personal and moving farewell talk with these leaders who met him at Miletus (20:17–35), Paul is represented as referring to them as "overseers" *(episkopoi)*—a responsibility that he says was given to them by the Holy Spirit (v. 28).

Paul presented himself as a faithful example of the kind of leader these elders should aspire to become. Among the recommended qualities are humility, compassion, readiness to do anything that is helpful and to endure trials, proclaiming the gospel and the "whole purpose of God," teaching both publicly and from house to house, coveting no one's silver or gold or clothing, working with one's hands to support oneself, watching over the house churches, and warning against "savage wolves"—as Paul himself did night and day with prayers and with tears. There is in this listing, however, no claim to any patriarchal type of authority.

Luke's Paul concluded this talk to the Ephesian leaders as follows: "In all this I have given you an example that by our work we must support the weak, remembering the words of the Lord Jesus, for he himself said, 'It is more blessed to give than to receive'" (Acts 20:35). Luke clearly intended this talk to define and inspire the leadership of his own time as well as to challenge traditional views of leading with an authoritarian manner.

According to his narrative in Acts, with regard to "the ministry" it seems evident that Luke valued ability and willingness to serve far more than office, in which he appears to have had limited interest. May the tribe of leaders he sought to shape by his powerful words increase and be richly blessed by the Holy Spirit, the presence of Ultimate Reality in our midst.

BIBLIOGRAPHY

Barrett, C. K. *Church, Ministry and Sacraments in the New Testament.* Exeter: Paternoster, 1985.

Bartchy, S. Scott. "A Community of Goods in Acts: Idealization or Social Reality?" Pages 309–18 in *The Future of Early Christianity: Essays in Honor of Helmut Koester.* Edited by Birger Pearson et al. Minneapolis: Fortress, 1991.

———. "The Credibility Factor: How Christian Practice Affected the Persuasiveness of Early Christian Preaching." Pages 151–81 in *Faith in Practice: Studies in the Book of Acts (Festschrift in Honor of Earl and Ottie Mearl Stuckenbruck).* Edited by D. A. Fiensy and W. D. Howden. Joplin, Mo.: College Press, 1995.

———. "*Agnostos Theos:* Luke's Message to the 'Nations' about Israel's God." Pages 304–20 in *Society of Biblical Literature 1995 Seminar Papers.* Edited by E. J. Lovering Jr. Atlanta: Scholars Press, 1995.

Bartlett, David L. *Ministry in the New Testament.* Minneapolis: Fortress, 1993.

Burkert, Walter. *Greek Religion: Archaic and Classical.* Translated by J. Raffan. Oxford: Blackwell, 1985.

Burtchaell, James T. *From Synagogue to Church: Public Services and Offices in the Earliest Christian Communities.* Cambridge: Cambridge University Press, 1992.

Campbell, R. Alastair. *The Elders: Seniority within Earliest Christianity.* Edinburgh: T&T Clark, 1994.

Clark, Andrew D. *Serve the Community of the Church: Christians as Leaders and Ministers.* Grand Rapids, Mich.: Eerdmans, 2000.

Esler, Philip F. *Community and Gospel in Luke–Acts.* Cambridge: Cambridge University Press, 1987.

Giles, Kevin. *Patterns of Ministry among the First Christians.* Melbourne: Dove-Collins, 1989.

Johnson, Luke Timothy. *The Acts of the Apostles.* Collegeville, Minn.: Liturgical Press, 1992.

Kee, Howard Clark. *Who Are the People of God? Early Christian Models of Community.* New Haven, Conn.: Yale University Press, 1995.

Krodel, Gerhard. *Commentary on Acts.* Minneapolis: Augsburg, 1986.

Lloyd-Jones, Hugh. *The Justice of Zeus.* Berkeley: University of California Press, 1971.

Lohfink, Gerhard. *Jesus and Community: The Social Dimension of Christian Faith.* Translated by J. P. Galvin. Philadelphia: Fortress, 1984.

Malina, Bruce J. *The New Testament World: Insights from Cultural Anthropology.* Rev. ed. Louisville, Ky.: Westminster John Knox, 1993.

Meeks, Wayne A. *The Origins of Christian Morality: The First Two Centuries.* New Haven, Conn.: Yale University Press, 1993.

Sandnes, Karl O. *A New Family: Conversion and Ecclesiology in the Early Church, with Cross-Cultural Comparisons.* Bern: Lang, 1994.

Schweizer, Eduard. *Church Order in the New Testament.* Translated by F. Clark. London: SCM, 1961.

Chapter 7

Congregation and Ministry in the Pastoral Epistles

I. Howard Marshall

The Pastoral Epistles stand out from nearly all the other New Testament letters in that they are addressed not to congregations but to individuals—that is, to two persons who were engaged in the oversight of existing congregations in the city of Ephesus and on the island of Crete and who did so in the context of opposition to the beliefs and practices of the Pauline churches. They were, therefore, intended primarily for church leaders, although there are various indications that they were also meant to be "overheard" by the congregations as a whole.

Our task here is to inquire into the nature of the congregational situations that formed the context of these letters and thus to understand better the patterns of ministry reflected in them. I will assume in what follows that the Pastoral Epistles reflect a situation that arose around the end of Paul's ministry and that the picture presented in them rests on the realities of that situation. For detailed discussions of this and other points made in this chapter, see the fuller treatments in my 1999 commentary, *The Pastoral Epistles*.

1. THE MISSIONARY SETTING OF THE EARLY CONGREGATIONS

All the New Testament documents came out of a missionary situation. This is especially true for the letters in the Pauline corpus, which arose out of Paul's mission and deal largely with internal growth problems of his young congregations. As Paul's mission continued its advance, his missionary concerns were reflected in his letters—particularly in his plans for the advance of his mission in such letters as Romans and Philippians. Paul's mission, however, included not only the winning of converts and the planting of churches but also the establishment of those churches that were planted.

Like the major missionary letters of the Pauline corpus, the Pastoral Epistles are documents that served the cause of Paul's mission and were themselves shaped by that mission—whether they were composed during the apostle's life-time or represent the work of his followers who were concerned to pass on his message for the church in the period after his death. It has been argued that the controlling factor in them is an opposition to Pauline Christianity that had a false understanding of the Christian faith. But even if such opposition was the occasion for the letters and shaped the response that the author gives, the writer's motive for dealing with that opposition was that it was threatening the mission of the church—that is, threatening the church's evangelism and the building up of gospel-based congregations. Thus the Pastoral Epistles must be seen as coming out of a missionary setting, with the fact of that mission having determined the nature of the response the author gives to that opposition.

The Pastoral Epistles, then, seem to have been affected by a specific polemical situation. So it follows that the instructions given in these letters must be understood as a response to a particular situation that was in some ways unusual. Some features of Paul's teaching may be emphasized more in them than would be usual in a different setting, and some of the responses to the opposition faced may be more of the nature of emergency measures than policies to be enacted at all times.

2. THE SOCIAL COMPOSITION OF THE CONGREGATIONS

On the basis of the information contained in the Pastoral Epistles, what can be known about the social composition of the congregations of Christian believers in the city of Ephesus (as reflected in 1 and 2 Timothy) and on the island of Crete (as reflected in Titus)? To begin with, it can be said that the congregations in both of these areas were mixed. In both there was a mixture of Jews and non-Jews, and in both there were people of all ages. Furthermore, there were sufficient widows at Ephesus, both young and old, to merit special attention.

At Ephesus

In the case of Ephesus we are dealing with an urban situation. The congregation included householders, out of whose ranks church leaders were chosen. These may have included people who were well-off, but this was not necessarily true of them all. It seems evident that there was a group of people who were comparatively wealthy. The remarks about women's clothing and ornaments in 1 Tim 2:9 would not have been necessary if there were no such people in the church. Similarly, there is the mention of widows who are well-off in 1 Tim 5:6. And there is explicit teaching addressed to the rich in 1 Tim 6:9–10 and 17–19, which covers both those who were already rich and those who were social climbers.

From 2 Tim 1:16–18 we learn that Onesiphorus had the resources to travel to Rome and was able to be hospitable in his own home to Paul. Some of the members (or erstwhile members) of the congregation were probably craftsmen or tradesmen, like Alexander the coppersmith (cf. 2 Tim 4:14). Furthermore,

Paul's missionary colleagues included people who had the means to travel and so were sent as the apostle's delegates to these congregations. Some of them also had professions, such as law (cf. Titus 3:13). These people may not have been extremely wealthy. Nonetheless, they seem to have been comparatively well-off in an urban setting.

At the same time, a considerable number of Christians living in Ephesus were not well-off. These included believing slaves, who would have had some security if they were in well-off households but would themselves still be of lowly means. The teaching about being able to subsist on a minimum of food, clothing, and shelter in 1 Tim 6:6–8 must have been relevant to a fair number of people. The remarkable thing is the coexistence of such a broad range of people within one congregation.

At Crete

The social situation of the church on the island of Crete, which is addressed in Titus, may be presumed to be similar. Here we are again dealing with congregations in town settings and composed of people of all ages, both young and old. There were married men with children. It may be significant, however, that these men are not said to be householders or slave-owners. There is nothing in Titus, in fact, to indicate that there were any especially wealthy people in the Cretan congregations, although there is no reason to think that they were made up entirely of people at the bottom of the social ladder. Rather, it appears that the congregations on the island of Crete, like those at Ephesus, comprised a wide social range and various types of people.

3. THE LIFE OF THE CONGREGATIONS

But what went on in these congregations? Here we can discuss the congregations of Ephesus and Crete together, since the evidence from 1 and 2 Timothy and Titus indicates that there were no significant differences between them— other than those to which I will draw attention later. And here we will be noting both those activities that actually did take place and those that the author encouraged as being appropriate in a healthy congregation.

Verbal Activities

It is evident that Christian believers met together in congregational groups, for the letters are concerned with what they did in such group meetings— whether in small house groups or larger congregational meetings, with the latter possibly including the members of several small house groups. The predominance of verbal activities in the house groups and congregational meetings is especially marked. There is, in fact, a wide and varied vocabulary for the different modes of verbal activity. These include "speaking," "reading aloud," "teaching," "rebuking," and "encouraging" (cf., e.g., 1 Tim 4:11–14; 2 Tim 4:1–5; Titus 2:1, 15).

Prophecy was known (1 Tim 1:18; 4:14; cf. 4:1), although there is some dispute as to how extensively it was practiced at the time when the Pastoral Epistles were written.

The particular activity mentioned in these letters is, for the most part, that of preaching. The speaking was done largely, though not exclusively, by the congregational leaders, with an emphasis being on teaching. Paul refers to his own role as an apostle, teacher, and herald (1 Tim 2:7; 2 Tim 1:11). Timothy and Titus, whether in their own personae or as role models, also had authoritative teaching roles (1 Tim 4:13; 2 Tim 1:13; 2:2, 24; 3:16; 4:2; Titus 2:1, 15; 3:8). But there was also teaching done by other people within their own local congregations (1 Tim 5:17; Titus 1:9), and individuals who were destined for future teaching were given special teaching (2 Tim 2:2).

The scope of teaching in these letters, however, is not confined to matters of faith, but also includes matters regarding proper behavior in the family and in society (Titus 2:1–15; 3:1–2). Specific teaching is given to various groups in the church as well as to the congregation as a whole (1 Tim 6:1–2; Titus 2:2–10; 3:1–8). In addition, the writer even sets out directives about dress and general decorum (1 Tim 2:9–10).

Prayer

As stated in 1 Tim 2:1–2, prayers are to be offered for all kinds of people, including rulers. 1 Tim 2:8 is a directive that tells us that prayers were certainly being offered in the congregations by men: "I want men everywhere to lift up holy hands in prayer, without anger or disputing." It is a directive that has in mind unspecified individuals actually taking part verbally in the worship of the various Christian communities, for the instruction hardly refers to members of the congregations simply listening silently while a leader prays. The most natural explanation of the way in which 1 Tim 2:9 follows this directive—"I also want women to dress modestly, with decency and propriety, not with braided hair or gold or pearls or expensive clothes, but with good deeds, appropriate for women who profess to worship God"—is that it refers to the appropriate comportment of the women when they too were praying.

Prayer was also part of the personal life of believers, there being no reason to suppose that only widows engaged in prayer (1 Tim 5:5; cf. 2 Tim 1:3). We do not, however, hear of any other activities that may broadly be described as "worship," such as the offering of prayers of praise and adoration and the use of hymns or other worship forms—though the doxology of 1 Tim 1:17 ("Now to the King eternal, immortal, invisible, the only God, be honor and glory for ever and ever. Amen") and the doxology of 1 Tim 6:15–16 ("God, the blessed and only Ruler, the King of kings and Lord of lords, who alone is immortal and who lives in unapproachable light, whom no one has seen or can see. To him be honor and might forever. Amen") may well reflect forms that were actually used in the congregational meetings.

Doxologies, Confessions, and Trustworthy Sayings

A further feature to note in the Pastoral Epistles is the presence of material capable of being memorized and recited, which suggests that there was congregational participation in the church's meetings. This material may have included such doxologies as found in 1 Tim 1:17 and 6:15–16 (noted above), as well as various communal confessions as found in 1 Tim 3:16 ("He appeared in a body, was vindicated by the Spirit, was seen by angels, was preached among the nations, was believed on in the world, was taken up in glory") and the "trustworthy sayings" of 1 Tim 1:15; 3:1; 4:9–10; 2 Tim 2:11–13; and Titus 3:8.

This evidence of doxologies, confessions, and trustworthy sayings, however, should be used with caution. For while such passages may be adaptations of existing materials, most of them—if not all—appear to be *ad hoc* compositions by the author. Furthermore, singing, which is typical of modern churches as a form of congregational participation, is not mentioned, although this may be a dubious argument from silence.

Baptism

The practice of baptism is implied in Titus 3:5, "He [God our Savior] saved us through the washing of rebirth and renewal by the Holy Spirit." There is, however, no explicit mention of the Lord's Supper. The reference to "everything" being "consecrated by the word of God and prayer" in 1 Tim 4:5 is not an allusion per se to the Lord's Supper. But congregational meals may be alluded to in 1 Tim 5:17—"the elders who direct the affairs of the church well are worthy of double honor, especially those whose work is preaching and teaching"—for it is plausible that the "double honor" for worthy preachers and teachers was a larger portion of food at the congregational meals, and that these meals may have had a eucharistic character.

Appointment of Leaders

The appointment of people to fill various leadership roles was done, at least in some cases, at meetings of the congregation that included a solemn laying on of hands. This seems evident in the admonitions directed to Timothy: "Do not neglect your gift, which was given you through a prophetic message when the body of elders laid their hands on you" (1 Tim 4:14); "Do not be hasty in the laying on of hands" (1 Tim 5:22); and "I remind you to fan into flame the gift of God, which is in you through the laying on of my hands" (2 Tim 1:6).

Women

Another feature of importance is the fact that women had an important place in the life of the congregations. Some of them cared for children, who were presumably orphans. 1 Tim 5:10 speaks of their providing hospitality for others and washing the feet of the saints, which was a necessary duty in the conditions of the ancient world. It is noteworthy, however, that in the congregational context it was not the task of slaves to wash the feet of others. The teaching of Jesus about humble service seems, at least to some extent, to have been taken seriously.

Furthermore, as 1 Tim 5:10 continues to mention, Christian women helped "those in trouble" and were generally active in doing "all kinds of good deeds." These were not, as is sometimes thought, the tasks of the widows, which they did in exchange for support from the church. Rather, as 1 Tim 5:3, 9, and 16 point out, they were the kind of things done by believing women in the past that entitled them to support from the congregation in their widowhood and old age.

The older women were responsible for training the younger women in the Christian life (Titus 2:4). Some women, however, had been giving teaching in the congregational meetings and are told in 1 Tim 2:12–14 to "be silent." This admonition must have been aimed against some particular existing practice, since the analogy of other New Testament situations indicates that women played a part in prophecy and teaching within Christian congregations.

It is unlikely that 1 Tim 5:13, which speaks of women "going about from house to house," refers to an organized system of pastoral visitation by women. It is more likely that it describes ordinary social intercourse.

Hospitality and Social Outreach

Hospitality was a duty of the leaders (1 Tim 3:2; Titus 1:8). This may refer to their readiness to accommodate meetings of believers. But it may also imply that leaders in the church were to provide hospitality for other Christians on their journeys, including that of hospitality to traveling teachers. More broadly, the congregations were to show practical care for the needy (Titus 3:14) and individuals were expected to use their resources generously to help other people in need (1 Tim 6:18–19). There was also congregational provision for the needs of widows.

How far social concern extended outside the congregations is not clear. Certainly there was concern for the outside world, which was expressed in prayer for rulers and for people of all kinds (1 Tim 2:1–2). It is possible, however, to pray for people and not be able to do anything more tangible—or not take initiatives and opportunities to do so.

Nevertheless, from the section about the widows we saw that a fairly far-reaching program of social care was envisaged in and around the congregation. This activity was probably centered on the Christian circle rather than being "social outreach" to the neighborhood. But the boundary line must have been somewhat fluid. Similarly, when Titus's congregations are told to apply themselves to "doing what is good" (Titus 3:14), this should not necessarily be seen as confined to inner-church activity.

The ancient world knew of the way in which better-off people acted as benefactors to the less well-off and expected some kind of recognition in return. The rich are reminded in 1 Tim 6:18–19 that they are to do good. The more probable interpretation of 1 Tim 6:1–2, in fact, is that the slaves are being told to act as benefactors to the rich—which is an astounding reversal of the normal direction of benefaction. But even if this interpretation is not assured (cf. the alternative rendering in NRSV mg.), slaves, at the very least, were to serve their non-Christian masters (and mistresses) well in ways that would be recognized as "good" by the expectations of the time—and so, as is plainly exhorted in Titus 2:9–10, to add luster to the gospel.

Discipline

Discipline had to be exercised, as is evident from such passages as 1 Tim 5:20; 2 Tim 3:16; 4:2; and Titus 1:11. There had to be restraint on people whose teaching was causing disruption in the congregations. The problem was twofold: their teaching could lead to a false understanding of how Christian believers should behave; and discussion of such false teaching was diverting the church from its serious business into endless arguments, which were ultimately futile because of the nonsensical character of the teaching. The responsibility rested on Timothy and Titus. It is not clear, however, whether the local congregations shared their responsibility (1 Tim 1:20).

In the first instance reasoned appeal was to be attempted. That there was to be no dialogue in the church at all, which is a view that has been often proposed, is at the very least exaggerated. Rather, the point is that church leaders are not to behave like their opponents, who engage in empty disputations that get nowhere, but are to act gently in the hope that they may lead their opponents to see their error (see especially 2 Tim 2:23–6; cf. 2 Tim 2:16–17; Titus 3:9). But where reasoned appeal failed, it was appropriate to refrain from futile discussions. And if individuals persisted in teaching that was a nuisance to the congregation and could lead to splits among its members, then it was right to warn them and even to exclude them from fellowship (Titus 3:10; cf. 1 Tim 1:20). The reference in 1 Tim 5:20 to bringing charges against sinners ("those who sin are to be rebuked publicly, so that the others may take warning") probably refers to moral misdemeanors.

4. SOME MISSING ELEMENTS IN THE LIFE
OF THE CONGREGATIONS

Although the Pastoral Epistles present a surprisingly full picture of what was taking place in the congregational life of Christians at Ephesus and Crete, we must be careful in evaluating that data. Furthermore, it is also important to take into account what is missing from this picture. Bearing in mind, therefore, that the picture is somewhat one-sided because of the brevity of the letters, that the situation addressed seems to have had certain distinctive, though unstated, peculiarities, and that arguments from silence may be dangerous, we may nevertheless note that there are some missing elements in our sources regarding the life of these congregations.

First of all it needs to be noted that the writer is generally opposed to discussion in the church. Teaching is to be conducted more by appropriate people giving authoritative instruction (like a modern sermon) than by group discussion. Since, however, it was the presence of the opponents and their teaching that had led to fruitless discussions and unedifying controversy (2 Tim 2:25; Titus 3:9), it would seem that the emphasis on a more authoritative kind of teaching was dictated by the situation rather than by a rejection of discussion absolutely.

Also to be noted is that there is no mention in the Pastoral Epistles of individual counseling or care for people with personal problems. Nor, as noted earlier, is the Lord's Supper explicitly mentioned, and there is no teaching that appears to reflect the occasion. The fact, however, that this item is also passed over in silence in other New Testament letters warns us to be wary about overconfident arguments from silence.

Furthermore, although I have argued for a missionary character to the theology that backs up the practical teaching and exhortation in these letters, there is little, if any, evidence of actual evangelism going on. In assessing this omission we must take into account the fact that the New Testament letters usually say next to nothing about evangelism that is carried on by the local congregations, as opposed to that of traveling evangelists. Yet concern for all people is to be both expressed in prayer and based on a belief that God wants all people to be saved (1 Tim 2:4–7). And Timothy himself is assigned the role of an evangelist (2 Tim 4:5).

More importantly, despite all that is said elsewhere in the New Testament about "oneness in Christ," it does not appear that the social differences between believers were altogether overcome in the Christian congregations at Ephesus and Crete. In general, leadership was in the hands of married men with children—and, as in 1 Tim 3:4–5, with "households." This strongly suggests that slaves were not appointed to such positions, except, perhaps, slaves who occupied responsible positions. And since the qualities required in deacons are virtually the same as those for overseers (cf. 1 Tim 3:8–13), there does not seem to be a leadership opening for younger men.

The subordination of children, of whatever age, to their parents was, of course, the assumed pattern of contemporary society. It was assumed, as well, that children would accept the Christian faith of their fathers (Titus 1:6).

The subordinate place of women is also inculcated (1 Tim 2:11; Titus 2:5). This takes place against the background of some women teaching in the congregations in a way that was considered to be an exercise of inappropriate authority over men in the congregations—including, presumably, their husbands. It is not certain whether the activity of some younger widows going around from house to house and talking inappropriately was a form of Christian teaching or simply—perhaps more probably—a matter of frivolous conversation (1 Tim 5:13). The author is clear that younger women should be married and bring up their families (1 Tim 2:15). And he commends the fulfillment of their domestic roles, including submission to their husbands (Titus 2:4–5).

5. IMAGES OF THE CHURCH

Now that we have seen something of the actual life of the congregations, we may go on to explore the underlying theology of the church. Of greatest relevance here is the text that stands at the center of 1 Timothy—that is, 1 Tim 3:14–16. For in verse 15 there are expressed three images of the church: "the household of God"; "the church of the living God"; and "the pillar and bulwark of the truth."

The Household of God

The dominant metaphor for the nature of the church in the Pastoral Epistles is that of the household. This emerges clearly in 1 Tim 3:15 where Timothy is being taught how to behave in the household of God, which is the church, the pillar and bulwark of the truth. The implication of this metaphor is that God is like a householder who exercises authority over his household, and so there should be appropriate behavior within the church. The metaphor can include both people and buildings simultaneously, and the latter element is not missing.

The picture is developed in one particular way in 2 Tim 2:20–21 where the metaphor of utensils used in a household is employed. A distinction is made between those utensils made of gold and silver, which are for "special" use (such as at a banquet), and those made of wood and clay, which are for dishonorable uses (such as containing garbage). And people are urged to cleanse themselves from iniquity—which in this context appears to refer primarily to false teaching—so that they may be for special use. The metaphor of utensils, however, is not expressed with great clarity and its implications are not drawn out. The warning seems to be that some people can be like garbage bags, which are thrown out with their contents—but with the fact of garbage disposal as a necessary household function not being taken into account. The metaphor deals only with material objects in the home, and so there is no development of the topic of personal relationships within the church.

Nevertheless, human family relationships are important. In particular, the role of Timothy's mother and grandmother in his spiritual upbringing is positively stressed (cf. 2 Tim 1:5 with 3:15). Furthermore, the picture of an extended household is applied to all the members of the congregations in Titus 2:1–10, where young and old, male and female, and even slaves have roles within the church and are exhorted to demonstrate the appropriate Christian qualities and virtues. The teaching here assumes that people can be categorized by age and sex and that there are appropriate virtues for them to demonstrate. The effect is to approve and maintain a *status quo* in which, for example, younger women are to be taught to be good at their domestic duties and to be subject to their husbands.

Similarly, respect is to be shown to older people and all others (1 Tim 5:1–2). This may appear at first sight to perpetuate social status. Rather, it is, in fact, straightforward teaching regarding respect for all people, which could fail to be shown if attention was not specifically drawn to it.

It is only the subordination of wives to husbands, with no mention of any reciprocal duties, that causes problems for modern readers. Some interpreters have gone over the top in seeing the Pastoral Epistles as being motivated, above all, by a desire to put recalcitrant women in their place. This interpretation, how- ever, fails to reckon sufficiently with the existence of a culture whose shortcom- ings—as we now see them in the light of the gospel—were no more evident in the first century than were the non-Christian character of slavery to many people in the nineteenth century or the non-Christian character of racism, tribalism, and nationalism to many in the twentieth century. And who knows in what other ways we are blind to the claims of the gospel today?

The positive advantage of the household image as applied to the church is that it develops the notion of care for those who are needy within the congrega- tion—in particular, indigent widows—in the same way as a household cares, or should care, for all of its members. Some commentators seem to think that the point could be made just as well by the use of the "body" metaphor, as found in 1 Cor 12, and that this metaphor would be more conducive to social equality in the church. It has also been suggested that the concept of "brotherhood," with all that this metaphor implies for being one in Christ, is deficient in the Pastoral Epistles. Yet 1 Cor 12:28 appears to state that some parts of the body come before others and to suggest that mutual care and honor does not rule out some differentiation of status.

The Church of the Living God

The term "church" *(ekklēsia)* is surprisingly rare in the Pastoral Epistles. In 1 Tim 3:15 "the household of God" is expressly defined as "the church of the living God." In the only two other uses of the term in 1 Tim 3:5 and 5:16 the ref- erence is to the local congregation, and we have the familiar idea that the church is constituted by the existence of a local group of the people of God. The full term used here, the "church of God," can thus refer to both the local and the universal—just like we use "bank" for the local branch and the whole organization.

The precise formulation of the phrase here—"the household of God, which is the church of the living God"—should alert us to the fact that some- thing with special significance is being stated. The household is said to be the church rather than that the church is the household. This indicates that the writer is saying something fresh here, and this is emphasized by the addition of "living": the household of God is the church of the living God.

Two points here emerge: First, the church is seen in Jewish terms as the Is- rael of God. This understanding is presupposed in the identification of believers as "God's own people" (Titus 2:14) and by the continuity that is seen between Paul's ancestors and himself (2 Tim 1:3). Second, "the church of God" is remi- niscent of the "the temple of God" (2 Cor 6:16). Since "house" can refer to the temple and the "pillar" may well also be temple imagery, it is difficult to avoid the thought of the church being the place where God is present with his people.

The addition of the adjective "living," in fact, heightens this emphasis, for it draws attention to God's activity (cf. 1 Tim 4:10; this is probably evangelistic language, as in 1 Thess 1:9). He is not an absentee landlord. His activity is to be seen in the way that the Holy Spirit is active "in us" (2 Tim 1:14; Titus 3:6) and speaks in the church (1 Tim 4:1). His Word is not chained, but is powerful and active (2 Tim 2:9).

The Pillar and Bulwark of the Truth

The church is also depicted in 1 Tim 3:15 as "the pillar and bulwark of the truth." This statement is the inverse of what might have been expected—that is, that the church is built on the foundation of the truth. On the contrary, the church is to be the guardian of the truth and the public sign of it. The "pillar" is probably not a structural part of the building that helps to hold the church up. Rather, it is a free-standing column, like the two pillars outside the Temple of Solomon. It is thus more of a public testimony to the truth. The "bulwark" is more like a foundation or structural support, but again it does not hold the church up. Rather, it buttresses and fortifies the truth that it is the task of the church to proclaim.

This truth is condensed in the immediately following statement of 1 Tim 3:16, where we have a missionary theology: "He appeared in a body, was vindicated by the Spirit, was seen by angels, was preached among the nations, was believed on in the world, was taken up in glory." The church's role in the preservation and proclamation of the gospel is thus emphasized. And it is this role that lies behind the major thrust of the Pastoral Epistles!

Summation

These three images of the church—(1) the household of God; (2) the church of the living God; and (3) the sign and upholder of the truth—give a thoroughly dynamic theology of the church over against accusations that the ecclesiology of the Pastorals is static and unadventurous. The emphasis on the role of the church with regard to the truth is ad hoc in view of the polemical situation.

The metaphor of the household may have several implications. It is used explicitly to indicate the importance of right conduct within the church—that is, "how one ought to behave." The major implication is that submission to God is required. Another possible implication of the metaphor is that the ancient household functioned as a school where education was practiced. There may, in fact, be a link between this function and the immense stress on the place of teaching in the church found in the Pastoral Epistles (cf. Young, *Theology of the Pastoral Letters*, 79–84).

There is, accordingly, a stress on truth and orderliness as marks of the church in the Pastoral Epistles. Such a stress, however, is not in principle different from that in 1 Cor 14:40, where everything in a congregational meeting is to be done "decently and in an orderly fashion."

6. THE NATURE OF LEADERSHIP

Against this background, we now must ask: What does the church require to be able to function in the interests of the gospel—and, correspondingly, in the interests of truth and order?

The Function of Leaders

The congregations of the Pastoral Epistles are understood in these letters to have been founded by Paul himself, either directly or through his delegates. Consequently, Timothy and Titus are set in place as supervisory church leaders and their functions are generally similar to those of the local leaders.

Timothy and Titus, of course, are not the only examples of Pauline coworkers in the Pastoral Epistles. The continuation of traveling workers on the pattern of the Pauline mission is assumed in 2 Tim 4:9–13, 19–21, and Titus 3:12–13. These people were evangelists whose task included the upbuilding of existing congregations, and their ministry formed a vital part of the total work among the congregations.

We can get some idea of the function of these leaders in the various congregations by looking at the role of Titus. His task was, first of all, to appoint elders in each town. He had responsibility delegated from Paul to see that church leaders were appointed. He was not told how to choose people or what the appointment procedures were, but simply what kind of people to appoint in terms of their character, Christian commitment, and personal endowments. The role of the local congregation in these appointments, however, is not discussed—though 1 Tim 4:14, which mentions "the body of elders" who "laid their hands" on Timothy, should be noted for the involvement of existing local leaders.

Furthermore, Titus was to give teaching to the congregations on the island of Crete, which teaching was to include "ethical" instruction in conformity with sound doctrine and rebuke or refutation of those who were teaching otherwise. He was also to deal with people who needed to be disciplined. And although the instruction regarding discipline was addressed to him, it was presumably to be put into effect also by the local leaders. Likewise, Titus is given instructions about his own personal Christian behavior in Titus 2:7–8.

Similar instructions are given to Timothy in 2 Tim 1:8, but at considerably greater length and with more stress on his task of witnessing in an environment that may be hostile (cf. 1 Tim 6:13).

Passing on Teaching to Faithful People

The picture in the Pastoral Epistles is of congregations founded during the Pauline mission and still under the pastoral oversight of its missionaries. Titus had a number of scattered congregations to look after. The same may be presumed for Timothy, though this is not a certainty but an inference. The scope of the work was such that an enlargement of the group of leaders was needed, and so a local leadership was in the process of being developed.

Consequently, in a somewhat informal and almost casual manner, Timothy is told to pass on the teaching that he received from Paul to "faithful people who will be able to teach others as well" (2 Tim 2:2). Although this passage is commonly understood to be providing for the *future* needs of the church by educating the next generation to be teachers, it should primarily be understood in the context of caring for the *present* needs of the church by enlarging the number of teachers who can complement the teaching given by Timothy and extend it— thereby continuing Timothy's role when he himself was not able to be present. Apostolic delegates travel and go where they are most needed; meanwhile, the existing congregations must continue to function.

Qualifications for Local Leadership

The congregations required, then, the appointment of local leaders whose duties might include teaching but were wider. In 1 Tim 3:1–13 and Titus 1:5–9 similar descriptions of the qualifications for leadership in the church are given.

Prospective elders/overseers are to be people, first of all, with a good reputation—not only within the congregation but also within society at large. This is a motif that recurs with the dual intent of safeguarding the congregation from slander and promoting the gospel by the quality of the lives of believers. And since the local leaders were "high profile" persons in the community, the point is emphasized. The function of congregational leaders as role models is represented concretely not only by Titus (Titus 2:7) and Timothy (2 Tim 4:12), but also by Paul himself (2 Tim 3:10–11).

Several of the desired qualities listed for leaders in the Pastoral Epistles are also found in similar listings for leaders in the Hellenistic world generally, including military commanders. This suggests that the kind of people being sought were ideally those with gifts of leadership, the capacity to guide and direct a group of people, the ability to set goals and organize people to achieve them, competency at practical tasks and procedures, and the ability to inspire others to action. These were qualities that the ancient world required of its leaders, and therefore what the church was looking for in its leaders as well. There may also be the implication that—like candidates for political office in the western world— they must have sufficient resources to be able to carry out their task, such as an adequate house for a church group to meet in.

The particular qualifications for a Christian leader include an upright married life and an orderly family. A person who could not control his household could not control God's church (1 Tim 3:5). So it must be assumed that the task of being a church leader is similar to that of managing an ancient household.

Certain more specifically "Christian" qualifications, however, are also listed in the Pastoral Epistles. One of these is being hospitable, which means the readiness to welcome guests and give them appropriate care—a quality that some people are better at expressing than others.

In addition 1 Tim 3:2 mentions, somewhat in passing, that a church leader must be good at teaching. The motif is more strongly expressed in Titus 1:9, which emphasizes that a leader must have a firm hold on the "word" so that he can be good at both teaching the truth and refuting those who contradict it. We get something similar in the description of a deacon, who must also "hold fast to the mystery of the faith" (1 Tim 3:9). This could, of course, simply refer to the need for any church leader to be "sound" in the faith, but it may also refer to a capacity to teach.

The Two Main Tasks of Local Leaders

What kind of tasks did people who were thus qualified do? Two main tasks of local leaders are given in 1 Tim 5:17–18: that of teaching and that of ruling. Admittedly, however, the interpretation of these verses is not unambiguous.

I take these verses to refer to a specific group of elders who are entitled to double honor, and that this group consists of those who are active in the word and teaching—that is, those involved in teaching within the congregation. The alternative interpretation is that the reference here is to elders who do the task of eldership (i.e., "rule") well, and especially those who teach. The task of teaching in a congregation was carried on, at least in part, by the elders, and so, on any interpretation of the language, a distinction can be drawn between those elders who taught and those who did not do so.

The verb *proistēmi*, "to rule," which occurs here, is also used in 1 Tim 3:4 for household management and is found elsewhere in Paul's letters as a general term for the exercise of leadership functions (cf. 1 Thess 5:12; Rom 12:8). It can include, therefore, both the care of other people and having an authoritative role. It has been surmised that it would involve general superintendency of a congregation's affairs—one that included discipline, pastoral oversight, and presiding at meetings.

Two Further Characteristics of Local Leadership

Two further characteristics of local leadership must also be noted: that of collegiality and that of oversight.

There is no indication in the Pastoral Epistles that a one-person ministry was appropriate. Rather, a prominent characteristic of leadership is *collegiality*. Titus was to appoint *presbyteroi*, "elders," in every town on the island of Crete, who were also known in terms of their function by the term *episkopos*, "overseer" or "bishop" (Titus 1:5–9). The shift from the plural "elders" to the singular "overseer" or "bishop" is natural in the detailed discussion of the qualities required. Furthermore, it is paralleled elsewhere—notably in 1 Tim 5:3–16, where the author oscillates between the singular and the plural with reference to widows (so, rightly, Michaelis, *Pastoralbriefe und Gefangenschaftsbriefe*, 49).

It is possible, of course, on the basis of the imagery of a steward in Titus 1:7, to argue that Titus was instructed to appoint only one elder/overseer per town. But the Greek of the passage does not require this. The clear picture elsewhere in the New Testament is of a plurality of leaders in a town—as, for example, in Phil 1:1 and Acts 20:17, 28; 14:23 (cf. 16:4). If *ekklēsia*, "church," is a collective term for a number of house fellowships in a particular locale (cf. 1 Cor 1:2), then, perhaps, oversight of the smaller units by a single leader is possible. In 1 Pet 5:3 there is a reference to "those in your charge" (literally, "the lots"), which might suggest individual areas of responsibility for each of the elders. But we lack sufficient information to be more specific.

Another important characteristic of local leadership has to do with *oversight*. The requirement that elders are to exercise oversight over congregations follows from the fact that they are identified as overseers. This is certainly the case in some of the other congregations reflected in the New Testament—as, for example, those attested in 1 Pet 5:1–2 and Acts 20:17, 28, which link an overseer's task with the language of shepherding the flock of God.

In Titus 1:5–7 specific qualities are desired in elders because an "elder," "overseer," or "bishop" must be a particular kind of person as God's steward. The only way around the apparent identification here would be if the choice of "elders" had to be made in the light of the fact that some of them would later become "overseers" or "bishops." But such an implication imports an alien feature into the discussion. For in 1 Tim 3:1 the concern is with a person desirous of exercising oversight in the church, and the use of the word *episkopos* to designate such a person assumes that the terminology is known.

We have, as well, a reference to "elders" in 1 Tim 5:17–20, and their tasks may include preaching the word and teaching. But the task of an "overseer" or "bishop" also includes teaching, as set out in 1 Tim 3:2—and the same may be true of a "deacon." Identity, therefore, seems likely, since to have a combination of overseers or bishops, deacons, and elders—with no explanation of their relationships—would be very odd. It would also be strange to deal with matters relating to elders in 1 Tim 5:17–20 as if that discussion did not apply as well to overseerers and deacons in 1 Tim 3:1–13.

One other possibility that should not be excluded is that the elders of 1 Tim 5:17–20 consisted of both the overseers and the deacons of 1 Tim 3:1–13— including, perhaps, female deacons. "Elders" would then be an inclusive term for all the leaders. In some congregations there could be a distinction between "overseers" and "deacons," which was apparently not the case in the less developed situation on the island of Crete.

Such a possibility should not be dismissed out of hand—although, admittedly, against it stands the way in which oversight is understood to be the task of all the elders in Acts 20 and 1 Peter 5. But if accepted, the equation would be only partial rather than total, and we would still have people who were known as "elders" or "overseers" as alternative designations. The advantage of this proposal is that it would explain why there is one set of terms in 1 Tim 3 and then a different set, for no apparent reason, in 1 Tim 5—rather than the view, which is fairly often proposed, that two different systems of church leadership are brought together in the Pastoral Epistles, which is a theory I consider unnecessary.

Remuneration

Paul and some of his colleagues were fully engaged in missionary work, even though in Paul's case he worked with his hands to maintain himself in some places and for some part of his time. We also know that some new congregations gave financial help to the missionaries. But what happened with regard to local church leaders?

It is very unlikely that local church leaders were paid officials. It is more likely that they were ordinary working people who did the work of the congregation in their "spare" time—though, of course, we need to be careful not to import anachronisms about employment, leisure, retirement, and holidays into the ancient world. The leaders of the congregations at Ephesus and Crete were in all probability people who had the work of the church to do in addition to their existing secular tasks. They may have received some small remuneration for their work, particularly if the time taken could otherwise have been used to their own profit. This may be what is meant by "double honor" being given to the elders in 1 Tim 5:17. It is more likely, however, as noted earlier, that their honor consisted of receiving extra portions of food at church meals.

Appointment

A clergy-laity distinction emphatically did not exist in the apostolic church. There is no indication of any church task that required what we call ordination. Nevertheless, there were some occasions, tasks, and/or positions for which the laying on of hands was appropriate. Being sent on a specific mission was one such occasion, as Acts 13:1–3 tells us. Timothy was appointed with the laying on of the hands of Paul and the elders (1 Tim 4:14; 2 Tim 1:6). And it is most likely that the appointment of local elders in the congregations of Ephesus and Crete was also recognized in this way (cf. 1 Tim 5:22).

From 1 Tim 4:14 we find that Timothy had been given a "gift" by the laying on of hands. Similarly, in 2 Tim 1:6 Paul comments on the gift of God that was in Timothy through the laying on of hands, and in the same context refers to the Spirit. The straightforward interpretation of these passages is that Timothy was commissioned and equipped for his work in the church by a formal action in which Paul and the elders laid hands on him and prayed for the gift of the Spirit to enable him to fulfill the tasks associated with that work.

The procedure is exactly as in Acts 13:1–3. It is important to note that in Acts such a formal act of commissioning for a special task stands alongside those passages where the Spirit came upon people in an "unasked for manner" for specific tasks of witness. There was no tension between these two types of empowering in the early church. It was entirely natural when a special task arose to pray especially for it. Elements of both authority and empowering are present. Furthermore, it appears that elders could be appointed in the same way (cf. 1 Tim 5:22), although the procedure was not necessarily confined to elders.

Does this mean that tasks and spiritual gifts were confined to people who had been appointed only in this more formal manner of the laying on of hands? As we have seen, there is flexibility in the portrayals of Acts, and persons performing tasks of ministry and formally appointed elders coexist in 1 Pet 4:10–11 and 5:1–4. Teaching was not confined to the elders. There were the opponents who were active in teaching, and nothing suggests that they were the only other teachers over against the elders. In fact, their activity would be hard to understand if only the heretics were free-riding teachers in the church. Teaching by women in the churches also leads in the same direction.

The appointment of elders/overseers who were apt at teaching suggests, therefore, that there was evidence of their ability to teach before their appointment. And when Timothy is told to teach faithful people who will be able to teach others also, there is, again, no necessary formality and appointment about this process.

7. SOME CONCLUSIONS

Theological Basis

The image of the church as "the pillar and bulwark of the truth" found expression in the need for a teaching ministry that expressed the gospel faithfully. The danger of opposition subverting the gospel meant that an orderly form of leadership and ministry had to be developed.

Furthermore, the image of the church as "the household of God," with its steward or stewards, was appropriate in the society of that time as a model for a congregation with recognized leaders providing care for its members. This feature is less obvious in the image of "the body." But even within the body imagery Paul recognized the existence of the more and less important, and saw no problem in reconciling the existence of varied, necessary gifts, with the position of "apostles first, prophets second, teachers third," and so on.

Likewise, the image of the church as "the church of the living God," within whose midst God himself is to be found, helped to preserve an emphasis on Christian ministry as inspired by the Spirit of God. There has been a tendency in some commentaries to understand the term "charisma" as meaning something like "office." This interpretation is valid in that the people who were recognized as having the spiritual gifts were to find expression for them in particular duties. But it is hard to resist the conclusion that the basic meaning of "charisma" is that of a particular empowering by the Spirit of God that was meant to be exercised in a specific way.

Social Pressures

The character of leadership and ministry in the Pastoral Epistles reflects, and to some extent is in tension with, the social situation of an urban environment. In the context of the patriarchal society of that day, it is significant that believers at Ephesus and Crete were appointed leaders in their respective congregations not simply because of their social position, age, or wealth but because of their appropriate qualities. Although the tendency of the time was to appoint people of social status, age, and wealth the examples of Timothy and (probably) Titus demonstrate the existence of leaders with none of these predispositions (cf. 1 Tim 4:12; Titus 2:15).

The question of the ministry of women is too large a subject to raise in the present context. I am persuaded, however, that the peculiarities of the local situation were largely behind the prohibition of their teaching found in the Pastoral Epistles—particularly as the positive role of women in the church is taken for granted elsewhere in the New Testament. In this specific context, it seems, teaching by women was flouting the social norms of the day in an unhelpful way and was associated with a particular false teaching that was then rampant. The implicit praise given to Eunice and Lois in 2 Tim 1:5, together with the references elsewhere in the New Testament to women who had worked effectively in the church (cf. esp. Rom 16:1–16), suggest that in another setting the author might have written 1 Tim 2:11–15 somewhat differently.

In any case, the prohibition is of women teaching men, not of women exercising other forms of ministry or holding some kind of office in the congregation. It is altogether more probable that the women in 1 Tim 3:11 were female deacons than simply the wives of deacons. And if the deacons were in some way assistants to the overseers, then the appointment of women deacons would presumably not constitute a problem. In the patriarchal society of that day it may have been too bold a step to appoint women as overseers. The force of this consideration should not be overlooked. Modern churches, sadly, have a worse history of not allowing black people to be leaders—as witness, for example, the fact that as late as the 1960s it was emphatically against Roman Catholic practice in Africa for a white priest to be under a black bishop!

From the beginning the Christian congregations of the Mediterranean world had a plurality of leaders. There is nothing unusual about this in comparison with other first-century groups, such as Jews and their synagogues. It follows that the leadership of the congregations in the city of Ephesus and on the island of Crete was no more monarchical than elsewhere in the New Testament churches, since leadership was not in the hands of only one person.

A Process of Transition

What we are observing in the Pastoral Epistles is a process of transition in which the congregations at Ephesus and Crete were being adapted to a new situation. It is a situation in which these congregations, which had been founded by missionaries who continued to exercise superintendence over them, were gradually developing greater and greater autonomy—and yet, at the same time, were still associated with one another and with their founding missionaries. It is entirely correct to see the Pastoral Epistles as reflecting a shift from the fairly close supervision exercised by Paul over the congregations to a situation in which he was no longer there to do so. His role was taken over by people like Timothy and Titus. But even their roles were not conceived as being permanent and all-pervasive.

With the development of autonomy, there was a corresponding development of structures within the individual congregations in order to stabilize them. This stability was centered on the gospel, as expressed in the teaching handed down from Paul. It should not need to be said that Christian congregations do need some structures that make for stability, continuity, and the maintenance of identity. The structure here is determined by the gospel, of which the church is the guardian and which in turn shapes the church. It finds expression in a corresponding human system consisting of people who demonstrate qualities of Christian character, capacities for leadership, and a fundamental loyalty to the gospel.

The emphasis on structure in the Pastoral Epistles is probably enhanced by the need to deal with the opposition to the Pauline gospel and teaching. In a setting where congregations were less threatened by such factors, it would undoubtedly be possible for the structure to be somewhat less rigid.

Some Apparent Omissions and Weaknesses

Earlier I drew attention to some omissions and oddities in the situation reflected in the Pastoral Epistles. It is now time to reconsider two of these.

Some of the perceived lacks in the life of the congregations at Ephesus and Crete may be due to our expecting first-century congregations be like modern Western ones. Thus we should not necessarily expect to find a developed social outreach to those outside the church—although it is possible to see elements of such a stance in the encouragement to good works of Titus 3:14. We must beware, however, of interpreting the passage against a background of anachronistic expectations derived from our own situation with its church centers, its neighborly help, its participation in politics both local and national, and so on. Even more, we should not expect to see the modern Western practice of learning by sharing and submitting ideas to be discussed. In any case, some criticisms of the author for forbidding discussion with the opponents rest on the assumptions that what they were saying was open to reasonable discussion, rather than being nonsense, and that deeper insights into truth might be reached through dialogue. But neither assumption appears to be justified in this particular case, although the possibility of some discussion with the opponents remains present.

A regrettable factor, however, is that the missionary implications of the gospel are not put more into effect in the admonitions of these letters. The situation resembles, at least in some ways, that in Jude, where the author is diverted from writing about the salvation shared by himself and his readers in his endeavors to deal with the corruption that was seeping into the church (cf. Jude 3). Yet the Pastoral Epistles continue to retain the conception of a mission being carried out by a movement that was to some degree separated from the local congregations but supported by them. This finds expression in the role of Timothy as an evangelist.

And there is also the pressing task of helping those people who have been led astray by wrong teaching to find their way back to a knowledge of the truth, as in 2 Tim 2:25–26.

The Permanent Value of the Teaching

The detailed pattern of community formation in the Pastoral Epistles was not necessarily intended to be prescriptive for the church, either then or now (cf. Lohfink, "Die Normativität der Amtsvorstellungen"). The emphasis on order, which is characteristic of these letters, together with the precise form of that order, must be seen as due, at least in part, to the need for defensive measures against the particular opposition encountered.

What is of permanent value in the teaching on church order in these letters are the underlying principles. The threefold imagery of the church has as its corollaries: (1) the maintenance of the truth of the gospel and witness to it; (2) the development of a ministry that will build up the church in faith, love, and unity, and that will provide for pastoral care for believers—with which may be linked practical care for material needs; and (3) the recognition of the presence of the Spirit of God in providing the gifts for Christian ministry and calling those who possess them to exercise them. The way in which this is done in the Pastoral Epistles was appropriate in the social setting and the specific situation of the congregations at Ephesus and Crete. The outworking of God's call, the Spirit's gifts, and Christian ministry in the church today must take these permanently valid principles seriously and contextualize them appropriately.

BIBLIOGRAPHY

Campbell, R. Alastair. *The Elders: Seniority within Earliest Christianity.* Edinburgh: T&T Clark, 1994.
Clarke, Andrew D. *Serve the Community of the Church: Christians as Leaders and Ministers.* Grand Rapids, Mich.: Eerdmans, 2000.
Fee, Gordon D. "Reflections on Church Order in the Pastoral Epistles, with Further Reflections on the Hermeneutics of *ad hoc* Documents." *Journal of the Evangelical Theological Society* 28 (1985): 141–51.
Ferguson, Everett. *The Church of Christ: A Biblical Ecclesiology for Today.* Grand Rapids, Mich.: Eerdmans, 1996.
Giles, Kevin. *What on Earth Is the Church? A Biblical and Theological Enquiry.* London: SPCK, 1995.
Lips, Herman von. *Glaube—Gemeinde—Amt: Zum Verständnis der Ordination in den Pastoralbriefen.* Göttingen: Vandenhoeck & Ruprecht, 1979.
Lohfink, Gerhard. "Die Normativität der Amtsvorstellungen in den Pastoralbriefen." *Theologische Quartalschrift* 157 (1977): 93–106.
Marshall, I. Howard, with Philip H. Towner. *The Pastoral Epistles.* International Critical Commentary. Edinburgh: T&T Clark, 1999.

Michaelis, Wilhelm. *Pastoralbriefe und Gefangenschaftsbriefe: Zur Echtheitsfrage der Pastoralbriefe.* Gütersloh: Bertelsmann, 1930.

Oberlinner, Lorenz. *Die Pastoralbriefe: Dritte Folge: Kommentar zum Titusbrief.* Freiburg: Herder, 1996. See esp. pp. 74–101.

———. "Öffnung zur Welt oder Verrat am Glauben? Hellenismus in den Pastoralbriefen." Pages 135–63 in *Der neue Mensch in Christus: Hellenistische Anthropologie und Ethik im Neuen Testament.* Edited by Johannes Beutler. Quaestiones Disputatae 190. Freiburg: Herder, 2001.

Oberlinner, Lorenz, and Anton Vögtle. *Anpassung oder Widerspruch? Von der apostolischen zur nachapostolischen Kirche.* Freiburg: Herder, 1992.

Roloff, Jurgen. *Die Kirche im Neuen Testament.* Göttingen: Vandenhoeck & Ruprecht, 1993. See esp. pp. 250–67.

Schweizer, Eduard. *Church Order in the New Testament.* Translated by F. Clarke. London: SCM, 1961.

Towner, Philip. H. *The Goal of Our Instruction: The Structure of Theology and Ethics in the Pastoral Epistles.* Sheffield: Sheffield Academic Press, 1989.

Verner, David C. *The Household of God: The Social World of the Pastoral Epistles.* Chico, Calif.: Scholars Press, 1983.

Young, Frances. *The Theology of the Pastoral Letters.* Cambridge: Cambridge University Press, 1994.

Part III

The Early Centuries

Chapter 8

Christian Ministry in Three Cities
of the Western Empire (160–258 C.E.)

Alan L. Hayes

The study of early Christian ministry has been complicated by the fact that most scholars of the subject have approached it with programmatic purposes. Some have hoped that new information about the early church would help reform and renew the church of their own day. An example is the Catholic reformer Erasmus, who in 1526 rediscovered and published Irenaeus' *Against Heresies*. Others have believed that the example of primitive Christianity would justify the ecclesiastical practices and forms of ministry of their own confessional tradition. Still others have used the sources to support a sociological theory or historical method.

In the twentieth century the force that most conspicuously motivated and shaped the historical study of ministry in the ante-Nicene church was the Liturgical Movement, which became prominent in the Roman Catholic Church after 1903 and soon spread to the Anglican, Lutheran, and other communions. This was a movement that sought to recast the theology and practice of contemporary worship according to the norms found in—or, perhaps, projected onto—the pre-Constantinian period. It was enormously influenced by the scholarly reconstruction between 1910 and 1916 of a text of the *Apostolic Tradition*, which was attributed to Hippolytus of Rome and dated about 215.

As the Liturgical Movement read it, the *Apostolic Tradition* presented a picture of an early Christian congregation in which (1) common worship was the central reality and (2) the chief ministers were a bishop, presbyters, and deacons, with each being ordained to his office and having a specific and distinctive role of liturgical leadership. Here, it seemed, was the true catholic norm of ante-Nicene Christianity. It was this picture that led the Roman Catholic Church to the liturgical reforms associated with the Second Vatican Council. It also inspired churches in the Anglican, Lutheran, Presbyterian, and Methodist communions, as well as others, to publish new liturgical orders of their own.

Paul Bradshaw has made the canny comment that most liturgists are "lumpers" while most historians are "splitters" *(Search for the Origins)*. From a historian's point of view, the generalizations made by scholars of the Liturgical Movement on the basis of a short, textually defective document of uncertain provenance were never very persuasive. And now that the Liturgical Movement has effectively run its course (see my "Tradition in the Anglican Liturgical Movement"), it is a good time to revisit the ministry of the early church.

As a "splitting" historian wary of the danger of premature generalization, I propose in this chapter to consider three specific situations of ministry in three early Christian communities of the western Roman Empire—that is, in communities at Lyons, Carthage, and Rome. These three Christian communities, which were located in the three major provincial capitals and commercial centers of the western empire, provide us with some of the earliest evidence we have of church order and ministry in the western Roman Empire. My opening date of 160 is just before the dawn of historical evidence for Christianity at Lyons and Carthage. My closing date of 258 is the death of Cyprian, who, I suggest, transformed the theory and dynamics of Christian ministry.

1. THE CASE OF LYONS (177–CA. 200 C.E.)

A Profile of the City and Its Populace

Lyons occupies a strategic position at the juncture of the Saône and Rhône Rivers. The first Roman colony was settled there in 43 B.C.E., under a mandate from the Roman Senate. The Roman builders set to work to turn the colony into a fine Roman city, with a theater, forum, imperial temple, public baths, and shops. They built several aqueducts, which were marvels of engineering. They constructed four major roads to the city. Lyons became a large manufacturing and distribution center for all kinds of consumer items. Augustus Caesar, sometime between 16 and 13 B.C.E., chose Lyons to be the capital of a province, and he established an important imperial mint there.

In 12 B.C.E. the area became, in effect, the religious capital of Gaul, thanks to a huge altar and sanctuary that the stepson of Augustus built for the imperial cult. The delegates of the sixty peoples of the Three Gauls were invited to celebrate the dedication, with the convocation of delegates becoming an annual event. In 19 C.E. the high priest of this "Federal Sanctuary of the Three Gauls" organized the construction of a huge amphitheater nearby—a monument that would later become notorious in church history. Every year, at the beginning of August, delegates from the sixty peoples convened at the sanctuary to participate in the cult, and then would assemble in the amphitheater to take council together—which was, as some say, the first French parliament.

By the 160s the population of Lyons numbered perhaps about 50,000. Racially and religiously the city was diverse, as one might expect in an administrative and commercial center on the outskirts of the Roman Empire. In addition to Celtic people who were native to this part of Gaul, the ancient inscriptions record Greek, Asian, and Latin names. From Phrygia in Asia came the cult of Cybele, and in the year 160 an inscription reports that one Carpus brought a pair of bull's testicles from Rome to be offered at the shrine of Cybele at Lyons. The cult of Mithra enjoyed strength in nearby Vienne.

In addition to the Roman cult, the Celtic cult, and the Asian cults, there was the small Christian community, which we now associate with the church father Irenaeus. Christianity must have arrived in Lyons by the 160s. It seems likely that it came with traders and immigrants from Greece and Asia, whose presence in Lyons is well attested. It is the earliest church in the western Roman Empire for which we have any certain evidence, aside from Rome itself.

The social, cultural, and linguistic diversity of the church of Irenaeus reflected the diversity of the larger population. In his preface to *Against Heresies,* Irenaeus tells us that he spent much of his time speaking the language of the barbarians, which presumably means Celtic. Whether any of the Christian community were Celtic-speakers, however, has been debated (cf. Frend, *Martyrdom and Persecution,* 3; Grant, *Irenaeus,* 5). An affirmative answer is suggested by Irenaeus's pride in the diversity of languages spoken by Christians in Gaul and elsewhere (*Against Heresies* 1.10.2).

In any event, a letter of about 177 from the Christians of Lyons and Vienne, which is transcribed by Eusebius in *Ecclesiastical History* 5.1, identifies Greek, Asian, and Latin Christians as being in the church at Lyons—including Attalus from Pergamum in Asia Minor, who had Roman citizenship; Alexander from Phrygia, a physician who had lived in Gaul for many years; Alcibiades, a Greek-sounding name; and Sanctus, who spoke to the authorities in Latin, although he refused to tell them his race or his city of residence.

The letter also reports the martyrdom of a number of Christians. Some were Roman citizens, who could suffer only imprisonment and beheading; others were not Roman citizens, and therefore were tortured and thrown to the beasts. Some were old, such as Pothinus, who was over ninety. He is generally believed to have come from Smyrna. Some were young, such as Ponticus, a boy of only fifteen. One, named Vettius Epagathus, was a young man of some social importance; another, the most famous of all, was Blandina, a slave, whose mistress was also a Christian.

Three Realities of Christian Experience

Three realities particularly converged on the little community of Christians at Lyons in the years after 165. One was persecution. While we do not know the formal grounds for the persecution of about 177, which is described in the letter transcribed by Eusebius, its general progress resembled persecutions elsewhere: the townspeople began gossiping about the little group of Christians, with increasing distaste and anxiety; Christians refused to join in propitiating the pagan gods, whose favor was considered essential to civic safety and prosperity; mob violence occasionally broke out; city officials intervened, and began demanding that the Christians renounce Christ and make sacrifices in the imperial cult; Christians began to be excluded from public places; rumors spread that

Christians were practicing cannibalism and incest; city officials confirmed the rumors by extracting evidence under torture from the slaves of Christians; and Christians were interrogated, imprisoned, and publicly executed, in scenes which modern sensibilities find grisly and shocking. The Christian martyrs of Lyons provided the principal entertainment for the assembly of delegates from the Three Gauls in the amphitheater at the beginning of August 177. We know the names of ten of them. From later sources we are led to believe that there may have been forty-eight martyrs altogether.

A second reality that characterized the little church at Lyons was spiritual gifts. The martyrs displayed perseverance under persecution, uttered prophecies, received visions, offered forgiveness, and practiced love. These were all seen as spiritual gifts. Moreover, spiritual gifts could become a theological issue. The Christians of Lyons involved themselves in controversies about prophecy—specifically, so Eusebius thought, about Montanism, the prophetic movement that originated in Phrygia around 170. Eusebius tells us that some of the confessors in prison wrote letters giving their opinion of Montanism.

The third reality facing Christians at Lyons was the rivalry of gnosticism, which was a diverse collection of beliefs and practices that they regarded as heretical distortions of the gospel. Irenaeus himself was most noted in the early church, as he still is today, for his five books against these heresies. The threat was by no means a distant one. Irenaeus tells us that a certain man named Mark, who was a disciple of the heretic Valentinus, was active "even in our regions of the Rhône" and attracted a number of Christians from the churches with which Irenaeus was identified (*Against Heresies* 1.13.7).

A modern reader can imagine the appeal of the gnostic heresies, for (1) they claimed a fuller wisdom of Christ and at least equal gifts of prophecy; (2) they were, according to Irenaeus, not overly scrupulous about moral discipline; and, perhaps most attractively, (3) their adherents were not being arrested and tortured and thrown to wild beasts (*Against Heresies* 3.33.9). They could avoid arrest because they did not share the views of Christians that confessing the name of Christ was a matter of principle, that sacrificing to the image of the emperor was a betrayal of the faith, and that to suffer torture and death for the truth was a participation in the redemptive death of Christ.

These three realities were not separate but intimately interrelated. Unity in orthodox doctrine helped the Christian community withstand persecution; persecution helped bring forth the spiritual gifts of God; and the spiritual gifts of God included the knowledge of orthodox doctrine.

Spiritual Leadership

If we were to begin our analysis of ministry at Lyons by looking for bishops, presbyters, and deacons, we would be missing the point, for the gnostics had their overseers, elders, and ministers as well, and so did other voluntary associations in the ancient world. Of these groups, of course, Irenaeus and his community maintained that they had neither the true Christian ministry nor the Holy

Spirit who gives the gifts of ministry. The most important spiritual leaders the Christians had, and the gnostics lacked, were confessors under persecution, and those who encouraged them. The authority and the importance of the confessor were unrelated to his or her status in society or institutional office or rank in the church. The author of the letter of 177 that Eusebius transcribes uses the female slave Blandina on two occasions to make the point that in Christ and in the church social roles had gone topsy-turvy, for it was this slave, who was small and weak and despised, and not her owner or the physician or the gentleman of importance, who demonstrated the most impressive spiritual gifts in the face of persecution. The letter preserved for us by Eusebius, in fact, describes her as a "noble mother" to her fellow sufferers—and it was in her, when she was hung on a stake, that the other martyrs saw the form of Jesus Christ. Among the martyrs, one is named as a deacon and one is named as having been entrusted with the ministry of *episkopē*. But neither of these quite attained the spiritual distinction of Blandina the slave.

There is no concern in the literature of this community for institutional rank as such. No distinction is ever drawn between the laity and the clergy, in the sense of the baptized and those ordained—either in the letter of 177 or in any of the writings of Irenaeus. The only use of the word "clergy," which is found three times in the letter transcribed by Eusebius, has to do with "the *klēros* ['allotted portion' here taking the meaning 'class' or 'order'] of the martyrs." Only a few years later, Christian writers will begin using *klēros* to mean a group of leaders distinct from the general laity, but in Lyons the closest thing to a clergy, in the sense of a group chosen for spiritual leadership, is the martyrs.

The Spirit is free to bestow gifts, and spiritual gifts cannot be controlled by organizational officials. Irenaeus and his community wanted to avoid the errors of the Valentinian community, where its leader Mark decided who would prophesy, what would be taught, and how their banquets would be organized. For Irenaeus, "the spirits who are ordered by such people and speak when they desire it, are feeble and powerless" (*Against Heresies* 1.13.4). If some Christians at Lyons assumed special roles of authority in worship, we do not hear about it. Irenaeus speaks briefly of the Eucharist and the liturgical sacrifices that are proper to Christians, but he does not hint that in the church's worship any roles are reserved to certain people. In fact, he calls those who offer worship "the disciples," or "the church," or simply "we."

Nor would there appear to be much need for administrators over a small group of people without property, wealth, social prestige, or worldly power. Those few instances of conflict within the group that can be discerned—for example, the martyrs in prison wishing that Alcibiades would be less austere in his diet—are resolved through peer negotiation, not through the exercise of authority.

The community does use the terms that we are accustomed to recognize as indicators of ecclesiastical office, such as bishops and presbyters (the same thing, perhaps) and deacons. But these terms do not signify anything of institutional importance. In fact, Irenaeus is wary of these offices. Presbyters, he says, can be puffed up with pride; when they are judged by the Word, it will be according to their heart, not according to their appearance (*Against Heresies* 4.26.3). The Christians of Lyons, toward the end of their letter introducing Irenaeus to the bishop of Rome, write: "We would have commended him in the first instance as a presbyter of the church, which indeed he is, if we knew that place could secure righteousness for anyone" (Eusebius, *Ecclesiastical History* 5.4.1).

If the most important ministry is confessing, there is always the danger that the confessors themselves become puffed up, try to exercise ecclesiastical authority, or denigrate and lord it over the faint-of-heart. Indeed, in other parts of the early Christian world, the claims of confessors to exercise authority were to become a theological and institutional issue. At Lyons, however, the confessors explicitly eschewed title and rank. They would not allow themselves even to be called martyrs. Christ, they said, was alone the true martyr, and they were only lowly and humble confessors. The letter of 177 emphasizes that the confessors of Lyons

> did not boast over the fallen, but from their own abundance supplied with a mother's love those that needed, and shedding many tears for them to the Father, they prayed for life, and he gave it to them. . . . They ever loved peace; peace they commended to us; and with peace they departed to God. (Eusebius, *Ecclesiastical History* 5.2.6–7)

Spiritual Gifts

Along with the ministry of confessing and encouraging the confessors, the exercise of other spiritual gifts, too, was given by God, not by human commission. The ministry of spiritual gifts was an essential confirmation of the community's claims about Jesus Christ. The gnostics pictured a docetic Christ who did not truly perform great works. Irenaeus demonstrated their error by pointing to the reality of spiritual gifts being exercised by Christ's disciples in the present. For he insisted:

> Receiving grace from Him, they [Christians] do in His name perform [miracles], so as to promote the welfare of others, according to the gift which each one has received from Him. For some do certainly and truly drive out devils, so that those who have thus been cleansed from evil spirits frequently both believe [in Christ] and join themselves to the Church. Others have foreknowledge of things to come: they see visions, and utter prophetic expressions. Others still, heal the sick by laying their hands upon them, and they are made whole. Yea, moreover, as I have said, the dead even have been raised up, and remained among us for many years. And what shall I more say? It is not possible to name the number of the gifts which the Church, [that is scattered] throughout the whole world, has received from God, in the name of Jesus Christ. (*Against Heresies* 2.32.4)

Miraculous and charismatic ministry, therefore, was of central importance in the church, because it verified the reality of redemption in Jesus Christ.

Preserving and Defending the Gospel

Finally, among the Christians of Lyons there were those who exercised the ministry of preserving and defending the truth of the Gospel of Jesus Christ. In writing *Against Heresies* Irenaeus was responding to a request from a fellow Christian. And his prayer was that this person, who is unidentified, "would successfully minister to serve others according to the grace given you by the Lord, so that people may no longer be taken captive by their persuasive talk" (1 *praef.* 3).

Here it appears, at least at first glance, that we finally have identified a familiar role for bishops and presbyters, for Irenaeus appears to appoint them the guardians of Christian doctrine. But here we encounter a well-known problem of translation. Is an *episkopos* the holder of an office (i.e., a bishop) or a person with a function (i.e., an overseer)? Is a *presbyteros* the holder of an office (i.e., a presbyter) or a person of venerable age with a long memory of agreed doctrine? Furthermore, is the term *episkopos* equivalent to the term *presbyteros?* The first person to be identified as bishop of Lyons is Pothinus, a man ninety years of age—which would certainly qualify him as an elder in point of age, but perhaps not as an active executive officer in the manner of a bishop today. These problems, which are much discussed, cannot be pursued here. Indeed, they appear to be intractable.

In any event, these bishops and presbyters—or overseers and elders, or elders who have a ministry of oversight—are privileged by Irenaeus as teachers of the truth of the Christian gospel. If we ask why they exercise this particular ministry and duty, summaries of the history of theology routinely report that Irenaeus understood them to be the successors of the apostles, and therefore the custodians of the apostolic tradition; and that his purpose was to discredit the gnostics, whose leaders stood well outside the line of succession. Such summaries often imply that Irenaeus's theology represents a step toward an understanding of apostolic succession that would give presbyters and bishops the authority to define truth and enforce unity. But Irenaeus would never have either expected or desired such a development.

Office and Apostolic Succession

In his own context, Irenaeus's claims for the doctrinal ministry of presbyters and bishops were more modest. In the first instance, his claim of apostolic succession was simply autobiographical. Irenaeus had been a protégé of Polycarp of Smyrna, and Polycarp had been a protégé of John, the disciple of the Lord. Apparently Pothinus, the first bishop of Lyons, had also been Polycarp's disciple. No Valentinian gnostic could make a like claim. Being connected to the risen Lord by one or two intermediary witnesses gave both Pothinus and Irenaeus unmatchable credibility. But this advantage obviously would dwindle after only a few generations.

Second, office and apostolic succession did not, by themselves, guarantee the authority of the bishops and presbyters. They must also demonstrate sound doctrine and virtuous behavior. "The truth," Irenaeus wrote, "is with those in whom the succession in the church from the apostles, unassailable integrity of behavior, and the incorruptible purity of the word are to be found" (*Against Heresies* 4.26.5). Or, again, "it behooves us . . . to adhere to those who, as I have already observed, do hold the doctrine of the apostles, and who, together with those appointed *presbyteroi,* display sound speech and blameless conduct for the confirmation and correction of others" (4.24.4). To test whether bishops and presbyters were truly teachers of sound doctrine by determining whether they taught sound doctrine may seem somewhat circular to us, but it clearly did not bother Irenaeus.

Third, no single elder or bishop possesses the truth. Irenaeus always speaks of their authority in plural number. Appointment to an office in itself confers no apparent authority of rulership.

We do not know whether at Lyons it made any difference from day to day whether a Christian were a bishop, a presbyter, or a deacon. Sanctus, the one who spoke to his accusers in Latin, is called a *diakonos.* But whether the word should be translated as "deacon" in the sense of an ecclesiastical office is not clear—and, if so, it is even less clear what a deacon is supposed to be or to do. To his accusers he identifies himself simply as *christianus,* that is a Christian.

Furthermore, the letter of 177 said of Pothinus that "the ministry of *episkopē* had been entrusted" to him. It is usually assumed that this means he was the bishop. But the text almost makes a point of identifying a ministry rather than an office of ministry. Irenaeus criticized the gnostics for distinguishing their leaders from the common adherents. And he and his community may well have wanted to avoid falling into the same trap themselves.

Summation

The forms and functions of Christian ministry at Lyons, therefore, seem to have been shaped—at least in large measure—by the character and agenda of the Christian community in that city. In character, the church was so socially, linguistically, and culturally diverse as to be relatively free from the influence of worldly principles of authority. More importantly, however, its agenda was focused on confession and resistance in the face of persecution, on prophecy and spiritual gifts, and on maintaining the faith.

The fortunes of the city of Lyons declined in 197 when it took the wrong side in a challenge to the imperial authority of the Roman emperor Septimius Severus. The decisive battle in the conflict took place just outside Lyons. Apparently the city was pillaged, its military cohort dissolved, and many of its citizens exiled. Nothing more is heard of the Christian community there until the middle of the fourth century.

2. THE CASE OF CARTHAGE (180–220 C.E.)

Profile of the City and Its Populace

Carthage, which is now a northern suburb of Tunis, was believed by the ancients to have been founded about 800 B.C.E. by adventurous Phoenicians. Its city center was a hill called the Byrsa, which overlooked the Mediterranean Sea. In 146

B.C.E., at the end of the third and last of the Punic Wars, the Romans leveled the city. But about 44 B.C.E. Julius Caesar recolonized it, and later Augustus Caesar had it rebuilt in the grandest of Roman style.

With growing government patronage, agricultural cultivation, and shipping interests, Carthage became one of the wealthiest centers in the western Roman Empire, second only to Rome. After a fire in the middle of the second century C.E., Antoninus Pius and his son Marcus Aurelius lavished on Carthage new public works, including a huge basilica, a great library, and public baths. With schools, theaters, bookstores, and an important library, it became one of the intellectual centers of the empire. There are no extant census statistics. A modern educated guess, however, is that the population of the late second-century city-state of Carthage, which extended scores of kilometers inland and included dozens of towns, may have been half a million.

Carthage was even more multicultural and multireligious than Lyons. Punic, African, Greek, and Latin languages were spoken. In religion, official municipal cults (the *sacra publica*) and the imperial cult were prominent. But native gods, who were often somewhat Romanized, were conspicuous. In addition, there were oriental religions, a large synagogue, and various philosophical schools.

Christianity at Carthage

No one knows whether Christianity came to Carthage through Rome, through Asian immigrants, through the Jewish community, or in some other way—or in some combination of such ways—and no one knows when. The first evidence of Christianity comes from a document that can be dated to 180 and is called the *Acts of the Scillitan Martyrs*—the adjective "Scillitan" evidently referring to an unidentified town near Carthage. The document appears to be a partial transcript of the interrogation of a group of Christians by the area's Roman proconsul. One of the Christians was in possession of the Scriptures of Paul when he was arrested. And so the Christians were condemned to death.

A second source of information about Christians at Carthage comes from a writing called the *Passion of Perpetua*, which was written about 203 and contains the diaries of two martyrs, Perpetua and Saturus, along with editorial material. This personal record is among the most remarkable of all the ante-Nicene documents.

Almost all the rest of the contemporary evidence for Christians at Carthage before 215 comes from Tertullian, the North African theologian, apologist, and controversialist. According to many older biographies, he was born about 155, presumably the son of a Roman centurion, and was trained in law. As an adult he converted to Christianity and later was probably ordained a priest. He became, however, increasingly disenchanted with the Catholic Church, and so became a Montanist. He died sometime in his seventies, perhaps about 230. Timothy Barnes, in his *Tertullian: A Historical and Literary Study,* has cast serious doubt on almost every element of this story. But no one has proposed a narrative of any higher probability to replace it. All that can be said about Tertullian with reasonable assurance is that he lived in Carthage around the year 200 and that he wrote more than thirty surviving tracts and treatises—most of which are in Latin, but three in Greek.

From the *Acts of the Scillitan Martyrs* and the *Passion of Perpetua* we can tell that Christians at Carthage were as diverse linguistically, culturally, and socially as those at Lyons. Among the Scillitan martyrs some names are apparently African and others obviously Latin. Perpetua herself was a married woman from a good family and a Roman citizen of high social standing. Among those arrested with her, however, were two slaves, Revocatus and Felicitas.

Ministries of the Christian Community

Interrogating the *Acts of the Scillitan Martyrs* (ca. 180) and the *Passion of Perpetua* (ca. 203), together with Tertullian's *Apology* (ca.197), we can discover the anxieties, values, and issues that shaped the Christian agenda at Carthage at the end of the second century. Some, it seems, were very much like the three realities of persecution, prophecy, and the defense of orthodoxy at Lyons. In fact, among Christians at Carthage can be found three corresponding ministries in prominence: the ministry of the confessor, the ministry of the prophet, and the ministry of the teacher.

As at Lyons, we hear about bishops, presbyters, and deacons at Carthage. But we cannot be sure of their respective functions, authority, or distinctions. Tertullian is proud to say that in at least one respect these church offices were different from civil offices in that they could not be gained by ambition or money, but proven good character was necessary (*Apology* 39). Furthermore, Christian ministry at Cathage was shaped by the functions of the Christian community, which we may summarize as being prayer, study, and service. Money was of little consequence. The church did, indeed, have its treasury, but it was used to assist the poor, orphans, the elderly, prisoners, and the shipwrecked.

Heresies and Disagreements

This is, however, perhaps too rosy a picture. Partly because Carthage was larger, more complex, and much more sophisticated than Lyons, the situation of ministry at Carthage was more complicated as well. There were also various Christian groups in the city that were in some degree of tension or rivalry. Some had become separated by heresy. "We ought not to be astonished at the heresies (which abound)," says Tertullian, "neither ought their existence to surprise us, for it was foretold that they should come to pass" (*Prescription against Heretics* 1).

But even within the community there were disagreements. Some may not have been particularly serious. In prayer, for instance, most Christians knelt for prayer, but "a very few" stayed off their knees on the Sabbath—which is "an opposing point of view," says Tertullian, "that is just now strongly defending itself in the churches" (*On Prayer* 23). Such differences mattered little, for, as Tertullian goes on to say, the minority may "maintain their own opinion without giving scandal to others." Whether in large things or small, however, Carthaginian Christians seemed to have quarreled. In the vision of Saturus, as recorded in the *Passion of Perpetua,* a group of angels compare the Christians of Carthage to people "returning from the games, fighting about the different teams" (*Passion of Perpetua* 13).

Signs of Transition

There are signs of transition in the understanding of Christian ministry around 200 at Carthage, but developments are hard to trace because the evidence is hard to date. Only two of Tertullian's writings can be confidently dated through internal evidence—*To Scapula* and *Against Marcion.* A few others appear to allude to one another, and so can be placed in a relative chronological order but not definitively dated. A more fragile criterion, though a rather common one, is to assign a relatively late date—somewhere between 208 and 212—to a number of works in which Tertullian is seething with anger toward the authorities of the Catholic Church. By contrast, works in which Tertullian seems reasonably content with the Church are assigned an earlier date. If we accept this arrangement—which is certainly not beyond challenge—we can recognize clear signs of mounting divergence in the understanding of Christian ministry at Carthage.

Two explanations are usually given for this divergence. The majority view is that between his earlier writings and his later writings Tertullian has become a Montanist, and has therefore come to value the prophetic gifts of the Spirit more highly than the established leadership structure and orderly administrative processes of the church. Against this view, however, are several considerations: that Cyprian, the bishop of Carthage after about 248, reportedly read Tertullian every day and regarded him as his master, which he would not have done had Tertullian been a schismatic; that there is no independent evidence of a Montanist group in Carthage; that Tertullian continues to speak as if the Catholic Church is his own church; and that there are arguably few discernible changes in Tertullian's actual theology in his later writings, but for the most part only a greater emphasis on prophecy and a greater stridency in tone.

These objections seem weighty. We may well prefer, therefore, the alternative explanation: that it was not Tertullian who was changing, but the church around him. Taking such a view, it may be postulated that in the years around 200 Carthage was experiencing an evolution in the ministry of the Church.

The editorial introduction to the *Passion of Perpetua,* which was composed about 203 and contains the diaries of Perpetua and Saturus, seems to reflect such a divergence in the understanding of Christian ministry. For while there are those who think that "supernatural grace prevailed solely among the ancients," the editor urges readers to reverence "the new visions"—those things "which we have heard and touched with our hands." Perpetua and Saturus have the spiritual gifts of confession, perseverance under persecution, and visions. And they are presented as great spiritual ministers, who will, indeed, continue to be so recognized in Africa in the years following.

There are some indications in this work that some Christians were rever-
encing the ministries of Perpetua and Saturus above that of the ordinary authority structure of the Church. Thus, for example, Saturus receives a vision in which
a bishop and a teacher have apparently been in discord, and they come to him and
Perpetua, kneel before them, and ask them to help reconcile them (*Passion of
Perpetua* 13). While there is more than one way to interpret this scene, the most
obvious explanation is that the bishop and teacher recognize their dependence on
the spiritual ministry of the martyrs.

Another example of the authority of the confessors is given by Tertullian,
who has the following explanation for the origins of the Valentinian heresy:

> Valentinus had expected to become a bishop, because he was an able man both in
> genius and eloquence. Being indignant, however, that another obtained the dignity
> by reason of a claim which confessorship had given him, he broke with the church
> of the true faith. (*Against the Valentinians* 4)

The ambitious and worldly, therefore, could not easily attain church office, because preference was given to those who have shown themselves ready to sacrifice
themselves in martyrdom. Appointment to church office did not confer spiritual
authority, but it recognized it.

Divergence and transition in the Christian understanding of ministry also
appear when Tertullian distinguishes between the roles of the clergy and the laity.
He is, in fact, the first Western theologian to make the distinction. He generally
uses the Latin term *ordo* for what we call the clergy and the Latin *plebs* for what
we call the laity—terms he clearly took over from the Roman civil constitution.
And he is the first Christian writer to use "ordination" in an ecclesiastical sense.
He uses it to mean not a liturgical rite, but a firm appointment to *ordo*. So he
speaks highly of the office of presbyter, for the elders, he says, have "double honors," being both "brethren" and officers (*Fasting* 17). Indeed, one of his criticisms
of the heretics is that they downplay distinctions between officers and laity:
"Today one man is their bishop, tomorrow another; today he is a deacon who tomorrow is a reader; today he is a presbyter who tomorrow is a layperson" (*Prescription against Heretics* 41). Nevertheless, Tertullian is strongly opposed to any
tendency toward absolutizing these distinctions.

Responsibilities, Obligations, and Authority of the Clergy

In at least one respect the clergy *(ordo)* have greater responsibility, in
Tertullian's view, than the laity *(plebs):* they are more clearly obliged to hold their
ground in times of persecution. After all, if "the very deacons, and presbyters, and
bishops" turn their backs and run, "who of the *plebs* will hope to persuade people
to stand firm in the battle?" (*On Flight in Persecution* 11). What we may call the
clergy, on the one hand, have a particular obligation to give strong moral leadership. On the other hand, with apparent consistency throughout his writings,
Tertullian denies to the clergy any inherent powers or rights. The distinction between the officers and the people of the church is purely an organizational one,

which is meant to ensure good order and avoid schism. It is the gospel that is important, and the church as a whole hears, proclaims, and ministers to the gospel. Within the church, however, the officers are expected to exercise certain ministries on behalf of the whole for the sake of good order.

Especially in what are often considered his later writings, Tertullian expresses concern that the officers of the church are claiming more authority than they rightly have. Four examples can be given, which may be expressed in the form of four questions debated by Tertullian.

1. Are the clergy subject to more exacting moral standards than the laity? Tertullian thinks not. In one of his most strident treatises, and therefore one that is usually dated late, he attacks the view that although lay people may marry a second time, bishops or presbyters may not. Against this view he contends that whatever moral standards govern the one must govern the other. Otherwise, he says, "are we to institute some special order of monogamists so that we may choose the clergy from its ranks?" (*Monogamy* 12.2).

2. Is the administration of baptism to be restricted to the clergy? Tertullian answers: as a matter of order, yes, but not as a matter of right. The laity, too, have the right to baptize, "for what is equally received can be equally given." Thinking of Paul's injunction that "all things are lawful, but not all expedient," Tertullian affirms that all can baptize, but, if a bishop is present, it is expedient to leave the matter to him, to avoid the danger of schism. Nevertheless, if no church officer is on the spot, Tertullian says, other disciples are called to the work, for baptism is the property of God, not of the clergy (*Bap.* 17).

3. Is the administration of the Eucharist restricted to clergy? Again, Tertullian's answer is that while it is a respectable custom for Christians to receive the Eucharist from the hands of what he calls the presidents (*On the Chaplet* 3), the power to celebrate the Eucharist is not intrinsically restricted to the *ordo*. He exclaims in a passage, which, admittedly, different translators interpret differently:

> Are we laity not also priests? . . . The authority and honor of the church, through the assemblies of the *ordo* consecrated to God, has established the difference between the *ordo* and the *plebs*. [But] where there is no assembly of the clergy of the church, you the layman offer the Eucharist and baptize; . . . in short, where there are three, there is the church, even if those three are laity. (*Exhortation to Chastity* 7)

This argument is in service of Tertullian's larger point that the laity should be held to the same moral standards as the officers of the church because at any time they may be called on to take leadership: "God wishes every one of us to be ready at all times to administer His sacraments properly" (ibid.).

4. May clergy absolve sin after baptism? In what is generally supposed to be an earlier treatise, Tertullian acknowledged that the church may absolve a Christian's sin after baptism, although he gives no hint as to the procedure that is to be followed or who exercises authority in the matter (*Repentance* 17). But in a later treatise *(On Modesty)* he is appalled that one of the bishops—at Carthage? or at Rome?—has taken on himself the authority to absolve. He quotes (or seems to quote) the bishop in question: "I remit, to such as have discharged

(the requirements of) repentance, the sins both of adultery and of fornication."
Unless Tertullian is embellishing, which is not impossible, this is the first clear instance in Christian literature of a clerical absolution, and it must have been a new
departure. Tertullian's vigorous opposition to this innovation is often used as an
example of his small-minded rigorism, as if he lacked compassion for the weakness of those Christians who may lapse into sin. But much of his argument is not
in favor of rigorism, but against episcopal pretension. God can absolve, and a
prophet might absolve on God's behalf. But bishops, he says, have only the functions of discipline—their power is to preside "not imperially, but ministerially."
The church, having the power of the keys, can absolve, but not the bishop, who is
only its servant. "For the right and arbitrament is the Lord's, not the servant's."

Summation

It is not easy to discern the patterns of ministry at Carthage, primarily because we see them almost entirely through the eyes of those who were criticizing
certain developments that were then current. Up until about 200 we see that confessors, martyrs, prophets, and visionaries were honored for their spiritual authority. We can identify a distinction being made between the church's officers
and its people. We recognize the same general functions of ministry as we saw at
Lyons at about the same time. And we hear of bishops, presbyters, and deacons,
but we can not be sure of who they were, what they did, how they were appointed,
or for how long they served.

Around 200, however, there appear signs of divergence of opinion within
the church at Carthage. Some are beginning to doubt the authority of then
present-day visions and prophecies. Others are ascribing special powers and responsibilities to the clergy. Tertullian thinks that at least some bishops are seeing
their role not only as *ministerium* but also as *imperium*. This divergence seems to
simmer for forty or fifty years before the personality of Cyprian and the persecutions of Decius bring it to a boil.

3. THE CASE OF ROME (160–C. 215 C.E.)

Early Textual Evidence

Unlike at Lyons or Carthage, Christianity at Rome is reliably attested from
New Testament times. Paul's letter to the Romans suggests the existence of several
house churches in Rome, including "those of Aristobulus's house" (16:10) and
"those of Narcissus's house who are in the Lord" (16:11). During the period when
the books of the New Testament were still being written, we know of the martyrdom—or, at least, the victimization—of Christians at Rome under Nero. The letter from the church of Rome to Christians at Corinth, which is called *1 Clement*,
may well have been composed around the year 100. Chapter 44 of that letter gives
tantalizing glimpses of Christian ministry. And while there is more than one
way to read *1 Clement* 44, most commentators—Roman Catholic as well as

Protestant—are now inclined to interpret it as describing the leadership of a college of presbyters. Furthermore, the arch-paulinist Marcion and the gnostic Valentinus can be found in Rome in the 140s.

Closer to the period that we are considering here is the *Shepherd of Hermas*—a work that places itself in Rome and (since the Muratorian canon declares it was written by the brother of Pius, a bishop in the church of Rome) is often dated about 148. In this work Hermas receives several visions, most notably a vision of a shepherd, the angel of repentance, who communicates to him several commands and parables. The work is addressed to a community that is being tested by persecution and is struggling with the unrighteousness of some of its members and the disappointing behavior of some of its leaders.

Like Irenaeus and Tertullian, the *Shepherd of Hermas* affirms the *ministerium* of vision and exhortation (*Similitude* 10.2, 4). And like Irenaeus, Hermas places no special emphasis on *episkopoi, presbyteroi,* and *diakonoi*—the categories that have often held most interest for church historians. Numerous references to the dignity and importance of male *presbyteroi* and female *presbyterai* invariably pose the problem of whether Hermas is speaking of older people in general or those who occupy the office of the presbyterate. There are references, as well, to *episkopoi,* but not enough to identify clearly their function. For instance, Hermas receives a vision of the building of a tower, which represents the church, and "fitting exactly into each other" he sees square white stones, which represent "the apostles and *episkopoi* and teachers and deacons" (*Vision* 3.5).

Eusebius, Justin, and Hippolytus

For the period 160–215 we have many more witnesses for Christianity at Rome than we have for Christianity at Lyons or at Carthage. The three most important are Eusebius, Justin, and Hippolytus.

Eusebius's *Ecclesiastical History* touches on the history of the church at Rome during the second century and transcribes a number of archival documents. Scholars now commonly trust Eusebius when he is directly quoting. But they are more suspicious of his interpretations, which he seems to have filtered through his experience of the church in his own day and bent to his historiographical agenda. Justin, who was a native of Palestine, arrived in Rome during the reign of Antoninus Pius (138–161), began a Christian school there, and wrote two apologies and a dialogue. The *Acts of Justin,* a later composition with reliable material, reports his martyrdom about the year 165, which was a dozen years before the martyrs of Lyons and fifteen years before the Scillitan martyrs at Carthage. At the end of the second and the beginning of the third centuries, the most important source for our period of 175–215 is Hippolytus—or, to be precise, the corpus of writings that have usually been attributed to someone named Hippolytus. If we have little contemporary evidence for Tertullian at Carthage, and less about Irenaeus at Lyons, their younger contemporary at Rome, Hippolytus, is very much a mystery.

Concerns of the Church

From these writings it seems evident that the concerns of Christians at Rome closely paralleled those of Christians at Lyons and at Carthage—that is, relations with the state, threats of persecution, the existence of heresy, gifts of the Spirit in general, and prophecy in particular. There are signs, too, that as the church in the capital of the empire, the Roman church felt some responsibility to give leadership in the wider church. *1 Clement,* for example, is a book of advice organized by the Romans for the Corinthians. Hermas, in one vision, receives a book that a Roman official is supposed to distribute across the empire. And Eusebius quotes a letter showing how Soter, who is described as a bishop of Rome about 168, sent charity to the provincial churches.

Ministry in the Church

It is notoriously difficult to construct a consistent picture of ministry in the Church of Rome during these years. On the one hand, Irenaeus and Eusebius speak of a succession of bishops at Rome, and this evidence may suggest a monarchical episcopate. On the other hand, *1 Clement* and Hermas describe an authority structure in Rome wholly devoid of a monarchical episcopate. Moreover, it is difficult to imagine how one person in an illegal, multicultural organization in a large city could force a general recognition of his personal authority—a feat that would later prove to be notoriously challenging for the bishops of Rome and Carthage in the 250s.

The recent trend in scholarship, which seems persuasive to me, is to date the emergence of a monarchical episcopate at Rome toward the beginning of the third century—or, indeed, even later. The interpretations of Eusebius are then explained as his more or less unconscious assimilation of earlier documents to fourth-century realities that were known personally to him. This assimilation also served his historiographical agenda of demonstrating that the ecclesiastical leadership of bishops was consistent from the beginning. As for Irenaeus, although he gives a list of bishops at Rome, he also, in one of his letters, affirms that it was actually presbyters who presided over the church there (cf. *Ecclesiastical History* 5.24).

The best evidence for the Church of Rome at the beginning of the period we are considering is that of Justin. No one doubts that Justin was an important literary figure in Christian history of the time. But since he is not identified as a bishop, a presbyter, or a deacon, those who assume that churches were always run by bishops, presbyters, and deacons have relegated him to a minor place in the institutional history of the Roman church. As the self-appointed leader of a Christian academic community, he has looked to many readers more like the founding principal of a rather marginal religious school than a major church leader. But what if the Christian community that he describes is not a mere historical sidelight but a paradigm? And what if all Roman churches were modeled on the philosophical schools of the day?

The model of the school that Justin founded was clearly that of the Greek philosophical schools. Justin, in fact, is described as wearing a *pallium*, which was the cloak of Greek philosophers. The philosophical schools were not, of course, value-free research and training centers but communities of masters and disciples intent on what we might call spiritual formation. Those in the Greek schools dialogued, took meals together, drank together, shared in household sacrifices together, and sometimes lived together. So did those of Justin's school, except that his community did not offer sacrifices.

The fact that Christian teachers and pagan philosophers had intellectual conversations with one another—as reflected, for example, in the writings of such Apologists as Justin himself and Minucius Felix—demonstrates that Christianity could look very much like a community of the disciples of a particular school of religious thought. Justin's favorite term for Christians was "disciples." In his extant writings, he never once speaks of *episkopoi* or *presbyteroi*. In his well-known description of worship in his *First Apology*, especially chapters 65 and 67, he describes the leader of the eucharist as a "presider" (*proestōs*)—a term often used in the philosophical schools of the day for their organizational head.

A Collection of Independent Voluntary Associations

Some recent historians have portrayed the church at Rome in the latter half of the second century as an associated collection of independent voluntary associations, which looked perhaps like house churches or perhaps like philosophical schools (cf. esp. Lampe, *Die stadtrömischen Christen;* Brent, *Hippolytus and the Roman Church*). These independent communities in Rome were, according to this picture, the origins of the well-known *tituli* churches of Rome, which in the *Liber Pontificalis* of the fifth and sixth centuries are described as *quasi diocesis*—that is, independent congregations with their own buildings, clergy, liturgies, and burial places. Perhaps twenty of these are pre-Constantinian.

Before Constantine, no bishop or body of presbyters in Rome enjoyed the legal authority to bring all these independent groups under uniform control. Rather, it seems more likely that the elders of each of the house-school churches met together from time to time in association. There are pieces of evidence to hint that one officer of this citywide association received money offerings from the various Roman congregations, administered charity, and corresponded with churches in other cities of the empire. As this secretary-treasurer's budget and correspondence grew, he became increasingly important and emerged as the chief "overseer" or *episkopos* of the churches of the city of Rome.

Against this understanding of the second-century church at Rome as being a highly decentralized association of independent house churches or school churches stands Eusebius's narrative of Pope Victor's role in the controversy about the date of Easter (*Ecclesiastical History* 5.23ff.), which suggests a monarchical episcopate. According to Eusebius, the dioceses of Asia were celebrating Easter on the fourteenth day of the moon, on whatever day of the week that might fall. Victor, however, apparently like most other westerners, supported those who required it to be celebrated on a Sunday. Victor felt so strongly on the matter that he "tried to cut off from the common unity the dioceses of all Asia" and composed letters of excommunication. But is it really possible that in the second century there was a Roman ecclesiastical leader who, with any credibility, could claim authority to excommunicate the entire Christian population of Asia?

Eusebius's interpretation has long been questioned (cf., e.g., Jalland, *Church and the Papacy* 115–222; McCue, "Roman Primacy"). His sources were likely authentic enough. He appears to have had a letter from Victor, which he does not quote, and a letter from Irenaeus, which he quotes at length. Irenaeus challenges Victor on the grounds that earlier presbyters of Rome were "at peace with those from the *paroikoi* in which [the fourteenth day of the moon] was observed," and that they "sent the eucharist" to them. Although *paroikos* is etymologically the root of our word "parish," for Eusebius a *paroikos* was a diocese—and so he apparently concluded that Rome had long observed the rather odd custom of shipping the Easter Eucharist overseas to the dioceses of Asia. But what if a *paroikos* for second-century Romans was a house church? And what if "sending the Eucharist" meant that the Roman house churches exchanged among themselves food from their Eucharists as a sign of their association?

There is perhaps a hint of such an exchange between house churches in Justin's *First Apology*, 65 and 67, when he says that his community sends a portion of the eucharistic bread and wine to those absent. And if such an exchange is what was really being referred to by Victor—who was the leader of one of the Roman congregations, and, perhaps, also the secretary-treasurer of the association of Roman congregations—the scenario should probably be seen as follows: that Victor was refusing to exchange a portion of the Eucharist with the Asian immigrant congregations in the city of Rome because they observed a different date of Easter, whereas Irenaeus was remonstrating with him against this unprecedented act of discourtesy. Mistaking the term *paroikos,* Eusebius, it appears, imagined that Victor was refusing eucharistic partnership with the dioceses of Asia.

The picture for second-century Rome, therefore, is an association of house-school churches, each with its own president and each with its own form of worship—all of them being generally indulgent of one another's idiosyncrasies in practice, until in the 190s when Victor attempts, apparently unsuccessfully, to secure uniformity among them regarding the date of Easter. The ministry of the Roman churches is focused on teaching and study, spiritual gifts, firmness under persecution, service, and love. The offices of bishop and presbyter are not specifically emphasized—or, as in the writings of Justin, not even mentioned—and clergy and laity are not distinguished.

The Evidence from The Apostolic Tradition

With *The Apostolic Tradition,* which is usually attributed to Hippolytus of Rome and generally dated about 215, we seem, on initial reading, to have reached a very different situation. As this work is usually read, bishops for the first time are clearly distinguished from presbyters; those ordained by the laying on of

hands are clearly distinguished in function and authority from those not ordained; and ordination entitles persons to take roles of liturgical leadership. Here,
at last, we seem to have a picture of an episcopally dominated, hierarchically ordered, liturgically centered Christian community—exactly the kind of community that leaders of the modern Liturgical Movement have thought the church
originally was and still ought to be. In his recent study of Hippolytus, however,
Allan Brent asks us to reread *The Apostolic Tradition,* putting away the lenses of
the Liturgical Movement, acknowledging textual difficulties, and recognizing the
difficulties of identifying the author with the Hippolytus later named as a schismatic bishop of Rome. The text itself pictures a close-knit Christian community,
the kind of house church or school church we have seen in the writings of Justin.
The communal supper or *agapē* meal, which is described in chapters 25–30, is
clearly in someone's house (see esp. ch. 27) and resembles the meal of Justin's
Apology 65 and 67—and, for that matter, the meals of the philosophical schools.
The offering called the *apophorēton* in chapter 28 may be a memento of a meal
such as we hear about in Petronius's *Satyricon* 56, or it may be a gift of food or
clothing for the poor analogous to offerings we hear about in the banquets of the
school of Epicurus.

In the community depicted in *The Apostolic Tradition,* opportunities for
ministry are reasonably numerous. Confessors are particularly honored, as are
those with spiritual gifts—notably, that of healing. There are also teachers, widows, readers, virgins, subdeacons, and those who host the *agapē* meals. Moral
standards are strict.

But is there a new note of sacradotalism in the understanding of Christian
ministry? In *The Apostolic Tradition* 3, the bishop's ministry is described in language that is unprecedented—that is, as the exercise of high priesthood, the offering of gifts, the propitiation of God, and the forgiveness of sins. Some researchers,
however, such as Paul Bradshaw (cf. his *Canons of Hippolytus*), are suspicious of
the text at this point.

Indeed, the text of *The Apostolic Tradition* as a whole is problematic, for it
does not exist in the original Greek, except in occasional fragments, but only in
later ancient translations. There are particular puzzles for chapters 2–3, which
comprise a rubric and prayer for consecrating bishops, and for chapter 7, which is
a prayer for consecrating presbyters. In particular, the prayer for bishops in chapter 3 is entirely lacking from two important ancient versions, the Sahidic and the
Arabic. The rubric in chapter 2 is quite corrupt textually, as Bradshaw has demonstrated. The prayer for presbyters in chapter 7 is introduced by a direction that
the bishop "shall say according to what was said above, as we said before about
the bishop," although what follows is not the same at all. Finally, although the first
prayer describes the bishop in priestly terms—drawing on Old Testament imagery concerning the ministry of the sanctuary, and distinguishing the episcopal office from the presbyteral office—the second prayer compares the bishop to
Moses, who was not a priest, and, using "us" language, emphasizes the similarity
of function of bishops and presbyters.

It begins, in fact, to look as if chapters 2–3 were not in the original of *The Apostolic Tradition,* and that chapter 7, with its "us" language, was originally a prayer for both bishops and presbyters, who were still not yet clearly distinguished. But if chapters 2–3 are set aside, then we are left to derive our understanding of bishops and presbyters from the prayer of chapter 7. And that prayer specifies no liturgical function for presbyters but regards them as governors and counselors—that is, as teachers and guardians of orthodoxy, just as they were for Irenaeus. So we are left without evidence for a sacerdotal, hierarchical understanding of ministry about the time of 215.

Another piece of questionable evidence in *The Apostolic Tradition* having to do with ordination being for a liturgical function is found in chapter 10, which prohibits the ordaining of a widow on the grounds that "she does not offer the offering, nor has she a *leitourgia.*" But *leitourgia* at this date need not demand the translation "liturgical duty," but may simply mean "office of ministry"—or, in its more ancient usage, "service to the community," as in *1 Clement.* And the offering may well be an offering of food or money to the poor, as in *1 Clement* (and probably in *The Apostolic Tradition* itself, chapter 28). Those entitled to ordination, then, would not be those contemplating a career of liturgical leadership but those called to collect and distribute relief for the poor and needy. We recall that Tertullian's *Apology* 39 also connected the ministry of the presbyterate with the disposition of the church treasury for the service of the poor, the imprisoned, and the shipwrecked.

Summation

In short, if we read *The Apostolic Tradition* without chapters 2–3, as it seems we must, the work supports the picture given for Rome by Justin of an early Christian ministry comparable to what we found at Lyons and at Carthage during approximately the same time period. Christians meet in house churches; the hallmarks of their common life are prayer, study, social service, and community meals; confessors, healers, and those with other spiritual gifts are much honored; the elders, having spent many years in Christian study and often having been called to confess the faith before persecutors, help keep the community centered in a tradition of orthodox teaching; and *episkopoi* are named, but are not readily distinguishable from presbyters.

4. CYPRIAN OF CARTHAGE (248–258 C.E.)

Carthage Christianity and Cyprian

The history of Christianity at Carthage is largely dark to us between Tertullian and Cyprian, who became bishop there about 248 and was martyred in 258. Cyprian had been a member of the Roman upper classes with a large estate and a high professional reputation in pagan Carthage. In the middle or late 240s, however, he embraced Christianity, and within a very few years, while still a relatively recent convert, he was elected bishop. In late 249 or early 250 the emperor Decius ordered a systematic persecution of Christians, and the imperial authorities in Carthage appear to have been particularly vigorous in administering it. Probably a large majority of Christians effectively renounced their faith by word or deed, and as a result church leaders found themselves overwhelmed with thorny pastoral, disciplinary, and theological issues.

In addressing these issues, Cyprian's approach was to affirm the authority of bishops. In his letters and treatises there appear a clear distinction between clergy and laity, the first clear assertion in the west of a monarchical episcopate, a hierarchical understanding of ministry, a condemnation of schismatics as people "from whose breasts the Holy Spirit has departed" (*Letter* 66.2.2), a liturgically oriented understanding of the presbyterate, a priestly interpretation of episcopacy, and glimmerings of a sacrificial understanding of worship. We finally, in fact, have in Cyprian's writings our first clear western source for an understanding of ministry that is consistent with what is described by the Liturgical Movement.

Cyprian and Institutional Authority

Was Cyprian simply the first witness to a development of institutional authority in the early church, which tradition is largely invisible to historians? Or was Cyprian himself the seminal influence in the establishment of this tradition? Most scholars have affirmed the former—but not, I think, persuasively. Thus W. H. C. Frend suggests that since between 212 and 250 the church enjoyed virtual freedom from persecution, and since therefore confessors and martyrs retreated from prominence, "sovereignty passed from the 'spiritual men' to the bishops and their clergy" (*Donatist Church*, 125). But if this were so, Cyprian would not have needed to present himself—as he did again and again—as a spiritual person who received private visions and dreams (see, e.g., his *Letters* 11.5–6; 40.7; 58.1; 63.1; 66.10).

It can be legitimately argued that with the decline of an urgent, external threat between 212 and 250, there was nothing to push Christians toward the kind of closely defined, institutionalized authority structure that bursts into the historical evidence with the works of Cyprian. Moreover, we have the apologist Minucius Felix—who apparently was an African living in Rome, possibly in the years following Tertullian—firmly making the point in his *Octavian* that Christians, as a matter of theological principle, worship and serve entirely without temples and altars.

Cyprian's View of Ordained Ministry

An excellent source for Cyprian's view of ordained ministry is his *Letter* 1. The occasion for the letter was the death of a Christian who had nominated a presbyter named Geminius Faustinus to be his family's guardian. Cyprian, however, was incensed about the nomination, for the office of a guardian was a time-consuming task and would take the presbyter away from his proper task—which Cyprian describes as "altar and sacrifices," "prayer and supplication."

Cyprian had in view at least two practical concerns in so writing. First, the clergy received an honorarium (which, it seems, was itself something of an innovation), and if they were being paid to do church work they should not, he argues in *Letter* 1, be spending their time instead on other tasks. Second, Cyprian's correspondence is emphatic that presbyters should be ruled by their bishop, and so, it seems, he worried that presbyters who work for and receive compensation from laypeople would no longer be so tractable with their bishop.

In arguing his case, Cyprian appeals to two authorities. One is the Old Testament. The tribe of Levi, he points out, was dedicated to the temple, and therefore received no distribution of land, "so that those who were engaged in the works of God should not . . . be compelled to turn their thoughts or energies to worldly affairs." The implication, confirmed in his other letters, is that Cyprian understood the Christian clergy to be in some sense successors to the priests and Levites of the Old Testament. His other authority is a council of bishops, which, he says, "some time ago" prohibited people from appointing clergy to serve as guardians.

The question is: Does this apparently new view of ministry actually reflect an established practice and consensus? At first glance it appears so, partly because of Cyprian's reference to a council of bishops "some time ago," and partly because, when historians see a change in circumstances and have no evidence to explain it, they usually would rather infer a gradual historical development than an abrupt departure. But Cyprian's vague allusion to an undated council looks suspiciously tendentious, and church history offers many examples of abrupt changes in policy and practice.

A closer look at the situation suggests that Cyprian's views of ministry and his way of exercising authority were, in fact, a widely unpopular innovation. Three lines of evidence can be appealed to in support of this understanding. First, it is clear from the letter that Cyprian enjoyed no real authority over either the presbyter or the presbyter's patron, for they were defying his wishes with impunity. His only recourse was to write to the particular congregation involved, evidently the patron's congregation, asking them to desist from praying for the repose of the patron's soul—which request may or may not have been honored.

Second, we know that Cyprian's claims to authority were widely resisted by both presbyters and laypeople. The theme of resistance recurs throughout his letters—as, for example, in *Letter* 43, where he describes "the spite and treachery of certain presbyters," their "plots" against him, and "their old venom against my episcopate." G. W. Clarke, somewhat hesitantly in the face of uncertain evidence, speculates that Cyprian at the time of *Letter* 43 had eight presbyters, of whom five were hostile to him (*Correspondence of St. Cyprian,* 1:41). What appears to be the recent innovation of giving the presbyters an honorarium provides Cyprian with the leverage of patronage. Otherwise, however, he must depend for his authority in large measure on his political savvy, his oratorical ability, his network of friendships, and his agile appeal to Scripture.

Third, the councils of African bishops, to which Cyprian is appealing in *Letter* 1, appear to have no authority other than what they give themselves, or what bishops such as Cyprian acknowledge. As instruments of ecclesiastical authority, councils do not clearly appear before Cyprian's lifetime. Evidence for councils before the third century is rare and sometimes debatable—as in the case of Eusebius's report of councils relating to Victor's actions on the date of Easter. Cyprian and later Augustine refer vaguely to a meeting of North African bishops that was convened by a bishop of Carthage named Agrippinus (perhaps between 195 and 235) to discuss topical issues. But attempts of scholars to derive from this shadowy event a fully developed and generally recognized instrument of church governance before Cyprian are unpersuasive.

Cyprian and Church Councils

Councils may have evolved as a mechanism to ensure that Christians disciplined in one congregation did not simply migrate to another congregation (cf. *Letters* 42; 55.21.1; 59.10.1). So far as we know, Cyprian was the first to appeal to councils of bishops as an independent authority for defining disciplinary standards. He himself convened councils to seek a common front of regional bishops on issues that were dividing Christians at Carthage in the wake of the persecutions—that is, regarding readmitting those who had "lapsed" under persecution, placing limits on the institutional authority of those who had confessed their faith in the face of persecution, and recognizing the baptism of those who had been baptized by schismatic bishops and presbyters.

Indeed, the councils that Cyprian convened seem to have been largely, though not entirely, inclined to follow his lead. But there was nothing to prevent bishops, presbyters, and laypeople who disagreed with Cyprian's councils from forming communions of their own. We know of several such alternative communions, each judging the others to be schismatic, and each denying in the others the hope of eternal life (cf., e.g., *Letters* 66.7.3). After 251 there were at least three rival bishops of Carthage. And the various rival associations of North African bishops seem to have sought partnerships among similarly oriented rival associations of Italian bishops (cf. *Letters* 59.9.3).

Cyprian and Episcopal Authority

Cyprian's strategic brilliance was that he sought and found a theological rationale for his unprecedented claims for episcopal authority—a rationale that was based on what was considered to be both inspired and authoritative by all Christians. It was not enough to appeal to the decisions of the councils of bishops, for episcopal authority itself was at issue and the Christian community in North Africa had rival councils of bishops. It was not enough to appeal to his own private visions and revelations, for other Christians had visions and revelations. It was not enough to claim that the visions of bishops were more dependable than the visions of other people, for this argument was not likely to impress those who did not already share his sense of the importance of the office of bishop. Rather, his great achievement was to see that the most effective rationale was sure to be one drawn from Scripture, the single commonly agreed authority among Christians.

The New Testament, however, was not helpful in this respect, and so Cyprian turned to the Old Testament. There he found that God had provided for a special caste of religious leaders—priests and Levites—who, by divine injunction, were entitled to the support and obedience of the community. Accordingly, Cyprian began to argue that in the community of the New Covenant bishops and presbyters had assumed the priestly and levitical office of ministering holy things. Here was a line of reasoning that definitively trumped confessors, martyrs, ad hoc prophets, lay teachers, and everyone else. The key to connecting the priesthood of Israel with the priesthood of the church was to connect the sacrifices of the temple typologically with the Eucharist. This Cyprian was glad to do. In *Letter* 63 he argues that the Old Testament sacrifices of Abraham, Judah, Melchizedek, and Solomon were types of the sacrifice of Christ, and that the sacrifice of Christ is consecrated and celebrated in the Eucharist. A priest like Melchizedek, who makes an offering that looks forward to Christ's sacrifice, is a type of a bishop like Cyprian, who makes an offering which looks back to it. With satisfaction, therefore, Cyprian contemplated Deut 17:12, which he quotes more than once in his *Letters* (e.g., 43.7.1): "In order that the Lord may pardon you, you must not abandon His priests, since it is written, 'And whatever man acts with such arrogance that he does not heed the priest or the judge, whoever he may be in those days, that man shall die.'"

Making Christian bishops successors to the high priests of Israel gave them divine sanction, based in Scripture, for claiming the obedience of the church. Making presbyters the successors of the Levites neatly demoted them, leaving them as cultic functionaries—a development that they themselves naturally resisted, as *Letter* 1 demonstrates. Cyprian also gave correspondingly greater weight to the Eucharist, which became the focus of Christian priesthood. In all the works of Justin, Irenaeus, and Tertullian, which total hundreds of pages, one would be hard pressed to find as many as a score of references to the Eucharist. But such references abound in Cyprian, and he gives us the first treatise on the Eucharist in the western empire (*Letters* 63).

Moreover, by identifying the church with its eucharistic offerings and its episcopal high priesthood, Cyprian was able to place those dissidents whom he had excommunicated entirely outside the grace of God, outside the presence of the body and blood of Christ, and outside the comfort of the Holy Spirit. Salvation itself was denied those who refused to acknowledge the authority of their bishops and to agree with their doctrine.

Summation

Evidence drawn from Cyprian's writings for a Liturgical Movement understanding of ministry, therefore, is not what it seems. Partly for temperamental reasons, as one who liked to have his leadership honored, and partly for what he conceived to be the good of the church in an apparently deteriorating situation, Cyprian made claims for the office of bishop not previously seen in the western empire. He supported these claims with an innovative—indeed, almost outlandish—appeal to the Old Testament, applying God's favor for the temple priesthood to Christian bishops. He treated his presbyters as his assistants, with possibly the majority of them resisting. He developed networks of like-minded bishops so that, meeting as councils, they might promote episcopal authority. He defended his approach by inventing tradition.

Cyprian was able to move his innovative ideas into the mainstream because of his dominating personality, his political savvy, his oratorical and theological skills, his social and professional eminence, his identification with the metropolitan city of North Africa, and, in the end, by the credibility of his martyrdom. In his own context he was resorting to desperate arguments in a fight against considerable odds for the church's survival. When Christendom dawned, his arguments would lay the foundation for a kind of hieratic totalitarianism.

5. CONCLUDING, RETROSPECTIVE POSTSCRIPT

At Lyons, Carthage, and Rome before 250, Christian ministry was shaped by its contexts and objectives. The primary functions of ministry were to confess, teach, and defend the faith, to encourage others to a holy life, to exercise spiritual gifts, to address disciplinary, pastoral, and theological issues as they arose, to maintain fellowship with distant churches, and to distribute relief to the poor. In these three multicultural cities, racial origin and social status were of little importance. Confessors, martyrs, prophets, healers, presbyters, and deacons could be found among Greek-speakers, Latin-speakers, Celtic-speakers, and African-speakers, among men and women, among slaves such as Blandina, and among nobles such as Perpetua.

The climate of persecution and tensions with paganism magnified the importance of the confessors. These ministers received their authority directly from God, and, if they were not martyred, they became influential figures in the church. The Spirit also gave gifts generously to prophets and healers. But since false prophets were not readily distinguishable from inspired prophets, prophecy sometimes divided the church into separate factions.

Along with these ministers, persons who had gifts of teaching and writing were also valued for maintaining the orthodox tradition of Christian teaching, which was the lifeblood of the Christian community. Irenaeus was the spokesperson for the churches of Gaul by 190; Justin presided over an influential and highly regarded house church; the school of Hippolytus was influential in the east as well as the west; and Tertullian, one of the most passionate of theologians, helped mold all western thought. Most clearly with Irenaeus, but also with Tertullian, the special role of the presbyterate was to maintain the doctrine of the apostles.

So far as early Christian literature is concerned, the character and privileges of ministerial office and the celebration of liturgy, which consume so much attention in the church today, were overwhelmed by other interests. The *Apostolic Tradition* appears at first to be a partial exception to this generalization, but a close critical reading brings it into consistency with the other contemporary evidence. Until about 190 distinctions between clergy and laity were scarcely known, and distinctions between bishops and presbyters, if they existed at all, evade definition. Until Tertullian there is no reason to believe that presidency at the Eucharist and ministerial office were formally connected. Afterward, it appears that eucharistic presidency was, indeed, restricted to ordained persons—as a matter of organizational expedience, but not, as Tertullian himself so strenuously insisted, as a matter of theological principle.

With Cyprian, however, the understanding of ministry changed. The elements of church life at Carthage were much the same. As at Lyons in 177, so at Carthage in 250, Christians taught and prayed and helped the poor, the mobs harassed, the authorities persecuted, the stalwart confessed, the weak lapsed, many of the confessors forgave the lapsed, leaders had visions, and rival Christian groups competed for followers. But the theology and dynamics of ministerial office were being transformed.

It is plausible to believe that social, economic, and political contexts in which the church found itself changed. But there is so little evidence for Christian developments at Carthage between the time of Tertullian and the time of Cyprian that we have left most of these considerations to one side. The three most obvious differences were these. First, the gnostic threat subsided, and so Christians who were once forced to make common cause against heretics now had the luxury to dispute with each other over points of ecclesiastical organization. Second, the church had grown, and so there were many more martyrs, many more lapsed, and much larger treasuries—with opportunities for tension and schism among Christians to grow at least proportionally, if not, indeed, exponentially. Third, there was Cyprian. For the first time in the western empire a metropolitan congregation had as its leader a person who by birth, wealth, professional training, political ability, intellectual discipline, administrative skill, and oratorical gifts would have made a fine provincial proconsul.

Indeed, Cyprian's approach to managing the church more than resembles a proconsul's approach to governing a province—except, of course, that Cyprian dispensed with his personal wealth. He is politically canny. He cultivates allies among fellow bishops, enlists friendly presbyters as his retainers, harangues or (if necessary) excommunicates unfriendly presbyters, and outmaneuvers and neutralizes the confessors who are his most dangerous rivals for spiritual authority.

Most enduringly, Cyprian develops a theology of the ordained Christian ministry as a successor to the cultic officialdom of the Old Testament temple. He presents bishops as high priests ruling with divine sanction and presbyters as a kind of levitical tribe. His purpose is to bring Christians to obedience in order to save the church. In restrospect, we may see dangers in his assimilation of the *imperium* and the *sacerdotium* to the episcopal office. But in Carthage in 250, how could he have foreseen such dangers? The church was too beleaguered and bishops had too reduced a life expectancy to realize their pretensions.

I began this chapter by saying that many Christians throughout the generations have looked to the first two or three Christian centuries for inspiration and direction—even for justification for their own ecclesiologies, polities, and programs. This approach, however, is problematic because the culture of antiquity was different from ours. Furthermore, the churches of antiquity had a social character and an understanding of themselves and their purpose that were somewhat different from, for example, churches of the Constantinian period, churches of the Protestant Reformation, or churches today. There are, therefore, dangers in drawing parallels between the forms and theories of early Christian ministry and those of modern Western Christian ministry.

It is possible, as I have argued, to distinguish between the model of ministry that operated in Irenaeus's church and the model that operated in Cyprian's church. But we should think twice before extracting those models—either or both—from their historical contexts and treating them as ideal types, and so translatable to other situations. Some sociologists of religion have described, for example, Irenaeus and his church as being "charismatic" and Cyprian and his church as "institutional," these being categories that may be helpful for the twentieth century. But Irenaeus, though a man of the Spirit, clearly recognized the importance of institutional safeguards for the preservation of orthodoxy and unity, and Cyprian, though canny about institutions, knew the importance of prophecy and the gifts of the Spirit.

Christians in the first centuries did not develop models of ministry in order to facilitate their organization or to optimize their social effectiveness. Rather, ministries and understandings of ministry developed around particular concepts of mission and the gifts of the Spirit. Before 250, the mission of Christians and the Christian church was seen primarily in terms of confessing Christ even under persecution, maintaining and studying the apostolic teaching, serving the needy, and building up the Christian community in love. With the Decian persecution, as we have seen at Carthage, maintaining ecclesiastical unity, pastoral integrity, and consistent standards of membership assumed urgency. In both situations, Christian ministry, leadership, and community relationships were shaped accordingly.

BIBLIOGRAPHY

Primary Materials in English Translation

Ante-Nicene Christian Library: Translations of the Writings of the Fathers Down to A.D. 325. 10 vols. Edited by A. Roberts and J. Donaldson. Edinburgh: T&T Clark, 1869–1883.

Correspondence of St. Cyprian. 4 vols. Edited by G. W. Clarke. New York: Newman, 1984–1989.

Early Christian Writings: The Apostolic Fathers. Translated by M. Staniforth and A. Louth. Rev. ed. Baltimore: Penguin Books, 1987.

Eusebius of Caesarea. *The Ecclesiastical History.* 2 vols. Translated by K. Lake. Cambridge, Mass.: Harvard University Press, 1959, 1964.

Secondary Literature

Barnes, Timothy David. *Tertullian: A Historical and Literary Study.* Oxford: Clarendon, 1971.

Bradshaw, Paul, ed. *The Canons of Hippolytus,* with translation by Carol Bebawi. Bramcote, Nottingham: Grove Books, 1987.

———. *The Search for the Origins of Christian Worship.* London: SPCK, 1992.

Brent, Allen. *Hippolytus and the Roman Church in the Third Century.* Leiden: Brill, 1995.

Fahey, Michael A. *Cyprian and the Bible: A Study in Third-Century Exegesis.* Tübingen: Mohr, 1971.

Frend, William H. C. *The Donatist Church.* Oxford: Clarendon, 1952.

———. *Martyrdom and Persecution in the Early Church.* Oxford: Blackwell, 1965.

Grant, Robert. *Irenaeus of Lyons.* London: Routledge, 1997.

Hayes, Alan L. "Tradition in the Anglican Liturgical Movement, 1945–1989." *Anglican and Episcopal History* 69 (2000):22–43.

Jalland, T. G. *The Church and the Papacy.* London: SPCK, 1944.

Lampe, P. *Die stadtrömischen Christen in den ersten beiden Jahrhunderten.* WUNT 2.18. 2d ed. Tübingen: J. C. B. Mohr (Paul Siebeck), 1989.

Les Martyrs de Lyon (177). Paris: Centre National de la Recherche Scientifique, 1978.

McCue, J. F. "The Roman Primacy in the Second Century." *Theological Studies* 25 (1964): 161–96.

Rives, J. B. *Religion and Authority in Roman Carthage from Augustus to Constantine.* Oxford: Clarendon, 1995.

Young, Frances. *Presbyteral Ministry in the Catholic Tradition, or "Why Shouldn't Women be Priests?"* London: Methodist Sacramental Fellowship, 1994.

Chapter 9

Ministerial Forms and Functions in the Church Communities of the Greek Fathers

Frances Young

Investigation of ministerial forms and functions in the early church is a subject that cannot escape revealing the interests of those who interpret the evidence. Historico-critical scholarship has sought to trace objectively the development of offices in the church. But what has most often emerged is a reflection of the investigator's own denominational face at the bottom of a deep well. More recently interest in the ordination of women has produced further debate, but with evidence all too often interpreted to suit the argument being made.

This more recent debate on the ordination of women, however, evidences a significant shift. For a search for precedents has tended to dominate these discussions. Yet discontinuity with a discredited patriarchal system may be as important for feminists as the discovery of particular continuities. And, indeed, interest in the early church as a social organization set in a very different kind of social order than we live in today has highlighted such discontinuities. The conclusions of older investigators, therefore, must be modified by taking seriously the "otherness" of the cultural world in which people then officiated—even if they held titles of which our titles "bishop," "presbyter" and "deacon" are direct descendants.

On this occasion a further factor encourages taking a less than conventional line, namely the explicit request to focus on the Greek fathers. It has been unusual in patristic studies of this question to distinguish between East and West, Greek and Latin. Once the so-called threefold ministry emerged early in the second century, with Ignatius providing the first clear evidence, parallel developments across the Roman Empire have been assumed. The contentious period has been that for which late canonical and early noncanonical texts overlap, and the argument has been mainly concerned with how early the episcopate emerged and whether certain offices can be proven from Scripture. Then Cyprian, the mid-third-century Latin father, has been seen as the key figure who shifted the "ministry" of the earlier period into a "priesthood" offering the "sacrifice" of the

Eucharist. To concentrate on the Greek fathers exclusively, therefore, is a challenge. And to do so effectively I will not confine myself to the pre-Nicene church fathers, for the relevant continuities and discontinuities are best highlighted by examining the better-documented period between the Council of Nicaea in 325 and the Council of Chalcedon in 451.

So what I aim to do in this chapter is to address old questions from newer perspectives, and, drawing on some of my previous work, to challenge conclusions that reflect both old and new interests.

1. BASIL OF CAESAREA: PORTRAIT OF A
FOURTH-CENTURY GREEK BISHOP

I begin by offering a portrait of a bishop in the latter part of the fourth century. The area is Cappadocia, a Roman province located in what we now call Turkey. The bishop is Basil of Caesarea, who purports to be the compiler of one of the liturgies used to this day by the Greek Orthodox Church. He was also founder of the dominant form of monasticism in the same ecclesial tradition. The portrait is drawn by his lifelong friend, Gregory of Nazianzus, which is a place also in Cappadocia. The two met as students at Athens. So the speech composed by Gregory in Basil's honor, *Oration* 43, probably for the anniversary of his death, provides a good first source. It will give us some insight into how Basil was perceived.

Family Background

Gregory was a well-trained orator and his speech follows the conventions of panegyric (i.e., "eulogistic" or "elaborate praise") rhetoric. Allowance has to be made for very different cultural expectations, and we will certainly not follow Gregory's speech blow by blow. Much of it rehearses Basil's ancestry, education, and career up to the time when he became bishop—highlighting the facts that this fourth-century bishop, like many another, came from a leading local family and had a first-class education according to the norms of the day. Gregory's recital of Basil's pedigree is nuanced with an emphasis on his martyr ancestors and saintly parents, who are depicted in terms of Christianized virtues and values. Nonetheless, the social superiority of Basil's background glints through the sackcloth, the biblical allusions, and the scriptural exemplars.

Unlike some other Christian leaders of this time, however, Basil grew up in a Christian family and was a baptized Christian and ordained to the presbyterate at the time of his election as bishop. Gregory expresses approval of the fact that Basil had not been advanced to "the holy thrones of the priesthood" too rapidly (43.25)—which provides Gregory the occasion for lamenting the "danger of the holiest of all offices" becoming, as he expresses it, "the most ridiculous among us. For promotion depends not on virtue, but on villainy; and the sacred thrones fall not to the most worthy, but to the most powerful" (43.26).

These words of Gregory were written just over half a century after the conversion of Constantine. Together with many other bits of evidence drawn from the period, they reflect the fact that offices in the church had come to be prized by the ambitious as well as to fall naturally to the local aristocracy. Imperial patronage had dramatically changed the social position of church leaders. Gregory and others recognized that this was a kind of betrayal. Yet they also prized the Christianizing of the elite culture to which they belonged.

Clerical Progression and Politics

Basil progressed through the ranks properly, being first lector, then presbyter, and eventually bishop—receiving this honor "not as human favor but as from God and divine" (43.27). But Gregory has jumped forward in his narrative, and so in what follows he retreats to describe Basil's withdrawal to live as a monk rather than get into an open dispute with the bishop who was his predecessor. At this stage Valens came to the imperial throne. From the point of view of Basil and Gregory, however, Valens was a heretic, and Gregory spares no rhetoric. Hostile rulers of the churches, as well as governors of the provinces, were out for political gain. So Basil returned to church politics (43.31). He was reconciled with his bishop and provided the mind and energy for resistance to the increasingly heretical world. Effectively, he already had episcopal control (43.34).

But what did resistance and episcopal control mean for Basil? It meant standing up to governors and powerful men in the city. It meant deciding disputes, supporting the needy, entertaining strangers, overseeing the care of virgins, challenging exploiters in times of famine, and providing the nourishment of God's Word (43.34–36). Little surprise, then, that Basil was the natural successor when Valens, his bishop, died. Gregory praises the virtue of Basil's private life and the way he increased in wisdom and favor, as well as stature—alluding in these expressions, of course, to Luke 2:52. Basil would now exercise his virtue on a wider stage and with greater power (43.38).

But Basil had opponents within the church that he had to appease. Gregory indicates that they surrendered to the superiority of his intellect and to the fact that his virtue was unmatchable. With internal rivalries suppressed, Basil became patron of the wider community, which was under pressure from the civil authorities. His first weapon was the pen; his second, what we would call networking. He also had profound differences with the state.

Statesmanship, Character, Roles

The emperor was using exile, banishment, confiscation, plots, persuasion, violence—and whatever else he could devise—against all those church leaders who would not tow his line. Gregory tells of Basil's famous refusal to kowtow to the emperor's prefect, and then of the way he outfaced the emperor himself on his appearance for the liturgy in Basil's cathedral (43.52). Other anecdotes indicate the pressures to which Basil was subjected because of his differences with the state, and these differences were reinforced by the rivalry of episcopal colleagues.

Indeed, the interlocking of state and church is revealed by a telling incident that Gregory handles with a certain degree of care. The emperor had decided to split the province of Cappadocia—the motive almost certainly being to curb Basil's power, for metropolitan boundaries followed those of the imperial provinces. (The word "diocese" originally had a secular connotation.) Basil's reply was to create a whole lot of new bishoprics. In so doing, he consecrated his friend Gregory to a diocese that Gregory himself regarded as a potty little place—a move that had considerable consequences for Gregory's later career and permanently damaged their relationship. Gregory admits to his pain, even as he commends Basil's political astuteness.

The rest of Gregory's speech is a rhetorical celebration of Basil's qualities—his holiness displayed in temperance and simplicity, his celibacy and leadership in the monastic movement, his philanthropy and support of the poor. Gregory defends Basil against the charge of pride, celebrating acts of condescension and suggesting that "what they [his defectors] term pride is, I fancy, the firmness and steadfastness and stability of his character" (43.64).

Basil is turned by Gregory into the ideal bishop, with the description reaching a climax in telling of his eloquence as a preacher and composer of discourses, his ability to move from scriptural exegesis to moral and practical homilies, and his panegyrics on saints and martyrs in the defense of orthodox doctrine. The ideal picture is confirmed by an extraordinary example of the rhetorical trick of *synkrisis,* in which Basil is compared to Adam, Enoch, Noah, Abraham, Isaac, Joseph, Job, Moses, Aaron, the judges, David and Solomon, Elijah and Elisha, the Maccabees, John the Baptist, Peter, Paul, the sons of Zebedee, and Stephen—with Basil often, according to Gregory, outdoing the biblical hero to whom he is likened.

For our purposes I need not dwell on the details of the deathbed scene with which Gregory's *Oration* 43 ends, except to draw attention to how all sectors of the community were called on to honor Basil as one of them. This list indicates the roles that were projected onto the bishop of the day—that he was to be lawgiver, politician and statesman, popular leader, educator, monk and ascetic, example to contemplatives, pastor and comforter, support to the aged, guide to the simple and the young, reliever of poverty and steward of abundance, protector of widows and father of orphans, friend of the poor, entertainer of strangers, physician to the sick, brother to all, and all things to all men (43.81). It all sounds very good. But even in the hands of the saintly Basil, such power over others could become imperious and damaging—as Gregory himself knew to his own cost.

The Monepiscopate: Basil and Ignatius

Gregory's portrait of Basil is not exactly the medieval prince-bishop of the West. But neither is it the bishop that Ignatius had in mind at the beginning of the second century. Ignatius, bishop of Antioch, was arrested and transported to Rome around 110, where he suffered martyrdom. On the way he wrote letters to various church communities in western Asia Minor. The burden of his message to the Ephesians is that they should be in harmony with their bishop, for he "speaks the mind of Christ." The presbytery are said to be "attuned to their bishop like the strings of a harp," with the result of such tuning being a hymn of praise (*Ephesians* 4). The Magnesians are to have respect for their bishop, despite his lack of years, and never to act independently of him (*Magnesians* 3, 7). The Trallians must be obedient to the bishop (*Trallians* 2). The Philadelphians are to follow their bishop like sheep (*Philadelphians* 2), while the Smyrnaeans will avoid faction by holding to the bishop's Eucharist (*Smyrnaeans* 8).

Ignatius's letters, being full of such advice, have usually been taken as evidence that the "monepiscopate" already existed before the time of this early bishop of Antioch, whereas they actually show that he was its first proponent. It seems likely that he urged the authority of the bishop precisely because it was contested rather than achieved. "To do everything in accordance with the bishop," therefore, should probably be seen as Ignatius's own solution to divisions and heresy in the churches to which he wrote. And so, in his view, the bishop was effectively the congregational leader.

But the social and political position of Basil within the Cappadocian church—let alone in relation to the Roman state—can hardly be compared with that of Ignatius, who was writing letters to obscure local communities as he journeyed on to Rome to die for Christ. We cannot generalize the forms and functions of ministry over several centuries without oversimplification.

2. THE APOSTOLIC CONSTITUTIONS: A FOURTH-CENTURY CHURCH MANUAL

Gregory's portrait of Basil combines temporal power in church and society with certain ideals of character drawn from Scripture. Another text from approximately the same period, the so-called *Apostolic Constitutions,* does much the same thing in ways that provide intriguing clues about both the origins of the forms of ministry that we find in the Greek fathers and the ideological milieu that produced a fourth-century Basil. Some understanding of this text, however, is required before we can explore what it has to say about the church and ministry (for a more extensive treatment, cf. my "*The Apostolic Constitutions:* A Methodological Case-Study").

Provenance and Value

The Apostolic Constitutions is, in reality, the end-point of a long process of development. It is a compendium that incorporates older texts and may loosely be described as collections of rules and canons about church order, ministry, and liturgy. The seventh book incorporates one of the earliest texts of this genre, the *Didache* or *Teaching of the Twelve Apostles* from the second century, which, since its rediscovery in 1873, is usually reckoned among the Apostolic Fathers—to which prayers, liturgical texts, and other odds and ends have been appended. The eighth book includes a third-century text known as the *Apostolic Tradition,* which was erroneously attributed to Hippolytus of Rome. The first six books largely reproduce another third-century writing extant in Syriac and known as the *Didascalia apostolorum.*

These older texts were not simply copied. Previous documents, which were thought to have apostolic authority, have been gathered together and reinforced with scriptural backing so as to create a community more in line with what was perceived to be apostolic intention. Scholars have plundered *The Apostolic Constitutions* to reconstruct what the church was like in the fourth century, and possibly before that to some extent. But the text is more prescriptive than descriptive. Furthermore, *The Apostolic Constitutions* rapidly lost influence, since the work in its final form was thought to be Arian.

Despite these reservations, however, *The Apostolic Constitutions* doubtless reflects the social world from which it came. It provides, therefore, a conservative and ideologically driven picture of a bishop's character and role to be set alongside Gregory's portrait of Basil. It also correlates the bishop's role with other ministerial offices in the context of the community as a whole.

The Church Community

The whole church in general is the opening subject of *The Apostolic Constitutions.* It is introduced as God's vineyard, containing the heirs of God's eternal kingdom—that is, those who are partakers of God's Holy Spirit, sprinkled by Christ's precious blood, and fellow heirs with God's beloved Son. Those who enjoy these promises are to do everything in obedience to God, so general commandments are assembled from Scripture, after which men and women are given advice appropriate to each.

Much of this material is about attitudes: not coveting, blessing those who curse you, loving enemies; the husband pleasing his wife and being compassionate to her; and the wife obeying her husband. The practical outworking of these exhortations is spelled out for each of those addressed in terms of not gadding about, not dressing up so as to attract others, sticking to proper tasks, reading the Bible rather than pagan literature, avoiding bathing in mixed company, and strengthening each other in the faith. The style is homiletic and reminiscent of ethical injunctions found in the New Testament and the Apostolic Fathers. Although often characterized as legislation for the laity, such a description hardly fits. Rather, these are exhortations intended to form a community with particular moral characteristics.

The Bishop and Other Officials

Uneven subdivisions make book 2 of *The Apostolic Constitutions* the most substantial part of the work. The focus is now on the bishop, with some relatively brief mention part way through of all those who perform functions in the church and share the tithes and offerings. These other officials include readers, singers, porters, deaconesses, widows, virgins, and orphans—along with bishops (as already mentioned), presbyters, and deacons. The latter three officials are designated high priests, priests, and Levites, respectively, and so a threefold ministry is here differentiated from other orders.

But emphasis on a threefold ministry is exceptional in *The Apostolic Constitutions.* The multiplicity of functions is more noticeable, as is the dominance of the bishop. In fact, the succeeding four books, books 3–6, revolve around the episcopal office, for the bishop holds responsibility for all the various things discussed—whether groups such as widows, or activities such as charitable works, or dealing with heresy and support of the persecuted.

Prime attention, however, is not given to the bishop's role or functions, but to his character. The characteristics required of a bishop mirror those stated in the Pastoral Epistles: he should not be fond of money, ambitious, double-minded, partial, or given to anger; rather, his character should be sober, prudent, decent, stable, generous, and humble. Scriptural quotes and examples enhance the picture of the one who rules and guides the community with wisdom, fairness, and patience. The bishop, in fact, represents God to the people. And he has God's authority to judge, exclude, govern, reform the penitent, and be the good shepherd of the flock.

In the words of book 2 of *The Apostolic Constitutions:*

> The bishop, he is the minister of the word, the keeper of knowledge, the mediator between God and you in the several parts of your divine worship. He is the teacher of piety; and, next after God, he is your father, who has begotten you again to the adoption of sons by water and the Spirit. He is your ruler and governor; he is your king and potentate; he is, next after God, your earthly god, who has a right to be honoured by you. (2.26)

Clearly, the bishop dominates the community. The social world that the author and his readers inhabited is taken for granted. That world was hierarchical and patriarchal. For as the father ruled a household, so the emperor ruled the world and God ruled the universe. People had roles within those structures under monarchical rule. In *The Apostolic Constitutions* all this is unquestioned. The text, in fact, suggests a series of overlapping discourses that indicate how the church mapped onto that world. The principal discourse would appear to be that of the household.

Servants in the Household of God

Sociological studies of the New Testament have demonstrated the significance of the household for understanding the church in its earliest phase. Not only did Christian groups meet in households, they also used familial language in designating God as Father and themselves as adopted sons and heirs through Christ, the Son of God, and in referring to each other as brothers and sisters in Christ. If Colossians, Ephesians, and 1 Peter deliver teaching in a form comparable with similar ethical discourse in the Greco-Roman world and dubbed "household codes," the so-called Pastoral Epistles display a kind of adapted "household code" for the needs of the Household of God.

Book 1 of *The Apostolic Constitutions,* as we have noted, begins with the whole church, which is constituted of people who belong to God's household and who also run households of their own. The analogy between God's household and their own households implies parallels in appropriate behavior and qualities of character. The very shape of the text rapidly becomes that of a "household code" in reviewing what is required of first the husband and then the wife. Thus the ordinary life of Christians is to be morally ordered in light of relationships established within the Household of God. The analogy between God's household and everyday households to which people belong also illuminates ministerial forms and functions.

It has been reckoned that the typical household in the Greco-Roman world consisted of about fifty persons. The immediate kin would constitute an extended family of at least three generations, in addition to which there would be servants, slaves, tenants, clients, and others. There would be male and female servants, all of whom might be called *diakonoi*—even though they would undoubtedly have had differing duties. Does that bear on the question about women deacons? I suspect it does. For starting from everyday household usage, our understanding of what will later become technical terms of Christian ministry must undergo some shift of perspective. Deacons were simply servants in God's household with a range of services to provide—some appropriately assigned to men, others to women. It is, however, somewhat misleading to look here for precedents when arguing for women's ordination in a very different social world.

Following the same principle, the *episkopos* would simply be the head steward, the top servant. But being a managerial slave in charge of others and representing the master could bring great authority in the households of antiquity. It could even mean holding the master's seal and being able to enter into business contracts on his behalf. When Paul speaks of himself as God's *doulos,* it is, as Dale Martin points out, a double-edged expression that adopts the humility of a slave while proudly claiming to speak and act on God's behalf (cf. Martin, *Slavery as Salvation*). It is hardly surprising, therefore, that the *episkopos* appears as representing God in early ecclesiastical texts, including *The Apostolic Constitutions.* God is, as it were, the *pater familias* in whose service bishops and deacons are employed. So the bishop is to be obeyed as one would obey God, for he is the steward who both represents God the Householder and serves the members of the household—administering funds and seeing to the family's needs, both temporal and spiritual.

Widows and Presbyters

The New Testament oscillates between the language of family and the language of service. So does *The Apostolic Constitutions.* Service would seem to be the context from which the titles "bishop" and "deacon" were drawn. But what about "widow" and "presbyter"? Were these terms drawn from the realm of family discourse?

Commentators have long been puzzled as to why, compared with bishops and deacons, presbyters hardly appear in *The Apostolic Constitutions*. It is worth considering whether this difference preserves the memory of a distinction in discourse that would clarify different ministerial roles. My suggestion is that "widows" and "presbyters" take their designations from the discourse of the family, by contrast with the discourse of service from which "bishops" and "deacons" received theirs.

Some seeking precedent for women's ordination have tried to prove that "widows" formed a kind of ministerial order in the early church (as, e.g., Thurston, *The Widows*). But widows in the relevant texts seem primarily to be those on a register to receive charity. Frequently they are bracketed with orphans, have to be needy and of a certain age, and are expected to reciprocate with prayers and proper behavior. This offering of prayers and their designation as "the church's altar" (*Apostolic Constitutions* 3.6.3, and elsewhere) have suggested, at least to some interpreters, a holy office of some kind. Yet the phrase "the church's altar" is also used of orphans, and so must surely have arisen from the view that almsgiving replaced sacrifice. What we find here, therefore, is not a ministerial "order" but an extension of the responsibilities of households and families to provide for their dependants.

But what about the elusive presbyters? Most remarkable is *Apostolic Constitutions* 2.28. The general context concerns the distribution of tithes and offerings, and soon we read that a double portion should be set aside for the presbyters. But first there appear *presbyterai*. The question is: Are these female presbyters or just old women? The matter at issue in the text concerns inviting these women to feasts—that is, that they should be women the deacons know to be in need.

So are male "presbyters" any more than "older men" who need support? Well, they are described as busy with the "word" and "teaching," as standing in the place of the apostles, and as counselors of the bishop. Are the presbyters, then, the revered elderly in the household of God—in particular, those who are the bishop's advisers because they carry the community memory? My suggestion is that these references in *The Apostolic Constitutions* allow us to discern a shift in the discourse whereby everyday terms drawn from the household and family become technical terms in a surrogate family community, which functions like a voluntary association.

God's People

In the Greco-Roman world, households were generally treated as analogous to kingdoms, and vice versa. So the members of the civil service, for example, were known as "Caesar's household," and the ideal philosopher-king was instructed to mirror the good householder who directed, cared for, even educated and trained everyone for whom he was responsible. Belonging to God's household, therefore, could easily slide into a sense of being God's people—a nation over whom God rules through earthly ministers.

This wider discourse, in fact, pervades *The Apostolic Constitutions* and undergirds its use of Scripture. For in *The Apostolic Constitutions* the institutions of ancient Israel are taken to have their counterparts in the church, which is now God's people, and Old Testament texts are used to shape the duties and obligations of the church's officeholders, who are now, as it were, officers of God's state. And the analogy between household and state is projected onto the universe.

Clearly, this perspective had already shaped a discourse that had already encouraged the conflation of Christianity with traditional state religion as practiced by imperial Rome. In book 7 of *The Apostolic Constitutions* one noticeable modification made to the *Didache* is the long insertion about fearing the emperor because he represents Christ. Yet the discourse of religion does not appear to be the most obvious for us to pursue in adopting a sociological approach to *The Apostolic Constitutions.*

Religion in antiquity was neither a matter of belief nor the preserve of a single institution. Rather, religion was woven into everyday life. At one level, it consisted of respect to the household gods; at another, civic festivals—all of which were seen as expressions of "piety" toward the traditions of the ancestors and obligations to the gods who protected the family and the nation. *The Apostolic Constitutions,* of course, projects a Christianized version of this general religious orientation. But that is because its fundamental discourse is that of household and people.

When Christians established places of worship, they adapted houses and built basilicas. Basilicas were public meeting places and places where teaching took place—not palaces for the gods, which were served by priests while the people remained in the courts outside. The voluntary associations or philosophical schools of the day are closer precedents for early Christian gatherings. These associations and schools had religious aspects, but they also provided precedent for a critique of religion, both public and private. For Christians, that critique was married with biblical opposition to sacrifice, such as is found in the Old Testament prophets (as we will see below).

The Community as "School"

The fact that the Christian community was a religious oddity is sharpened by the description of a church gathering in *Apostolic Constitutions* 2.57. The bishop is first described as the commander of a great ship. The building is to be long, with its head to the east, and the seating arrangements are to be such as to reflect the tasks of a captain and a ship's company—everyone in his or her own proper place. This prepares for the reading of Scripture and the exhortation of the presbyters, which are culminated with the discourse of the bishop who sits centrally as the commander.

The church is then likened to a sheepfold—with, again, the proper ordering of women, young people, and children capturing the headlines. Only now does attention turn to prayer, which is followed by the offering of the Eucharist. This climax may be analogous to religious rituals, but it is placed in a rather strange context. For while the language of sacrifice and priesthood permeates much of this text, it retains the sense of a community that has distanced itself from common religious practices. Furthermore, it has instruction at its heart and claims a more rational understanding of the universe and its relation to God the Creator.

All of this hints at another fruitful sociological model, namely the school. One of the most important themes in *The Apostolic Constitutions,* in fact, is knowledge. The very existence of "heresy" is an indication that the analogy with philosophical schools ran deep, for it was the schools that offered various "options" *(haereses)* and delivered rival "teachings" *(dogmata).* Indeed, placing a body of literature at the heart of the community and delivering exegetical discourses on such approved texts was analogous to school activity as practiced in the cities of the Roman Empire. *The Apostolic Constitutions,* in fact, presents the bishop as responsible for seeing that members conform to the teachings of the Christian "school" tradition.

What, then, of the liturgical texts incorporated into this compendium? Most work on these texts has been done by liturgiologists, whose interest has been primarily with the prayers themselves and tracing out the development of liturgy. It has been widely accepted that the prayers of book 7 have a strongly Jewish character, and doubtless that is an important clue with regard to origins. For certainly another discourse that shaped early Christian institutions was that of the Jewish synagogue.

Indeed, the precedent of the synagogue could account for many of the overlapping discourses we have been exploring. The Jewish people had lost their temple and land but, though scattered across the world, preserved their culture—including its religious traditions—through community institutions and regular gatherings for reading their sacred texts and praying without sacrifice. The Jewish community to many in the ancient world seemed like a school. Some, in fact, respected them for having a philosophical religion of a higher order than the rest of society since it was focused on monotheism and morality.

The interesting thing about *The Apostolic Constitutions* is what it takes for granted—that is, that these overlapping discourses make sense. A new discourse was emerging that would contribute to the formation of a new world in which imperial and hierarchical authority would be given apostolic and theological warrant. And it is *The Apostolic Constitutions* that enables us to explore the nature of the community within which ministers performed their functions, provides clues to the origins of the forms of ministry we find in the Greek fathers, and sets out the ideological background that produced such a man in the fourth century as Basil, bishop of Caesarea in the Roman province of Cappadocia.

3. OUTSTANDING QUESTIONS

It would seem that by the time Basil mounted the episcopal throne and *The Apostolic Constitutions* was compiled, the threefold ministry had been established. Bishops presided over cities with many congregations, and presbyters were local eucharistic ministers served by deacons. Those offering the Eucharist had become priests presenting a sacrifice. A pattern of hierarchical progression through the ranks of the clergy appears also to have established itself, though irregularities sometimes occurred. Yet, as we have seen, the conservative compendium of older texts called *The Apostolic Constitutions* only partially presents such a picture. For the bishop still appears to preside over a unitary community, being assisted by deacons, while the presbyters' role is mostly obscured.

We are left, then, with several pertinent questions: (1) How do the clues picked up from this text relate to other evidence, and how might they affect classic theories about the origin and development of the threefold ministry? (2) Was there—or, perhaps, at what moment in history did there develop—a rigid distinction between ordained clergy belonging to this threefold order and the many other functionaries and holy offices in the church, especially such as lectors, widows, virgins, and ascetics? (3) How was priesthood associated with church functionaries who apparently did not carry priestly titles, and what were the implications of this development? The remainder of this chapter will pursue these issues.

4. ORIGIN AND DEVELOPMENT OF THE THREEFOLD MINISTRY

As is well known, "elders" *(presbyteroi)* do not appear in the principal Pauline letters, but do emerge in the Acts of the Apostles and the Pastoral Epistles. In the latter, their relationship with an "overseer" or "bishop" *(episkopos)* is notoriously unclear. In Titus 1:5–9, we are given to understand that Titus was to appoint "presbyters" *(presbyteroi)* in each city in Crete, their character is briefly sketched, and then the text continues: "For a bishop *(episkopos)*, as God's steward, must be blameless" (v. 7). The little word "for" has suggested that the same subject is in view and that therefore *episkopos* may simply be an alternative term for *presbyteros.* So the standard theory (which is taken for granted elsewhere in this volume) is that a "college" of *presbyteroi* was presided over by one of their number known as the *episkopos.* Then, it is suggested, in the early second-century writings of Ignatius we see the situation developing, when he insists on the authority of the monepiscopate and reflects a threefold ministry.

Ignatius, however, twice produces a puzzling image of the Christian ministry in exhorting two of the churches he writes to in western Asia Minor:

> Hasten to do all things in harmony with God, with the *episkopos* presiding in the place of God and the *presbyteroi* in the place of the *synedrion* of the Apostles, and the *diakonoi,* who are most dear to me, entrusted with the *diakonia* of Jesus Christ, who was from eternity with the Father and was made manifest at the end of time. (*Magnesians* 6)

> Likewise, let all respect the *diakonoi* as Jesus Christ, even as the *episkopos* is the "type" of the Father, and the *presbyteroi* God's *synedrion* and as the *synedrion* of the Apostles. (*Trallians* 3)

Thus, in both *Magnesians* 6 and *Trallians* 3, he likens the *episkopos* to God, the *diakonoi* to Christ, and the *presbyteroi* to the apostles.

Reading Ignatius's comparisons in light of the developed clerical hierarchy, it seems odd that the deacons should apparently be ranked higher than the presbyters—as Andrew Louth has noted (*Early Christian Writings*, 82). This is not to be lightly explained away, for we find exactly the same oddity in *Didascalia* 9—indeed compounded—since deaconesses are there likened to the Holy Spirit! And this phenomenon is reproduced in *Apostolic Constitutions* 2.26, where priority is given to the Trinitarian representation in the ministry of the bishop (God the Father), deacons (Christ), and deaconesses (the Holy Spirit)—with presbyters appearing at the end of the list, almost as an afterthought.

The Pastoral Epistles

If we return to the Pastoral Epistles and read them in the light of this evidence, we can find there a distinction between bishops and deacons on the one hand, and presbyters on the other. In 1 Tim 3:1–13, which appears a bit like an ecclesiastical code, two kinds of "officers" appear, and only two: the *episkopos* and the *diakonoi*. This accords with the reference to *episkopoi* and *diakonoi* in Phil 1:1, where such officers are simply taken for granted—presumably by both the author and his readers, for no explanation or discussion is offered. *Presbyteroi* do not appear in this context in 1 Timothy, any more than they do in Philippians and the other principal Pauline letters. Elsewhere in the Pastoral Epistles, where they do appear, the duty lists are still very close to "household codes." Titus 2:1–15 is clearly talking about old men and women, as contrasted with young people and slaves, within the household community.

The situation elsewhere in 1 Timothy, however, is a bit more complex. The term *presbyteros* appears in chapter 5, and in the opening sentence of that chapter the natural sense of "senior" appears correct—for family relations are the subject and a presbyter is to be treated as a father, just as young men are to be treated as brothers, *presbyterai* (feminine plural) as mothers, and younger women as sisters. There follows, however, an extended passage on widows, after which we read that the *presbyteroi* who preside well are worthy of a double "honor" *(timē)*, especially those who labor in the word and teaching. Presumably, given the following justification in verses 18–19, the honor *(timē)* given is to be understood as pay or an honorarium for their teaching activities. Besides teaching, they also "preside." This, as well as the succeeding discussion of discipline, suggests we are no longer talking simply about "older men." And the reference in 1 Tim 4:14 to the *presbyterion* as laying on hands, presumably in some sense "ordaining," confirms this. Furthermore, we should note how closely the *Apostolic Constitutions* follows this text.

I have suggested that none of the solutions proposed so far really accounts for this complex evidence. The clue, however, is to be found in the curious statements of Ignatius, which are followed by the *Didascalia*. And the answer, I suggest, lies in the theory outlined earlier: that the *episkopos* and that the *diakonoi* were originally the only appointed "officers" of the congregation; and that the congregation was established as "God's household" (1 Tim 3:15), the *episkopos* being "God's steward" (Titus 1:7) and the *diakonoi* being the servants.

Presbyters as the Guardians of Tradition

As for the presbyters, the terminology was from the beginning ambiguous and basically suggests seniority. Confusion as to whether the term is to be used in a natural or a technical sense is already present in the Pastoral Epistles, as we have seen. "The Household of God" was a family community made up of older and younger people, both men and women. As the Pastoral Epistles indicate, seniority came with age and was to be respected. It seems entirely plausible that the "senior citizen" carried what we might call the community memory, and so was commissioned to teach the tradition.

That *presbyteros* was associated with tradition is clear from the fragments of the second-century writer Papias—though, of course, Papias' own use of the term is notoriously unclear:

> I shall not hesitate to furnish you, along with the interpretations, with all that in days gone by I carefully learned from the *presbyteroi* and have carefully recalled, for I can guarantee its truth. . . . And whenever anyone came who had been a follower of the *presbyteroi*, I inquired into the words of the *presbyteroi*, what Andrew or Peter had said, or Philip or Thomas or James or John or Matthew, or any other disciple of the Lord, and what Aristion and the *presbyteros* John, disciples of the Lord, were still saying. (Eusebius, *Hist. eccl.* 3.39)

The problem with this much-quoted passage is that *presbyteros* is used in two, if not three, different ways: (1) with reference to the apostles; (2) with reference to people who appear to be second generation Christians, where the phrase "the presbyter John" may or may not indicate that the term was used in a technical sense; and, perhaps also initially, (3) for "seniors" in general who authentically bear the tradition. The importance of the passage, however, is that it shows that in the second century the term was not simply used in a technical way for an "office," but was also used, apparently, to mean the senior members of the community who carried the community memory—indeed, in this sense, even for the apostles themselves. This explains the curious link between presbyters and apostles noted earlier.

It makes sense that as the generations passed the *episkopos* should appoint older, more senior members to act as an advisory council. It also fits with the problem at Corinth dealt with in *1 Clement* and with the response made in that writing—that is, that younger people should not rise in revolt against the senior people who carry the community memory and to whom the *episkopos* turns for advice, for they form the church council.

The Synagogue Analogy

But there is also another possible factor to be considered here, and that is the analogy of the Jewish communities in the Diaspora. It seems that such Jewish communities were governed by a council of elders who appointed the synagogue officials. And the early Christian evidence indicates that the presbyterate ordained the *episkopos*, though the *episkopos* appointed the presbyters.

My own admittedly tentative hypothesis is as follows: that the administrator of the church, who was called an *episkopos* by longstanding Christian habit, began to acquire the functions of a Jewish *archisynagogos* ("ruler/head/administrator of the synagogue"); and that *diakonoi* in the churches began to acquire the functions of the almoners and attendants in the Jewish synagogues—in addition, of course, to those associated with the Christian eucharistic meal. Meanwhile, Christians, who, like Jews, were excluded by their religious scruples from many normal civic functions, began to organize themselves as a kind of distinct "ethnic" community—later to be known as a "third race," which was neither Jew nor Gentile but professed a "heavenly citizenship." So their "seniors" were constituted into a kind of governing council for the community, with authority to appoint and advise the *episkopos*.

Whereas Jewish community leaders often obtained some constitutional recognition from the officials of the various cities, Christians lacked that privilege. Internally, however, they endeavored to organize themselves in a parallel way, and the apologists of the second century tried to claim that same right to recognition. So there is a perceptible shift in the way Christians were beginning to identify themselves socially—from "God's household" to "God's people."

So my suggestion (which I have spelled out more fully in "On *Episkopos* and *Presbyteros*" and *The Theology of the Pastoral Letters*) is that the origins of the presbyterate are distinct from those of the episcopate and the diaconate, the *presbyteroi* were originally a council of senior Christians, who were recognized as the bearers of the apostolic tradition, and, therefore, their association with the apostles was natural—indeed, that the very term *presbyteros* could be used of the apostles themselves.

5. FROM "MINISTRY" TO "PRIESTHOOD"

The shift from God's household to God's people is the key to answering our other questions, for not only did it allow the effective taking over of monarchical institutions from what was by now the Christian Old Testament, but by means of typology it also enabled the assimilation of the orders of ministry to the orders of priesthood under the Old Covenant. As already noted, the *Apostolic Constitutions* likened the bishop to the high priest, presbyters to priests, and deacons to Levites.

And this correlation of offices, I suggest, is what finally shaped the threefold hierarchy in its traditional ranking.

The distinction between "ministry" and "priesthood" has been important in post-Reformation debates. The churches of the Protestant Reformation, basing their arguments on key New Testament texts, have insisted that the priesthood belongs, on the one hand, to Christ and Christ alone, but also belongs, on the other, to all believers. The Roman Catholic tradition has associated priesthood with the presidency of the Eucharist, with the priest being a "type" of Christ in that context. If we were here taking into account the Latin fathers as well, we would find in Cyprian the earliest statements encouraging that view (cf. my brief excursus on Cyprian appended at the end of this chapter). Elsewhere I have argued that to use references to the priest as a "type" of Christ as an argument against women's ordination is to misunderstand typology—for all martyrs, whether male or female, were regarded as "types" of Christ. But let me not get diverted further, except to point out that, insofar as it claims to represent Christ's servanthood, this kind of typological modeling of ministry on Christ's ministry also undergirds Protestant ministry. The difference between Catholic and Protestant lies in the nature of the Eucharist as sacrifice.

My principal aim in referring to these matters is to highlight what I think is an important contrast—that is, that originally during the postapostolic period, and in the East predominantly, the priesthood attributed to officers of the church was validated not by an explicit reference to the eucharistic sacrifice, nor by reference to the person of Christ, but by means of Old Testament typology. As noted, the three orders *episkopos, presbyteros,* and *diakonos* were linked with the high priest, the priests, and the Levites of the Old Covenant, respectively. Already in the late first-century work known as *1 Clement* we have hints of what was to come, for in chapters 40–41 the author pleads for due order in the church and backs up his exhortations with allusions to the Scriptures. The church at Corinth, to which *1 Clement* is addressed, had at that time, it seems, a high priest, priests, Levites, and laity—each with particular offices to perform. The Eucharist is implicitly paralleled with the daily sacrifices of the Jerusalem temple. Scriptural typology, in fact, is the undergirding concept for the writer of *1 Clement*. And by the time of the *Apostolic Constitutions,* such a typological understanding was clearly written deeply into Christian tradition.

The Rejection of Sacrifice

To get all of this into perspective, it is important to realize that earliest Christianity had firmly rejected cultic worship, whether pagan or Jewish (cf. my *Use of Sacrificial Ideas in Greek Christian Writers*). Adapting the critique of the philosophers, early Christians claimed to offer a spiritual cult, prayers rather than sacrifices, circumcision of the heart rather than of the flesh, and the indwelling of the Holy Spirit—with the indwelling of the Holy Spirit making their bodies into spiritual temples. The antisacrificial passages of the prophets were cited as evidence, together with such classic texts as Ps 51:17: "The sacrifice acceptable to

God is a broken spirit; a broken and contrite heart, O God, you will not despise."
By contrast with both Greeks and Jews, Christians spoke of offering "bloodless
sacrifices"—that is, true spiritual praises and thanksgivings.

From the earliest days, Mal 1:10–11 had become an important text in the
church: "I will not accept an offering from your hands. For from the rising of the
sun to its setting my name is great among the nations, and in every place incense
is offered to my name and a pure offering." Gentile Christians now offered everywhere the pure spiritual worship that God required. Writing in the mid-second
century, Justin, who died a martyr at Rome in 165, notes that this pure offering is
made especially, but certainly not exclusively, at the thanksgiving "whereby the
passion which the Son of God endured for us is commemorated" (*Dial.* 117).

It is abundantly clear by the time we reach the *Apostolic Tradition* of (Ps.-)
Hippolytus that first fruits and other offerings in kind, as well as almsgiving and
charity, along with the Eucharist, were expressions of Christian sacrificial worship, and that these offerings were made through Christian "priests." Animal sacrifice was not reinstated, but a purified cult was being recommended as an
alternative. Second-century apologists used this Christian understanding of a purified cult as a powerful argument. Pythagoreans had long opposed animal sacrifice and practiced vegetarianism. Now for Christians the philosophical critique
and the prophetic condemnation of sacrifice came conveniently together.

Typology and Sacrifice

Nonetheless, even as this critique was being pressed home, the cultic system
of Leviticus was taken over as "type" or prefiguration of the Christian purified
way of worship. Origen's exegesis validated a typological approach to the Penta-
teuch. Almost two centuries later, a treatise such as Cyril of Alexandria's *On Worship in Spirit and in Truth* develops and sums up a whole tradition: that Old
Testament law points forward to its fulfillment in Christ and that Christian worship exemplifies the characteristics of true worship as foreshadowed in that law.

Already in the second century, this typological reading of sacrifice was leading naturally to the association of the Old Testament priesthood with the leaders
of the church, especially the *episkopos.* The Greek fathers, however, show little
sign of having associated particularly closely this reconstituted priesthood with
the Eucharist as such. There is nothing to suggest it in Gregory's portrait of Basil
or in the *Apostolic Constitutions.* Later we find John Chrysostom much exercised
by the question as to how there could be one sacrifice of Christ when the Eucharist is repeated in many places and at many times (*Hom. Heb.* 27). In fact, he is ad-
amant that Christ's one sacrifice is never repeated, and he resorts to *anamnēsis*
(memorial) as he searches for a way to safeguard that one, completed sacrifice.

Yet Chrysostom also wants to claim a mystic union of the many Eucharists
with the one sacrifice where Christ was both priest and victim (cf. my *Use of
Sacrifical Ideas*). And in his work *On Priesthood* he emphasizes the awe-inspiring
nature of the priest's duties at the Eucharist. Christian worship, it appears, was
increasingly assimilating the religious features of a dying paganism. Theologically,

however, it was as priests of the New Covenant that first bishops, and then presbyters, received their priestly designations, and not originally because they were eucharistic celebrants. Typology was the ancient and persisting justification for associating priesthood with the officers of the Christian community.

So the separation of the three orders from all the others who had roles in the church community arose from the association of bishops, priests, and deacons with the priests and Levites of the Old Covenant. To treat Cyprian as the one who turned ministers into priests, as is often done (cf., e.g., Hanson, *Christian Priesthood Examined*), is to miss the difference between Cyprian's position and the much more general acceptance of the typological character of the Old Testament Scriptures.

6. CONCLUSION

It is hardly possible to trace a simple linear development through the Greek fathers with respect to models of ministry and community formation. If we take seriously the potential for typological association, it is evident that the projection of Old Testament models of kingship and priesthood was almost inevitable. Monarchy and patriarchy were both biblically and socially sanctioned. They were reinforced by monotheism, as God's sovereignty was mirrored in the head of state, the head of the household, and the episcopal head of the church.

What we are to make of this in a world of democracy and equal opportunities is the challenging question we face today. Was it a sellout to the surrounding culture or a healthy "indigenization"? Should we seek parallel "inculturations" or cling to continuity with the past? Probably it is worth noting, in conclusion, that even the conservative *Apostolic Constitutions* did not avoid updating.

AN EXCURSUS

Cyprian was bishop of Carthage around 250 C.E.. In the Decian persecution he tactically withdrew from the city and left the presbyters in charge. His authority was challenged, particularly over the question of the readmission of "lapsed" Christians to communion. It is now widely thought that these events and Cyprian's response to them were instrumental in his developing of a situation where presbyters acted as local eucharistic ministers under the authority of the bishop, who had wider responsibilities—thereby establishing the monepiscopate and a clerical hierarchy.

Cyprian wrote treatises about the issues of his day, including *On the Unity of the Church*. Perhaps more important, however, are his letters, from which a detailed account of his struggles can be reconstructed. In his writings we find clear statements about priesthood: the priesthood is invested in the bishop, but presbyters share in the "priestly honor" of the bishop (*Epistle* 1.1, 61.3).

Epistle 63 is a key text for understanding what this means. Here Cyprian affirms that "the Lord's passion is the sacrifice we offer." This is prefigured in

Melchizedek's offering of bread and wine in Gen 14:18; it is "postfigured" in the Eucharist, where the priest "images" Christ:

> For if Christ Jesus our Lord and God himself is the High Priest of God the Father and first offered himself as a sacrifice to the Father, and commanded that this take place in his memory, that priest indeed truly functions in the place of Christ who imitates that which Christ did, and consequently offers a true and complete sacrifice in the Church to God the Father. (*Epistle* 63.14)

Because this imitation of Christ is occasionally described in rather literal terms, as if the priest were slaughtering the Lamb of God on the altar, this statement has often been interpreted in a rather literalistic way—that is, that only a man can "image" the man Christ. But typology, like metaphor and simile, is not meant to be taken literally, as if every point of comparison were valid. Martyrs, both women and men, were regarded as "types" of Christ as they suffered with him. No one quite meant that the Eucharist was a kind of "passion play." But Cyprian certainly implies that the terminology of priesthood is to be associated with eucharistic presidency.

My argument in this chapter has been that Cyprian's view was not only a novel view, but also one that remained somewhat marginal among the early Church Fathers. Old Testament typology, rather than Christology, was dominant in the postapostolic church's justification of the use of priestly language for ministerial functions.

BIBLIOGRAPHY

Primary Materials in English Translation

Clementines and *Apostolic Constitutions*, in *Ante-Nicene Christian Library: Translations of the Writings of the Fathers Down to A.D. 325*. Vol. 17. Edited by A. Roberts and J. Donaldson. Edinburgh: T&T Clark, 1870. Reprinted in *Ante-Nicene Fathers*. Vols. 7 and 8. Peabody, Mass.: Hendrickson, 1994.

Correspondence of St. Cyprian. 4 vols. Edited by G. W. Clarke. New York: Newman, 1984–1989.

Cyril of Jerusalem and *Gregory Nazianzen*. Vol. 7 of *The Nicene and Post-Nicene Fathers*, 2d series. Edited by P. Schaff and H. Wace. Peabody, Mass.: Hendrickson, 1994.

Early Christian Writings: The Apostolic Fathers. Translated by M. Staniforth and A. Louth. Rev. ed. Baltimore: Penguin Books, 1987.

Eusebius. *The History of the Church from Christ to Constantine*. Translated by G. A. Williamson. Baltimore: Penguin, 1965.

Secondary Literature

Burtchaell, James T. *From Synagogue to Church: Public Services and Offices in the Earliest Christian Communities*. Cambridge: Cambridge University Press, 1992.

Hanson, Richard. *Christian Priesthood Examined.* Guildford: Lutterworth, 1979.

Malherbe, Abraham J. *Social Aspects of Early Christianity.* 2d ed. Philadelphia: Fortress, 1983.

Martin, Dale B. *Slavery as Salvation: The Metaphor of Slavery in Pauline Christianity.* New Haven, Conn.: Yale University Press, 1990.

Thurston, Bonnie Bowman. *The Widows: A Women's Ministry in the Early Church.* Minneapolis: Fortress, 1989.

Torjesen, Karen Jo. *When Women Were Priests: Women's Leadership in the Early Church and the Scandal of Their Subordination in the Rise of Christianity.* San Francisco: HarperCollins, 1993.

Young, Frances. "The *Apostolic Constitutions:* A Methodological Case-Study." Pages 105–18 in *Studia Patristica,* vol. 36. Papers presented at the Thirteenth International Conference on Patristic Studies held in Oxford 1999. Edited by M. F. Wiles and E. J. Yarnold with the assistance of P. M. Parvis. Leuven: Peeters, 2001.

———. "On *Episkopos* and *Presbyteros.*" *Journal of Theological Studies* 45 (1994): 142–48.

———. *Presbyteral Ministry in the Catholic Tradition, or "Why Shouldn't Women be Priests?"* London: Methodist Sacramental Fellowship, 1994.

———. *The Theology of the Pastoral Letters.* Cambridge: Cambridge University Press, 1994.

———. *The Use of Sacrificial Ideas in Greek Christian Writers from the New Testament to John Chrysostom.* Philadelphia: Philadelphia Patristic Foundation, 1979.

Part IV

The Church Today

Chapter 10

The "Self-Organizing" Power of the Gospel: Episcopacy and Community Formation

John Webster

In one of the most potent and celebrated Anglican books on ecclesiology of the past century, A. Michael Ramsey set himself the following task: "to study the Church's order not in institutionalist terms but in terms of the Gospel, and to ask . . . whether Episcopacy tells us of some aspect of the Gospel which would lack expression if Episcopacy were to be abandoned" (*The Gospel and the Catholic Church*, vi). Though its conclusions are rather different from those that Ramsey reached, this chapter addresses itself to the same question: "What truth about the Gospel of God does the Episcopate, by its place in the one Body, declare?" (ibid., 8). My concern is to outline an evangelical theology of episcopacy.

The word "evangelical" is not used here as a term of discrimination—as, for example, over against "catholic"—but in a more primary sense. An evangelical theology is one that is evoked, governed, and judged by the gospel. In this sense, evangelical is simply equivalent to "Christian"—for all Christian theology, whatever its tradition, is properly speaking evangelical in that it is determined by and responsible to the good news of Jesus Christ. We might, of course, equally say that all Christian theology is catholic in that it seeks reflectively to trace the universal scope of the truth of the gospel. Here, however, my particular concern is to indicate how episcopal ministry can be considered an ordered, institutional implication of the gospel.

The argument proceeds, first, by articulating the relation of gospel and church, then, second, by outlining an evangelical account of ministerial order, before finally moving to an evangelical theology of episcopacy itself. The case is made by dogmatic description, not by historical defense. That is, the argument is not that—in the charmingly deceptive phrase beloved of Anglican apologists—"from the earliest times" the order of the church has been normatively mono-episcopal and that the structure and content of the office has exhibited a high degree of stability. It hasn't. Rather, the argument here is simply that a ministry of oversight is a necessary implication of the church's confession of the gospel.

1. GOSPEL, EPISCOPACY, AND THEOLOGY

A case for episcopal order in the church must be evangelical, simply because, as Edward Schillebeeckx has said, it is "by the heart of the gospel message
that any ecclesiology . . . can and must be measured" (*Church,* xiii). The task of
giving an account of episcopal order, therefore, falls within the realm of dogmatics. Dogmatics aims at the conceptual clarification of the Christian gospel that is
set forth in Holy Scripture and confessed in the life and practices of the church.
The task of an evangelical dogmatics of church order is to inquire into the entail-
ments of the gospel for the structure of the church as a political society. And in
the matter of episcopacy, such a dogmatics inquires into whether episcopal order
is (minimally) fitting or (maximally) necessary to the life of a community at
whose center lies the gospel of Jesus Christ.

The Need to Trace the Connection between Gospel and Order

An approach from this direction is required for at least two reasons. First, it
is vital to trace the connection between gospel and order if we are not to fall prey
to individualism or anticlericalism, which have affected a great deal of modern
Protestant theology and the historiography of ministry. The protests of the Protestant reformers against inflated claims for the mediating power of the church
and its orders of ministry have often been translated into assertions of the primacy of private (or, perhaps, congregational) judgment and the merely secondary character of community order in relation to the fundamental reality of
unmediated encounter with God in Christian experience.

The polemical use made by some Lutheran biblical and theological scholars
of the construct "early catholicism," which has been seen as a negative contrast to
the normative "charismatic" Pauline message, is merely one case in point. Such a
stance has sought to radicalize the contrast between the gospel, which is typically
construed as an eschatological word of deliverance and justification, and church
order, which is often construed as the routinization of the charisma—or, in other
words, of Paul versus Ignatius. This kind of contrast cannot be overcome by historical considerations alone—by pointing, for example, to the existence of some
kind of primitive catholic order in the Jerusalem church—because in the last re-
sort the contrast is parasitic on a normative claim that "charismatic" Pauline
Christianity *is* authentic Christianity. Rather, the contrast can be challenged only
by drawing attention to the gospel itself and seeking to indicate that order is an
ingredient within the gospel's logic.

Second, a dogmatic approach is also required if we are to disentangle discussion of episcopacy from the historical apologetics in which a good deal of
Anglican theology of episcopacy has become entangled. This entanglement
has been closely tied to the construal of the church's apostolicity through
ideas of "inheritance"—or, worse yet, of "pedigree." The difficulty into which
apologetics of this kind falls is not simply that of the near impossibility of the
task of furnishing incontrovertible historical warrants. Much more is it that the

search for origins is always driven by interests, so that doctrinal judgments masquerade as historical observations. Moreover, the pressure of historical apologetics has frequently skewed the content of a theological portrayal of episcopal office, turning it into something amenable to historical demonstration. Thereby, crucial theological considerations—in particular, the relation of episcopal office to the ministry of all the baptized and, most of all, to the continuing activity of the risen and ascended Christ through the Spirit—are pushed to the margins.

In such a scenario, episcopacy first migrates to apologetics and polemics; then, detached from dogmatics, apologetics and polemics rather easily strike up alliances with ideology—thereby furnishing retrospective warrants for the adequacy of existing institutional arrangements and grounds for denying adequacy to other arrangements that fail to conform, which is a point that even the most generous of the dominant conventions of Anglican ecumenical theology have been reluctant to register. The corrective, once again, is to develop an evangelical dogmatics of the order of the church—or, as Ramsey has aptly put it, "our view of the ministry had better be evangelical than archaeological" (*The Gospel and the Catholic Church*, 69).

The Critical Function of a Dogmatic Theology of Ministry

In this connection, it is important to lay some emphasis on the *critical* function of a dogmatic theology of ministry. It is not the task of dogmatics to underwrite the practices of the church, but to submit them to judgment. Dogmatics does so, of course, as part of the church, and the criterion by which it makes its judgment is none other than that under which the church as a whole has already been placed by its confession—that is, the gospel announced in Holy Scripture. But because it is in this way evangelical, dogmatics is also inescapably critical.

In the case of an evangelical dogmatics of church order, this may mean, for example, a quite sharp distinction between episcopacy as a given norm for the church's ministry and any particular contingent ordering of the episcopal office in a given context. But the church's capacity to draw such distinctions and to evaluate its practices critically depends, at least in part, on the existence of the instruments of reflection that dogmatics seeks to furnish. In short, it must be said that because dogmatics is evangelical, it is critical and reformatory.

2. GOSPEL AND CHURCH

Discussion of the relation of gospel and church must come before any discussion of ministerial order, because, as Paul Avis put it in a remark about Luther, "the Church precedes the ministry in the logic of grace" (*The Church in the Theology of the Reformers*, 111). What, then, is the place of the church in the structure of the gospel?

The Church as an Ingredient within the Divine Economy of Salvation

We might put the matter thus: The church is an ingredient within the divine economy of salvation, which is the mystery of God made manifest in Jesus Christ and now operative in the power of his Spirit. The revealed secret of God not only has to do with the unfathomable majesty of God himself; it also concerns that human society that the triune God elects, sustains, and perfects "to the praise of his glorious grace" (Eph 1:5). From this there emerge two fundamental principles for an evangelical ecclesiology. First, that there can be no doctrine of God without a doctrine of the church, for, according to the Christian confession, God *is* the one who manifests who he is in the economy of his saving work in which he assembles a people for himself. Second, that there can be no doctrine of the church that is not wholly referred to the doctrine of God, in whose being and action alone the church has its being and action.

Accordingly, we need to draw a fundamental distinction between the being and act of God and the being and act of the church. This is done in order to secure the vital consideration that the church is not constituted by human intentions or activities, on the one hand, or by institutional or structural forms, on the other, but by the action of the triune God, realized in Son and Spirit. As Edmund Schlink expressed it: "The Church is, because Jesus Christ, the Crucified and Risen One, acts upon her ever anew. . . . She was not before this action; and she is not for an instant without this action" ("Christ and the Church," 116).

This is what is meant by speaking, in company with the Protestant Reformers, of the church as "the creature of the Word"—that is, that the church is that human assembly generated and kept in life by the continuing, outgoing self-presentation ("word") of Jesus Christ. To quote Christoph Schwöbel in his attempt to recover the ecclesiology of the Reformers: "As the creature of the divine Word the Church is constituted by divine action. And the way in which the Church is constituted by divine action determines the character and scope of human action in the Church" ("The Creature of the Word," 122).

An evangelical ecclesiology, therefore, will have a particular concern to emphasize the asymmetry of divine and human action—that is, that God's work and the work of the church are fundamentally to be distinguished. They are, however, to be distinguished not in order to bifurcate them, which would undermine the fact that the church is indeed an ingredient within the economy of God's saving purpose, but in order to accord priority to the gracious action of God through which the church's action is ordered to its proper end in conformity with the will of God. The *distinction,* in other words, is for the purpose of recognizing a *right relationship.*

They are also to be distinguished in order to specify with the right kind of theological determinacy the respective characters of divine action and human, churchly action. Divine action is sheerly creative, uncaused, spontaneous, saving, and effectual, whereas human, churchly action is derivative, contingent, and indicative. All churchly action—whether cultic, moral, or diaconal—is thus characterized by "creative passivity," an orientation toward that perfect work that has been done and continues to be done for the church and to the church (cf. Jüngel, "Der Gottesdienst als Fest der Freiheit"). That orientation, of course, is what is meant by faith.

The Visibility of the Church

There is doubtless a danger of "spiritualizing" the church with such affirmations. It is clearly important that an emphasis on the priority of divine action over the church as an act of human association not be allowed to eclipse the "visibility" of the church. The polemical portrayal of Protestant religion as bare subjectivism without objective social form or endurance is doubtless a caricature. But it nevertheless identifies a potentially disruptive element in the dogmatics we have just outlined. Can a society that is in essence "invisible" ever be really human—that is, historical, material, or bodily?

In an evangelical ecclesiology, rhetorical and theological affirmations about the invisibility of the church must certainly be made. Indeed, their absence from one's doctrine of the church may be symptomatic of other disorders—such as a lavishly overrealized eschatology, or a suppression of the distinction between the gospel and its human representations, or an atrophied sense of the church's fallibility, or, perhaps above all, a routinization of the operations of the Spirit. Properly defined, the concept of the invisibility of the church is a standing denial of any easy identification of divine and human work. For talk of the church's invisibility secures the all-important point that, as Schwöbel expresses it: "Only as *creatura verbi divini* [creature of the divine word] is the Church an object of faith, because God's action in establishing and disclosing the true relationship between the creator and his creation that makes faith possible can be confessed as the content of faith" ("The Creature of the Word," 131).

Yet when this necessary statement of the church's invisibility takes over and is allowed to become the only constitutive moment for ecclesiology, other problems quickly emerge. Chief among these problems is that a picture of the church is promoted in which the human Christian community is unstable, liminal, and so incapable of sustaining a coherent historical and social trajectory. But the community that is constituted by the gospel is an ordered society. The church, in fact, is the event of the reconstitution of human fellowship by the saving acts of God that the gospel rehearses.

The "spirituality" of the church and the "visibility" or "order" of the church are not different entities—the latter, perhaps, clothing the former, but bearing no essential or intrinsic relation to it. Order does not constitute the church apart from the vivifying and sanctifying grace of the Spirit. Rather, the life and holiness that the Spirit bestows is ordered because that new life and holiness are expressed in forms that are human, social, and continuous. The danger of collapsing the Spirit into a human structure ought not to frighten us into the equally dangerous stance of a purely punctiliar or actualistic ecclesiology.

Church order is the social shape of the converting power and activity of Christ, which is present as Spirit. This is not to claim that the Spirit can be formalized or reduced to a calculable and manipulable element in what is envisaged as an immanent social process. It is simply to say, as does Miroslav Volf: "Without institutions, the church cannot become 'event.' This principle is correct, however, only if it is also reversible; unless the church becomes an event, it cannot be the kind of institution it is supposed to be" (*After Our Likeness*, 241).

3. GOSPEL AND MINISTRY

We may sum up the preceding two sections with some words from the Heidelberg Catechism, where in answer to the question "What do you believe concerning 'the Holy Catholic Church'?" the reply is:

> I believe that from the beginning to the end of the world, and from among the whole human race, the Son of God, by his Spirit and his Word, gathers, protects and preserves for himself, in the unity of the true faith, a congregation chosen for eternal life.

From this, we may formulate a dogmatic rule for ecclesiology: that an adequate doctrine of the church will maximize Christology and pneumatology, for it is Jesus Christ through Word and Spirit who "gathers, protects and preserves"; and will relativize—but not minimize or abolish—ecclesial action and its ordered forms. The question that arises, however, is: How does this ecclesial rule shape an evangelical theology of ministry?

Christ and the Spirit vis-à-vis Ecclesial Actions and Forms

At the heart of an evangelical theology is the axiom: Jesus Christ is himself the minister of the church; he is himself prophet, priest, and king; and so the ministry of revelation, reconciliation, and rule by which the church is brought into being, restored to fellowship with God, and kept under God's governance is the action of Christ himself, the risen and ascended one who is now present and active, outgoing and communicative.

Taking this point with full seriousness will entail wresting ourselves free from the notion, which has very deeply affected much of contemporary ecclesiology and theology of ministry, that at his ascension Jesus Christ resigned, as it were, his office in favor of human ministers, and that henceforth the church is the real center of ministerial agency. Without an operative theology of the present action and speech of Jesus Christ—which means, also, without an operative pneumatology—human acts of ministry threaten to assume Christ's role. The danger is present with special acuteness in those theologies of episcopal ministry that interpret the apostolicity of the church's ministry in terms of succession. Such accounts characteristically restrict the christological dimension of ministry to a dominical mandate given in the past. Furthermore, they run the risk of converting the pneumatological dimension of ministry into a mystagogical power transmitted through historical sequence. The christological inadequacy here is, very simply, an inoperative theology of the resurrection and the present activity of the glorified Christ. And the pneumatological inadequacy is that of construing the gifts of the Spirit as manipulable possessions rather than as events of relation.

By contrast, an evangelical theology of ministry will be, as Jürgen Moltmann has insisted, an "account of the history of Christ's acts" (*The Church in the Power of the Spirit*, 69). Because of this, the critical questions concern the relation of Christ's acts to the ministerial activities of the church. Here a number of lines intersect.

First, the ministerial acts of Jesus Christ in the Spirit, by which he gathers, protects, and preserves the church, are, properly speaking, incommunicable and nonrepresentable. That is to say, if by "communication" or "representation" we mean the assumption of Christ's proper work by agents other than himself, we may not make use of such concepts in a christologically and pneumatologically structured theology of ministry. The dogmatic premise of an evangelical ecclesiology—that as the risen and ascended Lord, Jesus Christ is present and active—does not permit any such transference of agency. Christ distributes his own benefits through his Spirit, that is, by his own hand. They are not to be thought of as some treasure turned over to the church for it to dispense. Whatever else we may wish to say about the mediating acts of the church's ministry, the barrier between Christ and the church must not be breached. It is at this point that the principle of *solus Christus,* or "Christ alone," finds its ecclesiological application.

It would, however, be illegitimate to use *solus Christus* in a way that disqualifies the real, though limited, ministerial activity to which the church is appointed by Christ as the vessel of his own ministry. For though the acts of Christ are incommunicable and nonrepresentable, Christ himself freely chooses to represent himself through human ministry. He does so sovereignly, graciously, and freely—that is, he does so as Lord. He is not delivered into the hands of his servants, who remain entirely at his disposal. But in his lordly freedom, he elects that alongside his triumphant self-manifestation there should also be human service in the church.

In an especially fine and discriminating discussion, John Calvin has succinctly put the matter as follows:

> He alone should rule and reign in the church as well as have authority or preeminence in it, and this authority should be exercised and administered by his Word alone. Nevertheless, because he does not dwell among us in visible presence [Matt 26:11], we have said that he uses the ministry of men to declare openly his will to us by mouth, as a sort of delegated work, not by transferring to them his right and honor, but only that through their mouths he may do his own work—just as a workman uses a tool to do his work.... "Christ ascended on high," Paul says, "that he might fill all things" [Eph 4:10]. This is the manner of fulfillment: through the ministers to whom he has entrusted this office and has conferred the grace to carry it out, he dispenses and distributes his gifts to the church; and he shows himself as though present by manifesting the power of his Spirit in this his institution, that it be not vain or idle. (*Institutes* 4.3.1, 2)

The Church's Subordinate Ministry

How, then, is this subordination of the church's ministry to be expressed? Thomas Torrance, a modern Reformed theologian, emphasizes that the church's ministerial acts are to be understood as *hypodeigma*—that is, as "patterns" or, perhaps, "tokens"—but not as *mimēsis*—that is, an "imitation"—of Christ's own perfect work (*Royal Priesthood*, 97). What is secured by this or similar distinctions is the *indirectness* of the relation between Christ's ministry and that of the church. Indirectness is not a denial of the real participation of the church in Christ, for, to quote again Torrance, "through the Spirit there is a direct relation of participation, but in the form of order the relation is indirect. The priesthood of the Church is not a transcription in the conditions of this passing age of the heavenly Priesthood of Christ" (ibid.). The real instrumentality of the church, therefore, is neither self-generated nor self-sustaining, for both its origin and its *telos* lie wholly beyond itself. So the ministerial action of the church is not in any fundamental sense "causative." Rather, it is appointed and empowered to present Christ's accomplishment, which lies entirely outside its own sphere of competence and responsibility.

Two things follow from this. First, ministerial activity shares in the asymmetrical character of the relation of Christ and the church. If an evangelical dogmatics of the church refuses to see the Christian community as coconstituted by Christ and the community as equal partners, an evangelical dogmatics of ministry similarly refuses to see the church's ministry as a coordination or cooperation between divine and human agents. Whatever else we mean by "fellow-workers of God," that we cannot mean.

Second, and more importantly, however, positing a limit to the action of the church's ministry by reference to the principle of "Christ alone" determines the task or content of the church's ministry. Ministry in the church "points beyond itself" (Torrance, *Royal Priesthood*, 97) to the action of another. Jesus Christ is not inert, but present with force, being active as prophet, priest, and king. The task of ministry, therefore, is not to complete that which he has done, or to accomplish that which Christ himself does not now do, but rather to indicate or attest his work both past and present. That to which the ministerial action of the church is ordered is the "showing" of Jesus Christ's self-proclamation in word, baptism and the Lord's supper. As such, as Oliver O'Donovan has highlighted, Christian ministry is "a *responsive* movement to the dynamic force of the Word of God" (*On the Thirty-Nine Articles*, 120).

The ecclesiological principle here is that the community is defined by its own Christological confession—that is, by dispositions and activities that give expression to the fact that the center of the church is not within itself but outside itself, being constituted, as it is, by the free event of Christ's self-bestowal in the Holy Spirit. The ministerial principle is that because the basic event of the life of the church is the event of Jesus Christ's self-communication, the task of ministry "is simply to serve this happening" (Barth, *Church Dogmatics* 4/3:833). Ministry is thus *ostensive*—that is, a work of testifying. Ministries in the church, as Ingolf

Dalferth points out, "exist not as visible signs or representations of the ministry of Jesus Christ, but as *ministeria verbi divini* ['ministries of the divine word'], that is to say, as *offices of service* of the actions in which and through which the ministry of Jesus Christ is accomplished" ("Ministry and the Office of Bishop," 42).

4. GOSPEL AND EPISCOPACY

We now reach, at an appropriately late stage in the present discussion, the question of episcopal ministry. The church is a political society—that is to say, it is a sphere of human fellowship, though one created not by natural affinity or association but by the gathering power of the gospel. And the church is commissioned to the task of bearing witness to the gospel—that is, of indicating in proclamation, sacrament, and service that "Jesus Christ . . . is the one Word of God which we have to hear, and which we have to trust and obey in life and in death" (Barmen Declaration). The ministry of the church, therefore, is an *ordered* ministry.

Episcopacy, or the Ministry of Oversight

Because the church is a visible and enduring arena of common life and action, authorized to indicate the gospel, "official" patterns of ministry are required. "Office" does not usurp the work of Christ or the Spirit. Nor does it take the place of the work of the whole church in witnessing to that work. Rather, it has the task of overseeing the unity and authenticity of the testimony of the church, and so of being caught up into Christ's own formation of his community.

In this sense *episkopē*, or "oversight," is the basic ministry of the church. Anterior to a functional differentiation of office (whether in the so-called three-fold office or in some other pattern) is the primary task of office to envisage, safeguard, and unify the church's fulfillment of its gospel mandate. This ministry, as Rowan Williams defines it, "is, under God, what draws together the community of faith and equips it to continue the mission and ministry of Christ in the world," and so is a ministry that "keeps alive the question of the community's integrity, by challenging its practice in the name of the gospel" ("Women and the Ministry," 13–14). What orthodoxy is in the realm of reflection, *episkopē* is in the realm of practice and order: an instrument through which the church is recalled to Christianness, that is, to the appropriateness of its action and speech to the truth of the gospel. Episcopal ministry "is that ministry whose special province is both to gather the believing community around the center which it proclaims, the preaching of the resurrection, and *in* that gathering, to make sure that this community is critically aware of itself" (ibid., 15). The gospel requires this simply because Jesus Christ elects to manifest himself to the world not without a visible human, historical society with a specific calling. And so the task of an ordered ministry of oversight is, very simply, "to minister to the Church's very identity" (ibid.). The issue, therefore, is not whether we can do without *episkopē*, but whether, as Karl Barth has expressed it, oversight can be exercised in a way that is sufficiently "loose" that "all encroachment on the lordship of the One who is alone the Lord is either avoided or so suppressed and eliminated in practice that there is place for His rule" (*Church Dogmatics* 4/1:723).

The Shape of Episcopal Ministry

What shape of episcopal ministry will best serve this "giving place" to the rule of Christ in the visible community of the gospel? This is a question that must be dealt with first of all from the perspective of Christian theology's Christological basis. For there is properly only one "overseer" of the church, Jesus Christ, "the bishop of our souls" (1 Pet 2:25).

To start from this point is immediately to make episcopacy contingent and relative to the headship of Christ. This, indeed, is part of the force of Calvin's rejection of any primatial understanding of episcopacy in his insistence that the church has no human head, that Christ does not transfer his headship to another, and so that there can be no single human primate:

> [The church] has Christ as its sole Head, under whose sway all of us cleave to one another. . . . Christ is the head, "from whom the whole body, joined and knit through every bond of mutual ministry (insofar as each member functions) achieves its growth" [Eph 4:15–16]. Do you see how he includes all mortals without exception in the body, but leaves the honor and name of the head to Christ alone? (*Institutes* 4.6.9).

Or as Calvin puts it in commenting on Cyprian, "he makes the universal bishopric Christ's alone" (ibid., 4.6.17). Such an extension of the doctrine of "Christ alone" is a significant counter to those theologies of episcopacy that expound the office of bishop as the sign or epiphany of Christ in the church.

One prominent example of a theologian who sets out the office of bishop as the sign or epiphany of Christ in the church is Rowan Williams, who depicts the church as a whole as a "showing" of that which lies at its heart: " 'Showing' is an effective, catalytic and transforming event, which draws new boundaries. . . . And to belong to the Christian community is to accept the paschal symbol as decisive" ("Authority and the Bishop," 95). As eucharistic president, Williams goes on to argue, the bishop is "the focal point around which the community gathers, overcoming its divisions, to affirm a single identity governed by the paschal symbol in its eucharistic shape" (ibid., 96). Such a depiction owes much to Eastern Orthodox theology (see Zizioulas, "The Eucharistic Community"; idem, "The Bishop") as well as to Ramsey's *The Gospel and the Catholic Church* (see esp. Williams, "Theology and the Churches"). If it fails to persuade, that is because it risks softening the distinction between Christ's self-presentation and the testifying acts of ordered ministry.

Williams, of course, insists that "no particular act of showing is of the same creative order as the paschal event itself, so that no act of showing has meaning independently of the generative event and the life of the community as a whole" ("Authority and the Bishop in the Church," 97). But even such a refusal to acknowledge the bishop as mystagogue does not secure the incommunicability—that is, the nontransferable status—of Christ's headship, which is primary for an evangelical account of ministerial order. We must, therefore, assert that the bishop is not an "effectual sign," for, as Torrance has aptly pointed out, "to make the bishop an 'effectual sign' of the unity and continuity of the Church and thus to give him independent significance in the role of a mediator . . . is to make the episcopate usurp the office of the One Mediator and to give it precedence over the Church which is His Body" (*Royal Priesthood,* 108).

The Function of the Episcopate

In its relationship to Christ, who alone is the church's prophet, priest, and king, episcopal order functions to "oversee" the Christian community. The episcopate is that official, ordered place within the life of the church as a whole where the church's oneness and genuineness are most directly addressed. But this takes place only where the episcopal office is understood to be indicatory or ostensive, and not epiphanic. The episcopate may serve unity and the continuation of apostolic authenticity, but it cannot secure those matters by its own existence. If it were able to do so as *alter Christus,* or "another Christ," then Christ would be pushed into inactive transcendence, and the Spirit would be reduced to simply the immanent animating power of an institution.

This means, consequently, that the unity of the church is not generated or kept by the episcopate. Unity is pure gift. It is brought about by Christ himself. For, as Edmund Schlink points out, "the unity of the Church is not primarily the unity of her members, but the unity of Christ who acts upon them all, in all places and at all times" ("Christ and the Church," 105). So we must say, with Ingolf Dalferth, that "the ministry of the church can neither create nor represent this unity, but only make it visible in that it points unmistakably away from itself and toward that which it serves—the present action of Christ in the proclamation of the Gospel through word and sacrament" ("Ministry and the Office of Bishop," 37).

Unity is evangelical. And it is to that unity, as established and formed by the gospel, that the ministry of episcopal oversight directs its own attention and the attention of the whole church. The office of bishop is not constitutive of the unity of the church. If it were, the church would indeed be "episcopocentric." But then the sole headship of the one Lord Jesus Christ would, to some degree, be compromised. Nor does the office of bishop symbolize the unity of the church—at least if by "symbolize" we mean "realize" or "actualize."

Furthermore, the office of bishop does not represent the unity of the church. Rather, the office *indicates* the unity of the church, testifying in a public manner to the oneness of the people of God as it is set out in the gospel. Episcopal office is thus a focused, public, and institutional place through which attention can be turned to the unity of the people of God through the Spirit, baptism, and confession. As such, episcopal office serves the unity of the church as it takes form in the congregation of the redeemed people of God—that is, those who are one body with one Spirit and who confess one hope, one Lord, one faith, one baptism, and one God and Father of all (Eph 4:4–6).

The episcopal office undertakes this function in a variety of ways. But it most centrally accomplishes it through teaching, presiding at the sacraments, commissioning an ordered ministry, and exercising discipline. The point can be illustrated by reference to the bishop as a teacher. For the teaching task of the bishop consists in the proclamation and safeguarding of the truth of the gospel. Accordingly, this involves—positively—the celebration of the sheerly authoritative goodness of the good news that the church is appointed to declare. It also involves—negatively—the defense of the gospel, particularly its defense from arbitrary, selective, or partial exposition. As teacher, however, the bishop is not to be considered as being in possession of something other than the truth of the gospel, which is to be set before the whole congregation. So it is the task of the office simply to encourage and defend by functioning as an exemplary instance of submission to the gospel's claim.

Ignatius in his *Letter to the Ephesians* was not reluctant to take the episcopal office quite seriously: "We should look upon the bishop as we would look upon the Lord himself" (*Ephesians* 6). Yet behind this statement is an important movement of deference: "I do not issue orders to you as if I were a great person," he says (ibid., 3). At the core of Ignatius's understanding of episcopal ministry is a renunciation—a following of the declared will of God, which is the true content of Christian teaching: "I have . . . taken upon me first to exhort you that you would all run together in accordance with the will of God. For even Christ, our inseparable life, is the manifested will of the Father, as also bishops . . . are so by the will of Jesus Christ" (ibid., 3). The bishop's authorization as teacher, in other words, is inseparable from submission to Jesus Christ, "the manifested will" of God. If, then, it is the task of the bishop to "form" the community, it is only by virtue of the fact that both bishop and community have already been formed by the divine self-manifestation of God in Christ and Spirit. As overseer, therefore, a bishop's task is to promote "unanimous obedience" to the one faith (ibid., 2).

Unity and Apostolicity

This function of the ministry of oversight with respect to the unity of the church is closely related to the church's apostolicity. Apostolicity, however, has less to do with transmission and much more to do with identity or authenticity—that is, with the "Christianness" of the church's teaching and mission. By its very nature, such authenticity cannot be "transmitted," because it is not capable of being embodied without residue in ordered forms. Forms cannot guarantee authenticity, simply because forms are themselves not immune to the critical question of their own authenticity.

Episcopal office is not a condensed form of apostolicity or a means of securing the apostolic character of the whole church. Rather, episcopal office oversees the life of the apostolic community as a whole, presides over the event in which the church becomes apostolic by consenting to the apostolic gospel of the resurrection, and gives itself to the apostolic mission of proclamation and service. In particular, because apostolicity is so closely tied to mission, the episcopate's ministry of oversight cannot properly be merely an internal oversight, but must always be directing the church's life toward an external orientation. For, as Karl Barth has rightly insisted, "As an apostolic Church the Church can never in any respect be an end in itself, but, following the existence of the apostles, it exists only as it exercises the ministry of a herald" (*Church Dogmatics* 4/1:724). If, therefore, the ministry of oversight is apostolic, it can only be so because it acts in relation to an externally oriented mission. Episcopal order without an externally oriented mission is simply not the order of the church—that is, the order of the community that is simultaneously gathered around and impelled outward by the uncontrollable compulsion of the Spirit of Christ. It is but mere form.

The episcopal office of oversight, therefore, is best understood as a function of the unity and apostolic character that the church has by virtue of its election, its gathering and sanctification, and its empowerment to know and to speak the gospel. Episcopacy does not secure the life of the church, but is an office of deference to the life-giving power of Christ. Episcopal office forms the church insofar as episcopacy itself is formed by the one bishop of the church, Jesus Christ. And episcopal office forms the church insofar as it testifies to the shaping power of the same Jesus Christ.

The Ordering of the Episcopal Office

How is the episcopal office, so conceived, to be ordered? Two basic principles are to be held together. First, there is a necessary distinction to be drawn between the *episkopē*, or ministry of oversight generally, and particular, contingent orderings of the episcopal office. I have suggested that oversight is a necessary implication of the gospel, through which the church is brought into being and which it is commissioned to proclaim. But this is quite other than, for example, a defense of a threefold order of ministry headed by a regional episcopate or of a "historic episcopate"—whether maintained by a laying on of hands or by the succession of a teaching office. Nor does it necessarily entail a synodical or congregational episcopate. Such orderings are *adiaphora*—that is, matters of relative indifference.

To say that the exact ordering of the episcopal office is a matter of relative indifference, however, is not to claim that the way in which oversight is ordered is purely arbitrary or driven by the exigencies and limitations of a particular historical or cultural context. If part of the function of the episcopate is to indicate the church's unity and apostolicity, and therefore its catholicity, its offices cannot be simply reinvented at will. Rather, freedom is given to the church to order its life *appropriately* in the light of its evangelical calling and mandate. Such freedom is not the freedom to invent, but it is freedom to structure responsibly the life of the church in view of the fact that "Christian believers *find themselves ordered* in a certain form of society precisely by the message which they believe and are charged to proclaim. And the decisive character of their order . . . is that it maintains the teaching of the truth of the gospel" (O'Donovan, *On the Thirty-Nine Articles*, 118).

Hence the second principle when asking about how the episcopate is to be ordered: the particular shape assumed by the episcopal office must be *fitting* to the church's identity, for episcopacy is the structural expression of what it means to be the church living out of and testifying to the converting energy of the gospel.

5. CONCLUSION

In the words of P. T. Forsyth, "episcopal order is indicative of the 'self-organizing' power of the gospel" (*Lectures on the Church*, 42). A dogmatic case for episcopal ministry such as we have offered here does not leave the exercise of the episcopal office undisturbed, for evangelical dogmatics is an aspect of the church's self-interrogation. An evangelical dogmatics of episcopacy, because it sets the office and its exercise in the light of the christological, pneumatological, and ecclesiological principles of the gospel, is quite far from those serene Anglican accounts of the history and practice of episcopal ministry in which the emergence of the monarchical episcopate is shown to be an entirely natural and unproblematic development from the earliest Christian impulse.

The naïveté of such accounts is not merely their reliance on the apologetic power of historical reconstructions, but their incapacity to envisage the history of episcopacy as political and ideological (cf. Roberts, "Lord, Bondsman and Churchman"). The church makes a move against the threats of ideology in this sphere, as in any other, by simply being the church—that is, by being attentive to word and sacrament, docile before the gospel, and, above all, prayerful for the coming of Christ and his Spirit. But theology, too, may have its part to play.

Sören Kierkegaard once famously remarked: "There is nothing so displeasing to God as official Christianity" (*Attack upon Christendom*, 210). If, on balance, he was more right than wrong, one way of heeding his lament is to make sure that the case for the episcopal office be made with the right kind of dogmatic precision and robustness.

BIBLIOGRAPHY

Avis, Paul D. L. *The Church in the Theology of the Reformers*. Atlanta: John Knox, 1980. Repr., London: Marshall, Morgan & Scott, 1981.

Barth, Karl. *Church Dogmatics* 4/1. Edinburgh: T&T Clark, 1956.

———. *Church Dogmatics* 4/3. Edinburgh: T&T Clark, 1961–1962.

Calvin, John. *Institutes of the Christian Religion*. Edited by J. T. McNeill. Philadephia: Westminster, 1960.

Dalferth, Ingolf U. "Ministry and the Office of Bishop according to Meissen and Porvoo." Pages 9–48 in *Visible Unity and the Ministry of Oversight*. London: Church House Publishing, 1997.

Forsyth, P. T. *Lectures on the Church and the Sacraments.* London: Longmans, Green, 1917.

Jüngel, Eberhard. "Der Gottesdienst als Fest der Freiheit." *Zeichen der Zeit* 38 (1984): 264–72.

Kierkegaard, Søren. *Attack upon Christendom.* Translated by Walter Lowrie. Princeton, N.J.: Princeton University Press, 1944.

Moltmann, Jürgen. *The Church in the Power of the Spirit: A Contribution to Messianic Ecclesiology.* Translated by M. Kohl. New York: Harper & Row, 1977.

O'Donovan, Oliver. *On the Thirty-Nine Articles.* Exeter: Paternoster, 1986.

Ramsey, A. Michael. *The Gospel and the Catholic Church.* London: Longmans, Green, 1936.

Roberts, R. H. "Lord, Bondsman and Churchman: Identity, Integrity and Power in Anglicanism." Pages 156–224 in *On Being the Church: Essays on the Christian Community.* Edited by C. E. Gunton and D. W. Hardy. Edinburgh: T&T Clark, 1989.

Schillebeeckx, Edward. *Church: The Human Story of God.* Translated by J. Bowden. New York: Crossroad, 1990.

Schlink, Edmund. "Christ and the Church." Pages 96–118 in *The Coming Christ and the Coming Church.* Edinburgh: Oliver & Boyd, 1967.

Schwöbel, Christoph. "The Creature of the Word: Recovering the Ecclesiology of the Reformers." Pages 110–55 in *On Being the Church: Essays on the Christian Community.* Edited by C. E. Gunton and D. W. Hardy. Edinburgh: T&T Clark, 1989.

Torrance, Thomas F. *Royal Priesthood: A Theology of Ordained Ministry.* Rev. ed. Edinburgh: T&T Clark, 1993.

Volf, Miroslav. *After Our Likeness: The Church as the Image of the Trinity.* Grand Rapids, Mich.: Eerdmans, 1998.

Williams, Rowan. "Authority and the Bishop in the Church." Pages 90–112 in *Their Lord and Ours.* Edited by M. Santer. London: SPCK, 1982.

———. "Theology in the Churches." Pages 9–28 in *Michael Ramsey as Theologian.* Edited by R. Gill and L. Kendall. London: Darton, Longman & Todd, 1995.

———. "Women and the Ministry." Pages 11–27 in *Feminine in the Church.* Edited by M. Furlong. London: SPCK, 1984.

Zizioulas, J. D. "The Bishop in the Theological Doctrine of the Orthodox Church." *Kanōn* 7 (1985): 23–35.

———. "The Eucharistic Community and the Catholicity of the Church." *One in Christ* 7 (1971): 314–47. Repr. pages 107–31 in *The New Man: An Orthodox and Reformed Dialogue.* Edited by John Meyendorff and Joseph McLelland. New Brunswick, N.J.: Agora, 1973.

Chapter 11

The Sanctified Life in the Body of Christ: A Presbyterian Form of Christian Community

David C. Hester

The context for a discussion of the Presbyterian form of Christian community is necessarily the affirmation of the Reformed tradition: *ecclesia reformata semper reformanda*—"the church reformed and always in need of being reformed." The church, in this reading, is at any time both being and becoming. Our beginning, historically, is with John Calvin and his doctrine of the church.

Calvin treats the doctrine of the church in the fourth book of *The Institutes*. His treatment of the church, however, is preceded by explications of the knowledge of God, the work of Christ, and the work of the Holy Spirit—and only after the nature and work of the Triune God has been explained through the interpretation of the Scriptures (which, in Calvin's view, is the only means to God's self revelation) does Calvin come to consider the nature and work of the church. Thus, since a biblically based understanding of God, Christ, and the Holy Spirit is necessary to a proper understanding of the church and its ministry, I will, in what follows, indicate how these doctrines inform a Presbyterian understanding of the church and the life of faith.

For Calvin, the form of the church's governance follows from the church's purpose and reason for being. In this chapter, therefore, I will attempt to show how the order of the Presbyterian Church is shaped by a Reformed ecclesiology—not only describing the "offices" and "ministries" (as Calvin called them) of the Presbyterian Church, but also pointing out the relationship of form to function. The hallmark of a Presbyterian form of government is "rule by representative elected elders" *(presbyteroi)*, who are organized in representative governing bodies in a connectional system of governance that links local churches in presbyteries, presbyteries in synods, and the whole church in a general assembly. It is a structure that reflects both Presbyterian theology, on the one hand, and historical tensions between church and state, on the other—which are factors I will also comment on throughout this chapter.

Finally, I conclude with an argument for the vitality and viability of the Presbyterian form of Christian community at this time in history and in light of complex challenges that must be faced both socially and globally today. The tension that Presbyterians work with is this: that a faithful identity is essential to the Presbyterian Church, yet the church must also be able to respond faithfully to new circumstances. The challenge for a Presbyterian form of church order and life—as, in fact, for every Christian communion—is to proclaim the gospel and practice governance for the sake of witness in ways that are, as James Sanders puts it in speaking of Israel's Torah, "adaptable for life."

1. REFORMATA SEMPER REFORMANDA: REFORMED AND ALWAYS IN NEED OF BEING REFORMED

Douglas Ottati, in his book *Reforming Protestantism: Christian Commitment in Today's World,* describes the present situation within Reformed churches as a tension between two competing impulses. One impulse is to conserve, to hold on tightly to the forms and traditions of the church, thereby seeking to preserve or recover the traditional identity of the Reformed church. Those responding to this impulse look to the church's historical faith, searching for the fundamentals of Reformed beliefs and practices in order to restore them to the contemporary church—which, they believe, has been led astray from its true identity by overassimilation and adaptation to modernism. The other impulse is to change, modernize, and reform the church—which, it is argued, requires responding to contemporary personal and communal needs and reflecting more accurately the character of a dramatically changed society and world. Those following a conserving impulse seek identity in the earliest church traditions. Those following a transformative impulse look to create a new identity for the church, one that is relevant to contemporary culture, in order to proclaim a gospel and live as Christians in ways that make sense of the modern world. While the conserving impulse draws the church away from worldly affairs, the transforming impulse asserts that the church's identity is necessarily linked to its being in the world.

Ottati claims that these two impulses in the church's life mirror a similar contemporary tug of war going on in society. In the United States, for example, this tension is evident in the significant shifts to the right in political thought and practice, which are countered on the left by the radical politics of such groups as the Libertine Party. In the political arena, and perhaps in the church, the stronger moves have been toward the right—that is, toward the conserving impulse. What both impulses have in common is that they represent reactions to complex changes taking place today within both nations and societies and to contemporary concerns of global economics and ecology.

Neither impulse is invalid under the circumstances. Each by itself, however, is an inadequate response to the complexities of change that confront both church and society today. On the one hand, followed to an extreme, the conserving impulse leads to a restrictive fundamentalism, which ultimately bifurcates tradition and social reality. On the other hand, the transformative impulse in its extreme threatens a loss of tradition and identity altogether—setting aside authority and embracing an extreme relativity with little common ground for decision making. Any adequate response to the challenging changes that are evident in modern life must honor both impulses: conserving the church's identity and the foundational traditions that inform it, and transforming the church's practices and reforming its identity through critical reflection on both the church's traditions and contemporary reality. For a reforming church, this means both an appreciation of and a critical reflection on Reformed theology and piety. Identity is crucial for the church if it is to minister effectively *as the church* in the world. At the same time, the church's engagement in the world must also be appreciative and critical, opening itself to learn from culture and society, yet committed to critical reflection in light of faith on cultural understandings.

As a Reformed and reforming communion, the Presbyterian Church today finds itself positioned in the midst of this conservatizing-transformative tension. The search for an identity that is relevant to the world in which the church lives and which the church serves is an urgent matter. Some seek recovery of our Presbyterian identity in a common theology and life of faith found by a conservative reading of Scripture and a strict adherence to the two documents of our church's constitution, *The Book of Confessions* and *The Book of Order.* Others, while affirming the authority of Scripture and the guiding direction of *The Book of Confessions* and *The Book of Order,* seek an identity for the church that celebrates the diversity of our traditions, highlights our freedom of conscience, and embraces the pluralism and diversity of the modern world. Both perspectives affirm that the mission of the Presbyterian Church is the proclamation of the gospel to the world and a life of witness to the saving work of God in Christ by living in the world as a visible sign of the reign of God.

As part of our Reformed tradition, Presbyterians embrace the affirmation *reformata semper reformanda*—that is, that we are *reformed* while always *in need of being reformed.* The grounds for this affirmation rest on the essential beliefs that the church belongs to God, that God may do with the church as God chooses, and that no form of the church is perfect and finished, because no form captures perfectly the intention of God or the holiness of God. The assumption that a reforming church must always exist within the tension of conserving traditions, on the one hand, and reinterpreting those traditions, on the other—so as both to retain and to transform the practices of faith in changing times and circumstances, in order that God's glory may be continually served—is itself a part of our Reformed tradition.

How Presbyterian tradition and governance function to respond faithfully to contemporary history is the burden of this chapter. A case to be made for a Presbyterian form of *ekklēsia* must always rest on the institutional church's adequacy to be the church and the institutional church's ability to carry out God's mandate for it in the midst of current forces and changes that challenge the church's identity and mission.

2. ENJOYING THE BENEFITS OF CHRIST

For Calvin, as well as for his Reformed and Presbyterian heirs today, several doctrinal convictions, particularly when taken together, imply the need for and work of the church.

The Sovereignty of God

At the heart of Reformed conviction stands the affirmation of the sovereignty of God. That God is Sovereign Lord over all creation and ruler over human history is affirmed by Reformed confessions across the ages. The Westminster Confession of Faith, for example, declares of God:

> God hath all life, glory, goodness, blessedness, in and of himself; and is alone in and unto himself all-sufficient, not standing in need of any creatures, which he has made . . . ; he is the alone fountain of all being, of whom, through whom, and to whom are all things, and hath most sovereign dominion over them, to do by them, for them, or upon them, whatsoever himself pleaseth. (*Book of Confessions* [hereafter *BC*] 6.012)

The most recent confession of the Presbyterian Church, A Brief Statement of Faith, expresses commitment to God's sovereignty in terms of trust:

> We trust in the one triune God, the Holy One of Israel,
>   whom alone we worship and serve.
>   . . . .
> We trust in God, whom Jesus called Abba, Father.
>   In sovereign love God created the world good and
>   makes everyone equally in God's image,
>   male and female of every race and people,
>   to live as one community.
>   . . . .
> We deserve God's condemnation [for our rebellion].
>   Yet God acts with justice and mercy to redeem creation. (*BC*, 10.1 and 10.3)

The Sovereignty of God is manifest in God's creation of all that is, including human beings, and, as their Creator, all things in turn belong to God. The Sovereign One is also the redeemer of creation—and, in particular, of human beings, who, though made in God's image, persistently refuse God's sovereignty and rebel against their creator, thereby distorting the very image in which they were made. Nevertheless, Reformed faith affirms, the Creator has redeemed human beings and all creation in Christ, exercising God's sovereignty through God's liberty to overcome human sin with grace, mercy, and love. Human beings now may live free from the Sovereign One's rightful wrath as persons re-created in Christ.

The sovereignty of God, in Presbyterian perspective, means that God rules our lives and our history. It means that we live by grace in Christ, set free for a life the chief end of which is "to glorify God and enjoy him forever" (The Shorter Catechism, BC 7.001). God's sovereignty affirms as well the providence of God, the ongoing care and work of God among God's creatures for the sake of God's reign on earth, and the new creation of all that now is.

The Authority of Scripture

While Calvin acknowledged that the wonder and design of creation pointed unmistakably to the Sovereign Creator, thereby leaving no one guiltless for not worshiping and obeying the Sovereign One, no true knowledge of God, he held, is possible apart from God's self-revelation. And apart from this act of grace, humankind is cut off from the One who is Other.

God's self-disclosure, which means the disclosure of God's purpose, nature, and will, is made known in Jesus Christ, the incarnation of the Holy One. Jesus Christ is God's means of salvation for humankind. He is the one through whom the creation has been redeemed and reconciled to God. Jesus Christ is the servant of God sent into the world to set captives free, to set at liberty those who are oppressed, to bind up the brokenhearted, and to give sight to the blind and to proclaim the time of God's favor (see Luke 4:16–19).

But we can know neither God nor Christ apart from the Scriptures, an affirmation that is also part of our Reformed heritage—*sola scriptura,* we live "by Scripture alone." The Confession of 1967 declares:

> The one sufficient revelation of God is Jesus Christ, the Word of God incarnate, to whom the Holy Spirit bears unique and authoritative witness through the Holy Scriptures, which are received and obeyed as the word of God written. The Scriptures are not a witness among others, but the witness without parallel. (BC 9.27)

The way to the knowledge of God is through Christ, and Christ is known and makes himself known to us through the Scriptures as interpreted through the power of the Holy Spirit. In the unparalleled witness of the Scriptures, the Triune God makes himself known through the witness of the Holy Spirit as Holy Other Creator and Redeemer in Jesus Christ.

Made in God's image as a human being, Christ lived in the image of God in perfect harmony with the Creator. And as Redeemer he has restored God's image for humankind, who through the power of the Holy Spirit may once more live in the image of God. For Calvin and the Presbyterian Church, Scripture is the preeminent authority for the church because its witness is the only way to know Christ and, in Christ, God, and is also the only way to understand what God requires of us to live obedient and faithful lives in the image of God as those in whom new life has begun.

Scripture must be interpreted for it to become the Word of God speaking Christ into changed times and circumstances. Only by the power of the Holy Spirit does this miracle of revelation occur—that is, that through the Scriptures the Word becomes flesh again and dwells among us in the decisions we make and the lives we lead. Calvin lodged the responsibility for interpretation in the community of faith under the prayer-sought guidance of the Spirit. Individual Christians are obliged to interpret Scripture as "the only rule of faith and life," but they are also bound to weigh their interpretations within the community of faith. So the will of God is sought effectively within the community charged with preserving truth and the discipline of Christian life.

Sola scriptura no doubt overstates the case for the singular authority of Scripture in Reformed piety, as if the voice of Scripture stood alone and apart from the historical context of interpretation. Nevertheless, the reformer's claim rightly points to the preeminent voice that Scripture has in fashioning the church's understanding of Christian faith and practice. In the context of a pluralistic world, Scripture stands in critical tension with the traditions of the church, on the one hand, and alternative readings of reality offered in society, on the other. Interpretation of Scripture under the guidance of the Holy Spirit, therefore, is critical to the identity of the church—particularly in its relationship to the world. At the same time, however, interpretation of Scripture in Reformed practice is also always transforming the church's identity as the body of Christ in the world.

The Church as Guide for the Sanctified Life

In the first three books of the *Institutes*, Calvin enumerates the great benefits that God has provided humankind through the life, death, and resurrection of Jesus Christ. These include the gift of faith, so that we may know Christ and, in Christ, God; justification or forgiveness and reconciliation, which have removed the threat of final judgment; regeneration or sanctification; restoration in the image of God, which has been distorted by human sin; and a new life in the Spirit of Christ. At the beginning of the fourth book, Calvin then turns to the means by which these great gifts may be enjoyed by those whom God has called in Christ.

For Calvin, the church is the external means by which the grace of God in Christ may be known and enjoyed. At the opening of book 4, he writes:

> As explained in the previous book, it is by faith in the gospel that Christ becomes ours and we are made partakers of the salvation and eternal blessedness brought by him. Since, however, in our ignorance and sloth [to which I add fickleness of disposition] we need outward helps to beget and increase faith within us, and advance it to its goal, God has also added these aids that he may provide for our weakness. And in order that the preaching of the gospel might flourish, he deposited this treasure in the church. He instituted "pastors and teachers" (Eph 4:11) through whose lips he might teach his own; he furnished them with authority; finally, he omitted nothing that might make for holy agreement of faith and for right order. (*Institutes* 4.1.1)

The purpose of the church, then, is to be a means of practicing our vocation. It is to be the guide for the sanctified life for all believers, through proclamation of the gospel, a right ordering of life in harmony with the gospel, and the practice of the sacraments as a means of maintaining the faith of believers and contributing to their sanctification.

The church is the earthly means by which God accomplishes the sanctification of those to whom he has given the gift of faith. Sanctification, for Calvin, is an ongoing process for believers. And "growing in faith" is a way of describing that process. Sanctification is a holy life in harmony with the image and will of God. It is the goal of faith, and it is the goal toward which life in the church is intended to nurture. Though justified by grace, living a sanctified life is a constant challenge for believers, for believers may still be drawn back into the "old life" rather than sustaining a new life in Christ. Sin, while shorn of its ultimate power by Christ's resurrection, nevertheless has destructive power still. The "old" has, in a profound sense, passed away—but the "new" is not yet entirely present. The church may be said to be the community of the faithful who are "being made new" in Christ.

Thus Calvin uses images for the church that depict it as a "nurturing mother" whose nourishment and guidance is needed all life long. Or, alternatively, the church may be thought of as the school for nurturing faith across a lifetime, God being the necessary teacher before whom believers are enjoined to have a "teachable spirit." In either case, the point cannot be missed. The church is a gift from God for the sake of those whom God has called to himself. It is the external means whereby those called may know and enjoy the benefits of God's grace in Christ. And it is the guide to the sanctified life in Christ whereby in faith believers may draw near to God to "glorify God and enjoy him forever," as the Shorter Catechism explains the "chief end of man." For these purposes God has instituted offices and order in the church, giving the church all that it needs to sustain the gospel and order the life of faith.

Calvin's view of sanctification is closely related to his doctrine of election and to the doctrine most popularly associated with Presbyterians—that is, predestination. A full discussion of the doctrines election and predestination would take us far afield. Yet the context seems to demand a brief word for the sake of imagining how "sanctification" remains an important and viable concern for the church in its contemporary ministry in largely "unchurched" communities. Presbyterians continue to affirm Calvin's claim that God has called to God's self those whom he chooses and has granted to them the gift of faith and the promises for life which the church embodies. Modern Presbyterians, however, have not felt it necessary to follow Calvin in dividing those whom God has called into those elected for salvation and those elected for damnation, which is the logical outcome of predestination. Rather, the church today sees foremost in the doctrines of election and predestination affirmations of God's sovereignty over our lives and God's radical rule of love and grace, which is constantly seeking to reconcile and redeem all humanity to God's self. The church's mission of proclamation and witness invites, in Christ's name, all who may hear into the church's fellowship to enjoy the benefits of God's liberating love in Christ and to join with the community in fashioning sanctified lives for faithful discipleship.

3. FORM FOLLOWS FUNCTION

We may now return to examine the offices that Christ has provided the church and their functions in light of the theological commitments highlighted above—especially in light of a Reformed understanding of the church as a means of grace and the God-ordained guide for the sanctified life in Christ. In particular, our focus will be on the Presbyterian form of church organization and life.

Preliminary Principles

The Presbyterian Church echoes Calvin's ecclesiology in its statement of "preliminary principles" that forms the foundation for an understanding of its governance (see *Book of Order* G-1.0000). The statement begins with the recognition that Christ is the Head of the church, which is his body. The sovereign God has made the resurrected Christ sovereign over all things, including the church. This principle positively affirms the community of faith under the lordship of Christ and, by calling it Christ's body, gives to the community its identity and purpose. For just as God was incarnate in Christ, so Christ is incarnate in Christ's church for the sake of the proclamation of the gospel in the world.

At the same time, however, the declaration of Christ's sovereignty over the church provides the standard by which proper leadership is to be exercised within the church and the context in which appropriate judgments are to be made. No one other than Christ is ruler over the church—a crucial concern historically in the church's struggle with civil authorities—and no officer of the church may fail to submit his or her authority to that of the sovereign Christ. No human being, in short, may claim sovereignty or the power to rule over the church, since Christ alone is head of the church. As the body of Christ, the community functions under the sovereign rule of Christ, carrying out its responsibilities for proclamation of the gospel, celebration of the sacraments, and faithful witness in the world as members of the body—with each person being valued in the body, but no one or several usurping the authority of the Head. In this declaration lie the seeds for the Presbyterian form of representative governance.

Following Calvin, Presbyterians state in a second principle of governance:

> Christ calls the church into being and gives it all that is necessary for its mission in the world, for its building up, and for its service to God. Christ is present with the church in both Spirit and Word. It belongs to Christ alone to rule, to teach, to call, and to use the church as he wills, exercising his authority by the ministry of men and women for the establishment and extension of his Kingdom. (*Book of Order* G-1.0100)

This statement points to the providential nature of the church—that is, that it is both called into being and equipped for its life by Christ. Christ is the living Lord of the church, ruling, teaching, calling, and making use of the church through the ministry of those who are members of Christ's body. The purpose of the church is here also clearly stated: Christ's exercise of authority through the church's ministry is intended for the "establishment and extension of his Kingdom."

Calvin seems to have limited the use of the term "ministry" to the offices that he believed were given by Christ for the proclamation of the gospel, the celebration of the sacraments, and the ordering or governance of the church's faith and life. The Reformation principle "the priesthood of all believers" he transposed to "the priesthood of all Christians," affirming by that expression the privilege of every Christian to offer to God all that he or she has and is—thereby using it to refer to the believer's sacrificial life in Christ. The gift of God's liberating salvation, with its attendant call for sanctification, Calvin saw as conferring the role of "priest" on all Christians—apart from any call to an ascetic life or any need for inordinate suffering.

The context for Calvin's reference to "the priesthood of all Christians" is his comparison of governance by presbyters and elders with the ecclesiastical orders of the Roman Church, particularly its office of "priest." Calvin argued that Christ, our High Priest, has already made the single, necessary sacrifice for our salvation, and therefore any priest offering the sacrifice of the mass was contradicting Christ's effective work. He concludes, "in him we are all priests [Rev 1:6; cf. 1 Pet 2:9], but to offer praises and thanksgiving—in short, to offer ourselves and ours to God" (*Institutes* 4.19.28). As priests in Christ, every member is also responsible for "public edification" according to the grace given to him or her, "provided he [or she] performs it decently and in order" (*Institutes* 4.1.12). Thus believers who participate in scriptural discussions, offering interpretations as the Spirit gives them insight, rightly share in "the priesthood of all Christians."

Calvin's distinctive use of "ministry," however, has been long lost in the common parlance of the church's discussion of ministry, so that today the word is regularly taken to mean the manifold ways in which believers live out their respective vocations, and thereby exercise their "priesthood." Calvin saw "ministers" as those whom God called to fulfill specific leadership roles in the church, each of whose ministries was practiced largely in the community of faith (the *koinōnia*) and in support of the institution of the church (the *ekklēsia*). The role of believers, however, was to live sanctified lives both in their own communities and in the larger world of their daily living, to admonish one another in matters of faith and practice, and to offer themselves and their work "wholly unto God" as a "worthy and acceptable sacrifice" to God (to paraphrase St. Paul).

At the same time, those called by God and elected to particular offices by the community of faith clearly share, as well, in the priesthood of all Christians. As officers and ministers, they have particular responsibilities for the community of faith. And as priests in Christ, they are called to perform their duties as those whom Christ redeemed through his sacrifice and in accordance with the particular gifts given them by the Spirit to carry out their duties. What results from the merging of "ministers" and their "offices" with "the priesthood of all Christians" is an affirmation of the unity in Christ that exists among all believers, which is coupled with the recognition of a diversity of ways of living out a common priesthood, with that diversity being seen as in accord with Christ's desire to make use of the church through a variety of gifts of the Spirit.

Therefore, the purpose or function of the church in Calvin's view—and, subsequently, in Presbyterian faith and doctrine—is to be the body of Christ in the world. This means proclaiming the gospel, safeguarding its truth, forming community through the sacraments of the Lord's Supper and baptism, and ordering its institutional and communal life so as to grow toward sanctification. It means bearing witness to the world of God's redeeming grace in Christ, for the sake of God's glory and the increase of the reign of God on earth. From these functions, it follows that governance of the church requires pastors and teachers to proclaim the gospel, teach the faith, and celebrate the sacraments, and others to whom responsibility for discipline, oversight of the church, and care for the poor may fall.

As with everything else, Calvin located in the Scriptures the authority for the offices and ministries that he believed Christ had ordained for the governance of his church. From Eph 4:11–16 he derived what he called the three "temporary offices"—that is, apostles, evangelists, and prophets—which were given for the particular needs of the early church, and the two "permanent offices"—that is, pastors and teachers—"whom the church can never go without" (*Institutes* 4.3.4). The pastor's responsibility is specifically the proclamation of the Word and the celebration of the sacraments, but it also includes oversight and discipline of church members. To these two permanent offices (which we will explore later in this chapter), Calvin added two more offices not directly related to the ministry of the Word, which he identified in the more extensive list of gifts in Rom 12:7–8: "government" (i.e., ruling elders) and "caring for the poor" (i.e., deacons).

Issues of Nomenclature and Social Location

John Calvin was clearly more concerned with the functions of these church offices than he was with the permanence of their nomenclature. Here we gain insight into his use of Scripture. For though he traced the nomenclature for the offices he deemed "essential" to scriptural passages, Calvin did not succumb to a slavish recapitulation of the church's early practices, as he understood them.

Thus Calvin sets out as being essential offices of the church first pastors and teachers, who are responsible for the ministry of the Word, including proclamation, sacraments, and guarding the truth of the faith through teaching, and secondly ruling elders and deacons, who attend to the discipline and witness of the people, apart from which those led astray from the gospel might never find their way back to the truth and life of faith. All who minister in the church do so according to the standard of Christ, "the pattern of the one who came 'not to be served but to serve'" (Matt 20:28; cf. *Book of Order* G-6.0100). But though he traced the nomenclature for the offices to scriptural passages that reflected the practices of the ancient church, Calvin also acknowledged differences between his own time and that of the apostolic church.

Indeed, Calvin interpreted Scripture in harmony with the Reformed principle of a "plain reading" of the text. But he also recognized that Scripture itself
provides a variety of ways of referring to those responsible for the ministry of the
Word and for discipline and order in the church. Thus he writes, "But in indis-
criminately calling those who rule the church 'bishops,' 'presbyters,' 'pastors,' and
'ministers,' I did so according to Scriptural usage, which interchanges these
terms" (*Institutes* 4.3.8). Here is an example of Calvin's effort to interpret Scripture in a way faithful to the gospel and the tradition, yet reforming or refashion-
ing earlier forms to meet the needs of the church in a different time and place—
the very project with which this chapter and others in this volume are concerned.

Calvin sought to maintain the roles that he saw as being necessary for a
faithful governance of the church—that is, those roles necessary to equip the
church to live as the body of Christ in the world and to grow up in every way into
Christ, the Head of the church. Yet the nomenclature used to designate those
roles and how they may be carried out by means of particular forms and practices
he understood as being open to ongoing interpretation under the guidance of the
Holy Spirit. Thus the offices in Reformed and Presbyterian churches are "authorized" by Scripture in two ways. First, they were congruent with the principles of
governance established in the early church, to which Scripture points. Second,
their identity and function, while derived from the early church's practices, are
continually being interpreted for ecclesiastical governance today under the authority of the Holy Spirit.

Therefore Calvin and his Presbyterian successors can say that their church
governance has been formed in obedience to the will of Christ for his church.
What that *does not say* is that a Presbyterian or Reformed way of governance is the
only scriptural form or the only form in conformity with the will of Christ. The
Book of Order expresses this point concisely: "The Church offices mentioned in
the New Testament which this church has maintained include those of presbyters
(ministers of the Word and Sacrament and elders) and deacons" (G-6.0103).

On the Terms Episkopos and Presbyteros

In a very helpful article, "On *Episkopos* and *Presbyteros*," Frances Young has
examined the role of presbyters in the Pastoral Epistles. She proposes, contrary to
Calvin, that the term *presbyteroi* ("presbyters" or "elders") in the Pastoral Epistles
does not seem to represent an "office," such as *episkopos* or *diakonoi* do. Rather, the
designation appears to refer in the first place, particularly when seen in the context
of the church as "the household of God" (cf. 1 Tim 3:15), to those who were older
in age—that is, to "elders" or those who had seniority in the community. Young
sees the presbyters' role as that of conserving the community's memory and teaching it to others. In addition, she contends, the Pastoral Epistles suggest that the
elders served as consultants or advisers to the *episkopos* or "steward." Thus, she concludes: "The origins of the presbyterate are . . . distinct from those of the episcopate
and the diaconate. They were originally a council of senior Christians recognized as
bearers of the apostolic tradition" ("On *Episkopos* and *Presbyteros*," 148).

Young's research into the social location of the presbyterate, using a household model for early church communities, provides insight not only into the origins of the "elders" as a distinct group in the church but also some clues regarding the development of the imagery of the term *presbyteros* into a designation for an office. Calvin, as we have seen, treated the nomenclature of the Pastoral Epistles as distinguishing ecclesiastical "offices," at the heart of which are functions essential to the right ordering of the community of faith. Thus, for him, "presbyter," "bishop," and "pastor" were interchangeable terms, since he failed to see distinctions in the texts on which he was relying. By so doing, he established a long-standing Presbyterian principle that sees bishop and presbyter as names for the same office.

In Presbyterian churches the presbyters, as ministers of the Word and sacrament and as ruling elders, remain responsible for the memory of the community, for teaching it to others, and for the oversight of the community's life—a role that is assumed to have been earlier played by the bishop. Moreover, the collective sense of the presbyterate remains in the Presbyterian concept of a local governing session of elders, which is composed of ministers of the Word and ruling elders, and in the presbytery, which is the governing body with oversight for a number of local churches. In recent conversations within the World Council of Churches, these representative bodies of elders have been taken to constitute the Presbyterian equivalent to the bishops of other confessions.

The Presbyterian Form of Calvin and Knox

Calvin's social location was the city-state of sixteenth-century Geneva, in terms of which he interpreted the offices and ministries he found in the New Testament witness, particularly the Pauline letters and the Pastorals Epistles. In this context, the "presbyter" was taken to be an office with distinct duties, and the presbyterate was understood as a body of elders, forming a governing council for the church—akin to the graded councils that constituted the governance of the city of Geneva. While Calvin insisted on the distinction between the church's governance and the authority of the city councils and the magistrate or syndic, there was no clear separation of church and state in Calvin's Geneva. On the contrary, when Calvin sought to reform the church in Geneva, he submitted his proposal, the *Ecclesiastical Ordinances* of 1537, to the various councils of the town. The magistrate, however, resisted any incursion of civil authority that could result from Calvin's formation of a consistory to govern the church in Geneva—even though the consistory consisted of the ministers of the city churches and twelve ruling elders, whom the civil council had approved. The civil authority ultimately recognized the authority of the ecclesiastical consistory to discipline believers, even to excommunicate them if necessary, while reserving judicial responsibility for lawbreakers to civil courts and councils. Calvin's "ruling elders" and the governing consistory consisting of elders and ministers must be located, then, in a different social configuration than that on which Young bases her analysis of the situation in the Pastoral Epistles, for it builds not on the "household" imagery of the ancient world but on the civic and social categories of a small city-state or limited nation-state of the Reformation period.

John Knox adopted Calvin's model of governance—resting on the need to ensure the proclamation of the gospel, the celebration of the sacraments, and a disciplined life of sanctification—in organizing the Reformed church in Scotland. Knox is most responsible for the use of the word "Presbyterian" to denote the form of the church polity under discussion. Tension between royal authority and the authority of the Presbyterian Church is vivid in Knox's preaching and ministry, particularly as the Scots opposed the English and the episcopal form of governance of the Church of England.

Like Calvin, Knox claimed the church's authority to admonish believers and hold them accountable to a life dictated by the gospel and the teachings of Christ. This was his warrant for public criticism of both royal authority and the behavior of Scottish citizens alike. Unlike Calvin, however, Knox was clear and unwavering in his refusal to recognize the authority of civil magistrates over the church. The magistrate is to be obeyed insofar as the civil authority is in conformity with the word and will of God in Christ. A Presbyterian principle of governance that emerged from this struggle between civil and ecclesial authority states unequivocally:

> God alone is Lord of the conscience, and hath left it free from the doctrines and commandments of men which are in anything contrary to his Word, or beside it, in matters of faith or worship. (*Book of Order* G-1.03.01)

This principle, coupled with the move toward a complete separation of church and state, reached its logical end in the Constitution of the United States, which formally declares that the state shall not establish any religion and that freedom of religion and worship is an inalienable right of all citizens.

Modifications in the Presbyterian Form of Calvin and Knox

With the movement of the Presbyterian form of ecclesial governance to larger geographic and national identities, the logic of Calvin's model has also been extended. The principle of governance by ruling bodies, including ministers and elders, has led to the creation of additional governing bodies, which are connected to one another through representative delegates. Thus the local church, which is governed by its session of ruling elders and ministers, belongs with other local churches to a presbytery, whose duties are those of oversight for the local churches. Presbytery membership consists of representative ruling elders and ministers of the Word and Sacrament (traditionally called "teaching elders"), who are drawn from the congregations. Presbyteries, in turn, are formed into a larger governing body called a synod, which has oversight responsibilities with regard to the presbyteries. Synod meetings are composed of representative elders and ministers sent by the presbyteries. Finally, the general assembly is composed of representative "ruling elders" and ministers of the Word and Sacrament sent by the presbyteries from across the whole national church. This body deals with issues, including initiating changes to the constitutional documents of the Presbyterian Church (the *Book of Order* and *The Book of Confessions*), which concern the whole church.

While these governing bodies increase in terms of their demographic and inclusive representation, they are not hierarchical in the sense that a higher body has more authority or power than a lower one. Only in terms of settling disputes or appeals unresolved at a lower level does a higher body have more authority. Indeed, the principal authority for ecclesiastical governance in the Presbyterian form remains in the presbytery and the local church. Notably, this series of connected governing bodies grew from the bottom up, from presbyteries meeting with one another in the British colonies in America. Freedom and flexibility remain available in the presbyteries to facilitate innovation today, while simultaneously reflecting on historic traditions and earlier practices.

Calvin's "officers" and ministries are now fully formalized in the Presbyterian form of the church. The present Presbyterian Church (U.S.A.) ordains by laying on of hands, as Calvin recommended. The presbytery ordains presbyters to proclaim the gospel, to see to the proper service of the sacraments, and to teach the gospel and ensure knowledge and practice of the faith (ministers of the Word and Sacrament). The church also ordains ruling elders and deacons to see to the governance of the life of the church, the faithful use of the church's possessions, and to care for those in need. All these officers are elected by the community of faith and granted authority by the congregation for the performance of their respective duties. Their election and ordination recognizes their gifts of grace for the office to which they are called and Christ's continual provision to the church for all that is needed to ensure the proclamation of the gospel, the sacraments of grace, and a right ordering of life together and individually as those sanctified by God in Christ and called to a new life in faith.

4. THE PRESBYTERIAN FORM IN THE CHURCH TODAY

The contemporary world is, of course, quite different from Calvin's Geneva, Knox's Scotland, or colonial America. Ours is a complex world of global interrelationships and economic interdependencies, with national boundaries collapsing before the interests of worldwide markets and possibilities for global ecological disaster. The social worlds of modern societies are largely demystified and secular. And the Christian church is no longer at the center of those societies but has moved unwillingly to their peripheries—retaining prominence, if at all, only in areas of individual and private needs.

In such settings, the church appears more like an "interest enclave" or "voluntary association," where those who are interested may belong and work together toward some common goal, but with minimal commitment to the enclave or association itself. What one chooses to be a part of, one may also choose to leave—particularly if perceived needs are not being met or interest lags. There is always another group to join, another interest to explore, or another means of exploring it. Such a pattern of belonging is typical of contemporary society in

North America. What is missing, at least in life in the United States, is the experience of community. Community depends on shared memories and values, a communal ethos and ethic, and a commitment to something of ultimate importance. Furthermore, community assumes lasting and valued relationships of mutual care and support.

What case can be made for a Presbyterian form of church governance in a setting such as this? In the language of the case as it has already been presented, we may put the question more sharply: Does the Reformed and Presbyterian understanding of the church as a gift from God for the sake of guiding believers in the way of a sanctified life in the world make sense in a world becoming postmodern? Can the Presbyterian Church be a means of grace, used by God to bring people to faith and the experience of God's liberating love, that they may live as holy children of God, trusting God and enjoying life, sharing in the goodness God intends for human life and all creation? It is the thesis of this chapter that the Presbyterian Church has the potential to provide this kind of community experience for a world much in need of it today.

The Church as the Body of Christ: Identity, Offices, and Reform

In the Presbyterian view the church is not an "interest enclave" or a "voluntary association." It is the body of Christ into which one is called, to which one is joined in holy covenant, and within which one finds the deepest meaning and purpose for life in service to God, by obedience to Christ's word, and in service as Christ's disciples to the world. The body of Christ is called and equipped by the Holy Spirit for the incarnation of Christ's ministry of love and liberation in the world. It is entrusted with the proclamation to all of the gospel of Christ, the celebration of Christ's presence in the sacraments of the Lord's Supper and baptism, and being a witness to everyone of new life in Christ through the daily lives of its members. Douglas Ottati describes this way of life as participation in the faithfulness of God, the purpose of which is the extension of the love of God and neighbor.

The Presbyterian community of faith begins with a declaration that resists the preeminence of personal choice. "In life and death," the church declares, "we belong to God." The sovereignty of God grounds all of life in the purpose of God. The modern world, no less than the world of the Gospels or the world of John Calvin, belongs to God. The sovereignty of God remains a fundamental truth claim. And if Christ is the One through whom the will of the Sovereign God is made known, then the church of Christ continues, quite rightly, to be a means of divine grace—a means by which the saving love of the Sovereign God takes form and flesh in those who live by faith in Christ.

The grace of God in Christ, which redeems a broken humanity and a broken creation, and the creation of the church for the continuing ministry of Christ through people whom God calls, are Presbyterian assumptions of faith with which community formation in the modern or post-modern world begin. The Presbyterian form of community has a basic commitment to governance by representative presbyters or elders, who are connected in governing bodies from the local church to a general assembly. This form grows out of the theological assumptions just mentioned. For its representative character safeguards the sovereignty of God, while taking seriously both the gifts of the Spirit in the church for ministry and the ever-present threat of sin to the sanctified life. Its offices of minister of the Word and Sacrament, ruling elders, and deacons provide for the continuing proclamation of the gospel, the mission and witness of the church as a sign of the present and coming reign of God, and the continuing interpretative search of the Scriptures under the guidance of the Holy Spirit so that Christ's word may indeed be a living word for faithful disciples in ordinary life.

The form argues for both a communal and an individual life of grace, which are open to the transforming will of God in Christ through the revelation of Christ's word in the Scriptures. It argues for being open to a reforming theology and practicing a reforming piety. It calls for a life of discipline, which is lived in covenant relationship with God and with one another, for the sake of full enjoyment and meaning in a life lived in harmony with God's good intentions for all creation. In the world we know, such a life, lodged in such principles of faith, can be welcome and creative. Trust in God, who alone is Lord, and respect for others that accompanies knowing the grace and promises of God encourages Presbyterians to welcome pluralism and multiculturalism. The conviction that Christ's word is always reforming and always creating asks Presbyterians to search the Scriptures together, to listen to teaching and preaching, aware that we live in today's world assured of Christ's presence while bound to Christ's leading in new directions.

Theological Identity and the Adaptation of Form to Function

The key to Presbyterian adaptation of form to function in the modern world does not lie in abandoning the church's confessions or its commitment to governance by presbyters. Rather, Presbyterian adaptability rests on clarity about its theological identity. This identity includes within it the seeds for being reformed as the need becomes evident to proclaim the gospel in a different world and to practice a life of faith in a changing context. Because the church is understood to be a guide for the sanctified life in Christ, Presbyterians, along with Calvin, recognize the need to provide for the proclamation of the gospel, the celebration of the sacraments, and the ordering of the Christian life in faith. And Presbyterians, along with Calvin, believe that Christ has given—and continues to give—all that is necessary for the church to be the body of Christ, thereby carrying out its mission and purpose in the world.

The officers historically drawn from the variety named in the Scriptures, together with the form of governance by presbyters formed into councils, have embodied the Presbyterian understanding of how Christ has provided for his church. What counts here, however, are the affirmations that Christ provides for all that the church needs, including its officers and its forms for governance, and that Scripture interpreted under the power of the Holy Spirit reveals Christ's will for the church in every time and place. The way is therefore open from within a Presbyterian form of Christian community to reform the offices of the church or change the form of governance that orders the church's life. Indeed, such a reforming is constantly going on as the *Book of Order* is altered or its practices of governance change in a local church or presbytery without any change in the *Book of Order* itself being required.

For Presbyterians, Scripture is the witness to Christ without parallel. And the interpretation of Scripture through the Holy Spirit by the community of faith is the way we know Christ's will in any new situation. Our doctrine and our discipline are shaped by the revelation of Christ's word in the Scriptures. The mission of the church remains steadfast: to preach the gospel and offer guidance in the way of sanctification for those who believe and walk by faith. But the forms and shape that such a community of faith gives to a Presbyterian church depends on how the Spirit of Christ leads us through the Scripture, in conversation with our doctrinal memories, to be reformed. The beginning word for the reformation church of Geneva is the beginning word for the contemporary Presbyterian community: *ecclesia reformata semper reformanda*—"always reformed, always in need of being reformed."

5. CONCLUSION

A Presbyterian form of Christian community has much to recommend it as a vital and viable form of church order and life for today. First, it is a representative form of governance. As such, it provides voice for a variety of perspectives represented within the contemporary church and, for that matter, society at large. Representative presbyters, however, while taking into consideration these diverse views, are expected to vote their own prayerful conscience after open debate and discussion. Representative governance entrusts decision making to community members without abnegating the individual right of conscience or point of view. Moreover, since the community elects representatives, they can be replaced if the electorate so wishes and if fair representation fails to occur. A representative system allows a smaller body of persons to meet to carry out most business, thereby moderating the potential ineffectiveness of a fully democratic system.

Second, the distinction between clergy and laity in the Presbyterian form is moderated by the inclusion in ordination of both ministers of the Word and ruling elders and deacons. Ruling elders and deacons are laypeople who have been elected from the local congregation. Yet they are ordained, and they share with the rest of the congregation in the election of ministers of the Word. In a Presbyterian church, moreover, the session of ruling elders is responsible for the governance of the church—including its worship, education, pastoral care, and mission. Only the explicit duties related to choosing preaching texts, preparing the sermon, proclaiming the word in worship, and celebrating the sacraments are reserved for the minister of the Word and Sacraments. The involvement of the laity along with the clergy in the interpretation of Scripture is underscored by the core responsibilities for governance that are assigned to all the presbyters, both clerical and lay, in the reformed doctrine of "the priesthood of all Christians," as previously noted.

Finally, the Presbyterian form of governing bodies of presbyters—who together search for the will of Christ in the Scriptures, seek to be guided by the historic and contemporary confessions of the church, and submit their wills to the leading of the Holy Spirit—creates a thoughtful and reflective atmosphere that honors tradition without being bound to it and effects changes carefully out of reverence for the holy work that is being done. Marginalized in the modern world, the church is in a situation very much akin to that of the churches at Ephesus, whose being "blown to and fro by every wind of doctrine" worried the Pauline writer of Ephesians. It is tempting in our time, especially for mainline Presbyterians, to search for quick solutions in order to restore lost members and lost authority in the public square. Church leaders run to discover the "needs" of modern "seekers" and to program congregational life in response. And some churches are having marked success as attendance numbers soar. Some lament that the mainline churches seem unable to face the changing realities of today's society, in which, as one scholar has put it, loyalty to tradition no longer may be assumed and where people feel free to pick and choose which traditions they wish to hold as meaningful.

The Presbyterian form of community bears within it the seeds for its own change. Its mission most certainly concerns proclaiming the gospel in articulate and convincing ways in the postmodern world and bearing witness to the goodness of God in Christ through life patterns that reflect the freedom and joy of being loved by God and bound to God in Christ in covenant community with others so loved. Still, the Presbyterian form, because it is linked so firmly to Presbyterian and Reformed doctrine, depends on tradition and memory being shared and insists on authority residing not in a tradition but in the living word of Christ, who is the image of the Sovereign God to whom we all belong. Presbyterian forms may change. We are warranted by our faith to do so. But institutional change moves slowly. Presbyterian forms are adaptable for life, but probably not at the speed of market analysis.

6. POSTSCRIPT

"A life of holiness" and "sanctification" are not expressions one hears in abundance in public or local church gatherings these days. What one does hear are heartfelt longings for life to have meaning and purpose. People talk painfully of their dissatisfaction with their work, even if it has proved lucrative. They lament their sense of isolation, of unfulfilled dreams, of life lived too hurriedly. All these feelings are taking form in a widespread longing for a deeper sense of faith, a quest for grounding life in something of ultimate and transcendent importance. The language of "spirit" and "spiritual" has been one popular way to speak of this longing.

In the language of Reformed theology, this quest for a spiritual life may fairly be called a desire to live a sanctified life that grows out of a relationship of knowing oneself to be loved by God. Spiritual disciplines are another way to describe the disciplined life in the Spirit that has concerned the Reformers and Presbyterians for a very long time. The Presbyterian Church, as a community of nurture and formation in the life of the Spirit, has within its traditions, its governance, and its calling to be the body of Christ in the world means of providing care and direction for many in the modern church and world longing to live as the beloved of God.

BIBLIOGRAPHY

Calvin, John. *The Institutes of the Christian Religion.* Edited by J. T. McNeill. Translated by F. L. Battles. *Library of Christian Classics* 20–21. Philadelphia: Westminster, 1960.

———. *Theological Treatises.* Translated by J. K. S. Reid. *Library of Christian Classics* 22. Philadelphia: Westminster, 1954.

Coalter, Milton J., John M. Mulder, and Louis B. Weeks, eds. *The Confessional Mosaic: Presbyterians and Twentieth-Century Theology.* Louisville, Ky.: Westminster John Knox, 1990.

———, eds. *The Pluralistic Vision: Presbyterians and Mainstream Protestant Education and Leadership.* Louisville, Ky.: Westminster John Knox, 1992.

———, eds. *The Presbyterian Predicament: Six Perspectives.* Louisville, Ky.: Westminster John Knox, 1990.

———, eds. *The Re-Forming Tradition: Presbyterians and Mainstream Protestantism.* Louisville, Ky.: Westminster John Knox, 1992.

The Constitution of the Presbyterian Church (U.S.A.). Part I: Book of Confessions; Part II: Book of Order. Louisville, Ky.: Office of the General Assembly, 1999.

Leith, John H. *Introduction to the Reformed Tradition: A Way of Being the Christian Community.* Atlanta, Ga.: John Knox, 1977.

McNeill, John T. *The History and Character of Calvinism.* Oxford: Oxford University Press, 1954.

Ottati, Douglas. *Reforming Protestantism: Christian Commitment in Today's World.* Louisville, Ky.: Westminster John Knox, 1995.

Small, Joseph D. *Committed Conversation.* Office of Theology and Worship Church Issues Series 2. Louisville, Ky.: Presbyterian Church (U.S.A.), 1999.

Smylie, James H. *A Brief History of the Presbyterians.* Louisville, Ky.: Geneva, 1996.

Trinterud, Leonard J. *The Forming of an American Tradition: A Re-Examination of Colonial Presbyterianism.* Philadelphia, Pa.: Westminster, 1949.

Wendel, François. *Calvin: Origins and Development of His Religious Thought.* Translated by P. Mairet. Grand Rapids, Mich.: Baker, 1997.

Wheeler, Barbara G., and Mark Achtemeier. *The Church and Its Unity.* Office of Theology and Worship Church Issues Series 1. Louisville, Ky.: Presbyterian Church (U.S.A.), 1999.

Young, Frances. "On *Episkopos* and *Presbyteros.*" *Journal of Theological Studies* 45 (1994): 142–48.

Chapter 12

Community Formation as an Image of the Triune God: A Congregational Model of Church Order and Life

Miroslav Volf

My topic here is the relation between persons and the community in Christian theology. The focus is on the community of grace, the Christian church. The point of departure is the thought of the first Baptist, John Smyth, and the notion of the church as a "gathered community" that he shared with the Radical Reformers. The purpose is to counter the tendencies toward individualism in Protestant ecclesiology and to suggest a viable understanding of the church in which both persons and the community are given their proper due. The ultimate goal is to spell out a vision of the church as an image of the triune God.

I will argue that the presence of Christ, which constitutes the church, is mediated not simply through ordained ministers but through the whole congregation; that the whole congregation functions as *mater ecclesia* to the children engendered by the Holy Spirit; and that the whole congregation is called to engage in ministry and make decisions about leadership roles. My primary objective in all of this is to contribute to the rediscovery of the church—both theologically, as the church seeks to understand itself, and missiologically, in developing an eccesiology that will facilitate culturally appropriate social embodiments of the gospel.

A major strand of my argument stands in close affinity with a "believer's church" ecclesiology and a feminist ecclesiology—particularly the "voluntarism" of the former (that is, that the incorporative act is deliberate on the part of the candidate and the community alike) and the "egalitarianism" of both (that is, that responsibility for the corporate life of the church ultimately rests on the broad shoulders of the whole community). My primary objective, however, is to contribute to a rediscovery of the church among "free churches"—that is, as the term primarily connotes, those churches that have a congregationalist church constitution, but also those churches that affirm a consistent separation of church and state. I would like to provide such churches with ecclesiological categories through which they might better understand themselves and live better as a community. For dispute concerning the church as community is simultaneously an ecclesiological dispute regarding the correct way in which the communal form of the Christian faith is to be lived authentically and a missiological dispute concerning how that faith is to be transmitted effectively today.

The material for this chapter has been abstracted from my book *After Our Likeness,* principally from part 2, and readers are directed to that volume for a more extensive, detailed, and nuanced presentation.

1. THE NATURE OF THE CHURCH

What makes the church the church? Our interest in this section is directed not toward how the church *ought* to live in the world according to God's will or how it *can* live successfully in the power of the Spirit, but rather toward the sine qua non of what it means for the church to call itself a church in the first place.

The all-embracing framework for an appropriate understanding of the church is God's eschatological new creation. According to the message of Jesus, the gathering of the people of God is grounded in the coming of the kingdom of God in his person. Commensurately, New Testament authors portray the church as the anticipation of the eschatological gathering of the entire people of God. Paul, for instance, understands the church as "the anticipation of the coming new, obedient world intended by God's *dikaiosynē* (righteousness)" (Stuhlmacher, *Gerechtigheit Gottes,* 214). The eschatological character of the church, therefore, demands that systematic ecclesiological reflection begin not immediately with the church itself, but rather with God's new creation in its relation to God's people.

What Is the Church?

The future of the church in God's new creation is the mutual, personal indwelling of the triune God and his glorified people, as becomes clear from the description of the new Jerusalem in the Apocalypse of John (cf. Rev 21:1–22:5). Participation in the communion of the triune God, however, is not only an object of hope for the church; it is also its present experience. "We declare to you what we have seen and heard so that you also may have fellowship with us; and truly our fellowship is with the Father and with his Son Jesus Christ" (1 John 1:3). Faith in this proclaimed "life"—that is, life with the Father and that appeared in this world in an audible and tangible fashion (cf. 1 John 1:1–4)—establishes communion between believers and the triune God, and therefore also among believers themselves. Present participation in the trinitarian *communio* through faith in Jesus Christ anticipates in history the eschatological communion of the church with the triune God.

Ignatius of Antioch, writing about 110 on his way to martyrdom at Rome, answered the question regarding the nature of the church by reference to the presence of Christ: "Wherever Jesus Christ is, there is the universal church" (*To*

Smyrna 8.2). Irenaeus, writing sometime between 182 and 188, answered it by saying: "Wherever the Spirit of God is, there is the church, and all grace" (*Against Heresies* 3.24.1). But reference to the presence of Christ or the Spirit—or, more precisely, to the Spirit of Christ—is not sufficient in identifying the church, for the presence of Christ and his Spirit cannot be restricted to the church alone (cf. Eph 1:22–23; Col 1:12–20). Hence one must distinguish between the general and the particular presence of the Spirit.

When one focuses on the particular presence of Christ and the Spirit, one can say: Wherever the Spirit of Christ is present in its *ecclesially constitutive* activity, there is the church. For the Spirit unites the gathered congregation with the triune God and integrates it into a history that extends from the Old Testament saints to the eschatological new creation. And this Spirit-mediated relationship with the triune God and the entire history of God's people—a history whose center resides in Jesus' proclamation of the reign of God and in his own death and resurrection—constitutes an assembly into a church.

But the presence of the Spirit of Christ cannot be directly ascertained, which is why this particular notion of the identity of the church cannot yet function as an answer to the question of its *identification.* If one is to speak meaningfully about the nature of the church, one must know not only what the church is but also how a particular group of people can be identified externally as a church—that is, one must also be able to say *where* a church is. Questions about the identity and the identification of the church are inseparable.

Where Is the Church?

Roman Catholic ecclesiology understands the church as constituted by the Spirit through the sacraments (principally baptism and the Eucharist) and the word. The office of bishop represents the indispensable condition of the sacraments and the word, since the bishop, standing in apostolic succession and communion with all other bishops, is the sign and guarantor of the universal character and divine origin of the sacraments and the word. Only those local fellowships of believers "united to their pastors" are, therefore, churches in the full sense of the word. This is why all other Christian fellowships—except the Eastern Orthodox Church, which seems to be something of an anomaly in Roman Catholic thought—exhibit merely more or less significant ecclesial elements, but do not qualify as churches.

Eastern Orthodoxy understands the church as being wholly eucharistic and "episcopocentric." The bishop functions in two ways: as *alter Christus* he mediates the presence of Christ and secures the catholicity of the local church; as *alter apostolus* he connects all the various local churches in time and space. In these two functions the bishop is indispensable for the event of a eucharistic gathering, and therefore also for the ecclesiality of every local church. From this it follows that no church standing outside the Orthodox communion of churches can be designated as a church—not even a church that stands in apostolic succession—because it lacks synchronic communion with all other churches.

In both Roman Catholicism and Eastern Orthodoxy the people or laity are also important—though not possessing, at least from a Protestant perspective, a particularly dignified status. According to Roman Catholic tradition, the real human subject of the liturgy is the entire *ecclesia sancta* and the individual priest is such only insofar as he embodies the larger church. That is why a congregation may not itself perform liturgical acts but must receive the liturgy from the universal church. According to Eastern Orthodoxy, there can be no eucharistic gathering without the presence of both the bishop and the people, for the "bishop-laity" relation at the level of the local church corresponds to the "Christ-church" relation at the level of the universal church.

Free church ecclesiology, however, takes as its departure point Jesus' words of Matt 18:20: "For where two or three are gathered in my name, I am there among them." This passage acquired importance quite early in church history. Ignatius of Antioch (d. ca. 110), for example, based his own ecclesiological principle on Matt 18:20: "Wherever Jesus Christ is, there is the universal church" (*To Smyrna* 8.2). So did Tertullian of Carthage (ca. 145–220), the great North African apologist and theologian, in declaring: "Where three are [with evident allusion to Matt 18:20], the church is" (*Exhortation to Chastity* 7; see also *Baptism* 6; *Modesty* 21). It was also important prior to, during, and after the Protestant Reformation. John Huss (1372–1415), the early Bohemian religious reformer, for example, declared: "From this [Matt 18:20] it follows that two righteous persons congregated together in Christ's name constitute, with Christ as the head, a particular holy church" (*The Church*, 2). Indeed, as Rudolph Sohm once noted: "This passage [Matt 18:20] traverses the entirety of church history" (*Wesen und Ursprung*, 49).

But it was particularly in the free church tradition that Matt 18:20 was accorded a key systematic role in ecclesiology. Based on this passage, John Smyth, who drafted the twenty articles of the *Baptist Confession of 1611*, defined the church as follows:

> A visible communion of Saints is two, three, or more Saints joined together by covenant with God and themselves, freely to use all the holy things of God, according to the word, for their mutual edification and God's glory. . . . This visible communion of Saints is a visible Church. (Whitley, *Works of John Smyth*, 252; see also 386–87, 403, 529, 548)

In fact, it was this verse that shaped the entire free church tradition. And I join this tradition by taking Matt 18:20 as the foundation not only for determining what the church is, but also for how it manifests itself externally as a church. *Where two or three are gathered in Christ's name, not only is Christ present among them, but a Christian church is there as well*—perhaps a bad church, a church that may well transgress against love and truth, but a church nonetheless.

The Church as an Assembly

The church is first of all an *assembly*: "where two or three are *gathered* in my name, I am there among them." The life of the church, however, is not exhausted in the act of assembling, for even if a church is not assembled it lives on as a church in the mutual service its members render to one another and to its common mission in the world. The church is not simply an act of assembling. Rather, it is the *people* who in a specific way assemble at a specific place for worship that constitutes the church's ecclesiality.

The New Testament use, and especially the Pauline use, of *ekklēsia* ("church") confirms this understanding of the church as an assembled community. Commensurate with secular Greek usage, according to which *ekklēsia* refers to the assembly of the free citizens of a city, *ekklēsia* in the New Testament refers almost exclusively to the concrete assembly of Christians at a specific place. And although the church is, indeed, always and emphatically "the church of God" (1 Cor 1:2), it is such only as it is the church of *those people* at a specific place—for example, the church of the Thessalonians or of the Laodiceans (cf. 1 Thess 1:1; 2 Thess 1:1). A church, therefore, is a concrete assembly of those who at a specific place "call on the name of our Lord Jesus Christ" (1 Cor 1:2).

The church nowhere exists *above* the locally assembled congregation, but exists *in*, *with*, and *beneath* it. A congregation *is* the body of Christ in the particular locale in which it gathers together (cf. Rom 12:5; 1 Cor 12:12–13). Despite the fundamental differences that exist between free church and Eastern Orthodox ecclesiologies, they agree on this important point: that the church in the real sense of the word is exclusively the concrete assembly. A particular denomination, the local churches in a cultural or political region, or the totality of local churches can be called "church" only in a secondary rather than a strictly theological sense.

The Church and the Confession of Faith

A church is an assembly, but an assembly is not yet a church. An indispensable condition of ecclesiality is that the people assemble *in the name of Christ*. Gathering in the name of Christ is the precondition for the presence of Christ in the Holy Spirit, which is itself constitutive for the church: "Where two or three are gathered *in my name,* I am there among them" (Matt 18:20).

Two conditions of ecclesiality emerge from the church's status as a congregation assembled in the name of Christ. First, since it is Christ in whose name Christians are assembled, the ecclesiality of a congregation is dependent on some doctrinal specification. For without such, Christ would not be identified as Christ. Second, to gather in the name of Christ means to have committed oneself to Christ. For in so assembling, Christians attest that Christ is the determining ground of their lives—that in him they have found freedom, orientation, and power. The first condition deals with cognitive specification of who Jesus Christ is, the second with personal identification with Christ. Without personal identification with Christ, cognitive specification of who he is remains empty. Without, however, cognitive specification of who Christ is, personal identification with him is blind.

The sacraments—baptism and the Lord's Supper—belong to the essence of the church, for they have to do with faith and its confession. Indeed, without baptism and the Lord's Supper there is no church. But the sacraments are an indispensable condition of ecclesiality only if they are a form of the confession of faith and an expression of faith. There is no church without sacraments. But there are no sacraments without the confession of faith and without faith itself. The church is wherever those who are assembled, be they only two or three, profess faith in Christ as their Savior and Lord through baptism and the Lord's Supper.

The Church, the Churches, and Humanity

The confession of faith, however, cannot be an idiosyncratic act of a local church. If this confession is constitutive for the church, then *every* church must be constituted by the *same* confession. The church's confession of faith in Christ not only distinguishes the church from the nonchurch, but it also simultaneously connects every church with all other churches. This raises the question of the sense in which the relations to other churches enter into the conditions of the ecclesiality of a local church, and on this matter three points need be made.

The first is that, while the whole Christ is present through his Spirit in every congregation assembling in Christ's name to profess faith in him—and so every local church is "independent" or "self-complete"—the independence of a local church does not mean that other churches are denied in every instance the right to intervene in its life. Other churches, however, can intervene in the affairs of a local church only *if the ecclesiality of that particular congregation is threatened*. This is the case when the integral confession of faith is distorted in a church through the loss of the substance of faith or through permanent resistance in practice to Christ's rule.

A second point that needs to be highlighted is this: that the same presence of Christ through the Spirit that makes each local church "independent" of other churches simultaneously connects them with one another. There is, as Lukas Vischer has observed, a broad consensus in the various churches "that the unity [of the churches] is given in Jesus Christ. It does not need to be created first" ("Schwierigkeiten bei der Befragung des Neuen Testaments," 34). Professing faith in the one Jesus Christ implies a unity with and openness to all other churches. What remains disputed, of course, is how this unity should be manifested concretely and how the various means of expressing it are related to the constitutive presence of Christ in a church.

A third point, however, needs also to be made: that professing faith in Jesus Christ as universal Savior and Lord implies, as well, an openness on the part of the church to all human beings. No one who professes faith in Christ should be denied entrance into the church and full participation in it. Just as Peter did not merely behave badly by refusing fellowship to Gentile Christians but actually betrayed the truth of the gospel itself (cf. Gal 2:11–14), so a discriminatory church is not merely a bad church, but no church at all—it is unable to do justice to the catholicity of the eschatological people of God.

Summation

The nature of the church, therefore, can be defined as follows: *Every congregation that assembles around the one Jesus Christ as Savior and Lord in order to profess faith in him publicly in pluriform fashion, including through baptism and the Lord's Supper, which is open to all churches of God and to all human beings, is a church in the full sense of the word, since Christ promised to be present in it through his Spirit as the first fruits of the gathering of the whole people of God in the eschatological reign of God.* Such a congregation is a holy, catholic, and apostolic church. One may rightly expect such a congregation to grow in unity, sanctity, catholicity, and apostolicity, but one may not deny to it these characterizing features of the church, since it possesses these on the basis of the constitutive presence of Christ.

2. THE PERSON AND THE CHURCH

In the early nineteenth century Friedrich Schleiermacher distinguished between two opposing forms of Christian communion: Protestantism, which "makes the individual's relation to the Church dependent on his relation to Christ," and Catholicism, which "makes the individual's relation to Christ dependent on his relation to the Church" (*The Christian Faith*, section 24). Such a distinction has been applauded by many. But only a simplistic theology contains the alternative "person-Christ-church" or "person-church-Christ." In the complex ecclesial reality of *all* churches, the relation of individuals to the church depends on their relation to Christ, just as their relation to Christ depends on their relation to the church. The two relations are mutually determinative.

Nonetheless, this issue of relations involves the central (and as yet insufficiently addressed) question in all contemporary ecumenical encounters—especially within the Protestant–Roman Catholic dialogue: Is the relation of human beings to Christ, which has often been seen within Protestantism to be individualistic, also mediated through their relations with one another, and does it not become real first only within these relations? It is this question regarding the person and the church that needs to be raised here.

Faith and the Church

It is obviously *human beings* who believe. Nonetheless, faith is not grounded in the activity of believing human beings. No one can give oneself faith. One must receive it from God precisely as one's own receptive activity. Faith is a work of God's Spirit and God's word. But presupposing the necessity of faith for the mediation of salvation, the question still arises as to *how* faith as a gift of God is mediated to human beings, and, especially, how the church participates in this mediation. The question is regarding the instrumentality of the church in the mediation of personal faith.

John Smyth in the early seventeenth century advocated the notion of God's
direct influence on human souls. Although he emphasized that those who have
not yet come to faith need the means of grace "to stir them up the better to perform the condition of repentance to the remission of sins" (*Works of John Smyth*,
743), he still insisted that "God the father, in our generation, *neither needed nor
used the help of any creature,* but that the father, the word, and the holy ghost *immediately* work that work in the soul" (ibid., italics added). When, however, a person has been born again, that person, according to Smyth, should no longer need
the means of grace, since he has "three witnesses in himself, the father, the word,
and the holy ghost, which are better than all scriptures or creatures whatsoever"
(ibid., 744). Yet Christians cannot do without such means of grace, because of
the "weakness of the flesh." For although they stand "above the law and scriptures," they are to make use of such means "for the gaining and supporting of
others" (ibid.).

According to Smyth, therefore, salvation takes place, at least ideally, between individual souls and God. Accordingly, the church emerges only through
the addition of those who, as isolated individuals, have become Christians and
now live as Christians. And such an individualistic understanding of the mediation of salvation is still advocated in some free church circles and within
Protestantism generally.

My own understanding of ecclesiality, however, is guided (as noted above)
by Matt 18:20, where Christ says: "For where two or three are gathered in my
name, I am there among them." According to this text, Christ's presence is promised not to the believing individual directly but to the entire congregation, and
only through the congregation to the individual. This is why no one can come to
faith alone and no one can live in faith alone. The church is not only the child
(filia) of faith—first of all of the Spirit and word of God, then also of faith itself—
but also the mother *(mater)* of faith (see Calvin, *Institutes* 4.1.4, and Luther,
Werke, 30/ I.188.24–25; 40/ I.664.18ff.; 47.20.20–21 on the church as the mother
of faith).

Appropriately understood, the motherhood of the church is a statement
that signifies that the transmission of faith occurs through interpersonal ecclesial
interaction. God's salvific activity always takes place through the multidimensional confession of faith of the community of faith *(communio fidelium).* The
sacraments, which no person can self-administer and yet which each person must
receive personally, symbolize most clearly the essentially communal character of
the mediation of faith.

It is from the church, therefore, that one receives the content of faith, and
it is in the church that one learns how faith is to be understood and lived. This
ecclesial activity of mediation is meaningful, however, only if it leads one to en-
trust one's life to God in faith. The goal of ecclesial mediation must be a person's own faith. Yet it is precisely this all-decisive faith, understood as a trust,
that the church cannot give to a person. For faith is exclusively a gift of the Spirit
of God. The church is not the subject of divine activity with Christ. Rather,
Christ is the *only* subject of such salvific activity and his divine salvific activity,

though always mediated, requires direct personal acceptance of saving grace by human beings.

The Motherhood of the Church and the Motherhood of Believers

Three affirmations need here to be made. The first is that one does not receive faith *from* the church, but rather *through* the church. A second is that because the church is a communion of persons rather than a subject, the character of faith as a gift does not require a priestly office fundamentally different from the general priesthood of believers through which God gives faith to individuals. A third is that the word of God, which creates faith, always comes to individuals through the multidimensional confession of faith of *others*. The mother church, therefore, does *not* stand *over against* individual Christians; rather, Christians *are* the mother church. For the mother church is the communion of brothers and sisters that has always existed vis-à-vis the individual Christian. And the universal priesthood of believers implies the "universal motherhood of believers."

Paul's use of the metaphor of conception and birth confirms this understanding of the motherhood of the church. Paul understands himself as father (1 Cor 4:14–15; 2 Cor 6:13; 2 Thess 2:11; Phlm 10) and mother (Gal 4:19; cf. 1 Thess 2:7) of his congregations and their members, since he was the first to preach the gospel to them and because their own spiritual birth occurred through him. There is no talk about the church as a subject acting with Christ. The apostle as *proclaimer* and as *individual apostle* is their father and mother. He did not baptize the Corinthians (1 Cor 1:14–17). His congregations had "not many fathers" (1 Cor 4:15), but only one. This is also why his fatherhood can be only "in Christ Jesus" and "through the gospel" (1 Cor 4:15). As C. K. Barrett correctly remarks, "Christ is the agent and the Gospel is the means by which men are brought to new life" (*Commentary on the First Epistle to the Corinthians,* 115).

Such a thesis of the universal motherhood of believers also corresponds to the actual practice of Christian churches. For the mediation of faith, for all practical purposes, proceeds less by way of officeholders than by way of the various Christian "significant others," such as family members or friends. And the mediation of faith is supported by this life of all the members of the church, who, among other things, also create the plausibility structures for the mediation of faith. Only within the framework of the motherhood of the local church, therefore, can one speak of the motherhood of individual Christians, for the universal motherhood of believers is bound to *common ecclesial* motherhood.

The Ecclesiality of Salvation

If salvation takes place between the lonely soul and its God, as John Smyth maintained (*Works of John Smyth,* 256–68), then it is individualistic and the purpose of church membership is only to support human weakness. The church is necessary—as John Calvin, in whose tradition Smyth stands, asserted—because Christians "have not yet attained angelic rank," but rather behave either as "infants and children," or as rebellious subjects (cf. Calvin, *Institutes* 4.1.1). Thus, according to Smyth, the visible church is not grounded in the positive experience of salvation, but rather in a *soteriological deficit.* The church is an "external aid" for a fuller experience of salvation, but salvation itself is asocial.

By contrast, the Catholic and Orthodox traditions insist on the essential sociality of salvation. Salvation *is* communion with God and human beings. The self-enclosed individual, in fact, is actually caught in the opposite of salvation. And even though the Catholic and Orthodox understandings of the church as communion must be judged as unpersuasive (see section on "The Nature of the Church"), this fundamental idea, grounded as it is in the very character of faith, should be affirmed.

The faith that human beings receive from God places them into a relation with God. To believe means to enjoy communion with God. Faith is not, however, merely the "flight of the alone to the alone" (Plotinus). Because the Christian God is not a lonely God, but rather a communion of three persons, faith leads human beings into the divine *communio.* One cannot, however, have a self-enclosed communion with the triune God—a "foursome," as it were—for the Christian God is not a private deity. Communion with God is at once also communion with others who have entrusted themselves in faith to this very same God. Hence, one and the same act of faith places a person into a new relationship both with God and with all others who stand in communion with God. Those others, as Eberhard Jüngel observes, "are discovered *equiprimally* with the new communion with God as one's neighbors, as those who belong to the same communion" (*Gott als Geheimnis der Welt,* 485, italics added). Inclusion into ecclesial communion is, accordingly, already given with the reception of salvific grace.

It is soteriologically and ecclesiologically inappropriate, therefore, to understand the church as an external aid to salvation. The church is not a mere training subject or training ground for the edification of pious individuals. As Emil Brunner correctly emphasized, the church is "not some *externum subsidium fidei,* but rather is the thing itself. . . . Being allied with one another is just as much an end in itself as alliance with Christ" (*Mißverständnis der Kirche,* 12, 15; I do not, however, share Brunner's hostility toward institutions). Salvation and the church cannot be separated. The old formula was *extra ecclesiam nulla salus* ("outside the church there is no salvation"). Freed from its element of exclusivity, which rightly has tarnished its reputation, the formula accurately expresses the essential communal character of salvation. Correctly understood— and as Dietrich Bonhoeffer formulated it, having picked up on it during the struggle between church and state during the period of National Socialism in Germany—the formula states that "salvation is inconceivable without the church, and the church is inconceivable without salvation" ("Zur Frage nach der Kirchengemeinschaft," 231). To experience faith means to become an ecclesial being. Nor can it be otherwise if the church is to be the proleptic experience within history of the eschatological integration of the entire people of God into the communion of the triune God.

3. THE TRINITY AND THE CHURCH

The thesis that ecclesial communion should correspond to trinitarian communion today enjoys the status of an almost self-evident proposition. Yet it is surprising that no one has carefully examined just where such correspondences are to be found, nor expended much effort in attempting to determine where ecclesial communion reaches the limits of its capacity for such analogy. The result is that reconstructions of these correspondences often offer nothing more than the platitude that unity cannot exist without multiplicity nor multiplicity without unity. The former, however, is so vague that no one cares to dispute it, whereas the latter is so divine that no one can live it.

The Correspondence between Trinitarian and Ecclesial Communion

Conceiving of the church in correspondence to the Trinity means both thinking about the Trinity and our social relations in light of the scriptural narrative of the triune God, and also thinking about such relations with theological consistency, all the while hoping that reality will not prove to be too recalcitrant. In substance, however, the correspondence is grounded in Christian baptism. For through baptism "in the name of the Father, of the Son, and of the Holy Spirit," the Spirit of God leads believers simultaneously into both trinitarian and ecclesial communion. Churches, therefore, do not emerge from baptism as images of the triune God that have been fashioned through imitation by human beings, but as those who are experiencing by the work of the Spirit communion with the triune God and God's glorified people (cf. 1 John 1:3–4; Rev 21–22).

If Christian initiation is a trinitarian event, then the church must speak of the Trinity as its determining reality. And because churches, in the power of the Holy Spirit, already form a communion with the triune God, ecclesial correspondence to the Trinity becomes not only an object of hope but also a task for human beings. Correspondence between trinitarian and ecclesial relationships, however, is not simply formal. Rather, it is "ontological" because it is soteriologically grounded—that is, as Alistair MacFadyen has argued, the Trinity is not merely a social model but "a consequence of God's redemptive and creative relationship with us" ("The Trinity and Human Individuality," 14). Jesus' high-priestly prayer, that his disciples might become one "as you, Father, are in me and I am in you, may they also be in us" (John 17:21), presupposes communion with the triune God, as mediated through faith and baptism, and aims at its eschatological consummation. Thus the already obtaining communion of the church with the triune God, which communion is directed at this consummation, implies that the correspondence between the Trinity and the church will be not purely formal, but that relations within the church—both with the triune God and with all human beings—will reflect the mutual *love* of the divine persons.

The idea of a correspondence between the Trinity and the church has remained, however, largely alien to the free church tradition. This is to be expected, for if one understands the church as arising only insofar as human beings make themselves into a church, as Smyth suggested, then one cannot understand the church in analogy to the Trinity. It is probably no accident, therefore, that A. H. Strong, the early twentieth-century Baptist theologian, did not mention the church in his analysis of the implications of the doctrine of the Trinity, even though he viewed the Trinity as the model of interpersonal love—"fatherly giving and filial receiving" (*Systematic Theology,* 351). In Strong's view, the church arises through human beings' constituting themselves into a church (ibid., 902). But were the divine persons to unite, as do converted Christians, into a fellowship—as the common free church ecclesial model has it—one would have not a Trinity but a tritheism.

My intention here is to make a contribution to the trinitarian reshaping of free church ecclesiology. I will try to show how those assembled in the name of Christ, even though they number only three, can be an "image" (Greek, *eikōn*) of the Trinity. Although this thesis may seem radical, it is not entirely new. Tertullian, albeit in his Montanist period, already brought into correspondence the ecclesial and trinitarian "three":

> For the Church is itself, properly and principally, the Spirit Himself, in whom there is a Trinity of one divinity, Father, Son and Holy Spirit. He unites in one congregation that Church which the Lord said consists of three persons. And so, from that time on, any number of persons at all, joined in this faith, has been recognized as the Church by Him who founded and consecrated it. (*Modesty* 21)

Tertullian's allusion to Matt 18:20 is unmistakable. It is precisely as the congregation assembling in the name of Christ that the church is an image of the Trinity. And in developing this correspondence of the church to the Trinity, I will relate John 17:21 ("as you, Father, are in me and I am in you, may they also be in us") to the following ideas: (1) the ecclesiality of the church, building on Matt 18:20 ("where two or three are gathered in my name, I am there among them"); (2) the mediation of faith, building on Gal 2:20 ("I live, but it is no longer I who live, but it is Christ who lives in me"); and (3) the structure of the church, building on 1 Cor 14:26 ("when you come together, each one has a hymn, a lesson, a revelation").

The Limits of the Analogy

Although the this-worldly character of God's self-revelation makes it possible to convert trinitarian ideas into ecclesiological ideas, it must always be recognized that this process of conversion has its limits—unless, of course, one reduces theology to anthropology or elevates anthropology to theology. Two considerations, in particular, are relevant here: first, that "person" and "communion" in ecclesiology cannot be understood as identical with "person" and "communion" in the doctrine of the Trinity, but rather only as *analogous;* and second, that human beings are creations of the triune God and can correspond to God only in a *creaturely* fashion.

A third point, however must also be added, one that is grounded in the difference between the historical and the eschatological being of Christians. For the correspondence of ecclesial to trinitarian communion is always lived out on the path between baptism, which places human beings into communion with the triune God, and the eschatological new creation, where this communion is completed. Here the correspondence acquires an inner dynamic that moves between the historical minimum and the eschatological maximum. It requires that we understand the church as a *sojourning* church, with the dilemma in such an understanding being this: If the church remains at a statically understood minimum of correspondence to the Trinity, it misses the possibilities that God has given it along with its being; but if it reaches for a statically understood maximum, it risks missing its historical reality, and its self-understanding turns into ideology. The relevant ecclesiological question, therefore, is this: How is the church to correspond to the Trinity *within history?*

Trinity, Universal Church, and Local Church

As is well known, the trinitarian theologies of the Christian West and Christian East differ in that for the West the unity of the divine essence is primary, whereas in the East it is the triplicity of the divine persons. This distinction explains the preference of the West for psychological analogies for the Trinity and the preference of the East for social analogies. But understanding the unity of God by way of the one substance of God seems, rather unavoidably, to establish the precedence of the one God before the three persons, and so to threaten the triunity of God. By contrast, one must insist with Jürgen Moltmann that "the persons themselves constitute both their differerences and their unity" (*The Trinity and the Kingdom,* 175). This presupposes that the divinity of the one God does not precede the divine persons, but that God exists concretely as three persons. And if this is the case, then God's being coincides with the communion of the three divine persons—which is what Eastern Orthodox theologians have rightly emphasized, even though their ecclesiological conclusions drawn from such a premise are not fully persuasive.

Within interpersonal relations there is nothing that corresponds to the numerically identical divine nature, as the divine nature is commonly presupposed by theologians of the West—unless one were to conceive of the unity of humanity anthropologically as the unity of one human nature and to assert that all human beings constitute "one single human being" destined to become one single human being in Christ, as is also commonly argued by theologians of the West. This theory of one single humanity destined to become one single human being in Christ has enjoyed a venerable history (see, e.g., Gregory of Nyssa, *Quod non sint tres dii* [*Patrologia graeca* 45.117ff.]). I believe, however, that such a notion is both anthropologically and ecclesiologically unacceptable. Therefore, for both trinitarian and ecclesiological reasons, the one numerically identical divine nature can play no role in the analogy between the Trinity and the church. Rather, one must understand relations within any given local church in correspondence to the *communion of the divine persons.*

Furthermore, it needs here to be said that the distinction between the universal church and the local church involves only the church that finds itself on the way to its eschatological future. When in the eschaton the whole people of God is assembled in the unity of the triune God, this distinction will be eliminated. Human beings will then live in perfect communion with the triune God and will reflect the communion of the triune God in their own mutual relationships.

Because, therefore, every local church is a concrete anticipation of the final, eschatological community, it is decisive that one understand and live *relationships within* a given local church in correspondence to the Trinity. These relationships between Trinity and church are eschatologically abiding. But those relationships between local churches as local churches are merely historically determined, and so transient. The Trinity indwells local churches in no other way than through its presence within the persons constituting those churches, since the church *is* those who gather in the name of Christ.

Trinitarian Persons and the Church

In their mutual giving and receiving, the trinitarian persons are not only interdependent, but also *mutually internal*—something to which the Johannine Jesus repeatedly refers: "So that you may know and understand that the Father is in me and I am in the Father" (John 10:38; cf. 14:10–11; 17:21). This mutually internal abiding and interpenetration of the trinitarian persons, which has been called *perichōrēsis* by theologians since Pseudo-Cyril, determines the character both of the divine persons and of their unity.

Perichōrēsis refers to the reciprocal *interiority* of the trinitarian persons: that in every divine person as a subject, the other persons also indwell; that all mutually permeate one another, though in so doing they do not cease to be distinct persons. It was used by the church fathers to mean, as G. L. Prestige has expressed it, "co-inherence in one another without any coalescence or commixture" (*God in Patristic Thought*, 298). This is why both statements can be made: "Father and Son are in one another," and "Christians are in *them*" (the plural "in *us*"; cf. John 17:21).

Being in one another does not abolish trinitarian plurality. Yet, despite their abiding distinctions as persons, their subjectivities overlap. For each divine person acts as a subject and, at the same time, the other persons act as subjects in that person. This is why the Johannine Jesus can say, in seemingly paradoxical fashion: "My teaching is not mine" (John 7:16). Such a statement acquires its full theological weight only if one does not attempt to resolve the tension between "mine" and "not mine" on one side or the other, but emphasizes both equally. For within the personal interiority of the divine persons, "mine" is simultaneously "not mine" without ceasing to be "mine," just as "not mine" is simultaneously "mine" without ceasing to be "not mine."

From this interiority of the divine persons there emerges what I would like to call their *catholicity*. "The Father is in me and I am in him" (John 10:38) implies that "whoever has seen me has seen the Father" (John 14:9–10). The one divine person is not only itself, but also carries within itself the other divine persons—and only in this indwelling of the other persons within it is it the person it really is. The Son is Son only insofar as the Father and the Spirit indwell him. Without the interiority of the Father and the Spirit, there would be no Son. The same applies to the Father and to the Spirit. In a certain sense, then, each divine person *is* the other persons—but is such in its own way, which is why rather than ceasing to be a unique person, in its very uniqueness it is a completely *catholic* divine person.

This reciprocal interiority of the divine persons determines the character of their unity. It is a unity grounded neither in a numerically identical substance nor in some accidental intentions of the persons, but rather in their *mutually interior being*. As Moltmann points out: "By the power of their eternal love, the divine persons exist so intimately with, for, and in one another that they themselves constitute themselves in their unique, incomparable and complete union" (*In der Geschichte des dreieinigen Gottes*, 124; see also *The Trinity and the Kingdom*, 174–75).

In a strict sense, of course, there can be no correspondence to the interiority of the divine persons at the human level. Another human self cannot be internal to my own self as the subject of my actions. Human persons are always external to one another *as subjects*. The indwelling of other persons, in fact, is an exclusive prerogative of God. Furthermore, even the divine persons indwell human beings in a qualitatively different way than they do one another.

At the ecclesial level (and at the creaturely level in the broader sense), however, the *interiority of personal characteristics* can correspond to the interiority of the divine persons. In personal encounters, that which the other person is flows, consciously or unconsciously, into that which I am. The reverse is also true. In this mutual giving and receiving, we give to others not only something, but also a piece of ourselves—something of that which we have made of ourselves in communion with others. And from others we take not only something, but also a piece of them. Each person gives of himself or herself to others, and each person in a unique way takes up others into himself or herself. This is the process of the mutual internalization of personal characteristics occurring in the church through the Holy Spirit indwelling Christians.

The correspondence of trinitarian and ecclesial communion, therefore, builds on the *catholicity* of the divine persons. Like individual persons, so also entire communities have specific identifying characteristics—which have been acquired either by way of the cultural context in which they abide or through exceptional personalities active among them. And like persons, they transmit these characteristics to other communities. By opening up to one another both diachronically and synchronically, local churches enrich one another, thereby increasingly becoming catholic churches. In this way, they also increasingly correspond to the catholicity of the triune God, who has already constituted them as catholic churches, because they *are* anticipations of the eschatological gathering of the entire people of God.

The Structure of Trinitarian and Ecclesial Relations

I have argued that we should conceive of the trinitarian persons and their relations as complementary, and I have defined the trinitarian persons as peri-choretic subjects (for a fuller treatment of these matters, see my *After Our Likeness,* 204–15). Father, Son, and Spirit are, as Wolfhart Pannenberg formulates it, not "different modes of being of the one divine subject," but rather "living realizations of separate centers of action" (*Systematic Theology,* 1:319). Accordingly, God also cannot act externally as the one tripersonal divine self, but only as a communion of the different persons existing within one another. But how are the relations of the divine persons as subjects structured?

There are two significant dangers to avoid when one thinks about the Trinity. One is dissolving relations between the divine persons into processions of the divine persons. The other is understanding processions of the divine persons as simply mutual relations. In the first case, the result is unilinear hierarchical relations between the divine persons—that is, the Father begets the Son and spirates (together with the Son?) the Spirit, and sends the Son and (with him?) the Spirit. In this scenario the Father alone is engaged in giving, and any retroactivity of the Son and Spirit on the Father appears as an anomaly. In the second case, the divine persons dissolve into a common divine nature—that is, all the persons mutually constitute and are conditioned by one another, and for that reason none can be distinguished from the others.

My argument, however, is that the one constituting and the one constituted are to be distinguished both conceptually and substantively from the constitutive process itself (cf. Moltmann, *The Trinity and the Kingdom,* 165–66, 175–76; also Siebel, *Der Heilige Geist als Relation,* 32ff.). This is why one must distinguish between the constitution of the divine persons and their relations. The Son and the Spirit are constituted by the Father. The Father is the source from which the Son and the Spirit receive their divinity—that is, it is the Father who constitutes the "hypostatic divinity" of the Son and and Spirit. But just *how* all three divine persons exist as God, or their "innertrinitarian form," is determined by their mutual relations—though, of course, the constitution of the persons and their relations are not to be conceived as two temporally sequential steps, but as two dimensions of the eternal life of the triune God. The constitution of the divine persons through generation and procession grounds the distinctions among the persons, who are simultaneously constituted as standing in relationship to one another. And these distinctions of person then manifest themselves in the salvation-historical differentiation of the divine persons.

If such a distinction between the "hypostatic divinity" of the trinitarian persons (i.e., the constitutional level) and their "innertrinitarian form" (i.e., the relational level) is persuasive, then it follows that unilinear relations disappear from any understanding of trinitarian communion, since maintaining that the

Father constitutes the Son and the Spirit says nothing as yet about *how* the relations between them are structured. In any case, within salvation history the divine persons do appear as distinguishable persons standing in reciprocal relationships to one another (see in this regard Pannenberg, "Der Gott der Geschichte," 123ff.; *Systematic Theology,* 1:308ff.).

Salvation history allows us to infer the fundamental equality of the divine persons in their mutual determination and their mutual interpenetration. For even if the Father is the source of the deity and accordingly sends the Son and the Spirit, he also gives everything to the Son and glorifies him, just as the Son also glorifies the Father and gives the reign over to the Father (cf. Matt 28:18; John 13:31–32; 16:14; 17:1; 1 Cor 15:24). Moreover, within a community of perfect love between persons who share all the divine attributes, any notion of hierarchy and subordination is inconceivable. Within *relations* between the divine persons, the Father is for that reason not the one over against the others, nor "the First," but rather the *one among the others* (so Moltmann, *Geist des Lebens,* 323). The structure of trinitarian relations, therefore, is characterized neither by a pyramidal dominance of the one, as in Catholic theology, nor a hierarchical bipolarity between the one and the many, as in Orthodox theology, but by a polycentric and symmetrical reciprocity of the many.

If one starts from the trinitarian model, as I have suggested, then the structure of ecclesial unity cannot be conceived by way of the one—be it pope, patriarch, or bishop. Every ecclesial unity held together by a mon-archy is monistic, and thus also untrinitarian. Reflecting on the fact that no *one* human being can correspond to the trinitarian relational network, Heribert Mühlen has concluded that ecclesiastical *office* is to be exercised collegially—even the office of the pope! *(Entsakralisierung).* This is a step in the right direction (for a discussion, see my "Trinity, Unity, Primacy"). Such a "trinitarianization" of office would correspond to the collegial exercise of offices in the early church (cf. Phil 1:1; 1 Thess 5:12; Rom 12:8; see also Fee, *First and Second Timothy, Titus,* 20ff., on the collegial exercise of offices in the Pastoral Epistles). Yet such a step will not suffice. For the correspondence between the structure of the Trinity and the church would still be conceived in an overly hierachical fashion. And though such a step would break the dominance of the one, the bipolarity between a "trinitarianized" determinative office and the congregation that says "amen" would remain. This is unavoidable if one distinguishes in principle, rather than in function, between the universal and the particular priesthood. The *ordo* of the priests then would correspond to the triune God and act in God's name over against the congregation.

Conceiving the structure of the church in a consistently trinitarian fashion means conceiving not only the institution of office as such, but also the *entire (local) church* itself in correspondence to the Trinity. The high-priestly prayer of Jesus brings all who believe in him into correspondence with the unity of the triune God (John 17:20; cf. 1 John 1:3). Paul, too, seems to be arguing from a trinitarian perspective when he admonishes the Corinthian congregation to unity (1 Cor 12:4–6; cf. Eph 4:3–6). The various gifts, services, and activities that all

Christians have correspond to the divine multiplicity. Just as the one deity exists as the Father, Son, and Spirit, so also do these different divine persons distribute different gifts to *all* Christians. That these gifts are distributed for the benefit of *all* (cf. 1 Cor 12:7), however, corresponds to the divine unity. For *the same* Spirit, *the same* Lord, and *the same* God (the Father) are active in all these different gifts. The symmetrical reciprocity of the relations of the trinitarian persons finds its correspondence in the image of the church in which *all* members serve one another with their specific gifts of the Spirit in imitation of the Lord and through the power of the Father. Like the divine persons, they all stand in a relation of mutual giving and receiving.

4. A PARTICIPATIVE MODEL OF COMMUNITY FORMATION

Ecumenical discussion about the church has in recent decades concentrated largely on the problem of ecclesial structures, and primarily on the question of office. It seems apparent enough why this is the case. Ecclesial life in most churches proceeds by way of priests and pastors and is realized in the proclamation of the gospel and in the celebration of the sacraments—primarily baptism and the Eucharist, events in which officeholders play key roles. Thus ecumenical dialogue concerning the question of office not only takes place around a well-defined issue but is also immediately relevant for the life of local churches. At the theological level, as well, the question of office is fertile ground for ecumenical discussion, since an entire ecclesiology is always reflected in a certain understanding of office—that is, of what officeholders are to do in the church and how they are to become officeholders.

Reflection on ecclesial structures, however, presupposes reflection on the church. For if the structures of the church are really to be the structures *of* the church rather than structures *over* the church, then the church must take precedence over its structures. That is why I have dealt first with what the church is (section 1), how salvation is mediated within it (section 2), and how it is to correspond to the Trinity as its ground and goal (section 3). Only after dealing with these fundamental ecclesiological questions can one reflect meaningfully on the structures of the church.

In this final section I will examine ecclesial structures by addressing the problem of participation in church life. Discussions about ordination, election, ecclesial offices, and the allocation of persons to particular roles in the church I must, of necessity, leave to more extensive treatments in my book *After Our Likeness* (esp. pp. 245–57). Nor will I, in view of my own primary interest in relations between persons, expressly examine the sacraments, which together with offices are part of the structures of the church. All of these matters are extremely complex. But in a study of the church as communion, it should suffice merely to point out which consequences regarding a theology of office can be drawn from the basic ecclesiological decisions I have presented in the preceding three sections.

A Polycentric Church

The church lives through the participation of its members, both laity and officeholders, and is constituted through them by the Holy Spirit. All churches agree on this point. What is disputed is *how* this occurs.

Catholic and Orthodox ecclesiologies are emphatically *episcopocentric.* And though he may play a somewhat different role in their respective understandings, the bishop's preeminent position in the church for both Catholic and Orthodox ecclesiology is decisively associated with the notion of the church as a subject— which, in turn, is a view sustained by the idea of the "whole Christ," head and members. The church, therefore, needs the bishop as the one human subject in order itself to be concretely capable of acting as a subject. The bishop acts *in persona Christi* and simultaneously *in persona ecclesiae.* These two are as intimately connected as are the head and body in the one organism of Christ, which is the church.

Over the course of this chapter, however, I have tried to show that the church is not a single subject, but a communion of interdependent subjects; that the mediation of salvation occurs not only through officeholders, but also through all other members of the church; and that the church is constituted by the Holy Spirit not so much by way of the institution of office as through the communal confession in which Christians speak the word of God to one another. From these three basic theological convictions, it follows that the life and structure of the church cannot be episcopocentric. The church is not a monocentric-bipolar community, however articulated, but fundamentally a *polycentric-participative community.*

Paul seems to envision such a model of ecclesial life when he tries to reestablish peace within the enthusiastic and chaotic congregation at Corinth (see 1 Cor 14:33). As a kind of summary of his instructions in 1 Cor 12–14, he writes: "When you come together, *each one* has a hymn, a lesson, a revelation, a tongue, or an interpretation. Let all things be done for building up the congregation" (1 Cor 14:26; cf. 1 Pet 2:5–10; 4:10). During the Protestant Reformation, Martin Luther rediscovered this polycentric-participative model of ecclesial life with his notion of the universal priesthood of believers—a priesthood he never understood merely soteriologically, but always also ecclesiologically. In the German-speaking sphere, it was Philipp Jakob Spener, Nicholas Ludwig Graf von Zinzendorf, and Johann Hinrich Wichern, in particular, who tried to vivify Luther's ecclesiological insight. Such an insight, however, was unable to establish itself fully within Protestantism. In the English-speaking sphere, it was the various free church groups who undertook to endue with renewed life this understanding of the universal priesthood of believers, such as the Baptists, Congregationalists, Quakers, and Pentecostals.

A Charismatic Church

Because the church is born through the presence of Christ in the Holy Spirit, the thesis that the church is constituted by way of the entire called and charismatically endowed people of God presupposes that the exalted Christ himself is acting in the gifts of the Spirit. According to the Pauline understanding of the charismata, this is indeed the case, since, as Ernst Käsemann emphasizes, a gift of the Spirit is "the specific portion of the individual in the dominion and glory of Christ" ("Amt und Gemeinde," 111). This is why the charismata are not gifts that can be separated from the concrete presence of Christ in human beings and so be at the latter's free disposal. Christ himself is "present in his gifts and in the ministries attesting those gifts and made possible by those gifts" (ibid., 118). And since all Christians have charismata, Christ is also acting through all the members of the church, and not merely through its officeholders.

A number of features identifying the charismata need here to be highlighted. One important feature is the *confession of Christ as Savior and Lord*. This is, in fact, the indispensable feature distinguishing the charismata from other activities in which people engage in the church and the world (cf. 1 Cor 12:2–3). It cannot be otherwise. For if Christ is to act in the charismata, then he must be implicitly and explicitly confessed by charismatics themselves through their charismatic activities as the one who he is, namely, Savior and Lord. Just as every charisma is a concrete manifestation of Christ's grace, so also is every charismatic activity a concrete form of confession to him.

A second identifying feature of the charismata is their *universal distribution*. According to the New Testament, the charismata are not phenomena limited to a certain circle of persons, but are universally present in the church (cf. 1 Cor 12:7; Rom 12:3; Eph 4:7; 1 Pet 4:10). In the community as the body of Christ, there are no members without charisma. The Spirit poured out on all flesh (cf. Acts 2:17–21) also distributes gifts to all flesh. This is why a division of the congregation into those who serve and those who are served is ecclesiologically unacceptable, for every person is to serve with his or her specific gifts and every person is to be served in his or her specific need.

The universal distribution of the charismata implies *common responsibility* for the life of the church. It cannot be the task of leaders, ordained or not, to do everything in the church themselves. This would lead to the hypertrophy of one member of the body of Christ and the atrophy of all other members. The task of leaders, rather, is to animate all the members of the church to engage in their pluriform charismatic activities and to coordinate these activities. It is also the task of leaders to be responsible for a mature church that is called to test every manifestation of the Spirit (cf. 1 Thess 5:21).

Furthermore, common responsibility implies *mutual subordination* (cf. Eph 5:21). Although Paul demands that his congregations acknowledge certain members and be subordinate to them (cf. 1 Thess 5:12; 1 Cor 16:15–16), the authority of these members is relativized in several respects, and thereby also protected. Such authority is not absolute, since the members of the church owe unconditional obedience only to their common Lord. Likewise, the authority of certain members is based less on their formal position than on their active service in the congregation (cf. 1 Thess 5:13). Ultimately, however, obligatory subordination to leaders stands within the framework of the obligatory mutual subordination of all, which is why Christian obedience can only be, as Hans Küng points out, free "obedience to the respectively different charismata of others" (*Die Kirche*, 474).

A third characteristic feature of the charismata is their *interdependence*. All members have charismata, but not every member has all charismata. The fullness of gifts is to be found in the entire (local) church. Paul emphasizes in several passages that, commensurate with their functions, the members of the body of Christ have "*different* gifts" (Rom 12:6; cf. 1 Cor 12:7–11). The church is not a club of universally gifted people or self-sufficient charismatics, but a community of men and women whom the Spirit of God has endowed in a certain way for service to each other and to the world in anticipation of God's new creation.

Since the members of the church are interdependent, their lives must be characterized by mutuality. The church is a community "of giving and receiving" (Phil 4:15), and the "charismata of office" must be integrated into this mutuality. Officeholders do not stand opposite the church as those acting exclusively *in persona Christi*. Since the Spirit of Christ acts in them not by the power of their office, but in the execution of their ministry, their actions do not differ in principle from those of any other member of the church.

A fourth feature of the charismata is this: that the *sovereign Spirit of God* allots the charismata "as the Spirit chooses" (1 Cor 12:11). The Spirit works, first, *as* the Spirit chooses. No church—neither an entire (local) church nor any stratum in the church—can prescribe which gifts the Spirit will bestow on which members. Furthermore, the Spirit works *when* the Spirit chooses. The church cannot determine at what time the Spirit will bestow its gifts. This clearly reveals that the church lives from a dynamic that does not derive from itself. Questions regarding who is to do what in the church, in a real and important sense, are not church matters at all. It is not the church that "organizes" its life, but the Holy Spirit. Hence the *pneumatological structure* of the church follows from the sovereignty of the Spirit in the bestowal of charismata.

Charismata for a specific ministry in the church and world, however, are not "irrevocable" (cf. Rom 11:29). Various charismata can replace one another over time, which is something implied by the interactional model of their bestowal. Over the history of the congregation, the charismata with which its individual members serve can change. Certain charismata may come to the fore at certain times, while others may become unimportant—either for the congregation itself or for the bearers of these charismata. This does not mean that the divine calling and endowment for a certain ministry cannot be a lifelong affair. But it is not *necessarily* so. There is no correlation between the permanence of a particular charisma and its divine origin. The Spirit of God is the Spirit of life, and the Spirit's gifts are accordingly as varied and dynamic as is ecclesial life itself.

The Trinity as Model for Church Structures

An appropriate answer to the question of the character of the church as an institution must finally be given through reference to the doctrine of the Trinity.

For the church reflects in a broken fashion the eschatological communion of the entire people of God with the triune God in God's new creation. Its institutions, therefore, should correspond to the Trinity as well. That they are able to do so derives from the character of the charismata that structure the church—with relations between the charismata, as I have tried to show above, being modeled after trinitarian relations.

The institutionality of the church can be conceived in correspondence to the Trinity only because the Trinity itself is, in a certain sense, an "institution." This becomes apparent as soon as one understands institutions as stable structures of social interaction. For the Trinity is inconceivable without stable relations between the divine persons—that is, the identity of the divine persons cannot be determined without such stable relations. Nonetheless, the Trinity is an institution only analogously. The divine persons do not, for example, exhibit any possibility for a *typology* of agents of the sort required for institutionalization, since, by definition, only one divine person is available for any one trinitarian "role." Their "roles" are not interchangeable, since their respective uniqueness as distinct persons is defined by their "roles."

Furthermore, we must note that the correspondence of ecclesial institutions to the Trinity cannot be determined just "from above," from the Trinity itself. The limits of analogy applicable to the church must also be considered—that is, limits grounded in the church's creaturely and historical nature. Hence a double access to the institutionality of the church is necessary: it must be viewed both as a communion living from its fellowship with the triune God and as a human social phenomenon. Just as an exclusively sociophilosophical grounding of its institutionality would neglect the inner essence of the church as a communion with the triune God, so an exclusively trinitarian grounding would fail to do justice to the character of the church as a human community on its way to its goal.

The character of an institution depends primarily on two factors: the pattern of power distribution and the manner of its cohesion. With regard to the distribution of power, one can distinguish between symmetrical-polycentric and asymmetrical-monocentric models. With regard to cohesion, one can distinguish between coerced and freely affirmed integration. The combination of these factors in their implementation yields the multiplicity of institutional forms seen throughout history. The two extreme models—which, of course, never occur in reality in their pure forms—are (1) institutions with an asymmetrical-monocentric distribution of power and (formally or informally) coerced integration, and (2) institutions with a symmetrical-decentralized distribution of power and freely affirmed integration.

In concert with Jürgen Moltmann, I have taken as my premise the symmetrical relations within the Trinity. This yields the ecclesial principle that the more a church is characterized by a symmetrical and decentralized distribution of power and by a freely affirmed interaction, the more it will correspond to the communion that exists within the Trinity. Furthermore, relations between the charismata, which are modeled after the Trinity, are reciprocal and symmetrical. Thus, since all members of the church have charismata, all are to engage their charismata for the good of all others.

Ecclesiastical "offices" are a particular type of charismata. Like any other ministry in the church, the ministry of officeholders is based on the one baptism common to all Christians and on the charismata bestowed especially on officeholders. Since *all* Christians are not only baptized but also have the various charismata specific to each of them, there can be no difference in principle between officeholders and other members of the church. The distinction between the general and the particular priesthood does not divide the church into two groups— one of which has merely the general priesthood, while the other has also the particular priesthood—but rather refers to *two dimensions in the service of every member of the church*. On the basis of a common baptism, all Christians have become priests and all realize their priesthood in their own way on the basis of their respective charismata. Hence all members of the church, both officeholders and "laypersons," are fundamentally equal.

5. A POSTSCRIPT

Trinitarian relations serve as the model for the institutions of the church because the triune God is present in the church through the Holy Spirit, shaping the church in the image of the Trinity. Through this activity of the Spirit, salvific grace is mediated and the church is constituted. A participative model of the church, therefore, requires more than just values and practices that correspond to participative institutions. The church is not first of all a realm of moral purposes. Rather, it is the anticipation, constituted by the presence of the Spirit of God, of the eschatological gathering of the entire people of God in the communion of the triune God. Hence the church needs the vivifying presence of the Spirit, for without this presence even a church with a decentralized participative structure and culture will become sterile—perhaps more sterile than even a hierarchical church. It will either have to get along without the participation of most of its members, or it will have to operate with more subtle and open forms of coercion. Successful participative church life must, therefore, be sustained by deep spirituality. Only the person who lives from the Spirit of communion (cf. 2 Cor 13:13) can participate authentically in the life of the ecclesial community.

BIBLIOGRAPHY

Barrett, C. K. *Commentary on the First Epistle to the Corinthians*. London: A. & C. Black, 1968.

Bonhoeffer, Dietrich. "Zur Frage nach der Kirchengemeinschaft." *Evangelische Theologie* 3 (1936).

Brunner, Emil. *Das Mißverständnis der Kirche*. 2d ed. Zurich: Zwingli. 1951.

Calvin, John. *The Institutes of the Christian Religion.* Edited by J. T. McNeill. Translated by F. L. Battles. *Library of Christian Classics* 20–21. Philadelphia: Westminster, 1960.

Fee, G. D. *First and Second Timothy, Titus.* Peabody, Mass.: Hendrickson, 1988.

Huss, John. *The Church.* Translated by D. S. Schaff. New York: Harper & Bros., 1954.

Jüngel, Eberhard. *Gott als Geheimnis der Welt: Zur Begründung der Theologie des Gekreuzigten im Streit zwischen Theismus und Atheismus.* 3d ed. Tübingen: Mohr-Siebeck, 1978.

———. *Wertlose Wahrheit: Zur Identität und Relevanz des christlichen Glaubens.* Munich: Kaiser, 1990.

Käsemann, Ernst. "Amt und Gemeinde im Neuen Testament." In *Exegetische Versuche und Besinnungen.* Göttingen: Vandenhoeck & Ruprecht, 1970.

Küng, Hans. *Die Kirche.* Munich: Piper, 1977.

McFadyen, Alistair I. "The Trinity and Human Individuality: The Conditions for Relevance." *Theology* 95 (1992): 10–18.

Moltmann, Jürgen. *The Church in the Power of the Spirit: A Contribution to Messianic Ecclesiology.* New York: Harper & Row, 1977.

———. *The Trinity and the Kingdom: The Doctrine of God.* New York: Harper & Row, 1981.

———. "Einführung: Einige Fragen der Trinitätslehre heute." In *In der Geschichte des dreieinigen Gottes: Beiträge zur trinitarischen Theologie.* Munich: Kaiser, 1991.

———. "Die einladende Einheit des dreieinigen Gottes." In *In der Geschichte des dreieinigen Gottes: Beiträge zur trinitarischen Theologie.* Munich: Kaiser, 1991.

———. *Geist des Lebens: Ganzheitliche Pneumatologie.* Munich: Kaiser, 1991. ET *The Spirit of Life: A Universal Affirmation.* Minneapolis: Fortress, 1992.

Mühlen, Heribert. *Entsakralisierung: Ein epochates Schlagwort in seiner Bedentung für die Zukunft der christlishen Kirchen.* Paderborn: Schöningh, 1971.

Pannenberg, Wolfhart. "Der Gott der Geschichte: Der trinitarische Gott und die Wahrheit der Geschichte." In *Grundfragen Systematischer Theologie: Gesammelte Aufsätze.* Göttingen: Vandenhoeck & Ruprecht, 1980.

———. "Person und Subjekt." In *Grundfragen Systematischer Theologie: Gesammelte Aufsätze.* Göttingen: Vandenhoeck & Ruprecht, 1980.

———. "Reich Gottes, Kirche und Gesellschaft in der Sicht der systematischen Theologie." Pages 119–35 in *Christlicher Glaube in moderner Gesellschaft: Enzyklopädische Bibliothek in 30 Teilbanden.* Vol. 29. Edited by F. Böckle, et al. Freiburg: Herder, 1982.

———. *Systematic Theology.* 3 vols. Grand Rapids, Mich.: Eerdmans, 1991–1997.

Prestige, G. L. *God in Patristic Thought.* London: SPCK, 1956.

Schleiermacher, Friedrich. *The Christian Faith.* Translated by H. R. Mackintosh and J. S. Stewart. Edinburgh: T&T Clark, 1928.

Siebel, W. *Der Heilige Geist als Relation: Eine sozial Trinitätslehre.* Münster: Aschendorff, 1986.

Smyth, John. *The Works of John Smyth.* Edited by W. T. Whitley. Cambridge: Cambridge University Press, 1915.

Sohm, Rudolph. *Wesen und Ursprung des Katholigismus.* 2d ed. Leipzig: Teubner, 1912.

Strong, A. H. *Systematic Theology: A Compendium Designed for the Use of Theological Students.* Old Tappan, N.J.: Revell, 1907.

Stuhlmacher, P. *Gerechtigheit Gottes bei Paulus.* 2d ed. Göttingen: Vandenhoeck & Ruprecht, 1966.

Vischer, Lukas. "Schwierigkeiten bei der Befragung des Neuen Testaments." Pages 17–40 in *Sie aber hielten fest an der Gemeinschaft: Einheit der Kirche als Prozess im Neuen Testament und heute.* Edited by C. Link, U. Luz, and L. Vischer. Zurich: Benziger, 1988.

Volf, Miroslav. " 'The Trinity Is Our Social Program': The Doctrine of the Trinity and the Shape of Social Engagement." *Modern Theology* 14 (1998).

———. *After Our Likeness: The Church as the Image of the Trinity.* Grand Rapids, Mich.: Eerdmans, 1998.

———. "Trinity, Unity, Primacy: On the Trinitarian Nature of Unity and Its Implications for the Question of Primacy." Pages 121–84 in *Petrine Ministry and the Unity of the Church.* Edited by J. F. Puglisi. Collegeville, Minn.: Liturgical Press, 1999.

Wainwright, Arthur W. *The Trinity in the New Testament.* London: SPCK, 1962.

Index of Subjects

Abraham's descendants, 75
angels, 30
anticlericalism, 180
apostle(s), 73, 83–83, 91, 96–100, 108, 143, 165, 170, 203, 215, 221
apostle to the Gentiles, 83–84
apostolic succession, xv–xvi, 135–36, 184–85, 190–91, 215–16, 229, 231
apostolicity, 190–91
Aristotelians, 4
Artemis, 42
ascetics, asceticism, 5, 160, 168, 202
associations, 3–18, 27–28, 36–37, 39–40, 42–43, 46–49, 165–66, 207–8
association buildings, 40–54
Attis, 48, 53
authority of scripture, 198–99, 210

baptism, 53, 85, 99, 101, 109, 133, 141, 151, 158, 186, 198–90, 203, 208, 215, 217–19, 223, 225, 230, 235
Baptist, 213, 216, 220, 224
basilica(s), 36, 39–40, 45, 50, 52, 54, 166
Believer's Church, 213
Bellona, 48, 53
bishop(s) (see also overseer; perhaps also presbyter), xii–xiii, xv, 129, 132–33, 135–36, 138–42, 144–54, 157–60, 162–71, 174, 188–91, 204–5, 215–16, 229, 231
body of christ, xvi, 73, 76–77, 80–81, 121, 199, 201, 203–4, 208–9, 212, 217
burial societies (Jewish), 28

Catholic, catholicity, 179, 191, 215, 218–19, 227–28
celibacy, 160
charisma, charismata, 121, 180, 231–35
charismatic-pneumatic community, 231–35

charismatic-pneumatic ministry, xv–xvi, 134, 180, 183
children, 109, 112
Christology, 184–85, 188, 192, 194, 198, 201, 217, 219
church, nature of the, 181–92, 194, 196, 199–200, 213–22
church councils, 151
church of the living God, 114–15, 121
clergy, 101–3, 133, 140–42, 146, 149–50, 154, 168–69, 174, 210–11
clerical absolution, 141–42
collegiality/mutuality, 118, 233
communal meals, 4, 6, 8, 25, 37, 45, 52, 133, 147–48
community of faith, 199–200, 205, 208, 210
community of grace, 213
community of the Spirit, xvi, 79–80, 95
compassion, 91, 102
confession(s), 109, 186, 209
confessor(s), 133–34, 138, 140, 142, 147–49, 151–55, 281, 220, 231–32
Congregational, xiv, 180, 191, 213
contextualize, contextualization, xvii–xviii, 73, 83, 86–87, 105–6, 122–24, 136, 153, 157, 174, 191–92, 185–96, 204–6, 209, 211–12
conversion, 32–34
cosmopolitanism, 32–33
coworkers of Paul, 84, 116–22
creativity, 82, 86, 182–83, 209
Cybelism, cult of Cybele, 40–41, 48, 53, 130–31
Cynics, 4

deacon(s), xii, 112, 118–19, 122, 129, 132–33, 136, 138, 140, 142, 144, 153, 157, 163–65, 168–71, 174, 203–10
deaconess (see perhaps also deacon), 162, 169

depostism/totalitarianism, 97, 153
diaconate, xii, 84–85, 171
Dionysus, Dionysian cult, 43, 45, 47, 53
discipline, 111, 116, 118, 149, 151, 153,
    190, 199, 204, 206, 209, 212
divine origin and control of the church,
    80–81
doxologies, 108–9
due, fees, collections, 16

"early catholicism," 180
ecclesiality of salvation, 221–22
ecumenism, ecumenical, 214, 219, 230
egalitarian, egalitarianism, 5, 14, 97, 213
elders (see also presbyters), xii, 99–100,
    102, 109, 116, 118–21, 140, 145, 148, 168,
    194, 202–10
elect, election, 75, 200
Epicureans, 4, 7–8, 17
episcopacy, episcopal (see also episcopate),
    179–81, 184, 187–92
episcopate (see also episcopacy and
    monepiscopate), xii, xiv, 84–86, 150, 157,
    171, 179, 189, 191–92
episcopocentric, 189, 215, 231
eschatological community, xvi, 30, 34,
    79–80, 214, 219–21, 226, 228, 235
Essenes (see also Qumran), 20, 22, 30, 94
Eucharist (see also Lord's Supper), 133,
    141, 146, 152, 154, 158, 161, 167–68,
    171–75, 188, 215, 217–19, 230
evangelical, 179–86, 189, 191–92
evangelism, evangelists, 112, 123, 203
excommunication, 16, 111, 146, 152, 154,
    205
exorcism(s), 63, 71

faith, 199–200, 208, 214, 219–22
fellowship, 4, 7, 65, 71, 85, 90, 153, 187,
    200–201, 214, 224
feminist ecclesiology, 157, 213
food prohibitions, 30–31
forgiveness, 64–66, 67–68, 71, 132, 147
Free Church, 213–14, 216–17, 220, 223–24,
    231
freedom of conscience, 196

gathered/assembled community, 25, 213,
    216–19, 224, 226
general assembly, 206–7, 209
gnostic, gnosticism, 132, 134–36, 143, 154
God, character of, 90–92, 196–98, 208
God: Trinity, triune, 182, 194, 197–98,
    213–15, 222, 225–28

grace, 200
guardians/defenders of the faith, gospel,
    orthodoxy, 134–35, 138, 140–41, 148,
    153, 155, 160, 187, 190, 203, 215
God-fearers, 26–28, 42

healing(s), 63–65, 67, 71
hellenization, 32–33
hierarchy, hierarchical (see also monar-
    chy), 14, 163, 167–69, 207, 229, 134–35
home (Jewish), 28–32
honor-dishonor, 93–96
hospitality, 25, 109–10, 117, 159–60
house church(es), xvii, 36, 39–40, 52, 54,
    85, 92, 96–98, 101–2, 107, 119, 142,
    145–48, 153, 166
households, 7, 28–29, 77, 102, 106–7,
    113–15, 117, 163–66, 174
household of faith/God, 77, 113–15, 121,
    164–66, 170–71, 204–5

in Christ, xvi, 73, 76–78, 82, 221
inclusivity, 90, 99
individualism, individualistic, xvii, 32–33,
    180, 213, 220–22
initiation rites, 16–17
interpersonal relations, 90
Isis/Sarapis, 43, 45, 47–48, 53
Israel of God, 75, 114

justice, 90–91

kingship/reign of God, 61–63, 65, 68–69,
    71
kinship: language, loyalties and obliga-
    tions, 16, 93–95, 97–98

laity, 26, 133, 140–42, 146, 149–51, 154,
    162, 210–11, 216, 231, 135
laying on of hands, 109, 116–17, 120,
    146–47, 169, 191, 207
leadership models, 6, 8, 10–12, 14–17,
    23–24, 26, 33, 81–85, 89, 94–103, 109,
    112, 116–23, 132–36, 138–42, 144–55,
    160–63, 168–71, 187–93, 201–7, 210–11,
    230–35
lectors, 168
Levites, 23, 150, 152, 171–72, 174
liturgical movement, 129–30, 147, 149
local leaders, 84, 96–97, 102, 109, 116–22,
    231–33
Lord's Prayer, 68
Lord's Supper (see also Eucharist), 82,
    85–86, 109, 112, 186, 203, 208

love, 7, 68–69, 132, 134, 146, 155, 162, 200–201, 208, 211–12, 216, 223–24, 227, 229

martyr(s), martyrdom, 70, 131–34, 140, 142–43, 148–49, 152–54, 158, 160, 172, 175
mercy, 90–91
mikveh (Jewish baptismal font), 29
ministers, 204, 206, 213
ministry, ministries, 59–61, 63–66, 69–71, 79, 83, 89, 103, 105, 120–21, 124, 129–30, 132–33, 136, 138–40, 142, 144, 148–50, 153–55, 157, 161–62, 168, 171–72, 179, 181, 184–87, 189–91, 194, 200–202, 213
miracles, 134
missiology, missiological, 213–14
Mithraism, cult of Mithra, 37, 48–49, 52–53, 131
modernization, 33
monarchy, monarchical (see also hierarchy), xiv–xv, 97, 122, 144, 149, 163, 171, 174, 192, 229, 234–35
monasticism, 39, 52, 54, 158, 160
monepiscopate, monoepiscopal (see also episcopate),160–61, 168, 174, 179
monotheism, 89–90, 92, 167, 174
Montanism, 132, 137, 139
motherhood of the church, 213, 220–21
multiculturalism, 209
mystery religions, 9–11, 16, 40, 53–54

new creation, 214–15, 225
non-patriarchy/antipatriarchal, 97–98, 102–3, 122

oligarchy, oligarchical (see also presbyterian), xiv, 97
order / orderly, 6, 11, 16, 77, 81, 108, 115, 117, 121, 124, 139, 167, 172, 180, 183–84, 187, 189, 190–91, 194, 200, 202–4, 207, 209, 213
ordination, 120, 133, 140, 147–48, 154, 157–58, 169, 207, 210, 213, 230
orphans, 138, 160, 162, 165
overseer(s) (see also bishop; perhaps also presbyter and elder), 112, 117–19, 121–22, 132, 168, 188, 190–91
oversight, 119, 187–91, 203, 205–6

pastor(s), 199, 203–5, 215, 230
patriarchy, patriarchal, 97, 102, 121–22, 157, 163, 174

patron(s), patronage, 15, 37–41, 43, 45–48, 51, 53–54, 94–96, l110, 137, 150, 159
people of God/God's people, xvi, 75–76, 79–81, 114, 165–66, 171, 214–17, 228, 232
perichoretic subjects, 226–28
persecution, 131–32, 136, 138–39, 143–44, 146, 148–49, 151, 153–55
persons/people and community/church, 213, 216–17, 219
Pharisees, 22, 31, 33–34, 65–67
pillar and bulwark of the truth, 115, 121
Platonists, 4
pluralism, 196, 199, 209
pneumatology, 184–85, 192, 194, 199
polytheism, 90
poor/needy, 91–92, 106–7, 110, 114, 138, 147–48, 153–54, 159–60, 165, 203, 207
prayer, praying, prayers, 25, 39, 52, 108, 112, 165, 167, 172, 192
preaching, proclamation, 5, 190–91, 196, 200–203, 206–10
predestination, 200
presbyterate, xii, xiv, 85–86, 148–49, 153, 158, 161, 171
Presbyterian (see also oligarchy), xiv, 194–96, 198, 200–201, 203–12
presbyters (masc.; see also elders), 129, 132–36, 138, 140–54, 157, 159, 163–66, 168–71, 174, 202, 204–5, 208–11
presbyters (fem.; perhaps see also presbyters and elders), 143, 165, 169
presbytery, presbyteries, 205–7, 210
priest(s), priesthood, 10, 14, 23, 59, 70, 102, 137, 147, 149–50, 152, 157–58, 166–68, 171–75, 184, 186, 189, 202, 216, 230, 235
priesthood of all believers, 78, 141, 172, 202–3, 211
prophet(s), prophecy, 101, 108, 132–33, 136, 138–39, 142, 144, 152–53, 155, 166, 173, 184, 186, 189, 203
purity, purification, 5, 12, 23, 28–31, 66–68, 79
Pythagorean(s), 4–6, 17, 173

Qumran/Dead Sea covenanters (see also Essenes), 23, 30, 37, 39, 63–64, 94

Radical Reformers, 213
reciprocity, 94, 97
reformed, reforming, 181, 194, 196, 209–10
remuneration, 120, 150

representative governance, 194–95, 201, 208–10
rich/wealthy, 106–7, 110–11
righteousness, 90, 134

sacradotalism, 147–48
sacraments (see also baptism and Eucharist/Lord's Supper), 190, 200–204, 206–7, 209–10, 215, 217–18, 220, 230
sacrifice(s), 11, 24, 30, 41, 53, 66, 69–71, 78, 132, 145, 149, 150, 152, 157, 165–68, 172–74, 202
sanctified/sanctification, 194, 200–203, 206–12, 219
school(s)/study, 4–8, 12, 25, 28, 51–52, 144–45, 166–67, 200
secularization, 33
separation of church and state, 213
servant, 69
service, 69–71
Shekinah (God's presence), 21–23, 31
skeptics, 4
slave(s), slavery, 12, 107, 110–13, 131–33, 153, 164, 169
social compact theory, 81
social concern and outreach, 110, 114, 123, 148
sojourning church, 225
solidarity, 91, 97, 99
spiritual gifts (see also charisma), 132–34, 136, 139, 144, 146–48, 153, 155
spontaneity, 82, 86
Stoics, Stoicism, 4
symmetrical-participative model of the church, 229, 231, 234–35

synagogue(s), xvii, 12, 25–29, 31–32, 36–42, 44, 46, 48–52, 54, 81, 137, 167, 171
synod, 206–7

teacher, teaching, 101, 107–8, 112, 116–18, 121–22, 133–39, 143, 146–48, 152–54, 159–60, 165, 190, 199–203, 206–7, 209
temple (Jerusalem), 21–24, 31–32, 66–68, 81, 150, 172
temple of God, 78–79, 81, 114, 172
temple, 46–47, 53
Therapeutae, 39, 63
tithes/offerings, 30–31, 66, 165
Trinity and the church, 223–30, 233–35
true circumcision, 75
trustworthy sayings, 109
Twelve, the, 97, 99–101

unity, 189–91, 218–19, 223, 225, 227, 229–30
unity and diversity, 82–83, 86, 202–3

virgins, 147, 159, 162, 168
vision(s), visionaries, 132, 139, 142–43, 149, 151, 154
voluntarism, 213

widows, 106, 108, 110, 112, 114, 118–19, 147–48, 160, 162–65, 168–69
women, 8–9, 11–14, 16, 26, 37, 43, 47, 65–66, 77, 82, 84–85, 96, 100–101, 106, 108, 110, 112–14, 119, 121–22, 133, 153, 157, 162, 164–65, 167, 170, 172, 175, 187, 213
worship, 9, 12, 63, 66–69, 82, 90, 129, 133, 149, 166, 172–74

Index of Modern Authors

Avis, Paul D. L., 181

Barnes, Timothy, 137
Barrett, C. K., 74, 102, 221
Bartchy, S. Scott, 91, 92, 95
Barth, Karl, 186, 187–88, 191
Bartlet, Vernon, xv, xvi
Bartlett, David L., 100
Beck, Roger, 37
Best, Ernest, 75, 77
Beyer, Hermann Wolfgang, 60
Bornkamm, Gunther, 85
Bradshaw, Paul, 129, 147
Branick, Vincent, 85
Brent, Allen, 145
Brooten, Bernadette J., 26
Bonhoeffer, Dietrich, 222
Brunner, Emil, 222
Burkert, Walter, 9, 10, 90

Calvin, John, 185, 188, 194, 198, 199–200,
   201–7, 209, 220, 221–22
Campbell, R. Alastair, 102
Clarke, G. W.
Cotter, Wendy, 37
Culpepper, Alan, 4, 5, 7, 8, 17

Dalferth, Ingolf U., 186
Davies, W. D., xi–xii, xvi
DeWitt, Norman W., 8
Dodd, C. H., xv

Ellis, E. Earle, 84

Fee, Gordon D., 229
Ferguson, Everett, 9
Flew, R. Newton, xv
Forsyth, P. T., 192
Frend, William H. C., 131, 149

Gore, Charles, xi
Grant, Robert, 131

Haenchen, Ernst, 102
Hanson, Richard, 174
Harnack, Adolf, xii, xv, xvi, 83
Hatch, Edwin, xii–xiii, xiv, xv, xvi, 83
Hayes, Alan L., 130
Heinrici, George, xii, xvi
Heuchan, Valerie, 37
Hort, F. J. A., xiii–xiv, xv, xvi, 81, 87
Huss, John, 216

Jalland, T. G., 146
Johnson, Luke Timothy, 95
Johnston, George, xv
Jüngel, Eberhard, 183, 222

Käsemann, Ernst, 232
Kierkegaard, Søren, 192
Kirk, Kenneth E., xi, xiv
Kloppenborg, John S., 37
Knox, John, 206, 207
Krodel, Gerhard, 91
Küng, Hans, 233

Lampe, Peter, 145
Levine, Lee I., 25
Lightfoot, J. B., xii, xiii, xiv, xv, xvi, 83, 85,
   87
Linton, Olof, xi–xii
Lloyd-Jones, Hugh, 90
Lohfink, Gerhard, 101
Longenecker, Richard N., 81
Louth, Andrew, 169
Luther, Martin, 220, 231

Malherbe, Abraham J., 85
Malina, Bruce J., 93
Manson, T. W., xv
Marshall, I. Howard, 105

Martin, Dale B., 164
Mason, Steve, 37
Mattila, Sharon Lee, 37
McCue, J. F., 146
McFadyen, Alistair I., 223
McKelvey, Richard J., 78
McLean, Hudson, 37
McReady, Wayne, 37
Meeks, Wayne A., 90
Meyer, Marvin W., 10–11
Michaelis, Wilhelm, 118
Minear, Paul, 76
Moltmann, Jürgen, 185, 225, 227, 228, 229, 234
Mühlen, Heribert, 229
Mussell, Mary Louise, 49–50

O'Donovan, Oliver, 186, 191–92
Ottati, Douglas, 195

Pannenberg, Wolfhart, 228, 229
Parker, Thomas, 49–50
Prestige, G. L., 226

Ramsay, A. Michael, xiv, 179, 181, 188
Ramsay, William M., 84
Redlich, E. Basil, 84
Remus, Harold, 37
Richardson, L. Jr., 47
Richardson, Peter, 37, 49
Roberts, R. H., 192

Safrai, Shmuel, 25, 29
Sanders, James, 195
Sanday, William, xii

Schillebeeckx, Edward, 180
Schleiermacher, Friedrich, 219
Schlink, Edmund, 182, 189
Schnackenburg, Rudolf, xvi, 76, 80
Schuller, Eileen, 37
Schweizer, Eduard, xvi
Schwöbel, Cristoph, 182, 183
Segal, Alan F., 34
Seland, Torrey, 37
Siebel, W., 228
Smyth, John, 213, 216, 220, 221, 224
Sohm, Rudolf, xii, xv, xvi, 216
Spener, Philipp Jakob, 231
Streeter, B. H., xii, xiv, xv, xvi
Strong, A. H., 224
Stuhlmacher, Peter, 214

Thurston, Bonnie Bowman, 165
Torance, Thomas F., 186

Vischer, Lukas, 218
Volf, Miroslav, 184, 214

Walker-Ramisch, Sandra, 37
Whiteley, D. E. H., 85
Wichern, Johann Hinrich, 231
Williams, Rowan, 187, 188
Wilson, Stephen G., 37

Young, David C., 115
Young, Frances, 161, 171, 172, 173, 204–5

Zinzendorf, Nicholas Ludwig Graf von, 231
Zizioulas, J. D., 188

Index of Ancient Sources

OLD TESTAMENT

Genesis
14:18   175

Exodus
24:8   70
28:35   59
28:43   59
29:30   59
30:20   59

Leviticus
21:16–24   67
22:17–25   67
26:12   78

Numbers
3:6   59

Deuteronomy
10:8   59
15:4–5   92
15:7–8   92
15:11   92
15:21   67
17:12   152
26   67
26:3   66
26:13–15   66

2 Samuel
5:8   67

2 Kings
9:16   60

Esther
2:19   60
6:10   60

Job
10:22   81

Psalms
51:17   172–73

Proverbs
14:19   60
19:6   60
29:26   60

Isaiah
26:19   64
35:5   64
40:9   62
52:7   62
53:5   64
54:17   60
58:6   65
61:1–2   61, 62, 65
63:16   77

Jeremiah
31:31   70
32:38   78

Ezekiel
37:27   78

Daniel
7:9   70
7:10   60
7:13–14   64

Hosea
11:1   77

Zechariah
9:11   70

Malachi
1:10–11   173

APOCRYPHA

1 Esdras
1:4   60

Tobit
1:7   60
12:3   60

Judith
11:17   60

Wisdom of Solomon
10:9   60
16:12   60

Sirach
18:19   60
35:16   60
38:7   60
51:10   77

Baruch
6:25   60
6:38   60

1 Maccabees
11:58   60

2 Maccabees
7:33   70
7:37–38   70

PSEUDEPIGRAPHA

Jubilees
1:17   78

1 Enoch
90:28–29   78
91:13   78

Testament of Benjamin
7:5   93

4 Maccabees
18:11   93

DEAD SEA SCROLLS

1QS
VIII, 5–6   78

1QS^a
II, 3–7   67

1QM
VII, 4   67

4Q521   63–64

4QMMT   23

11QT   23

NEW TESTAMENT

Matthew
5:23–24   68
5:48   34
6:9   77
6:9–13   68
7:12   68
9:2   64
9:6   64
10:21   94
11:5   61, 64
11:19   65, 66
12:28   62
18:20   216, 217, 224
18:23–35   68
19:28   70
20:28   70, 203
21:12–13   21
21:14–15   67
23:9   97
23:11–12   69
26:11   185
27   21
28:18   229

Mark
1:14–15   61
2:1–12   64
2:15–17   65
6:1–6   61
7   67
7:14–23   66
8:34   70
9:35   69
10:38–39   71
10:43–44   69
10:45   70
12:30–31   68
13:12   94
14:22   76
14:24   70
14:36   71
14:58   21, 78

Luke
1:17   75
2:52   159
3:23   59
4:16–19   198
4:16–30   61
4:18–19   62
5:20   64
5:24   64
6:13–16   99
7:22   61, 64
7:34   65
7:35–50   65
9:59–60   97
11:2   77
11:2–4   68
11:20   62, 63
12:37   69
14:11   69
14:26   97
18   67
18:9–14   66
18:14   69
18:18–25   95
21:16   94
22:26   69
22:27   69
22:28–30   70, 98

John
7:16   226
10:38   226
13:31–32   229
14:9–10   227

14:10–11   226
16:14   229
17:1   229
17:20   229
17:21   223, 224, 226

Acts
1:13   99
1:15   92
1:16   98
1:21–22   100
1:21–26   98
2   94
2–5   98, 99
2:17–18   101
2:17–21   232
2:33–47   95
2:42   85
2:46   94
2:46b–47a   86
2:47   92
3–4   99
4   94
4:26–37   95
4:32–35   91
4:34   92
4:36–37   94, 95, 96
5:1–11   94, 95–96
6:1–6   97
6:2   69, 101
6:2–6   99
6:7   102
7:28–8:3   98
8   99
9   98
9–12   98
9:10–19   96
9:27   96
10:47–48   99
11:1–18   99
11:22–30   86, 96
11:25–26   96
11:28   96
11:30   85
12:1–2   99
12:12   94
12:19   99
12:25   96
13–28   98
13:1   96
13:1–3   86, 96, 120
13:2–3   96
13:4–12   96

13:7   96
13:42–52   96
14:4   98, 100
14:12–20   96
14:14   98, 100
14:23   85, 119
15   99, 101
15:2   85
15:2–35   96
15:4   85
15:6   85
15:13–21   86
15:14   75
15:19   100
15:20   89
15:22   100
15:22–23   85
15:23   99
15:36–39   96
16:1   96
16:4   85, 119
16:14   96
16:40   96
17:14–15   96
17:16   89
17:23   89
18:2   97
18:5   96
18:8   97
18:18   97
18:26   97
19:22   96, 97
19:32   14
20:4   96, 97
20:17   85, 97, 102, 119
20:17–35   102
20:28   97, 119
20:31   102
20:35   103
21:8–9   101
21:9   96
21:10   96
21:18   85
21:29   97
22:12–16   96

Romans
1:5–6   84
1:7   74
1:13   84
4:16   75
6:3–7   85
7:4   76

7:24   76
8:14   77
8:15   77
8:33   75
11:29   233
12:1   76
12:1–2   78
12:3   232
12:4–5   75, 76, 77
12:5   217
12:6   233
12:6–8   83
12:7–8   203
12:8   118, 229
15:15–16   84
15:25–26   85
15:25–32   83
16:1–2   84
16:1–16   122
16:3–5   85
16:7   100, 101
16:10–11   85, 142

1 Corinthians
1:2   74, 119, 217
1:4–17   85
1:13–17a   75
1:14–17   221
1:23   75
2:2   75
3:4–9   84
3:5–9   80
3:16–17   78
4:1   80
4:1–13   84
4:14–15   221
4:15   83
4:17   84
5:4–5   84
5:9   78
6:12   84
6:12–20   76
6:15–17   77
6:19–20   78
9:5–6   100
9:6   84
10:16–17   76
10:17   77
11:3   81
11:4–5   82
11:5   101
11:11–12   81
11:17–34   85, 86

11:24   76
11:27   76
11:29   76
12:2–3   232
12:4–6   80, 229
12:4–11   83
12:7   230, 232
12:7–11   233
12:12–13   217
12:12–27   75, 76
12:12–31   77
12:28   83, 114
14:16   81
14:26   81, 224, 231
14:26–40   81
14:33   81, 231
14:40   81, 115
15:23   81
15:24   229
15:35–50   76, 81
16:1–3   83
16:1–4   85
16:10–11   84
16:15–16   232
16:19   85

2 Corinthians
1:1   74, 84
1:8–11   83
1:19   84
2:13   84
2:15–16   78
4:8–12   83
5:1–4   82
5:18–20   83
6:13   221
6:14–7:1   78
6:16   114
6:16–7:1   78
6:18   77
7:6–7   84
7:13–16   84
8:1–9:15   83
8:6   84
8:16–24   84
8:18–19   85
8:23b–24   100
9:11–15   78
11:2   80, 84
11:23–33   83
12:18   84
13:13   235

Galatians
1:2   74
1:15–16   83
1:18–20   86
1:19   99,100
2:1   84
2:1–10   86
2:6–9   83
2:9   84
2:11–14   218
2:12   86
2:13   84
3:1   75
3:1–4:31   79
3:26–28   75
3:28   82
3:29   75
4:5–7   77
4:13–16   83
4:19   83, 221
4:26   80
4:26–28   75
5:1–6:10   79
5:25   79
6:10   77
6:16   75

Ephesians
1:1   74
1:4   75
1:5   182
1:22–23   75, 77, 215
2:11–12   82
2:19   77
2:20–22   78, 80
4:3–6   82, 229
4:4   75, 77
4:4–6   190
4:7   232
4:10   185
4:11   83
4:11–16   80, 203
4:12   75, 77
4:15–16   188
4:16   75, 77
5:2   78
5:19   81
5:21   232
5:23–33   75, 77
6:21   84

Philippians
1:1   74, 84, 85, 119, 169,
  229

2:17   78
2:19–23   84
3:3   75
3:20   80
3:21   76
4:2   84
4:3   85
4:15   233
4:18   78

Colossians
1:2   74
1:3–9   84
1:12–20   215
1:18   75, 77
1:22   77, 78
1:24   75, 77
2:5   81
2:11   75, 77
2:17   77
2:19   75, 77
3:12   75
3:16   81
4:7   84
4:10   84
4:12   84
4:14   84
4:15   85
4:16   81

1 Thessalonians
1:1   74, 84, 217
1:9   92, 115
2:7   221
2:7–12   83
2:13   79
3:2–6   84
4:8   79
4:15–17   81
5:12   118, 229, 232
5:12–13   84
5:13   232
5:19   79
5:21   232
5:27   81

2 Thessalonians
1:1   74, 84, 217
2:11   221
2:13–14   79
3:7–10   83

1 Timothy
1:15   109
1:17   108, 109
1:18   108
1:20   111
2:1–2   81, 108, 110
2:4–7   112
2:7   108
2:8   108
2:9   106
2:9–10   108
2:11   112
2:11–15   122
2:12–14   110
2:15   112
3:1   109
3:1–13   117, 119, 169
3:2   110, 118, 119
3:4   118
3:4–5   112
3:5   114, 117
3:8–13   112
3:9   118
3:11   122
3:14–16   113
3:15   114, 115, 170, 204
3:16   109, 115
4:1   108, 115
4:5   109
4:9–10   109
4:10   115
4:11–14   107
4:12   122
4:13   81, 108
4:14   108, 109, 116, 120,
  169
5:1   85
5:1–2   113
5:3   110
5:3–16   118
5:5   108
5:6   106
5:9   110
5:10   109–10
5:13   110, 112
5:16   110, 114
5:17   85, 108, 109, 120
5:17–18   118
5:17–20   119
5:18–19   169
5:19   85
5:20   111
5:22   109, 120
6:1–2   108, 110

6:6–8   107
6:9–10   106
6:13   116
6:15–16   108, 109
6:17–19   106
6:18–19   110

2 Timothy
1:3   108, 114
1:5   113
1:6   109, 120
1:8   116
1:11   108
1:13   108
1:14   115
1:16–18   106
2:2   108, 117
2:9   115
2:11–13   109
2:16–17   111
2:20–21   113
2:23–26   111
2:24   108
2:25   112
2:25–26   124
3:10–11   117
3:16   108, 111
4:1–5   107
4:2   108, 111
4:5   112
4:9–13   116
4:12   117
4:14   106

Titus
1:11   111
1:5–6   85
1:5–7   119
1:5–9   117, 118, 168
1:6   112
1:7   170
1:8   110
1:9   108, 118
2:1   107, 108, 108
2:1–10   113
2:1–15   108, 169
2:14   75, 114
2:15   107, 108, 122
2:4   110
2:4–5   112
2:5   112
2:7   117
2:7–8   116

2:9–10   111
3:1–8   108
3:5   109
3:6   115
3:8   108, 109
3:9   111, 112
3:10   111
3:12–13   116
3:13   107
3:14   110, 110, 123

Philemon
2   85
8–21   82
10   221
23   84
24   84

Hebrews
4:9   75
8:10   75
13:3   76

1 Peter
2:4–10   78
2:5–10   231
2:9   202
2:9–10   75
2:25   188
4:10   231, 232
4:10–11   121
5:1–2   119
5:1–4   121
5:3   119

1 John
1:1–4   214
1:3   229
1:3–4   223
3:12   93

Jude
3   123
11   93

Revelation
1:6   202
21–22   223
21:1–22:5   214
21:3   75

RABBINIC LITERATURE

Babylonian Talmud
Berakoth
28b   67

PAPYRI

Oxyrhynchus
40   61
1088   61

Karanis
575   15

London
7.2193   17

Turin
1.ii.22   61

**OTHER ANCIENT
JEWISH, CHRISTIAN,
AND GRECO-ROMAN
LITERATURE**

Apostolic Constitutions
1   164
2   162–63
2.26   169
2.28   165
2.57   166
3.6.3   165
7   166, 167

Apuleius
Metamorphoses
18   9

Cicero
On Goals
1.65   7

John Chrysostom
Homilies on Hebrews
27   173

1 Clement
4:17   93
40–41   172
44   142

Cyprian
Epistle
1   150, 151, 152
1.1   174
11.5–6   149
40.7   149
42   151
43   150
43.7.1   152
55.21.1   151
58.1   149
59.9.3   151
59.10.1   151
61.3   174
63   152, 174–75
63.1   149
66.2.2   149
66.7.3   151
66.10   149

Didascalia
9   169

Diogenes Laertius
8.10   5

Eusebius
Ecclesiastical History
3.39   170
5.1   131
5.2.6–7   134
5.4.1   134
5.23ff   145
5.24   144

Preparation for the Gospel
8.11.1   63
14.5   7

Gregory of Nazianzus
Oration
43   158–60

Hermas
Similitudes
10.2   143
10.4   143

Visions
3.5   143

Hippolytus (Pseudo)
Apostolic Tradition
2–3   147–48
7   147–48

25–30   147
28   148

Iamblichus
Life of Pythagoras
6   5
17   5
18   6
21   6

Ignatius
Ephesians
2–3   190
4   161
6   190

Magnesians
3   161
6   168
7   161

Philadelphians
2   161

Smyrnaeans
8   161
8.2   214–15, 216

Trallians
2   161
3   169

Irenaeus
Against Heresies
praef. 3   135
1.10.2   131
1.13.4   133
1.13.7   132
2.32.4   134
3.24.1   215
3.33.9   132
4.24.4   136
4.26.3   134
4.26.5   135

Josephus
Antiquities
1.52–66   93
4.242–243   66–67
13.171–172   63
13.298   63
14.235   36, 44
15.371   63
17.150   61

War
2.136   63

4.618   64
4.656–657   64

Justin
Dialogue
117   173

First Apology
65   145, 146, 147
67   145, 146, 147

Letter of Aristeas
92–99   24

Ovid
Metamorphoses
1.127–51   93–94

Passion of Perpetua
13   139, 140

Pausanius
Description of Greece
4.33.3–6   10

Petronius
Satyricon
56   147

Philo
De vita Mosis
1.1   63
1.2   63
2.10   63

Quod omnis probus
12.75   63
12.87   63
13.91   63

Plato
Euthyphro
13a   61
13d   61

Pliny the Elder
Natural History
5.17.4   63

Seneca
Epistles
25.5   8

Shemoneh Esreh
Benediction 6   77

Strabo
17.1.8   17

Suetonius
Divus Vespasianus
7.2–3   64

Tacitus
Ann.
14.7.4   47

Tertullian
Against the Valentinians
4   140

Apology
38.1.5   17
39   138, 148

Baptism
17   141
6   216

Exhortation to Chastity
7   141, 216

Fasting
170   140

Modesty
21   216, 224

Monogamy
12.2   141

On Flight in Persecution
11   140

On Prayer
23   138

On the Chaplet
3   141

Prescription against Heretics
1   138
41   140

Repentance
17   141